THE BLACK CIRCLE

Alexandre Kojève, Boulogne-sur-Seine, July 6, 1930. Anonymous photo. Bibliothèque nationale de France, Fonds Kojève.

THE BLACK CIRCLE

A LIFE OF ALEXANDRE KOJÈVE

JEFF LOVE

Columbia University Press
New York

Columbia University Press
Publishers Since 1893
New York   Chichester, West Sussex
cup.columbia.edu
Copyright © 2018 Columbia University Press

Library of Congress Cataloging-in-Publication Data
Names: Love, Jeff (G. Jeffrey), author.
Title: The black circle : a life of Alexandre Kojève / Jeff Love.
Description: New York : Columbia University Press, 2018. |
Includes bibliographical references and index.
Identifiers: LCCN 2018007435 | ISBN 9780231186568 (cloth : alk. paper) |
ISBN 9780231546706 (e-book)
Subjects: LCSH: Kojève, Alexandre, 1902–1968. |
Philosophers—France—Biography.
Classification: LCC B2430.K654 L68 2018 | DDC 194—dc23
LC record available at https://lccn.loc.gov/2018007435

Columbia University Press books are printed on permanent
and durable acid-free paper.

Printed in the United States of America

Cover design: Julia Kushnirsky
Cover image: *Black Circle* by Kazimir Malevich © State Russian Museum

FOR GLORIA, JACK, DYLAN, AND GARRETT

CONTENTS

III. THE LATER WRITINGS

ACKNOWLEDGMENTS

This project began with a seminar on historical narrative that took place in Beijing during the summer of 2013. I owe a debt of thanks to the organizer of that seminar, my colleague Yanming An. I also wish to thank the resourceful staff at the National Humanities Center, where I spent a year (2014–2015) as a John E. Sawyer Fellow and managed to complete an initial draft of the book in the ideal working conditions created by the Center. Vladimir Alexandrov, Caryl Emerson, Michael Forster, Markus Gabriel, Ilya Kliger, Nina Kousnetzoff, Bill Maker, Donna Orwin, Lina Steiner, and William Mills Todd were all instrumental at various stages in the project, as were Jon and Nancy Love. Finally, I have benefitted a great deal from the unflagging encouragement of António Lobo Antunes as well as from the many astute comments and questions of my colleague and serial collaborator, Michael Meng. The latter have left their impression on virtually every page of this book.

Wendy Lochner has been an ideal editor—patient, thorough, and generous with her time.

I have used available English translations for material quoted in other languages throughout the book and have frequently modified them.

ABBREVIATIONS

CTD   Alexandre Kojève, *Le concept, le temps et le discours*, ed.
Bernard Hesbois (Paris: Gallimard, 1990).

EHPP   Alexandre Kojève, *Essai d'une histoire raisonnée de la
philosophie païenne*, 3 vols. (Paris: Gallimard, 1968–1973).

EPD   Alexandre Kojève, *Esquisse d'une phénoménologie du droit*
(Paris: Gallimard, 1981).

IDH   Alexandre Kojève, "The Idea of Death in the Philosophy of
Hegel," trans. Joseph Carpino, *Interpretation* 3, no. 2/3
(Winter 1973): 114–156.

ILH   Alexandre Kojève, *Introduction à la lecture de Hegel*, ed.
Raymond Queneau, 2nd ed. (Paris: Gallimard, 1968).

IRH   Alexandre Kojève, *Introduction to the Reading of Hegel*, ed.
Allan Bloom, trans. James H. Nichols Jr., 2nd ed. (Ithaca,
NY: Cornell University Press, 1969).

OPR   Alexandre Kojève, *Outline of a Phenomenology of Right*, trans.
Bryan-Paul Frost and Robert Howse (Lanham, MD:
Rowman and Littlefield, 2008).

OT   Leo Strauss, *On Tyranny*, ed. Victor Gourevitch and Michael
Roth (Chicago: University of Chicago Press, 2013).

TW   Alexandre Kojève, "Tyranny and Wisdom," in Leo Strauss, *On
Tyranny*, ed. Victor Gourevitch and Michael Roth, 135–176
(Chicago: University of Chicago Press, 2013).

THE BLACK CIRCLE

INTRODUCTION

A Russian in Paris

The pagan way: become what you are (as idea = ideal). The Christian way: become what you are not (yet): the way of conversion.

—ALEXANDRE KOJÈVE

lexandre Kojève was one of the twentieth century's most brilliant, elusive, and wide-ranging thinkers. He exerted a profound influence on a generation of French intellectuals through the lectures he gave on Hegel's *Phenomenology of Spirit* at the École Pratique des Hautes Études in Paris, from 1933 to 1939. His audience included André Breton, Georges Bataille, Henry Corbin, Jacques Lacan, and Maurice Merleau-Ponty.[1] These lectures were published, after the Second World War, by another of Kojève's students, Raymond Queneau, and they constitute a classic work on the *Phenomenology* that has divided Hegel scholars not only in terms of what the lectures say about Hegel but also in regard to the claim that they are merely commentary. Among contemporary Hegel scholars, Robert Pippin, for one, finds Kojève's reading of Hegel tendentious, while his colleague Michael Forster takes almost the opposite view, suggesting that Kojève's reading of Hegel is broadly justified within its own terms.[2] Whatever the final judgment, few scholars have taken the commentary as a "literal" reading of Hegel, citing a plethora of influences, from Martin Heidegger to Karl Marx, that shape Kojève's approach.

Surprisingly, one important stream of influence has been habitually neglected: the Russian literary, theological, and philosophical tradition from which Kojève sprang. This is an extraordinary omission, because Alexandre Kojève was born Aleksandr Vladimirovich Kozhevnikov, in Moscow, in 1902, and belongs to a dynamic generation of Russian artists, writers, musicians, poets, theologians, and thinkers. Indeed, the title of this book alludes to a painting by a distinguished artistic revolutionary of this generation, Kazimir Malevich, whose depiction of circular darkness offers an enticing visual metaphor for the final extinction of individuality that is a key feature of Kojève's thought. This generation flourished during the first quarter of the twentieth century despite the turmoil of the early postrevolutionary years and an increasingly violent imposition of doctrinal conformity in the Soviet Union. Although these difficult circumstances contributed to the undeserved obscurity of several important members of this generation, it is also not unfair to say that the omission is all too typical, another example of Western neglect of the richness, originality, and complexity of the Russian intellectual heritage.

The aim of this book is to correct this omission with regard to one of the more striking intellectual figures of this generation and to assert that Kojève is not merely a commentator on Hegel but also, as some have suspected, a provocative thinker in his own right, worthy of our attention. Kojève's substantial archive of material, largely unpublished in his lifetime, reveals a polymath who wrote thousands of pages on Hegel and other philosophers as well as a prescient book on quantum physics, book-length studies on problems of the infinite and on atheism, and shorter works on the Madhyamaka tradition in Mahayana Buddhism (for which he learned Sanskrit, classical Tibetan, and Chinese). Kojève emerges as a highly unorthodox and playful thinker, in the best Russian tradition, whose commentary on Hegel blends distinctively Russian concerns with the end of history in complete self-overcoming (or self-abnegation) into the thought of the ostensibly universal philosopher. The eccentric persona Kojève cultivated—he refused to publish his own work because, as he said, he did not want to take himself too seriously[3]—reflects an insouciant, subversive ambivalence toward European cultural norms that extends to his commentary on one of its foremost figures.

This book is divided into three parts, each dealing with a different facet of Kojève's thought. It is expressly interdisciplinary, merging intellectual history, close textual analysis, and philosophical speculation just as Kojève himself did. The main thread that ties these parts together is the distinctive form of speculation about the proper ends of human life, which emerged in Russia during the latter half of the nineteenth century as a debate about the nature of genuine human emancipation.

Before proceeding to a brief description of each of these parts, let me provide a biographical sketch of this most unusual man.[4]

BENE VIXIT QUI BENE LATUIT

Kojève had what we may call a storied life, the end of which reflects an intriguing and enduring discord, barely hidden under the surface.[5] He died suddenly, on June 4, 1968, while giving a speech in Brussels at a meeting of an organization he had done much to create and foster: the European Common Market. He was born in Moscow sixty-six years earlier, into an affluent family of the high bourgeoisie. His uncle was the famed painter Vasily Kandinsky, with whom the young Kojève corresponded. Like so many others of his generation, his properly Russian life ended with the revolution, although he did not leave the Soviet Union until 1920. He left in most inauspicious circumstances, fleeing, along with a friend, through Poland to Germany, where he stayed until 1926, mainly in Berlin but also in Heidelberg. During that period, he lived well on investments of the proceeds from valuables he managed to smuggle out of Russia, and he pursued an astonishing variety of studies, ranging from Kant to Buddhism, Vedanta, and other religions, to the languages of the Far East. He finally obtained a doctorate in philosophy from the University of Heidelberg, in 1926, under Karl Jaspers, with a voluminous study of Vladimir Soloviev.

In that same year he moved to Paris, where he continued his studies in Eastern thought as well as in mathematics and quantum mechanics. The stock market crash of 1929 ruined him, and he had to cast around for income to survive. Finally, in a remarkable twist of fate, fellow émigré Alexandre Koyré asked him to take over his seminar on the religious philosophy of Hegel at the École Pratique des Hautes Études for one year, in 1933. Of course, this seminar continued until 1939, with its varied and distinguished audience. Kojève became a legend.

But the convulsion of the Second World War changed his life again. He was drafted into the French army but saw no action. After the invasion of the Soviet Union in 1941, he fled to Marseilles, where he lived until the end of the war. While accounts differ, he seems to have been active in the French Resistance and, perhaps, in Soviet intelligence as well.

After the war, he was asked by a former student, Robert Marjolin, to join him in the Direction des Relations Économiques Extérieures as an "adviser." From this time on, Kojève seems to have played a role of considerable importance in the postwar French government, shaping economic policy, promoting the common market, the General Agreement on Tariffs and Trade, and support for third world development. Anecdotes abound regarding his influence on French policy making, the 1957 creation of the European Community from the Coal and Steel Treaty, and his unusual position as a feared and enigmatic éminence grise who, together with Bernard Clappier and Olivier Wormser, dominated French economic policy for more than a decade.

By all accounts, Kojève fascinated, with his secretive, charismatic personality, his coruscating irony, and the capacious mind that Raymond Aron, for one, considered the most extraordinary he had ever encountered (and in express comparison with Jean-Paul Sartre and other luminaries). Georges Bataille confirms this impression in one of his more florid letters. Kojève also was the only person whom Lacan always referred to as "mon maître." In these and many other cases, his students remained in thrall to the unusual master who elaborated, in six years of lectures, a remarkable reading of Hegel that addressed basic questions of the ostensibly modern project of emancipation, declaring that history had come to an end.[6]

STRUCTURE OF THE BOOK

The first part of this study addresses these questions in the Russian context, providing a brief orienting review of Plato and the Platonic notion of perfection or divinization that has played such an important role in

Russian religious thought. From this introduction, the text moves on to Fyodor Dostoevsky, who lays the foundation for the subsequent Russian debates about divinization—whether human beings should strive to be like gods or should create a community that embodies that striving through a unified adherence to a divine ideal.[7] The basic question here—whether we should pursue the transformation of the human being into a god literally free of the limitations that beset our mortal existence or create an emancipatory community of equals—drives the exploration of two Russian thinkers much influenced by Dostoevsky, Nikolai Fedorov and Vladimir Soloviev. Fedorov claims that the only emancipatory ideal for humanity is to achieve universal immortality (and universal resurrection of the dead) through technological advancement; Soloviev argues that this comes about through adherence to a divinely inspired community: one becomes God by embodying his law and, in so doing, freeing oneself of the self, along with the suffering that originates in the self. This rich and radical heritage of emancipation through divinization emerges in Kojève's commentary on Hegel and sheds light on some of the characteristics of that commentary that have most angered or mystified critics, such as Kojève's notorious end-of-history thesis, which is both a commentary on and an extension of his Russian predecessors.[8]

The second part of the book examines the commentary itself, providing a close reading of the introduction and, thereafter, of the lectures from 1938 and 1939 that are the commentary's culminating point. By examining these texts, I focus on the two principal narratives developed by Kojève: the narrative of the master and slave, culminating in the creation of the universal and homogeneous state, and that of the final ascent to wisdom that ends history in complete self-transparency. This close reading is not an attempt to ascertain whether Kojève "got Hegel right" but proceeds as an extension of the discussions carried out in the first part. As such, this reading is an independent investigation into aspects of the commentary that have bothered its critics or been ascribed to Kojève's alleged Marxism or Heideggerianism or, indeed, to extravagant simplification. The discussion of the master-slave relation for which Kojève is so famous thus emerges in the context of the Christian community advocated by Dostoevsky in *The Brothers Karamazov* and by Soloviev in his lectures on divine humanity. Moreover, the discussion of the sage, central to the 1938–1939 lectures, emerges from the account of divinization articulated throughout the first part of this book, most radically in the discussions of Alexei Nilych Kirillov, the theoretical suicide in Dostoevsky's novel *Demons*, and the doctrine of universal resurrection advocated by Fedorov.[9]

In both cases, my intention is not to show that other readings of Kojève's commentary as Marxist or Heideggerian are wrong or unjustified, but rather to supplement or transform these readings by clarifying the largely hidden Russian context. My intention is also more general, for the provocative end of these lectures, which equates emancipation at the end of history with the complete abandonment of the self, our individuality, is a searching rebuke of Hobbesian self-interest and a form of suicide or self-annihilation that reflects the influence of many religious traditions. The end of history, for Kojève, is to end history. As Kojève hauntingly notes, history is nothing more than the persistence of error, understood by Kojève as the adherence to ways of justifying self-preservation. The task of coming to wisdom is to correct history by ending it and, therewith, the dominion of self-preservation.

The final part of the book examines Kojève's later work and, more extensively, the central question of perfection or complete emancipation that informs all his work, from the Hegel lectures to his remarkable 900-page manuscript called *Sophia, Philosophy, and Phenomenology* (still largely unpublished), written at white heat in Russian in 1940–1941; to *Outline of a Philosophy of Right*, a 500-page treatise on law from 1943; to his final examination of the Western tradition, the enormous *Attempt at a Rational History of Pagan Philosophy*, published largely after his death in 1968. By focusing on the latter two texts, I develop the relation between the universal and homogeneous state and the temporalizing of the concept—the liberation from eternity—that constitutes a crucial narrative nested within the narrative of the ascent to wisdom. The difficult and broader question here is profoundly Kojèvian: How does one abandon the individual self's need for permanence, or freedom from death, while still living? Kojève provides no unified answer to this question. To the contrary, he ends up most frequently in irony, the irony that arises from describing the final state as something that dispenses with further descriptions. In other words, the final state is one in which the only possible discourse is repetition. By the mere fact of proclaiming that history, and with it the possibility of novelty, is over, one risks ending up in irony, inevitable and mocking—repetition offers the illusion of the eradication of the self that cannot but return to talk about itself.[10] If Kojève indicates that the end of history eradicates further reflection, then continued talk about that end postpones it, perhaps indefinitely, as the individual clings to her fear of death.

The book itself comes to a close by placing this discourse of discursive finality and self-abnegation in explicit contrast to Kojève's antipode, Martin Heidegger.[11] One can argue, indeed, that Kojève's thinking as a whole presents a hidden polemic against Heidegger, whose claims against the possibility of finality, of an end that merely repeats what has come before, offer a strong challenge to Kojève's advocacy of finality.[12] If Heidegger speaks of an end as well, it is only to come to another beginning that is like the first only in regard to the openness it promises. For Kojève, this other beginning requires an impossible transition, a forgetfulness of history that is a tempting ruse and deception. Yet, as we have seen, Kojève confronts the very same problem, because the moment of the end that leads to repetition of what has come before requires a similar forgetfulness.

In the end, we have two kindred attempts to be free from history and thus to be free, one where freedom is predicated on emancipation through extinction of the self, the other presuming a similar extinction but promising another beginning of history, not an end for all times. It seems to me that this contrast brings to the fore a powerful commentary on the nature of freedom and the possibility of revolutionary change that shows the full extension and challenge of Kojève's work. While I begin by attempting to recover aspects of Kojève's thinking that have been neglected, in the end I attempt to stress the more general provocation of his thought. Few contemporary philosophers, indeed, would openly equate freedom with a kind of suicide, as Kojève does; fewer still might associate suicide, literal or figurative, with final and full emancipation. In this sense, the end of history is clear and perpetually shocking, an affront to self-interest and common sense that recalls the genuine radicality of Dostoevsky and Fedorov.[13]

THE SENSE OF AN ENDING

Kojève's insistence on finality and repetition is untimely. It reveals the way in which Kojève's thought is deeply hostile to the governing dogma of our time, a dogma anticipated trenchantly by Dostoevsky's underground man: that freedom is continuous striving without limits; that, in a pregnant phrase, error is freedom. The praise of error or errancy is everywhere in evidence; it is virtually the rallying cry of modern emancipatory French philosophy, with several notable exceptions, largely from the Marxist camp.[14] The truth as truth has become tyrannical, terrifying. One seeks "infinite play," polysemy, *différance*, the free creation of concepts, or various kinds of transgression that satisfy our demand for freedom from hegemonic narratives.[15] Finality is to be rejected in favor of lasting openness, nonfinality, a horizon of possibility that beckons, seduces us to what *might* be rather than what *must* be.

Surely, this way of thinking is to be preferred to Kojèvian irony, to the notion that freedom may be finally achieved only through self-immolation, the abandonment of the self entirely to a final narrative from which no deviation is possible other than as nonsense or madness. And here is the most potent challenge to modern philosophy posed by Kojève. For Kojève calls into question, in the most aggressive way possible, the cherished basic atomic unit of modern thought: the free historical individual. Kojève questions each element of this atomic unit, and when Kojève declares dramatically the death of the human, he is speaking directly of the death of this particular view of the human, a view born from a radical commitment to the individual self or, in Kojève's terms, to the primacy of animality.[16]

Kojève reverses the basic, often deeply hidden, assumption informing much of modern social theory: that self-interest can lead to a stable political order and that society is the creation of mutual self-interest because society protects individuals from their greatest fear—death and, in particular, violent death. The modern political compact as established by Thomas Hobbes identifies genuine freedom as having a fundamental precondition: freedom from the fear of death. For Kojève, such freedom is in reality the most abject slavery.[17] Rather than becoming free to live one's life as guided by precepts formulated without reference to an underlying fear of death or other finite limitation, the ostensibly free historical individual enslaves herself to the most primitive animal desire for self-preservation. In the guise of freedom to pursue whatever they may like, modern human beings have enslaved themselves so completely and convincingly to the animal desire for self-preservation that they take what is perhaps the most extreme collective expression of this desire, modern consumer capitalism, to be the greatest and most noble "system of freedom" that history has ever known. This is so because modern consumer capitalism allows us the freedom to pursue our desires as we see fit, granting us the illusion of possessing a power over the world itself that a finite creature cannot possibly have. The freedom to proliferate desires, to indulge them endlessly, is the wellspring of an illusion of power, flattering to human hopes of longer, if not continuous, well-being, the precondition of which is the preservation of the self as an animal being.[18]

Kojève's essential challenge, then, does not end in a sort of skulking skepticism or pessimism about human life, though these elements of Kojève's thought should not simply be ignored as irrelevant. To the contrary, Kojève's essential challenge is to the reign of self-interest in its most profound form, self-preservation, as well as to the hegemony of the self, understood as devoted to its own flourishing and expansion at almost any cost, whether that relates to other human beings or to nature. Nothing could be further from Kojève's development of Hegel than the notion that there can be a "self-interest well understood," a selfishness that is praiseworthy, the bedrock of political union.[19]

Kojève's critique of self-interest merits renewal in a day when consumer capitalism and the reign of self-interest are hardly in question, either implicitly or explicitly, and where the key precincts of critique have been hobbled by their own reliance on elements of the modern conception of the human being as the free historical individual that have not been sufficiently clarified. Kojève's thought is thus anodyne: far from being "philosophically" mad or the learned jocularity of a jaded, extravagant genius, it expresses a probing inquiry into the nature of human being that returns us to questions that reach down to the roots of the free historical individual. Moreover, it extends a critique of self-interest deeply rooted in Russian thought, and Kojève does so, no doubt with trenchant irony, in the very capital of the modern bourgeoisie decried violently by Dostoevsky in his *Winter Notes on Summer Impressions*.[20]

Yet, there is of course another nagging irony in Kojève's later career as bureaucrat and "Sunday philosopher" who seems to shed the purported masks of the earlier Kojève, evoking what has become a cliché of twentieth-century philosophy: Did Kojève in effect accept the failure of revolution, of complete, final, and universal emancipation, and acquiesce in "bourgeois" philosophy? As everyone knows, we have paradigmatic examples of the earlier and later divisions in Heidegger, Georg Lukács, and Ludwig Wittgenstein, each in some way featuring an indissoluble opposition between the two different periods as an incentive for interpretive speculation. In the case of Kojève, however, it is quite clear that the later writings are a painstaking and extensive development of his earlier views. The generic peculiarity and enormous size of Kojève's final project, *Attempt at a Rational History of Pagan Philosophy*, suggest an uneasy irony: Why should Kojève need to prove to us that wisdom has come, so vehemently and at such length, if it indeed has come? Kojève's comprehensive, unfinished attempt to impose finality seems to be an uneasy contravention of the declaration that history and thought have come to an end. Is it indeed possible ever to say that *last* word? Or does Kojève not merely say it again and again? After all, once the truth is settled, there is nothing left but repetition in the final state, the universal and homogeneous state that is the home of wisdom having been achieved at last.

Here is Kojève the "enlightened" and implacable Stalinist, and one wonders to what extent Kojève's supposed irony is not merely a protective mask for his creation of a distinctive, philosophical Stalinism. Kojève's final order, the universal and homogeneous state of human beings freed of Hobbesian self-interest, is a radical project indeed, for Kojève thinks through to its conclusion the achievement of truth as finality: a state of endless repetition where all citizens have freed themselves of self-interest and thus of the fear of death—the foremost sting of individuality. Whatever Kojève's intentions may be, his project throws down the gauntlet to modes of thinking rooted in the appeasement or cultivation of self-interest and, as such, Kojève, the "modern," finds himself in the sharpest opposition to modern "bourgeois" narratives of self-creation, emancipation, and advancement.

THE RECEPTION OF KOJÈVE IN ENGLISH

There is no comprehensive account of Kojève as a philosopher in his own right that delves into the Russian context of his thinking in detail and focuses on his challenge to the modern free historical individual that he describes in his Hegel lectures. Indeed, most writing on Kojève in English comes from students of Leo Strauss, who write about Kojève mostly in terms of his relation to Strauss and of Kojève's famous debate with Strauss collected in the book *On Tyranny*.[21] Though Kojève can count among his many admirers figures as diverse as Jacques Lacan, Carl Schmitt, and Jacob Taubes (who considered Kojève the greatest eschatological thinker of his time), comprehensive English-language accounts of Kojève from other perspectives are rare. The only—and best—English accounts of Kojève's Russian roots come from chapters in books dealing with other issues, such as Boris Groys's *Introduction to Antiphilosophy* and Stefanos Geroulanos's *An Atheism That Is Not Humanist Emerges in French Thought*.[22]

Geroulanos's extremely perceptive discussion of Kojève is oriented primarily toward his influence in France. Notwithstanding that orientation, Geroulanos recognizes the Russian element in Kojève's thought, primarily by addressing Kojève's critical relation to Soloviev. He does not examine the crucial Dostoevskian background, nor does he consider Fedorov. Moreover, Geroulanos's notion of the death of the human, while firmly grounded in Kojève's Hegel lectures, tends to turn away from Kojève's central thesis that problematizes the very notion of the "free historical individual" that Geroulanos defends. In this respect, Kojève ultimately repudiates the equation of the human with the free historical individual, understood as the self-interested modern actor, central to Geroulanos's argument. To assert that Kojève announces the death of the human is thus somewhat questionable since, as I have said, Kojève announces what amounts to the death of only one notion of what is human as essential to becoming *truly* human, and does so with considerable irony. Nonetheless, one of the many signal virtues of Geroulanos's interpretation of Kojève is his recognition and characterization of the different responses Kojève offers regarding the end state, from the "citizen soldier" to the "bodies without spirit" of the 1939 lectures.

Groys refers to the influence of Soloviev as well, specifically to Soloviev's text *On Love* as well as to his sophiology. These are important references that the present study expands in its close reading of a text that was central both for Soloviev and Kojève, the *Lectures on Divine Humanity* from 1877 to 1878. Groys has also attempted to give a novel reading of Kojève's concern about originality by suggesting that, like Jorge Luis

Borges, Kojève's originality consists precisely in his claim not to be original.[23] While I have alluded to this issue in the preceding section, the emphasis in my book is not so much on the issue of originality and repetition as on the problem of finality itself, and I shall argue that this problem was central to Kojève's later thinking.

In general, my study seeks to offer a different perspective on Kojève's thought as a whole, by enriching the account of the Russian context as well as by discussing a somewhat wider selection of texts from the later Kojève. As such, it seeks to complement the pioneering work of Groys and Geroulanos while departing from them in its greater emphasis on the nature and consequences of human emancipation. Rather than viewing Kojève as one whose originality resides in his claim not to be original or in his declaration of the death of man, the book explores the consequences of radical emancipation as both a correction of history and the purest expression of the truly human power to counter natural necessity. In this respect, the question about finality (and repetition) emerges as a question not only about the possibility of complete emancipation but also about its desirability. Kojève sets us a most difficult task: On the one hand, complete emancipation, full self-transparency, appears to extinguish our very consciousness of ourselves as such—we become free, universal beings at the expense of knowing what we are and might be. On the other hand, the failure of such emancipation bequeaths us instability and endless conflict as we attempt to find a sense to our lives that might allow us to accept an essential inconclusiveness. Put in the language of revolution so important to Kojève, we are stuck between the choice of a success that overcomes us as a being or failure and, indeed, a fetishizing of failure that is indistinguishable from the punishment imposed on Sisyphus. Which should be our destiny?

A NOTE ON THE TEXTS

Kojève wrote a great deal but published very little in his lifetime—only two major texts, in fact: the famed *Introduction to the Reading of Hegel* (first published in 1947 at the behest of Raymond Queneau and consisting mainly of lecture notes reviewed by Kojève), along with the first volume of *Attempt at a Rational History of Pagan Philosophy*, which came out shortly after his sudden death in 1968. If the former was released with not much more than Kojève's desultory approval, the latter seems to have been published as part of a larger publication plan. Kojève also published several articles, among which the most well known are no doubt his "Tyranny and Wisdom," included in the book *On Tyranny*, which features a debate between Kojève and Leo Strauss, and "Hegel, Marx and Christianity," a condensed epitome of Kojève's thought that first appeared in Bataille's journal *Critique* immediately after the war.

Since Kojève's death, a number of the unpublished works have appeared. Aside from the final two volumes of the *Attempt* and a volume on Kant (1973) that is likely the final installment in that history, *Outline of a Phenomenology of Right* was published in 1981. Since that time, there has been a steady stream of publications, including *Atheism* (1931/1998), *The Concrete Paintings of Vasily Kandinsky* (2002), *The Concept, Time, and Discourse* (1953/1990), *The Idea of Determinism in Classical and Modern Physics* (1929/1990), *Identity and Reality in Pierre Bayle's Dictionary* (1937/2010), and *The Notion of Authority* (1942/2004).

Despite these publications, the archive at the Bibliothèque Nationale in Paris still contains a wealth of as yet unpublished material, of which the manuscript *Sophia, Philosophy, and Phenomenology* is perhaps the most notable example. There is also the substantial store of writings I have mentioned as well as an immense cache of meticulous notes for the Hegel lectures, drafts of the postwar "system of science," together with notebooks, book reviews, and various opuscula.

In this book, I have chosen to concentrate my account of Kojève's thought on what I consider to be his principal published works, *Introduction to the Reading of Hegel, Outline of a Phenomenology of Right*, and *Attempt at a Rational History of Pagan Philosophy* (including the volume on Kant). I do so because, in my view, these works provide the most comprehensive account of the two dominant narratives of Kojève's mature philosophical work: the struggle for recognition between master and slave, terminating in the universal and homogeneous state; and the ascent to wisdom or, in terms worked out exhaustively in the *Attempt*, the completed story of the radical temporalizing of the concept.

Nonetheless, while I focus on these volumes, I have not hesitated to refer to other works where that reference might assist in clarifying the principal narratives. And while I discuss *Sophia, Philosophy, and Phenomenology* in very general terms in chapter 8, I have not endeavored to give any greater account of that work, which, to my knowledge, remains as yet unavailable in anything other than manuscript form. As for *The Concept, Time, and Discourse*—a very intriguing text to be sure, and one soon available in translation—I have avoided any detailed discussion because many (though by no means all) of its arguments are taken up in somewhat greater detail in the *Attempt.*

In general, I have sought to appeal to a heterogeneous audience whose only common feature is likely a level of interest in the cultures and issues involved. The result of attempting to appeal to such a broad audience is a certain lack of balance; some discussions will prove too detailed, others not detailed enough. The latter response seems to me particularly likely with regard to my consideration of Kojève's later works, which I confine to one long chapter (chapter 8). Proper consideration of the richness of those works belongs to an extensive separate study, and I have covered them only in broad strokes and in conformity with the purposes of this book.

I

RUSSIAN CONTEXTS

❖

1

MADMEN

Behold Kazimir Malevich's provocative painting *Black Circle*. What may we say of it? An ordinary circle, a period, a pothole, dark sphere, spherical blackness, emptiness, void, pinhead, oil droplet, pupil, and so on. Yet we have here merely an ordinary circle against a white square frame—simplicity itself. What may we say of it? Nothing more than a minimal contrast of color and shape, it is certainly not depicting anything from nature, anything in our everyday world, any objects we encounter at home or on the way to work—indeed, any objects we encounter outside of a book or a museum. But it also may be seen in almost all of them. What may we say of it? All or nothing. Its simplicity is the simplicity of extreme abstraction, two of the most basic shapes, two of the most basic colors, nothing more, nothing less. The abstraction is arresting and estranging, reducing the profligate plurality of our everyday experience to a set of basic components, like a mathematical equation, at once beautiful and ugly, orderly and mad.

THE MAD DREAM OF PERFECTION

Madness plays a significant role in Kojève's thought.[1] In his dispute with Leo Strauss over the political commitments of the philosopher, Kojève's most striking argument against the sheltered, contemplative philosophical life is that it cannot successfully differentiate itself from madness. Kojève maintains that the philosopher's isolated judgment that his knowledge is superior—that he or she knows something more—is invalidated by the fact that there is madness, "which, insofar as it is a correct deduction from subjectively evident premises, can be 'systematic' or 'logical.'" The philosopher who claims to know is simply not that distant from "the madman who believes that he is made of glass, or who identifies with God the father or with Napoleon."[2] There is biting irony in these comparisons, since they call into question the authority of several leading figures in the Western tradition as well as a key element in the philosophical tradition, the divine madness or θεία μάνια that compels the genuinely philosophical mind to look beyond appearances, to resist the rule of the given by attempting to understand it—that is, by attempting to know something *more*.

While Kojève's argument clearly alludes to Plato (and Christ), he also alludes to one of the dominating figures in Russian literature, Fyodor Dostoevsky, whose brooding creation, the theoretical murderer Rodion Romanovich Raskolnikov, very much identified with Napoleon Bonaparte.[3] But there is another character in Dostoevsky's work who may hold even more significance for Kojève in this respect: Alexei Nilych Kirillov, the theoretician of suicide in Dostoevsky's third large novel, *Demons*. By tracing the link between these references to Plato and Dostoevsky, in the next several chapters, I aim to reveal how Dostoevsky's development of the notion of madness creates a framework articulating essential issues at stake in the subsequent Russian debates about the proper ends of human life—and the end of history—as a prolegomenon to consideration of Kojève's reading of G. W. F. Hegel.

To anticipate, I argue that Dostoevsky revives and clarifies the association of the striving for perfection, either as a striving to found the perfect city or to overcome all limitations of finite existence, with madness, albeit madness touched by the divine. Dostoevsky portrays this madness in a decidedly negative light, offering in its stead a portrait of radical finitude. Dostoevsky thus sets off an ambiguous hero of nonfinality against the hero of finality, perfection.[4] Two of the main lines of thought emerging in his wake, that of Vladimir Soloviev and of Nikolai Fedorov, develop this Dostoevskian problematic, if in radically opposed ways, as we shall see. For his part, Kojève reprises substantial elements of the

Dostoevskian position in his interpretation of Hegel by interpreting the ascent to absolute knowledge as a philosophical, even atheist, variant of deification, of becoming wise or a god on earth—a terminal, finite one.[5] Here the ambiguity of Kojève's approach is particularly evident. One may read Kojève as both repeating and overturning the Dostoevskian critique, as positing the sheer madness of striving to assume the role of an embodied god as the wise man—the σοφός—or its supreme sanity as the proper end of distinctively human life.

In this respect, Kojève's Hegel dares to conclude the extraordinary and complicated history of both philosophy and deification in one stroke, fulfilling the promises and warnings made in Plato's two fundamental works about love, the *Phaedrus* and the *Symposium*. It is surely no accident that these works lay the foundations for central narrative patterns of Western action and thought by eroticizing both, a move whose extraordinary strangeness Kojève recovers in his commentary on Hegel and in the later works that I will discuss in chapter 8, with a fundamental difference: if deification ends up in silence for Plato, in Kojève it is the result of a comprehensive Hegelian *discourse* narrating the ascent to wisdom as our gradual assumption of divine identity.

PLATO

The problem of madness appears frequently and in many guises in the Platonic dialogues. The philosopher appears to the uninitiated, after all, as having lost his bearings. Nothing could make this point more starkly than the descent of the enlightened prisoner back into the cave after having glimpsed the "things higher up" (τὰ ἄνω ὄψεσθαι).[6] The other prisoners seek to kill the one who has seen the higher realm. They fear and loathe him, giving birth to the cliché, flattering to the followers of Socrates and to many others claiming similar privilege, that the prophet of the truth is immediately decried by the many who are incapable and, therefore, unwilling to understand the truth brought to them. It is but a short step to the conclusion that the bearer of truth is a madman, for in the eyes of those who cannot conceive of any reality other than the one before them, such a figure may only be mad.

Plato makes this notion of madness central to the *Phaedrus*, where he famously refers to the striving to attain a vision of the "things higher up" as a blessed or divine madness, that is, a madness coming from the gods themselves.[7] What this provenance suggests for Plato, as opposed to the Greek tradition, may be gleaned from the narrative about the nature of the soul that Socrates provides in the dialogue. It is well to recall here that the dialogue takes place outside the city walls, near a stream infused with narrative, particularly the narrative of the snatching away of Oreithyia by Boreas, the north wind. As other commentators have noted, situating the dialogue outside the city in a place of rapacious mythic abandon is highly significant, for it emphasizes the tension in the dialogue between emancipation and restraint, which is arguably one of its most important thematic structures. The tension may be best described as one between license, the apparent freedom to let one's desires express themselves as they will, and the restraint that comes from reining in those desires so as not to harm others, so as to live tolerably well within the city according to its laws.

This tension emerges directly in the discussion of eros itself as a way of referring to the impulsion to throw off restraint, not only in the pursuit of given objects, like the girl Oreithyia, but also, more fundamentally, in pursuit of emancipation from restraint of any kind other than the restraint imposed by the pursuit of emancipation itself. This latter pursuit seems to be associated with the divine—as if one were stung by the god—because it seeks to partake in the radical freedom the gods enjoy, perhaps the most radical freedom imaginable: the freedom from death.

Socrates's expression is telling. After listening to Phaedrus's reading of a speech attributed to Lysias and making a speech of his own, the notoriously uncreative, maieutic gadfly creates in his second speech a remarkable counternarrative. Socrates begins this narrative by asserting that the divine is soul and that "all soul is without death" (ψυχὴ πᾶσα ἀθάνατος).[8] The Greek suggests a unified, atemporal "thing," which, as such, cannot really be a thing at all. More curious still is that this unique, invisible, unimaginable thing is what the erotic seeker or lover pursues, namely, communion with the deathless or, in the more common Latinate paraphrase, immortality itself. Yet if the object defines the quest—and surely it must, for the quest depends entirely on the object, without which it would not take place at all—then this quest is of a most unusual kind. What is it, after all, to pursue immortality as communion with something that cannot be a thing, whose identity is perhaps best described as a resistance to identity?

The most obvious response is that such a quest is simply mad. It carries within itself a contradiction or problem that belies the appeal of immortality as the proper end of human activity. If Plato notes elsewhere that the governing eros of human activity is oriented toward immortality, he is rather more reticent to clarify what the consequence of this activity might be. And there is good reason for such reticence, since the quest for immortality seems indistinguishable from the most complete eradication of oneself as a being in time and space, having a particular language, gender, age, and color. Put more bluntly, the quest for immortality is in this sense the most radical expression of the eradication of the seeker or the lover—what we may now call the self. The quest for immortality is a quest for self-immolation: suicide.

Divine madness is madness precisely because it beckons the seeker or lover to suicide. The philosopher as the most genuine avatar of the seeker is the most avid suicide of all. As such, why would the philosopher ever return to the cave, to the city? What drives the philosopher away from the highest, most noble goal?

Socrates is clear on this: the body. The primary reason that the philosopher is unable to retain his relation to the soul as the inviolate, invisible immortal is because of the interference of the body. The image of the soul losing its wings, an image worthy of Aristophanes's version of the erotic being in the *Symposium*, is central to Socrates's narrative in the *Phaedrus*. Not only does this image anchor the narrative but also it is a figuration of that narrative itself. Let me explain this latter point first.

Socrates emphasizes that the narrative is little more than a figuration. "So, then, concerning the immortality of the soul this is enough; but concerning its appearance [ἰδέα], one must speak as follows. To tell what it really is would be matter for an immense and divine description, while what it is like belongs to a human and lesser one."[9] This reduction to human terms is in itself as grotesque and inhuman as the image of the soul provided by the description itself—it is evident that no merely human description may do justice to the soul. Narrative or myth, that is, can be little more than an approximation, and, even as such, this approximation is problematic because it borders on the edge of the ridiculous to translate into an image that which by definition has and can have no image.

This proviso about the mythic narrative suggests that it is little more than a fiction making a promise it cannot possibly keep. If one were less charitable, one could argue that the proviso tells us that the mythic narrative is merely a lie, a cousin to the necessary or noble lie (γενναῖον ψεῦδος) that features so prominently in the *Republic*.[10] Insofar as it is a lie, it is a necessarily grotesque distortion of what it purports to describe. This is worth keeping in mind.

The narrative itself is quite simple:

> We will liken the soul to the composite nature of a pair of winged horses and a charioteer. Now the horses and charioteers of the gods are all good and of good descent, but those of the other races are mixed; and first the charioteer of the human soul drives a pair, and secondly one of the horses is noble and of noble breed, but the other quite the opposite in breed and character. Therefore in our case the driving is necessarily difficult and troublesome. Now we must try to tell why a living being is called mortal or immortal. Soul, considered collectively, has the care of all that which is soulless, and it traverses the whole heaven, appearing sometimes in one form and sometimes in another; now when it is perfect and fully winged, it mounts upwards and governs the whole world; but the soul which has lost its wings is borne along until it gets hold of something solid, when it settles down, taking upon itself an earthly body, which seems to be self-moving, because of the power of the soul within it; and the whole compounded of soul and body, is called a living being, and is further designated as mortal.[11]

This living or mortal body is beset by conflict because it brings together heterogeneous elements. Whereas the divine intelligence beholds what is unchanging and thus perfect because it is free of the interference of the body, the mortal intelligence cannot free itself of this interference. Therefore, the mortal intelligence is not capable of sustaining perfection; the most it can do is glimpse the perfection that it cannot durably possess. Socrates continues:

> Of the other souls, that which best follows after God and is most like him, raises the head of the charioteer up into the outer region and is carried round in the revolution, troubled by the horses and hardly

beholding the realities; and another sometimes rises and sometimes sinks, and, because its horses are unruly, it sees some things and fails to see others. The other souls follow after, all yearning for the upper region but unable to reach it, and are carried around beneath, trampling upon and colliding with one another, each striving to pass its neighbor.[12]

This mythic narrative, which may have once seemed so dangerous as to merit the execution of its author, is now the stuff of cliché. The narrative of the errant soul—errant because embodied or "fallen"—striving to return to its origin in a perfect heavenly realm may be found hidden in almost countless forms, from the remnants of Christian narrative to the progress narratives that still hold sway in the secular imagination as narratives of self-improvement or, perhaps most ironically, of sensual satisfaction.

The majority of these narratives express little more than a desire to be freed of limitations associated with our emplacement in the physical world. They are in this sense dreams of another world. Their relation to the world of quotidian experience is effectively a nonrelation for those who spot the contradiction inherent in identifying a world of pure form in terms of a world of impure forms, a contradiction that otherwise might be expressed as one between a world outside and a world inside of time. That a world outside of time might even exist is a logical problem that narrative works to conceal or disguise. And this may be said for Plato too. The Platonic narrative that purports to describe the perfect realm must be false, since perfection—pure unity—cannot be described without transforming it into what it is not.

Madness is thus a decidedly uncritical affair. To be stung by the gods is to be intoxicated with lies, stories, possibilities that may never be realized. But, as Socrates says, "Madness that comes from a god is superior to sanity, which is of human origin" (τόσῳ κάλλιον μαρτυροῦσιν οἱ παλαιοὶ μανίαν σωφροσύνης τὴν ἐκ θεοῦ τῆς παρ' ἀνθρώπων γιγνομένης).[13] Better to be mad than reasonable; better inspired than prudent; better filled with fictions than fixated (dully) on what is already "real."

What are we to make of this madness, then? On the one hand, we might read this divine madness through one of its successors, the romantic notion of inspiration or genius, according to which an individual expresses, as if chosen by the muses, the universal current of our lives otherwise hidden in their particularity. The artist is in this sense the privileged vehicle of the divine, the one who divines in the smithy of his soul the "uncreated conscience" of the race.[14] On the other hand, we might read this divine madness as the most powerful expression of the desire to free ourselves from all limitation, as I have suggested. But this freedom also has several facets: it can be a freedom expressed as a freedom to create whose most radical, far-reaching, and disturbing facet is the attempt to create ourselves wholly anew, a self-creation that transforms the human being, stuck in mortality, into a being no longer stuck in mortality but no longer recognizable, either.

This dual quality of erotic ascent is even clearer in the celebrated "ladder of love" example from the *Symposium*, a work traditionally linked to the *Phaedrus*:

> "A lover who goes about this matter correctly must begin in his youth to devote himself to beautiful bodies. First, if the leader leads aright, he should love one body and beget beautiful ideas there; then he should realize that the beauty of any one body is brother to the beauty of any other and that if he is to pursue beauty of form he'd be very foolish not to think that the beauty of all bodies is one and the same. When he grasps this, he must become a lover of all beautiful bodies, and he must think that this wild gaping after just one body is a small thing and despise it.
>
> "After this he must think that the beauty of people's souls is more valuable than the beauty of their bodies, so that if someone is decent in his soul, even though he is barely blooming in his body, our lover must be content to love and care for him and to seek to give birth to such ideas as will make young men better. The result is that our lover will be forced to gaze at the beauty of activities and laws and to see that all this is akin to itself, with the result that he will think that the beauty of bodies is a thing of no importance. After customs he must move to the various kinds of knowledge. The result is that he will see the beauty of knowledge and be looking mainly not at beauty in a single example—as a servant would who favored the beauty of a little boy or a man or a single custom (being a slave, of course, he's low and small-minded)—but the lover is turned to the great sea of beauty, and, gazing upon this, in unstinting love and wisdom, until, having grown and been strengthened there, he catches sight of such knowledge, and it is knowledge of such beauty."

What is this beauty?

"First, it always is and neither comes to be or passes away, neither waxes nor wanes. Second, it is not beautiful in this way and ugly that way, nor beautiful at one time and ugly at another, nor beautiful in relation to one thing and ugly in relation to another; nor is it beautiful here but ugly there, as it would be if it were beautiful for some people and ugly for others. Nor will the beautiful appear to him in the guise of a face or hands or anything else that belongs to the body. It will not appear to him as one idea or one kind of knowledge. It is not anywhere in another thing, as in an animal, or in earth, or in heaven, or in anything else, but itself by itself with itself, it is always one in form; and all the other beautiful things share in that, in such a way that when those others come to be or pass away, this does not become the least bit smaller or greater nor suffer any change."

Then a summary:

"One goes always upwards for the sake of this beauty, starting out from beautiful things and using them like rising stairs: from one body to two and from two to all beautiful bodies, then from beautiful bodies to beautiful customs, and from customs to learning beautiful things, and from these lessons he arrives in the end at this lesson, which is learning of this very Beauty, so that in the end he comes to know just what it is to be beautiful."[15]

Beauty is both plenitude and nothingness, positive and negative perfection. It does not take much effort to conclude, however, that positive and negative perfection are in fact one and the same, since full identity is no more capable of being grasped as a thing than full nonidentity. Both exceed what we may understand by a thing, that is, by any particular thing in the world. If we cannot understand perfection in terms of things or objects, then we are hard pressed to understand what perfection may mean, for understanding requires a syntax or "logic" of relations that the notion of perfection, predicated on pure self-consistency, must exclude as its very condition of possibility, to employ a Kantian turn of phrase. The striving for perfection, either as plenitude or nothingness, then, is madness insofar as it seeks in either case the completely unconditioned, the absolute, what has no relation to anything else—the very antithesis of sociality, of life.

Beauty in itself as plenitude, being, perfection, whatever one may like to associate with finality, is riven by a startling ambiguity: it is at once beautiful and terrible or, indeed, sublime. It is so because in its perfection or completion it represents a radical abstraction from anything we experience in the world. To make this beauty the highest "object" of human striving is to identify the only striving that truly counts with overcoming the world of everyday experience. The imperative is clear: one must seek union with beauty, with being, with the eternal and unchanging. As the mystical tradition well understood, this imperative leads to annihilation of the self, to silence, to *fanā*.[16] The imperative is in this sense a directive to leave one's life behind, and what a mystic may perform as a metaphoric instantiation of this annihilation comes down to a simple act of suicide in its literal and most violent incarnation. Beauty is indeed at once beautiful and ugly, beguiling in its perfection and terrifying in its distance from, or negation of, lived life.

The Platonic challenge is clear: to pursue beauty in itself is madness, but it is also the only sense-giving pursuit for the one who seeks to engage in philosophy, for beauty is one way of describing that wisdom, or *Sophia*, after which the philosopher seeks as a lover of wisdom, as one in search of the perfection that is wisdom. This perfection liberates one from the imperfection of the world of appearances—the pursuit of beauty in this respect is the pursuit of the most radical emancipation from imperfection, the difficult life lived down here below. From this perspective, the life lived down here below is itself ugly because imperfection is ugliness, first and foremost, the horrid ugliness imposed on each one of us by disease and death, the collapse of our corporeal existence. Here we have a reversal that turns on a negative evaluation of the life down here below based on its limitation, its finitude. And, indeed, the notion that the highest goal of human striving should be the acquisition (in whatever form) of perfection presumes that the imperfect life—the life of the finite, embodied individual—must be overcome. We must become free, just as gods or madmen are free.

The challenge is quite literally breathtaking. It is a call to revolution that bids us to leave behind our lives in the muddle of the imperfection that is our world down here below. It is a call to throw away what we have in pursuit of an existence that cannot be even tolerably clear to any of us, since what is clearest to us in our everyday world must be quite unclear to the one having seen the sun, having possessed the absolute vision that seems to condemn us to silence or chatter in the cave, the underground. This call echoes through two millennia. Perhaps all of Western culture has been colonized by Plato, and so it is in the Eastern Christian lands as well. If Heidegger makes the former point with succinct force in his celebrated essay "On Plato's Doctrine of Truth," Kojève seems to insist on it as well in his writings on Vladimir Soloviev and, indeed, in his commentary on Hegel.[17] Yet, in doing so, Kojève opposes Hegel to Plato in the sense that, for Hegel, final wisdom is attainable in discourse.

THE UNDERGROUND MAN

The radical desire for freedom from the muddle of indefinite existence seems to be one of the core concerns of Dostoevsky's fiction, demonstrated most memorably by his persistent interest in crime. Dostoevsky is not only a virtuoso of suicide; his fiction also presents a series of absorbing portraits of what extreme emancipation might look like, a gallery of myths of ascent to perfection, of dreams and obsessions, that rival their most imposing literary models, including those of Plato himself. Before proceeding to a discussion of two of those myths—that of the theoretical murderer Raskolnikov and the theoretical suicide Kirillov—I turn to the work that opens up the questions animating these mythic responses, *Notes from Underground*, a text exploring the life down here below, "liberated" from any ideal or ostensibly palliative myth of emancipation.

Indeed, *Notes from Underground* sets out a countervailing, perhaps "antimythic" portrait of emancipation as emancipation from the very striving for emancipation—freedom is to be sought not in the self-immolation that is the final end of self-perfection but precisely in avoiding the temptation to attain perfection as final freedom from the muddle of life down here below. Dostoevsky challenges the venerable tradition that views divine perfection as the highest of all values by presenting, in the extraordinary figure of the underground man, a view that celebrates, however ironically or morosely, finitude, the freedom that comes from being unable to finish, to achieve perfection. To the grand myths whereby man seeks to become a god or God, Dostoevsky opposes a humbler, uglier, less tragic tale—that of the imperfect being, the being in need of other beings, the being whose freedom is experienced as insecurity and suffering, a being that can be underground or, in its more positive form, very much in the world.

In this respect, it has become a commonplace of Dostoevsky criticism to maintain that *Notes from Underground* first opens up the various veins of ore later mined by the immense novels that constitute Dostoevsky's primary achievement.[18] I think that this commonplace, like many, is justified. *Notes from Underground* first posits the questions about this life down here below, its value and justification, that occupy the heroes of the subsequent novels. In short, *Notes from Underground* sets for the later novels a framework of response that is remarkably dialectical.[19]

FREEDOM AND NATURE

What could be more humiliating, boring, and ridiculous than our abject servitude to nature? We all have a "toothache," as the underground man puts it, using a simple example to make a crucial point: that pain reminds us uncomfortably of the natural necessity we cannot easily overcome, if we can overcome it at all. It hurts, and we moan, and "in these moans is expressed, first, all the futility of our pain, so humiliating for our consciousness, and all the lawfulness of nature, on which, to be sure, you spit, but from which you suffer all the same, while it does not."[20]

The lawfulness of nature and futility are closely related for the underground man. If nature is lawful, then there is no deviation from its laws; there is no act that can contravene nature. Put simply, we are entirely at the mercy of nature's laws, which prescribe, first and foremost, that we must die. A toothache is but a symptom of a far more comprehensive illness. One is reminded here of the celebrated final line of Plato's *Phaedo*, where Socrates's "cheerfulness" about his death comes out awkwardly as a withering judgment about life as an illness from which one is cured only at the end. Or, at least, this is how Friedrich Nietzsche interprets

Socrates's final words to Crito, and Nietzsche's interpretation seems quite persuasive.[21]

Yet the underground man says more. Not only do we suffer and moan about our suffering. We also derive pleasure from our moaning. We turn our moaning into sweet music that consoles us. While the transformation of pain into sweet music is a commonplace, arguably a romantic one,[22] it also points to another dimension of lawfulness that is very important for the underground man: repetition. While the "iron law" of nature may well prescribe our death, it also enforces a strict conformity on our life, a routine, that is likely the most powerful reminder of its sovereign authority in our everyday experience (precisely as everyday). Where there is only repetition, there is no novelty, no possibility of the new. Where there is no possibility of the new, there is only repetition (for a being subject to time). What sweet music can one possibly make out of repetition? What is sweet about repetition? If one rolls the boulder up the hill only to have it come down each time, why not simply fall under the boulder and be done with it?

The curious fact is that this tale of futility is in fact a tale. Why tell such a tale? Is it sweet music? It may not be sweet, but it is a kind of music, and it is sweet insofar as it is a consolation—surely, the underground man is percipient in this claim.[23] Otherwise, it would be very hard to understand why anyone would seek to record his or her pain, as the underground man does. Why create a record of one's moans if there is nothing consoling in it? Why write if writing changes nothing?

We look to look away.[24] Is this not the cardinal injunction? Is "sweet music" little more than a diversion from what we "always already know"? The underground man is, however, quite unable to listen to the "sweet music," to enjoy the pleasure his pain seems to inflict on him. One has only to recall the opening lines of the novella: "I am a sick man . . . I am a wretched man. An unattractive man."[25] The underground man is unable to look away. He is insufficiently mad. And yet he wears a conventional face of madness, as the one who cannot become anything, "not even an insect," as the one who hesitates, mired in indecision and apparent impossibility.

As the indecisive one, the underground man contrasts himself with those who have no difficulty making decisions, the "ingenuous people and active figures" who are able to act precisely because they do not think, precisely because they have rejected endless discourse in favor of action. The underground man is blunt about these active people: "As a consequence of their narrow-mindedness, they take the most immediate and secondary causes for the primary ones, and thus become convinced more quickly and easily than others that they have found an indisputable basis for their doings, and so they feel at ease."[26] These are the truly mad ones, the "charging mad bulls" possessed by an idea, possessed by the truth, those that have achieved or are on their way to achieving a final, decisive point in their lives.

The underground man, on the contrary, cannot stop thinking,

> Well, and how am I, for example, to set myself at ease? Where are the primary causes on which I can rest, where are my bases? Where am I going to get them? I exercise thinking, and, consequently, for me every primary cause immediately drags with it another, still more primary one, and so on ad infinitum. Such is precisely the essence of all consciousness and thought. So once again it's the laws of nature. And, what finally, is the result? The same old thing.[27]

Stuck in interminable, impotent discourse, the underground man cannot help but speak, and, in doing so, he seems to do little more than repeat his moan, his lament, even in different forms, as if to alleviate his boredom. Though he seems unsatisfied with his complaints, he seems equally unsatisfied with the prospect of liberation from them. He cannot decide; indeed, he turns the notion of decision upside down by emptying it of any positive criteria by which to make a final decision or even to make sense of decision as such.

Viewed from this perspective, the basic opposition developed by the underground man is at first blush a venerable one: the theoretical man is to be distinguished from the practical one. Theory and practice are, indeed, not unified but desperately, even comically, incommensurable.[28] When one thinks, one cannot act, and when one acts one cannot think. The examples may be multiplied, but one has only to recall a celebrated moment in the *Symposium* when Socrates, prior to entering Agathon's house to begin the festivities, mysteriously halts. Socrates halts, it seems, so as to consider his action. One cannot act and consider action at the same time, a point made twenty-five hundred years later by Martin

Heidegger, who noted that philosophy as such is a vexatious activity because it halts activity; one cannot reflect on the basis of a particular way of being without somehow stepping out of it while one considers it.[29] Reflection and action are thus incommensurable. The meditation that aims at synoptic understanding is at odds with action that is always within a context, in a given place and time—in a word, *involved* or *partial*.[30]

Perhaps the most sardonic play on this old distinction in *Notes from Underground* comes in the second part, where the underground man and the prostitute Lisa engage in no discourse at all while they are otherwise engaged in that most basic of actions, intercourse. The discourse "blooms" only after the act that first brings them together has in fact been completed. This play is indeed all the more sardonic because the underground man's discourse seems to be a cynical and impromptu performance, a feigning of sympathy for the prostitute's plight, which appears to have a transformative effect on her. Of course, in the end, the speech leads to no direct change in the underground man, who, in a grotesque repetition of their original encounter, is happy to have sex with Lisa again when she comes to him, having taken up his offer to leave her previous life. But he ends up dismissing her rudely and returning to the world of endless discourse that is his underground, the world of fiction, of literature, of the intellectual and the man of letters. The underground man cannot relinquish his freedom, and, in this respect, he is a perhaps grotesque example of negative freedom, of negation transformed into a "positive" criterion for action.

FREEDOM AS HESITATION

The underground man insists on the distinction between the man of action and the man of discourse. But rather than deciding which is to be preferred, the underground man treats the distinction from the standpoint of hesitation and in fact transforms hesitation into a principle of action itself. Is this a sort of trick, the play of a sophistical imagination? One might argue that the latter is indeed the case, and a number of studies decry the futility and sadness of the underground man's dilemma.[31]

There is nevertheless one nagging problem here: the underground man does not really fit this kind of characterization. Indeed, he seems to mock the interpreter who might make the very clichéd claim that the underground man's hesitation, his inability to make clear decisions, are reflections of profound or existential despair, a kind of paralyzing nihilism. The underground man seems far too cheerfully nihilistic in this sense. He is very much the forerunner of Louis-Ferdinand Céline's Bardamu and Samuel Beckett's Molloy, and perhaps others in the twentieth-century pantheon, for although he bemoans his situation in the world, his misery, he also mocks it.[32]

Put simply, the underground man tries to subvert the very opposition he otherwise affirms. Does he succeed or fail? And what might success or failure mean? The answers to these questions will turn us back to the guiding thread of my account, madness, which I described as the radical quest for freedom, the most complete emancipation. Is not madness as a radical desire for emancipation a desire for freedom from narrative that need not make sense of itself, that is, in this sense, the most beguiling nonsense? Is not the radical desire for emancipation a kind of madness precisely because it values nonsense above sense?

To escape restraint, we charge headlong into nonsense. This is the heritage of the underground man that works itself through Russian thought and up to the one who perhaps most perfectly realized its consequences, Kojève. And Kojève is, in this respect, both an exemplary and apostate disciple of Dostoevsky. This is so because Dostoevsky recognizes at once the madness of the man of action who stops thinking, who decides to act without grounding that action in reason, that is, by acting in accordance with a proper reason; likewise, Dostoevsky recognizes the madness of the one unable to find or depend on any reason whatsoever. We have here two kinds of freedom, one positive, pursuing a more or less mad ideal, the other negative, resisting any ideal. As Dostoevsky puts it memorably in chapter 9 of the first part of *Notes from Underground*:

Perhaps you think, gentlemen, that I am mad? Allow me an observation. I agree: man is predominantly a creating animal, doomed to strive continuously towards a goal and to occupy himself with the art of engineering—that is, to eternally and ceaselessly make a road for himself that at least goes *somewhere or other*. But sometimes he may wish to swerve aside, precisely because he is *doomed* to open this road, and also perhaps because, stupid though the ingenuous figure generally is, it still sometimes occurs to him that this road almost always turns out to go *somewhere or other*, and the main thing is not where it goes, but that it should simply be going, and that the well-behaved child, by neglecting the art of engineering, not give himself up to pernicious idleness. Which, as is known, is the mother of all vice. Man loves creating and the making of roads, that is indisputable. But why does he so passionately love destruction and chaos as well? Tell me that! But of this I wish specially to say a couple of words myself. Can it be that he has such a love of destruction and chaos (it's indisputable that he sometimes loves them very much; that is a fact) because he is instinctively afraid of achieving the goal and completing the edifice he is creating?

The underground man then makes his famous claim that while "two times two is four is an excellent thing," one might also say that "two times two is five is sometimes also a most charming little thing."[33] Here is the most radical claim of the underground man, that perfection is a deadly thing, perhaps beautiful in its purity but ugly insofar as it can bring only stasis or a living death to which the nonsense, the sheer absurdity of a sentence whose sense is to be empty of sense, is a life-giving antidote.

FREEDOM AS NONSENSE

The underground man frames this famous praise of nonsense, his *stultitiae laus*,[34] most respectably by reference to another venerable opposition: that between freedom and necessity. He starts out with the conventional and oft-noted critique of rational self-interest. The argument runs roughly as follows. The pursuit of rational self-perfection leads to the essentially algorithmic governance of human behavior and action; indeed, it is in this sense the perfection and thus elimination of the divide between theory and practice that we have already discussed. That is, the reconciliation between theory and practice, the impossibility of which seems to be crucial to the mytheme created by Plato and affirmed through many avatars in our tradition, becomes first possible as a dream or end in the guise of rational self-perfection.

This rational self-perfection, as Dostoevsky indicates, relies on mathematics and, in particular, on an algorithmic point of reference that can reduce all behavior types to a discrete calculus of relations.[35] Rather than dismissing this position as absurdly naive, the central thrust of the underground man's argument is to take it very seriously indeed. And he does so with good reason, since one may argue that such a calculus of relations is in fact a sort of synecdoche for profound currents in modern rationalism whereby the final end is a *characteristica universalis*, a sort of universal grammar, that has banished the possibility of error. The universality of this grammar is predicated on the impossibility of error. All minds that use this grammar—and all minds must use it—are brought together as one in every speech event. There is no isolated speech event, no speech event that cannot be made transparently clear to all. There are thus no idiolects, no accentuations of given conventions, no dialogues that do not repeat countless previous dialogues—there is and can be nothing particular, nothing extraordinary, nothing new.

The underground man's response to this solemn perfection is a radical challenge to it, so radical that many might think it merely spurious or mad.

> But I repeat to you for the hundredth time, there is only one case, one only, when man may purposely, consciously wish for himself even the harmful, the stupid, even what is stupidest of all: namely, so as *to have the right* to wish for himself even what is stupidest of all and not be bound by an obligation to wish for himself only what is intelligent. For this stupidest of all, this caprice of ours, gentlemen, may in fact be the most profitable of anything on earth for our sort, especially in certain cases.[36]

Perhaps nothing can be more profitable for us than nonsense. What could be more profitable, more exhilarating, even divine, than not having to make sense? For all sense is a kind of coercion, a straitjacket in which we supposedly must work if we are to work at all, if we are to *be* at all. But must we follow these strictures? May we not contravene them? By contravening them, do we not merely reassert their coercive power so that our impetus to move beyond or escape them becomes nothing else than a topic of mockery or, in the worst cases, punishment?

These sorts of questions get to the very core of *Notes from Underground*, an essential argument for freedom that equates freedom with the most extreme dismissal of any restraint on our human volition, such that volition cannot even make sense to itself anymore and, indeed, should not have to do so. To be free, in its fullest and most radical sense, is to not have to give an account of oneself to anyone, including oneself. A completed grammar or calculus of relations, as complete, transparent self-knowledge, is thus turned hollow, and Nietzsche likely praised the "un-German music" of *Notes from Underground* precisely on that basis—as a devastating parody of the injunction repeated in the *Phaedrus*, "Know yourself" (γνῶθι σεαυτόν).[37] Let me explain by returning our discussion to its original starting point in the *Phaedrus*.

Kojève notes, at the very beginning of a still largely unpublished manuscript from 1940–1941, that central to the concept of wisdom (*Sophia*) in the Greek tradition is the acquisition of self-knowledge, the fulfillment of the injunction to know thyself.[38] If one is to attain wisdom, one must acquire perfect self-knowledge. Kojève defines this perfect self-knowledge as the ability to answer any question that may be posed about one's actions. When one has answered all such questions satisfactorily, there is literally nothing more to do. Any further action can be nothing more than repetition or affirmation of what one always already knows. All knowledge has this revelatory quality insofar as we come to understand explicitly what was already implicitly "there." Philosophy as the pursuit of wisdom is in this sense a prolonged enterprise of making ourselves explicit to ourselves, and it assumes that we do in fact do so.

The echo of Platonic *anamnesis* (ἀνάμνησις) in this way of thinking is hard to miss. Coming to know, for Plato, is an act of recollection of what the soul always already knew in the hyperouranian realm, prior to the catastrophe of embodiment that so distorted the soul's previously clear vision that it forgot many of the things it had seen before, and had seen in their perfect form rather than in the form distorted by the contingencies of existence in the world of becoming—the world, as we say now, of time and space. Likewise, coming to know, even in the sense of responding to questions or otherwise interpreting one's surroundings, seems to be predicated on the discovery of things that are "there" waiting to be discovered, that are latent in our everyday experience, which, from this point of view, is a kind of blindness.

The central assumption here is that we are in a latent sense complete; thus, it is the work of a life, if it is to be an examined one, to effect completion by bringing into the light or making explicit the implicit aspects of ourselves. All knowledge is in this sense either recollection, as Plato suggested, or an act of making explicit whatever was for some reason implicit in our lives—the essence of rationality is self-explicitation.[39] If we return to the modern dream of a complete grammar or calculus of relations as a philosophical project, we might add that the same impulse to completion and full explicitness is evident there as well, but in a way that applies not only to our own consciousness of ourselves but also to ourselves as microcosmic representatives of the whole. Each one of us both expresses and mirrors the whole; we contain everything and everything is contained in us. This symmetry entails that self-knowledge is knowledge of the whole and that knowledge of the whole is self-knowledge, an equation that became much more celebrated in Hegel, as we shall see.

The underground man dares to upset this structure by insisting that the highest goal is not self-knowledge but in fact the rejection of self-knowledge insofar as self-knowledge is merely another way in which one can become a piece of a machine, a piano key.[40] The polemical use of the term "piano key" in *Notes from Underground* stems from the concern that the striving to achieve complete knowledge of the human being must lead to a transformation of the human being into an object, all of whose characteristics are settled. Here the underground man makes a connection between the attainment of knowledge and becoming a thing: to know results in reification.

Perhaps the most important aspect of the striving to become a thing, to become complete as a referent in a *characteristica universalis*, is that the notion of thinking itself must change. Perhaps the correct nature of thinking will become clear. For thinking, in this context, is precisely the correct and complete relation of all things to each other such that nothing can be changed, added, or subtracted. Change is indeed only possible as error, a limit, an outside. The basic claim here is that as long as we are a thinking thing, we must think in the way that is prescribed, the way that is correct or, as we say, "logical."

There is nothing surprising about this. We are supposed to think correctly, and as the political slogan might have it, correct thought begets correct action. To think correctly, moreover, is to think in a way that clearly grasps what was "always already there." This addition is necessary because of a formidable problem: to think correctly presupposes that no counterexamples exist, and to be sure that no counterexamples exist, one must have covered all possible counterexamples. Otherwise, one cannot be sure that one is thinking correctly, because, after all, a counterexample *may* be produced. To think correctly thus presupposes totality, that the correct mode of thinking that establishes the norm is not capable of being refuted by any possible counterexample. But this is the problem: How, then, is it possible for anyone to be incorrect if the correct is the true and complete account? If the account is true and complete, how can anyone do other than follow that account?

There are two separate issues here. On the one hand, there is the case where one thinks correctly but is simply not aware of the way of thinking as such; the one who reveals the principles of correct thinking as being themselves a component of that thinking is merely making explicit what is implicit in our thinking. Thus, the examination of thought makes us conscious of the principles that govern that thought. We become aware of the rules and that is all, for even our awareness is governed by those rules. One cannot separate the examination of the rules from the rules themselves—this kind of knowledge is completely circular, even viciously so. On the other hand, there is the case that one thinks incorrectly and learns the correct way by being referred to what was always already there. Still, in this case, it is difficult to explain how the incorrect, or error, seeps into the world.

This is no idle question. The seepage of error into the world resembles, on the cognitive level, a question that emerges on the ethical level: Whence evil?[41] The major difference is that one denies the importance of volition to cognition but not to ethics. In other words, there is a long tradition that places the introduction of error into the world clearly in the hands of one who concretely acts, the finite human being. The human being may act differently than he or she should, and the disunity that this possibility implies plays a key role in distinguishing the human from the divine, for the capacity to act incorrectly stems from a defect or imperfection in the human being that obviously cannot exist in the deity whose perfection rules out the very possibility of defect. In the deity, there can be no variance between thought and action, while in the human being, the lack of such variance would be a most striking possibility—a lack belonging to saints and madmen.

FREEDOM AND DIALECTICAL REASON

There is yet another problem, which takes the issue even further: How is it that we may think meaningfully about correctness and error? The very capacity to think about correctness and error seems to bring up the specter of a way of thinking that is beyond both. What is thinking beyond correctness and error? Is it still thinking? And here we return to the problem of defining what thinking is, a problem that is central to *Notes from Underground*, where various kinds of attitude to thought are brought forth, some connected very closely with action, some incapable of such a connection. The structure that emerges reinforces the impression of a marked dialectical tendency in Dostoevsky's narratives, a tendency that emerges in those narratives in a way that both reflects the German tradition of dialectical thought and calls it into question. Given the considerable importance of this structure for the series of arguments that will build on it in what follows, culminating in Kojève's own refashioning of dialectical reason, I want to examine this aspect of *Notes from Underground* in somewhat more detail, before moving on to the later novels.

If we look at the two perspectives that the underground man contemplates, we come to a complicated view of the options offered in the novella. Basically, there are three options: thought and action are one, thought and action are not one, or thought and action are not all.

1. Thought and action are one. The unity of thought and action is the outstanding characteristic of the man of action. This unity consists in the fact that the man of action has chosen a set of norms that govern his actions more or less completely and is unlikely to be moved by counterexamples because he interprets them in terms of what he already takes to be the case. The man of action is thus generally impervious to change and incapable of recognizing the counterexample as constituting a threat to his way of action. For these reasons, the man of action no longer needs to think, other than to think in the ways already prescribed by the chosen norms. Put differently, the man of action exercises a variant of calculative rationality because, for him, thinking is merely meeting those norms or affirming them by transforming something that may be other than those norms into those norms. The problem, however, is that the man of action has chosen not to think further. He has adopted those norms on a basis that is not subject to those norms; indeed, that basis may not be subject to any norms. His choice of those norms is not explicable within their terms, and as such it is not normative or not rational—it is mad.

2. *Thought and action are not one.* The disunity of thought and action is the outstanding characteristic of the man of inaction, "the man who sits with folded arms," in the words of the underground man.[42] The man of inaction is literally unable to decide how to act. All action is thus reactive, compelled by circumstances beyond the control of the man of inaction, who prefers to avoid entanglements of this or any sort because they compel action that the man of inaction cannot condone. Indeed, the man of inaction must regard any of his actions as being a betrayal of his intellectual probity, and this notion of betrayal sets up yet another tension that can never be resolved. The man of inaction is a locus of inexhaustible tension because the disunity of thought and action guarantees constant and irremediable tension. The underground man is a hero of negation, so much so that he rejects or negates his own negation. In this sense, he is mad, because he is incapable of assuming any regime of reason, even the one he uses to justify his negative stance.

3. *Thought and action are not all.* This is perhaps the most curious position. What is beyond thought and action? Here the question comes down to the problem of reflection: What exactly is reflection? One would have to argue that reflection is thought, not action, and, if so, then it seems that reflection, to the extent activity must be halted so that one may reflect, is merely a variant of the kind of thinking already discussed. Reflection might be this disruptive thinking par excellence, a kind of thinking that never gets anything done. But is that really so?

If the position that gives us the relation of thought to action is not in fact subsumed by that relation, then it is very hard to describe exactly what it is. Let me put the matter clearly: thought about the relation of thought to action must be either a further replication of that thought or outside the notion of thought defined as replicable in that way. But if that thought is merely a further replication of the thought it describes, one may wonder how description can in fact proceed, because it seems to be predicated on some distinction between the thought reflecting upon and the thought reflected upon that cannot be resolved; if it were resolved, the reflective relation would itself be dissolved. This is a crucial point: the point of view of thought reflecting cannot be the same as the thought reflected upon. If it were, the relation could not exist, because the difference crucial to it between observer and observed could not be constituted successfully.

The upshot is provocative: either reflection is impossible or it is possible only on the basis of the impossibility of identifying the reflecting agency fully and finally—and if the reflecting agency cannot be identified in terms of the agency being reflected upon, then the basic problem of identity cannot be resolved. This is merely to underscore the impossibility of reflection as a kind of thinking and thus, once again, the impossibility of reflection itself.

What, then, is reflection? What is this point of view that lies beyond all points of view? If it is not an identity or a nonidentity, then what is it? One thing is sure: what it is not. It is not a thinking *I* that can come to understand itself. On the contrary, I cannot know myself, I cannot get clear about myself, I remain and must remain a mystery to myself. The wondrous and terrible consciousness of self as self is impossible.

Notes from Underground seems to bring together all three positions: that of the unthinking actor, of the thinker who cannot act, and of the one who reflects on the actor and thinker from a position that is not resolvable into or "coextensive" with either. The third position, if it is one, is perhaps the least convincing, however, and we shall have to deal with it with some care. First of all: just "who" is this third, not resolvable into the positions given in the text? The most obvious and the simplest response to this question is that this person is none other than the author, whom we know to exist both as a real person and as the creator of the fictional world that is *Notes from Underground*. One of the terminologies that enables us to describe the author of the text when he or she hides behind the narrator is that of the "implied author." There are many ghostly echoes here, for we may not be able to say much more about the implied author than that he or she *is*—and in a way other than that of the characters who are "within" the fiction itself.

But this implied author draws attention to himself (for we are speaking of Dostoevsky here) right at the beginning of the work, with a peculiar note that merits being quoted in full:

> Both the author of the notes and the *Notes* themselves are, of course, fictional. Nevertheless, such persons as the writer of such notes not only may but even must exist in our society, taking into consideration the circumstances under which our society has generally been formed. I wished to bring before the face of the public, a bit more conspicuously than usual, one of the characters of a time recently passed. He is one representative of a generation that is still living out its life. In this fragment, entitled "Underground," this person introduces himself, his outlook, and seeks, as it were, to elucidate the reasons why he appeared and had to appear among us. In the subsequent fragment will come this person's actual "notes" about certain events in his life. –Fyodor Dostoevsky

The note itself employs some of the same cloying techniques as the underground man. A primary example of this is the impression of contradiction created by the first two sentences. On the one hand, Dostoevsky openly declares that the work is fictional, while, on the other, he also ensures us that this fiction has purchase on social reality insofar as the main character "not only may but even must exist." Of course, the use of the two modal expressions only muddies the waters further. This is so because they indicate not simply that this character exists (and if he did, why not merely tell his story as a newspaper might?) but also that his existence is both possible and necessary, thus suggesting an ideological commitment that serves to undermine the notion of the author as impartial and external to the work. Indeed, the injection of authorial intention into our reading of the work at its beginning has the same effect. While one should probably not go so far as to claim that this insertion of authorial presence and intent has the effect of the comic parabasis, it nevertheless exerts an ironic influence on the work because it interrupts the fictional compact—the suspension of disbelief—both implicitly, as an author's note, and explicitly, in terms of the content of the note itself.

This ironical attitude is of course matched by the hesitations of the underground man himself; and one might be tempted to view the underground man as an authorial disguise created for prudential purposes. But this identity is not a sure one—irony or dissimulation cannot finally be ruled out. And this seems to be the central point we may make about the figure of the author, the one who presents the conflict between the active and the theoretical man: he is both part of that conflict and beyond it. Like irony itself, he seems to both participate in and reject the fiction he ostensibly creates. Here is the role of this peculiar third, at once assenting to and rejecting his creation as such.

What is the significance of this position that denies that it is one? The most obvious and important significance is to suggest that there is in fact some position beyond all positions or, better, one that cannot be defined in terms of those positions other than as an X that is their very condition of possibility and, as such, cannot be qualitatively identical to them. The elusiveness of the fictional author mirrors the elusiveness of the author of the given, which, as author, cannot be qualitatively identical with what is given. In both these cases, a basic Christian proposition is at work, according to which creation is possible. I do not add here the usual complement, "ex nihilo," because that is the heart of the issue. For, if creation means that something new emerges, then the source of that emergence must also be like the new; that is, it can have no relation to anything that already is, other than as a nonrelation (and even this is open to question). If creation, then, is creation of the new—and what other creation can there be?—then its basis must be in what is utterly different from what is, something akin to nothing, though this nothing cannot be a quality or attribute but rather the absence of both.

Dostoevsky thus creates a peculiar version of a familiar structure in *Notes from Underground*. We find the opposition of theory to practice described ultimately from a point of view that subscribes fully to neither and which, moreover, cannot even give an account of itself.

KOJÈVE'S CLOSED LOGIC OF SENSE

This problem will return in Kojève's development of Hegel's dialectical logic. Kojève will attempt to refute what he appears to consider the most important issue in the dialectical logic: whether it is a closed or open logic. What this means, from our current standpoint, is that a closed logic is one in which the "observer," the one developing the logical structure itself or the one telling the story, folds himself neatly into the story. An open logic is one in which the observer or storyteller cannot be folded up or otherwise absorbed into the logic itself but remains, in a necessarily obscure way, outside that logic. The closed logic is a circular one in which the end returns us to a beginning. The open logic may have an apparently circular form, but the difference is that the circle cannot close back on its beginning but repeats itself, without final resolution of any kind being available.

Thus we find already, in *Notes from Underground*, the basic dialectical structure that will emerge in Kojève's work and that informs other aspects of Dostoevsky's fiction—which, to no one's surprise, has a profoundly dialectical structure. The fictional practice we examine next sheds light on Dostoevsky's pronounced focus on heroes of action, like Raskolnikov and Kirillov, and heroes of thought or negation, like the underground man and, in a much more complicated way, Nikolai Stavrogin. Dostoevsky creates a model of dialectical movement that opposes these heroes of action who seek perfection to those who negate that perfection. Dostoevsky calls into question, in the most candid way, both the striving for completion and the countervailing striving for incompletion in an attempt to find a proper end to this conflict, a reconciliation or equilibrium.

It is not clear that Dostoevsky resolves this conflict. As we shall see at the end of chapter 2, he offers a brilliant attempt at resolution, though it may prove inconclusive. This problem of inconclusiveness proved vexing to Dostoevsky's successors and is decisively challenged by Kojève, who transforms the intractable problem of completion and noncompletion, or finality and nonfinality, in his lectures on Hegel. At stake is the definition of the human itself. Is the human something to be overcome or should it continue in its flawed, seemingly nomadic, wandering? Is human imperfection to be preferred over human perfection, whatever form that might take? Or is equilibrium possible?

2

THE POSSESSED

If death is so terrible and the laws of nature are so powerful, how can they be overcome?

—FYODOR DOSTOEVSKY

s a self-proclaimed "paradoxalist," the underground man creates a series of arguments that undermine the striving for perfection associated with divine madness in the *Phaedrus*. The underground man is a distant cousin to Socrates himself, who was wont to claim, with all due irony, that his distinctive wisdom consisted in his knowing that he did not know, did not possess wisdom as perfect knowledge. Similarly, the impossibility that emerges in the discourse of the underground man, his savage parody of self-knowledge, is also an affirmation of the unattainability of final knowledge, that vision of the forms which is the sting of the god. Yet the sting of the god retains its power. The hesitation of the underground man and of Socrates is unlovely—recall that both Socrates and the underground man are ugly, unattractive. One may say the same of the praise of nonsense, for in what sense can nonsense ever claim to beauty? The necessarily inchoate notion of divinity one may associate with nonsense is recondite and unlikely to attract.

And, indeed, it is the great dark heroes of Dostoevsky's fiction who prove to be most beguiling, the ones who seek to step over the frontiers set by man and God. These heroes are great criminals, and they are great precisely because they dare to disobey, to say a new word, as one of these heroes, Rodion Romanovich Raskolnikov, notes at the beginning of *Crime and Punishment*.[1]

RASKOLNIKOV AND THE NEW JERUSALEM

Raskolnikov is a response to the underground man. We first encounter Raskolnikov in a situation closely resembling that of the underground man. Even the language is similar, because it is a language of indecision, hesitation. The opening paragraphs of *Crime and Punishment* are striking examples of the same technique of hesitation one finds in *Notes from Underground*. The intricate syntax of the opening sentence underlines this: "At the beginning of July, during an extremely hot spell, towards evening, a young man left the closet he rented from tenants in S—y Lane, walked out to the street, and slowly, as if indecisively, headed for the K—n Bridge."[2]

The subsequent paragraphs sustain the atmosphere of hesitation and indecision: Is Raskolnikov cowardly or brave? Is he downtrodden or bold? Is he crushed by poverty or not? None of these questions receives a clear answer. Raskolnikov is enigmatic until he acts decisively—to kill the pawnbroker. Raskolnikov's new word, the decision that extricates him from his kinship with the underground man, is of course the decision to murder the pawnbroker. Raskolnikov's new word issues in crime.

Of course, there is nothing unusual about the identification of crime with novelty. Raskolnikov seems to allude to Niccolò Machiavelli when, much later in the novel, his article "On Crime" emerges, in which Raskolnikov praises the one who introduces "new modes and orders," the legislator or lawgiver.[3] To be a founder, a "prince" in the full sense of this word, is to advocate new laws that contravene the old. Raskolnikov's justification for novelty—or, at the least, for ensuring that the new, while criminal, may be justified as such—is that the new laws are the creation of the exceptional man, such as Napoleon.

The exceptional man, the genius, is, as I have already suggested, the modern, romantic equivalent of the one stung by the divine in the

Phaedrus. The essence of the justification is that superior knowledge gives one authority to commit crime if, by doing so, that superior knowledge may be more effectively realized. In a way very reminiscent of Friedrich Nietzsche—and, as such, not overtly Christian—Raskolnikov's article condones the death of hundreds, if not thousands, should that death help the new word to institute itself.[4]

If one has something akin to that vision of the forms that Socrates describes in the ascent of the soul to the hyperouranian realm, one is entitled to bring it back to the world and to quell resistance—to kill—in order to disseminate it throughout the world. In this sense, Raskolnikov takes the universal claim for authority to its proper level as a measure for all of humanity. And, of course, the problem with this measure is quite obvious: How is one to know that it is the truth?

This question returns us to Kojève's characterization of madness. Implicit in Kojève's characterization is a claim about what constitutes authority. For Kojève, the "vision" or deduction of the isolated thinker has utterly no validity as truth in and of itself, no matter how universal that claim is supposed to be. How can one extend one's immediate certainty to all human beings? On what basis do all others have to accept this subjective certainty as a truth? It is in this sense no accident that the vision of the hyperouranian realm in the *Phaedrus* is presented in mythic form. There is no argument to defend the authority of the vision; rather, there is nothing more than bare assertion.

The equivalent, in action, to bare assertion is aggression, physical coercion. The most extreme form of bare assertion is murder. Finished with discourse because it cannot lead to a durable assertion of authority, Raskolnikov moves to action, declaring himself, by his act alone, to be the authority he thinks he is. Lest one reject as fanciful this characterization of Raskolnikov, we ought to examine it within the context of others who transform their vision of the truth into action as a means of asserting an authority that discourse alone cannot seem to achieve.

Raskolnikov gives us an easy and pertinent modern example: Napoleon.[5] Of course, the myth of Napoleon stands by itself as one of the crucial myths of the nineteenth century. As a myth, it seeks to impose in discourse the very authority that Napoleon sought to wield through his military conquests. At the foundation of the myth is pure self-assertion founded on genius or innate superiority. There is no external authority, no truth outside of the simple fact of greater ability, that serves Napoleon as a justification—or at least this may seem to be the case initially. But Raskolnikov does not focus on this aspect of the Napoleon myth. One might infer that he does so only in response to the questioning of his nemesis, Porfiry Petrovich, who attempts to reduce the defense of Napoleon, or the extraordinary man, to the argument for authority based solely on superior ability. Raskolnikov, on the contrary, supplies a crucial element to the argument. He does so by making references to the discoveries of Johannes Kepler and Isaac Newton, scientific discoveries whose truth is confirmable by evidence that compels *universal* assent. Raskolnikov insists that the discovery of these universal truths is sufficiently important to merit the elimination of all those who might resist those truths, if only "out of spite" or a love of nonsense.

But what can Napoleon possibly have in common with Kepler and Newton? What is Napoleon's great discovery or new thought? Napoleon's greatness seems to reside in his attempt to realize a universal empire, a New Jerusalem; his great deed is to announce a new word (that will also be a *final* word). Napoleon will bring about the end of time. Raskolnikov indicates as much:

> "As for my dividing people into ordinary and extraordinary, I agree that it is somewhat arbitrary, but I don't really insist on exact numbers. I only believe in my main idea. It consists precisely in people being divided generally, according to the law of nature, into two categories: a lower or, so to speak, material category (the ordinary), serving solely for the reproduction of their own kind; and people proper—that is, those who have a gift or talent of speaking a *new word* in their environment. The subdivisions here are naturally endless, but the distinctive features of both categories are quite marked: people of the first, or material, category are by nature conservative, staid, live in obedience, and like being obedient. In my opinion they even must be obedient, because that is their purpose, and for them there is decidedly nothing humiliating in it. Those of the second category all transgress the law, are destroyers or inclined to destroy, depending on their abilities. The crimes of these people, naturally, are relative and variegated; for the most part they call, in quite diverse declarations, for the destruction of the present in the name of the better. But, if such a one needs, for the sake of his idea, to step over a dead

body, over blood, then within himself, in his conscience, he can, in my opinion, allow himself to step over blood—depending, however, on the idea and its scale—make note of that. It is only in this sense that I speak in my article of their right to crime. (You recall we begin with the legal question.) However, there's not much cause for alarm: the masses hardly ever acknowledge this right in them; they punish them and hang them (more or less), thereby quite rightly fulfilling their conservative purpose; yet, for all that, in subsequent generations these same masses place the punished ones on a pedestal and worship them (more or less). The first category is always master of the present; the second—master of the future. The first preserves the world and increases it numerically; the second moves the world and leads it towards a goal. Both the one and the other have a perfectly equal right to exist. In short, for me all men's rights are equivalent—and *vive la guerre éternelle*—until the New Jerusalem of course."

"So you still believe in the New Jerusalem?"

"I believe," Raskolnikov answered firmly.[6]

Raskolnikov's defensive irony notwithstanding, this is a bold assertion of the intrinsic value of the New Jerusalem, of the universal state in which history and the state itself will be dissolved. Not stated quite so openly is the implicit premise that all merely particular forms of resistance must be eliminated for the sake of the universal state. What exactly does this mean, if its meaning is not readily apparent on the surface? And is it?

The commonsense view may be that Raskolnikov merely advances a variant of "typical" political expediency arguments, reduced nicely into the formula "The ends justify the means." While Raskolnikov's argument contains this thought, it also goes further by identifying the end as the creation of the New Jerusalem—not merely a particular political order that may itself yield to other political orders in an endless struggle for dominion of one kind or another, but a political order that brings a close to all politics in a final apocalyptic transformation, in the establishment of a final universal order, the heavenly city.[7]

The distinction Raskolnikov makes between the ordinary, who adhere to repetition, conservation, and continuity, and the extraordinary, who are such precisely because they disrupt continuity, seems most intriguing in this context. It is difficult, if not impossible, to grasp what the final order may be if it is anything other than the final or definitive establishment of flawless repetition—the final state is akin to the kind of state we may associate with the triumph of the rule of flawless, self-regulating reason. What is new about the New Jerusalem?

The most provocative response to this question is the most obvious: it is universal. How can a state be universal and still be a state? How can one square universality with repetition of anything that has had an origin? Put more simply, how can one square something that is by definition not in time or not temporal (as an end of time) with anything that has ever been or still is in time? How is it even possible for us to imagine something as a thing that is not in time?

Perhaps it is the very definition of madness to think in this way. Let us recall the *Phaedrus*. The vision of the hyperouranian realm is just that: a vision of what is timeless. If the hyperouranian realm were in time, it could not be what it is. But as it is something that is by definition not in time, one has to wonder what it possibly can be. And here, of course, the wonderful story that Socrates tells, the myth, allows one to skate over these difficulties, provided one does not think too closely about them. But if we do, we come once again to a fateful question: May one give form to what has no form?[8] Plato does not allow this question to be raised directly, since he populates the hyperouranian realm with the forms. Plato takes a different tack, allowing a different question—that of the forms' possible relation to the things of which they are the "ideal" or "perfect" form—to be raised in other dialogues, most famously in the *Parmenides*.

For Dostoevsky, this question is fundamental, and Dostoevsky makes explicit the connection between madness and crime that Plato is also much more reticent to make. Yet there is another connection to be made here as well, between madness, crime, and novelty, the "new" word. The new word is new precisely because it can never become routine, can never be made fully accessible to routine, because the grand, atemporal realm of the universal, the final state, is strictly speaking unimaginable; it is transcendent.

Here we enter into the oldest of arguments, and they turn on what the transcendent, the universal, the infinite—that which is in some manner outside our experience or any possible experience—can possibly be for us. When imagination cannot be translated into any form of possible experience, this is madness in its clearest and most disturbing form. This is indeed the notion of madness that Kojève develops in a subtle way in his essay "Tyranny and Wisdom."[9] To madness, Kojève opposes visions of the way things are, which can be translated into experience and become models for political behavior. While this point may simply seem to develop the usual ironies about the difference between the theoretical and the practical man—which it indeed does, with ironic delight—there is a more biting subtext: that madness is precisely the fixation on a view that cannot be translated into experience, that rejects myth, that rejects intellectual probity, that holds itself out in pursuit of a vision that in the end simply cannot be a coherent vision.

In this respect, as we look back and read Dostoevsky through Kojève, we may argue that this is exactly the point Dostoevsky's complex presentation of Raskolnikov makes. And the key piece of evidence for this claim is the remarkable emphasis throughout *Crime and Punishment* on novelty, on the new word that can never really be uttered, can never come to speech and, indeed, comes to be "uttered" as an unspeakable act of murder—not the translation into experience of a higher ideal but rather the elimination of experience as having any relevance in the first place. For murder in this sense, as the refusal to engage any others in one's own vision except so as to exclude them, to create the cloister of one, is the real essence of the mad visionary, the great criminal, and the prophet of novelty, at least as they emerge in the fictional world of Dostoevsky.

The creator of the new word is a master of nonsense who does not leave things at discourse. But the appeal of nonsense is evidently formidable enough to motivate the most radical political action, murder, or physical elimination of others. The master of nonsense seeks a freedom that is so complete, so universal, that it can resemble only the freedom of a god shorn of Platonic myth to appear as what cannot appear, as the god and freedom of mystic communion.

KIRILLOV: SUICIDE AS BECOMING GOD

If Raskolnikov presents the incoherent coherence of the striving for the universal as a striving for unbridled freedom in the establishment of the New Jerusalem—as the establishment, then, of a divine and perfect city—another important character presents this striving in its full splendor as a striving to overcome God: Alexei Nilych Kirillov. Raskolnikov's position remains within a primarily political context, the highest end being the establishment of a heavenly city that brings the kingdom of God to earth or represents the final fusion of the two, while Kirillov's more directly points beyond the political to metaphysical freedom. Put differently, Raskolnikov tests the boundaries of freedom, understood in the context of our relations to other human beings, whereas Kirillov squarely tests the boundaries of our relation to God or to any of his stand-ins, such as Being or nature.

Unlike Raskolnikov, Kirillov appears as a peripheral character. He is merely one of those characters in *Demons* who seems to be in the orbit of the novel's central character, Nikolai Stavrogin. But his primary concern, suicide, is central to the novel, as central as Stavrogin, who ends up committing suicide and is perhaps more consistent than Kirillov in that respect. Though I will return to Stavrogin—one of the most beguiling and complicated characters in all of Russian literature—I want to prepare that discussion by first examining Kirillov, especially given the interest that Kirillov has solicited from so many quarters, and from Kojève as well.[10]

Kirillov has got to be the most unusual "structural" engineer in literature. He is the theoretician of suicide, itself a provocative combination. While everyone may read Camus's revision of Hamlet's great question, there is still a decision at stake in Camus that Kirillov has definitely made.[11] For Kirillov, suicide is not a question but an imperative, and in this lies his curious "dark" appeal. Indeed, for Kirillov, suicide is the most significant imperative of all, quite a bit more significant than the injunction to "Know thyself" or to "Do unto others" and so on. Forget morality, the relation to others; Kirillov concerns himself with the only relation that matters: our relation to God. Of course, this aspect of the relation may leave those who have freed themselves of God blithely unaffected. Kirillov's concern with God may seem quaint and old-fashioned. God is dead, after all, and we have killed him. But Kirillov's concern with God is subtler. It is a concern with what God represents.

> "There will be entire freedom when it makes no difference whether one lives or does not live. That is the goal to everything."

"The goal? But then perhaps no one will even want to live?"

"No one," he said resolutely.

"Man is afraid of death because he loves life, that's how I understand it," I observed, "and that is what nature tells us."

"That is base, that is the whole deceit!" His eyes began to flash. "Life is pain, life is fear, and man is unhappy. Now all is pain and fear. Now man loves life because he loves pain and fear. That's how they've made it. Life now is given in exchange for pain and fear, and that is the whole deceit. Man now is not yet the right man. There will be a new man, happy and proud. He for whom it will make no difference whether he lives or does not live, he will be the new man. He who overcomes pain and fear will himself be God. And this God will not be."

"So this God exists, in your opinion?"

"He doesn't, yet he does. There is no pain in the stone, but there is pain in the fear of the stone. God is the pain and fear of death. He who overcomes pain and fear will himself become God. Then there will be a new, a new man, everything new. . . . Then history will be divided into two parts: from the Gorilla to the destruction of God, and from the destruction of God to . . ."

"To the Gorilla?"

". . . to the physical changing of the earth and man. Man will be God and will change physically. And the world will change, and deeds will change, and thoughts, and all feelings. What do you think, will man then change physically?"

"If it makes no difference whether one lives or does not live, then everyone will kill himself, and perhaps that will be the change."

"It makes no difference. They will kill the deceit. Whoever wants the main freedom must dare to kill himself. He who dares to kill himself knows the secret of the deceit. There is no further freedom; here is everything; and there is nothing further. He who dares to kill himself is God. Now anyone can make it so that there will be no God, and there will be no anything. But no one has done it yet, not once."[12]

The magnificent phrase "God is the pain and fear of death" rings throughout this passage and recalls a remarkable passage from Herman Melville that makes quite a similar point: "Faith, like a jackal, feeds among the tombs, and even from these dead doubts she gathers her most vital hope."[13] The pain and fear of death create God as a repository of hope, the hope that pain and death will not prevail, a hope that one might find patently ridiculous were it not enshrined in doctrines such as the Platonic immortality of the soul or Christian resurrection. Kirillov is not a creature of ridicule or irony, however comic or mad he may appear to those inclined to see him in that way. On the contrary, Kirillov shows a distinctive lack of affect when he discusses his all-consuming idea, and appropriately so, we may surmise, since the primary attitude he insists on is one of resolute indifference, a peculiar combination in its own right. Kirillov needs to prove his indifference, his freedom from all merely worldly interests, particularly those generated by fear, and the only way he can do so definitively is to commit suicide.

We do not typically associate suicide with indifference, however, because we do not typically associate action with indifference. If we return for a moment to dwell again on the difference between the theoretical and the practical attitude, we may note that the theoretical attitude observes and does not act, or sees no reason to act, because there is in fact a tension between contemplation and action. One contemplates the whole, and in order to contemplate the whole, one must suppress the kind of interestedness that obscures that contemplation of the whole or transforms it into observation from a perspective whose limits are dictated by the interests that prescribe what it may see. The notion implicit here is that my wants and needs determine how I look at things. Thus, the only way to see things "as they are" is to be free of the wants and needs that otherwise obscure my vision (belonging, as they do, to the animal imperative to survive). This way of thinking is obviously indebted to Plato and of course to the myth of the charioteer in the *Phaedrus*, where the pure vision of the hyperouranian realm—vision that is defined by its lack of perspective, the proverbial and contradictory notion of the all-seeing eye—is limited, if not completely blocked, by the passions that tear one away from this pure vision and force one to work with a limited recollection of it.

Suicide seems to be an action formidably entrenched in passion and, if we take the word literally at its root, in suffering. How, then, may suicide act as a proof of indifference? Must suicide not undermine the purpose to which Kirillov puts it? One may discern, in this respect, a failure of logic, a contradiction, and dismiss Kirillov as a madman, as one of those possessed by an idea that is quite literally incoherent. He, too, speaks nonsense in an effort to liberate himself from the humiliating recognition of nature's authority. Or perhaps his praise of suicide is a perverse form of that sweet music that the underground man described in connection with toothache. Perhaps the matter should not be left there. For Kirillov, indifference is freedom, and the highest freedom, the most complete indifference, can only emerge if one is unafraid to take one's life or to die, pure and simple.

Still, the nagging question remains: Why? Which interest impels one to seek liberation from all interests? Why would one have an interest in disinterest? And, indeed, what interest could be more powerful, more direct, and less easy to dissemble or sublimate than the fear of death? Melville seems to be correct in connecting vitality with the fear of death—we act in order to overcome the fear of death, to take it away, to hide it—and all these actions come from an overwhelming interest in turning or looking away from death.

Kirillov appears to be caught up in an ugly irony, a perversely "sweet music" indeed. This sweetness turns to the monstrous, however, in one of the most eerie and powerful scenes in the novel, when Pyotr Stepanovich Verkhovensky pushes Kirillov to make good on his promise to transform theory into practice by committing suicide. Kirillov resists Pyotr Stepanovich. Why he does so may be indicated by his own admission:

"There are seconds, they come only five or six at a time, and you suddenly feel the presence of eternal harmony, fully achieved. It is nothing earthly; not that it's heavenly, but man cannot endure it in his earthly state. One must change physically or die. The feeling is clear and indisputable. As if you suddenly sense the whole of nature and suddenly say: yes, this is true. God, when he was creating the world, said at the end of the day of creation: 'Yes, this is true, this is good.' This . . . this is not tenderheartedness, but simply joy. You don't forgive anything, because there's no longer anything to forgive. You don't really love—oh, what is here is higher than love! What's most frightening is that it's so terribly clear, and there's such joy. If it were longer than five seconds—the soul couldn't endure it and would vanish. In those five seconds I live my life through, and for them I would give my whole life, because it's worth it. To endure ten seconds one would have to change physically. I think man should stop giving birth."[14]

Kirillov hesitates. He makes a crucial distinction. The harmony he describes is intolerable for us in our earthly state. We cannot live harmony of this kind unless we physically change; that is, metaphysical transformation precedes political transformation. Without the radical freedom afforded by the transformation of the human being into a being capable of harmony, the political dream of harmony is nothing more than that—a dream. In that case, suicide, too, is merely a comfort offering an illusion of radical freedom. Even here, the freedom is so radical that one cannot even begin to describe it, presumably, for more than five seconds. Here we have nonsense again, a dreadful nonsense, evinced, moreover, by Kirillov's unusual language, a Russian that begins to lose syntactic integrity because it represents, as best as one can do in language, the disintegration of language as the foremost social bond that ties Kirillov to others, a tie that both discloses and restricts. In his headlong progress to emancipation from all limitation, Kirillov also emancipates himself from discourse—Kirillov moves from sense to nonsense. Rather than achieving a status equivalent to that of a god, Kirillov merely bestializes himself; he becomes a monster.

And so we return to the culminating scene of Kirillov's life. This scene develops the central difficulty of Kirillov's "theory," that he cannot make sense of his pursuit of indifference other than by revealing its rootedness in an overweening desire to live without the pain of limitation. We might assume that it is a simple matter for Kirillov to end his life, as Pyotr Stepanovich expects, in order to provide a necessary alibi. But Kirillov's theory itself emerges as a mask for a tyrannical desire to live. After all, the simple objection is devastating: Why make a theory about an act whose essential nature is to repose in silence? The genuine suicide need not speak, need not proselytize—the cultivation of indifference makes little sense if one may simply "get things over with."

Kirillov's mask falls off. He becomes animal. Pyotr Stepanovich waits for him to complete his promised suicide. But he hears nothing.

Though he was reading and admiring the wording, he still kept listening every moment with tormenting alarm and—suddenly got furious. He glanced worriedly at his watch; it was a bit late; and it was a good ten minutes since the man had gone out. . . . Grabbing the candle, he made for the door of the room where Kirillov had shut himself up. Just at the door it occurred to him that the candle was also burning down and in another twenty minutes would go out entirely, and there was no other. He put his hand on the latch and listened cautiously; not the slightest sound could be heard; he suddenly opened the door and raised the candle: something bellowed and rushed at him.[15]

This "something" is of course Kirillov, having become animal—no longer, it seems, capable of speech other than bellowing or shouting. Kirillov, indeed, barely utters another word in the novel (other than to shout "Now, now, now, now") and he dissolves into a something that Pyotr Stepanovich cannot even recollect or describe properly.

> Then there occurred something so hideous and quick that afterwards Pyotr Stepanovich could never bring his recollections into any kind of order. The moment he touched Kirillov, the man quickly bent his head down, and with his head knocked the candle from his hands; the candlestick fell to the floor with a clang, and the candle went out. At the same instant, he felt a terrible pain in the little finger of his left hand. He cried out, and all he could remember was that, beside himself, he had struck as hard as he could three times with the revolver on the head of Kirillov, who had leaned to him and bitten his finger. He finally tore the finger free and rushed headlong to get out of the house, feeling his way in the darkness. Terrible shouts came flying after him from the room.[16]

After this miserable drama, Kirillov manages to shoot himself. Long gone, however, is the rational suicide, the one who dies in order to be freed of the kind of impassioned, bestial action that his final moments seem to exemplify. The frenzied anger of the beast rather than the cool determination of the suicide prevails.

STAVROGIN, THE HERO OF EMPTINESS

Kirillov is merely a satellite. Stavrogin is the center, the "sun" around which all the other characters revolve.[17] Yet Stavrogin is a peculiar center. He is another master of nonsense, and the central role he plays in the novel has much to do with this enigmatic quality. Nietzsche is once again helpful. He maintains, in an aphorism from *Twilight of the Idols*, that those who are never understood have authority precisely for that reason— the authority of the enigmatic, mystery.[18] This aspect of Stavrogin comes clear very early on in the novel, when the narrator informs us of three striking and peculiar incidents. Immediately before he recounts the three incidents, the narrator provides a description of Stavrogin that makes an important point, one applicable to Kirillov as well: "I was struck by his face: his hair was somehow too black, his light eyes were somehow too calm and clear, his complexion was somehow too delicate and white, his color somehow too bright and clean, his teeth like pearls, his lips like coral—the very image of beauty, it would seem, and at the same time repulsive, as it were. People said his face resembled a mask."[19]

The combination of beauty and repulsiveness, as if at one and the same time Stavrogin is beautiful and repulsive (or twisted: отвратительный), does not make sense. How can one be, at one and the same time, both beautiful and repulsive? Does this not contravene the hallowed law of contradiction? Of course the claim that Stavrogin is dissembling, wearing a mask, serves to obviate the contradiction. In this case, Stavrogin is merely a creature of irony, *dissimulatio*, and nothing more. This notion of irony as one kind of sense hiding behind another seems far more comforting than the more radical notion of irony, according to which all varieties of sense hide, to a greater or lesser degree, a primordial absence of sense. In both cases, there is a ready distinction between sense and nonsense that affirms that there is a border between the one and the other that protects the integrity of each in relation to the other. However, this is not the case if one takes Stavrogin's peculiar ambiguity as encroaching on the tolerably clear divisions created by the law of contradiction. The greater and more disturbing import of this latter possibility is that the distinction between sense and nonsense begins, itself, to dissolve.

But this problem is only hinted at in the initial description. The three incidents that follow the description all seem to suggest that Stavrogin is a little mad in a conventional way, insofar as he engages in what we nowadays might call "random acts." These random acts are not kind ones, however, in which case their chance character might be passed off more easily. Rather, they are violent incursions, all the more violent because they do not seem to follow any logic. In this respect, the sheer menace of seemingly unmotivated action as dissolutive is much clearer. The first of these incidents involves a nose, the second a wife, the third an ear. All are darkly comic.

In the first instance, Stavrogin literally drags someone by the nose. This person, a respected elderly man, has the habit of accompanying his statements by the phrase "No, sir, they won't lead me by the nose!" Stavrogin at one point counters this statement by quite literally taking hold of and pulling the elderly man by the nose. The incident causes titters but it also disturbs, not for the reasons we might expect—such as Stavrogin's anger—but primarily because Stavrogin shows no anger whatsoever: "All this was very silly, to say nothing of its ugliness [безобразие]—a calculated and deliberate ugliness, as it seemed at first sight, and therefore constituting a deliberate and in the highest degree impudent affront to our entire society."[20] The claim made here applies to the other ostensibly "disturbed" actions of Stavrogin, both of which are violent, if in different ways, with the essential violence emerging either as a contravention of expected codes of conduct or of expectation itself. Stavrogin's love of novelty is a locus of crime, a calculated ugliness or nonsense.

Calculated ugliness is as unusual a combination as beauty and ugliness, although the connection may not be immediately evident. There is, however, nothing unusual about the association of beauty with order, an association that, as we know, stretches back to Plato and is a key aspect of the power that the hyperouranian realm may exert on those who have glimpsed it. The supreme order is beautiful because it is order, perfection, finality. Likewise, calculation depends on order—one may not calculate where there are no fixed rules of combination. If we accept that ugliness is the contrary of beauty, then it seems that ugliness denotes a lack of order. But, if that is so, calculated ugliness is itself difficult to understand. The orderly display of disorder? Is this not a sort of nonsense that implodes the boundaries on which both terms depend?[21]

The argument is this: Stavrogin plans his seemingly random acts. He is an agent of disorder. Yet to refer to Stavrogin as an agent of disorder is to reduce him to the very terms he seems to seek to deny. The deliberate perpetuation of nonsense is caught in the very logic it seeks to mock or overcome. This argument has been leveled at the underground man as well, and it is a variant of another argument: one cannot speak of nothing consistently because to speak of nothing is to transform it into what it is not by definition supposed to be. To speak about nothing is to speak nonsense.[22] Nothing cannot readily have sense unless it is not what it is. But if it is not what it is, then what is it?

These complicated ontological concerns need not detain us for the moment. The immediate point is that the narrator indicates that people seek to impute to Stavrogin a comprehensible identity, applicable to his seemingly random actions, as a way of dismissing the far more radical possibility his behavior raises—that there is no reason at all for it, that his behavior is simply an expression of chance, an expression of something that can have no coherent expression, that is the reverse of coherent expression. We return once again to the basic question: How may one give form to what has no form? And, in this respect, perhaps crime is the attachment to formlessness, the liberation from form.[23]

Kirillov and Stavrogin have in common an attachment to crime, insofar as both seem to be creatures of negation—Kirillov as the theoretical suicide and Stavrogin as a character who has no character, recalling the underground man's insistence that the intelligent man of the nineteenth century can only really be characterless. Stavrogin is a hero of nonidentity, a hero, in other words, whose identity is not to have an identity. In the guise of the hero, the beautiful individual, he is the very embodiment of ugliness or, perhaps more significantly, the embodiment of an irresolvable contradiction—or a contradiction resolvable only through suicide. In the end we learn that Stavrogin commits suicide, although we never really learn why he does so. One presumes that he could have remained in his own underground for as long as he wanted.

Stavrogin's suicide is much more enigmatic than that of Kirillov. Kirillov's suicide is not really what it appears to be: an act of theoretical freedom. It is not an acceptance of death being more beautiful than life, a point clarified by Kirillov's hesitation at the very end as well as by his incessant talk about his intention to die. In Kirillov's case, theory is a substitute for practice, not an overcoming of it. After all, this overcoming could only be forthcoming through suicide.

Stavrogin's enigmatic quality is indeed quite different. Boredom seems to overtake Stavrogin. Kirillov's "holy terror" before pain is worlds away from Stavrogin's descent into indifference. Kirillov is a good deal more like the active figures whom the underground man ridicules, whereas

Stavrogin is a brilliant avatar of the underground man himself, "shining darkness" or "beautifully ugly." But he is bored—and boredom, is it not ugly too?[24]

The sage can only be bored. The sage realizes the emptiness of all attachment (as Kirillov, for example, does not). The sage, beyond being and nonbeing, "is"—but in what sense? The sage is the characterless being or a being that *is*, insofar as it recognizes the emptiness of all merely specific shapes of being. The sage is in a sort of suspended animation, a figure that is detached, that offers no soothing tales, that provides no one with an impetus to act or not to act; the sage does not theorize. The sage is boredom itself, since for the sage there is nowhere to go and where he has come from can be little more than a history of error, comic error, for one who sees how all errors are merely comic attempts to give purpose, to alleviate boredom—and the terror of death is one of the great incitements to purpose. The sage is a variant of the last man, but a very complicated one, though they might appear to be exactly alike.

FINAL HARMONY

Theory and practice may not be reconciled. Or we may put the issue in different terms: reason and will may not be reconciled. There is a series of other couplets we may cite whose relation turns on a similar problem: that finality is both coveted and rejected. Though we may covet the harmony exhibited by God as at the very least a metaphor for perfection and an end to struggle, the effect of imitating that final harmony is boredom or unrelenting repetition, from which we seem to seek relief at all costs, as the underground man suggests.

How, then, do we approach this basic problem? Do we suggest that this structure is somehow fixed in human nature or in the metaphysical determinacy that we cannot overcome? Or is this structure itself merely a narrative behind which lies nothing at all other than a contingent history? These questions, largely of an epistemological nature, ask whether freedom is indeed possible, and possible other than as nonsense, as negation. If freedom is only possible as nonsense or negation, then we must return to question our definitions, because nonsense would seem to refer to the limits of our definitions rather than constituting a definition itself. A positive definition of a negative capacity is transformative, and hence impossible, because it gives that negative capacity a positive identity.

Yet if freedom is indeed possible other than as nonsense, then the question emerges as to why freedom matters. What matters about freedom such that we might desire to be free? Indeed, the question arises in either case because the fact is that we are talking about freedom, and in talking about freedom we reveal an interest in it that is more than a little pressing. Dostoevsky himself makes freedom into the highest aim of human activity. Dostoevsky installs the desire for freedom, even when that desire dissolves into nothingness, as the sine qua non of human activity. No other activity matters so much; will is more important than reason.

If we take the underground man and the other dark heroes of Dostoevsky's fiction at face value, we are compelled to conclude that they seek freedom from the humiliating force of nature described so eloquently by the underground man. Nature humiliates, and on top of that, human beings as natural beings humiliate each other in their attempt to overcome nature, to escape from its suffocating embrace. Here the link Gottfried Leibniz makes between metaphysical limitation and moral and physical evil is palpable.[25] Our metaphysical limitation—our imperfection or inability to overcome nature—is the fount of the kind of rebellion that moves Dostoevsky's heroes. But there is no necessity in the desperate striving of these Dostoevskian heroes; they may come to a different view, one which requires them to subordinate themselves to the whole, to leave behind will, defined as the marking point of disobedience in Dostoevsky just as it is in Augustine.

THE OTHER DOSTOEVSKY: ZOSIMA

There is also another Dostoevsky, who offers a response to the problem of freedom that is radically different from the one we have examined thus far. I have focused my account of Dostoevsky on a central difficulty, expressed clearly in Notes from Underground and in the triumph of violence—or will—in both Raskolnikov and the heroes of Demons. In all cases, this central difficulty, the conflict between reason and freedom or reason and will, proves to be incapable of resolution—one must opt for suicide or for the muddle of the underground man, who is incapable of resolving anything.

This other Dostoevsky transforms the muddle in a remarkable way. He does so by transforming the notion of freedom from one exclusively oriented to a freedom *from* limitations in any of the more or less utopian dreams of his heroes of will or nonsense to that of a notion of freedom *to* commit to a certain way of living that emerges as a practical *project*. Dostoevsky places the emphasis not on a terminal and absolute freedom—a kind of freedom that by definition can find no place in the world—but on a freedom that is worked out primarily as a freedom in relation to and among others. This kind of freedom, which takes as its condition of possibility the impossibility or incoherence of the absolute freedom sought by the Dostoevskian heroes of will—emerges in what Mikhail Bakhtin refers to as the "dialogicity" of Dostoevsky, a complicated notion, to be sure.[26] For the moment, however, I want to illuminate the basic distinction Dostoevsky draws between the hero of will, as one who strives for absolute freedom, and the much less dramatic hero of social freedom by reference to an intriguing example in Dostoevsky's last novel, *The Brothers Karamazov*: the enmity between Father Ferapont and the elder Zosima, which creates an astonishing counterpoint in part 2 of the novel, a "pro et contra" that deserves careful attention.

Father Ferapont is introduced in book 4 of part 2, the famous book entitled "Strains" or "Lacerations" (надрывы),[27] although he is mentioned earlier in the novel as an opponent of the institution of elders in general and an adversary of the elder Zosima in particular. Prior to presenting a detailed account of Father Ferapont, the first chapter of this book affords a glimpse of the elder Zosima's primary idea, which appears most clearly the closer he comes to death:

"Love one another, fathers," the elder taught (as far as Alyosha could recall afterwards). "Love God's people. For we are not holier than those in the world because we have come here and shut ourselves within these walls, but, on the contrary, anyone who comes here, by the very fact that he has come, already knows himself to be worse than all those who are in the world, worse than all on earth. . . . And the longer a monk lives within his walls, the more keenly he must be aware of it. For otherwise he had no reason to come here. But when he knows that he is not only worse than all those in the world, but is also guilty before all people, on behalf of all and for all, for all human sins, the world's and each person's, only then will the goal of our unity be achieved. For you must know, my dear ones, that each of us is undoubtedly guilty on behalf of all and for all on earth, not only because of the common guilt of the world, but personally, each one of us. For all people and for each person on this earth."[28]

Zosima's basic assertion here is that we all have a responsibility to each other, a proposition that has attracted substantial attention—one could argue that it is a cornerstone of Emmanuel Levinas's philosophy.[29] The basic notion is that we come first to recognize others in terms of our having a responsibility to them. Others are not there "for us"; on the contrary, others are "for us" only to the degree that we identify ourselves as being responsible or answering to them. Levinas is quick to identify the essentially social orientation of Zosima's simple exhortation. We are not monastic creatures but rather creatures whose primary devotion to God is expressed as devotion to others and not solely to God. The relation to others defines one's piety and godliness.

Father Ferapont represents a rigorist rejection of that notion; it is God who must take precedence over other human beings. The relation to God trumps the relation to other human beings. Individual salvation is central, not salvation as a group project, as a project that constitutes a community as such. Father Ferapont is a "great faster and keeper of silence" whose rigorous asceticism and eccentricity qualify him to be a "fool in Christ," one touched directly by the divinity. He lives apart from others and does not seek to deal with them.

Father Ferapont never went to the elder Zosima. Though he lived in the hermitage, he was not much bothered by hermitage rules, again because he behaved like a real holy fool. He was about seventy-five years old, if not more, and lived beyond the hermitage apiary, in a corner of the wall, in an old, half-ruined wooden cell built there in ancient times, back in the last century, for a certain Father Iona, also a great faster and keeper of silence, who had lived to be a hundred and five and of whose deeds many curious stories were still current in the monastery and its environs. Father Ferapont had so succeeded that he, too, was finally placed, about seven years earlier, in this same solitary little cell, really just a simple hut, but which rather resembled a chapel because it housed such a quantity of donative icons with donative icon lamps eternally burning before them, which Father Ferapont was appointed, as it were, to look after and keep lit. He ate, it was said (and in fact it was true), only two pounds of bread in three days, not more; it was brought to him every three days by the beekeeper who lived there in the apiary, but even with this beekeeper who served him, Father Ferapont rarely spoke a word. . . . He rarely appeared at a liturgy. Visiting admirers sometimes saw him spend the whole day in prayer without rising from his knees or turning around. And even if he occasionally got into conversation with them, he was brief, curt, strange, and almost always rude.[30]

Father Ferapont is a kind of madman or fool in Christ precisely because he takes no notice of other human beings. He mortifies himself and refuses to speak except in puzzling ways that others may try to interpret—the mantic speech of the "divine" madman is most frequently gibberish (and obscene) when one chooses to ignore the divine message supposedly locked therein. In this regard, Father Ferapont is also a purveyor of nonsense, and this nonsense together with his isolation are forms of freedom from the bonds of society that bear some resemblance to the kind of freedom enjoyed (and bemoaned) by the garrulous underground man. The dialogue with the northern monk that follows the description is one of Dostoevsky's great comic moments. But it is also revelatory of the peculiarity of Father Ferapont, who seems to have invented his own version of the Holy Spirit, the Holispirit, a comic play on words in the Russian (святой дух as apposed to святодух). Invention is, however, not a virtue of the truly pious, and there are more than a few hints that Father Ferapont's ostentatious piety is theatrical in a mocking sense that one would not associate with God but with human vanity, the very same vanity that propels Dostoevsky's other heroes to challenge God. In this respect, the elder Zosima, despite his position of authority, proves to be much more humble, much more aware of the distance between the disharmony and disorder of human reality and the divine harmony.

Zosima's project of humbling oneself before others is indeed a project of overcoming the tendency, natural as it may be, to place oneself before others: the tendency toward vanity. One way of acquitting oneself of vanity is to speak clearly so that all may understand, not in parables or riddles like Father Ferapont. For that matter, Father Ferapont's silence may just as easily be interpreted as rejection of speech, as rejection, thus, of the simplest element of relation to others. In the end, Father Ferapont's rejection of community tends to resemble contempt for the other, not true understanding. Only God is fit for Father Ferapont, who sees devils everywhere, especially in the cell of the elder Zosima, who has inadequately inoculated himself against others by actively advocating community.

The denouement of the tension between the elder Zosima and Father Ferapont constitutes a classic Dostoevskian "scandal" or "crisis" scene and serves to highlight the significance of the opposition between the two men as radically different ways of viewing Christianity, with Zosima oriented to largely "horizontal" relations, whereby the construction of faith is evidenced by the construction of a community, while Father Ferapont is oriented toward community with God, exclusive of any other kind of community. The section that immediately precedes the scandal scene provides an elaborate and remarkable narrative of crime and redemption, involving both the youthful indiscretion of the elder Zosima and a haunting murder tale of a mysterious stranger. It is certainly of special significance that Zosima's primary idea, the responsibility of each one of us to and for the other, for all others, seems to have particular resonance for this stranger.

> "Paradise," he said, "is hidden in each one of us, it is concealed within me, too, right now, and if I wish, it will come for me in reality, tomorrow even, and for the rest of my life." I looked at him: he was speaking with tenderness and looking at me mysteriously, as if questioning me. "And," he went on, "as for each man being guilty before all and for all, besides his own sins, your reasoning about that is quite correct, and it is surprising that you could suddenly embrace this thought so fully. And indeed it is true that when people understand this thought, the Kingdom of Heaven will come to them, no longer in a dream but in reality."[31]

The delicacy and simplicity of this thought seems belied by the reaction to Zosima's death, which follows this narrative. Zosima's corpse begins to smell. Questions arise about his sanctity, because there is no miraculous lack of smell and hence no miracle to provide a divine sign that Zosima is not merely human but somehow above the human. The focus on the supernatural, a focus away from Zosima's simple message, is clearly related to a rejection of that message as relying on mere human effort to bring forth a final kingdom without positive proof that doing so will in fact be a divine project. Those who seek to realize this project must rely on an essentially groundless conviction alone. Father Ferapont intrudes to raise the question of Zosima's sanctity and, by doing so, he instills doubt in many of those present. In response to a question put to him by one of Zosima's close associates—"And who can say of himself, 'I am holy?'"—Father Ferapont makes these telling comments:

> "I am foul, not holy. I would not sit in an armchair, I would not desire to be worshipped like an idol!" Father Ferapont thundered: "Now people are destroying the holy faith. The deceased, your saint here," he turned to the crowd, pointing at the coffin with his finger, "denied devils. He gave purgatives against devils. So they've bred like spiders in the corners. And on this day he got himself stunk. In this we see a great sign from God."[32]

Father Ferapont uses his authority as a great faster and keeper of silence to mock Zosima and his message of social harmony as the true import of the Christian project. One could just as easily argue that Zosima's insistence that we are guilty before and for all suggests that we make each other into idols and have a responsibility for the whole that encroaches, however subtly, on God's authority. Father Ferapont reaffirms the significance of individual salvation as primary against the salvation of all in a community of equals—we are slaves to God, not to men.

VERTICAL AND HORIZONTAL *ERŌS*

The distinction one finds in *Notes from Underground* undergoes a remarkable metamorphosis in *The Brothers Karamazov*, for the active man becomes a new kind of hero in *The Brothers Karamazov*, based on a notion of action whose end is radically different from that pursued by

Dostoevsky's heroes of will. The latter strive to attain an ideal that by its very nature leads beyond the human world, refusing to accept its imperfections in a pursuit that manifests the tensions we noted in the Platonic challenge. The attempt to achieve perfection, the ideal of beauty, ends up in the wholesale rejection of all that is imperfect, ugly, unnecessary—it is a call to eliminate finite life and, in this sense, it is a murderous, destructive call. In *The Brothers Karamazov*, in contrast, the ideal is incarnated in the other—one strives to redeem one's guilt toward the other, to perfect oneself by recognizing one's indissoluble debt to the other, what Zosima, in a significant passage, calls "active love," whereby one may truly become convinced of "the existence of God and the immortality of the soul."[33] Moreover, this notion of action as project leads one away from the vitiating indecision of the underground man and Stavrogin—one becomes God not by engaging in a necessarily impossible imitation of divine freedom, understood first and foremost as being free of the need to act, but by acting to bring about a perfect community where action will no longer require decisions, where action will become "second nature," and all the bitter questions of self-consciousness will resolve themselves in a finally finished compact in which all citizens will accept themselves in the other and the other in themselves. Theory and practice, reason and will, come together in a final synthesis.

Still, one cannot easily forget the underground man's declaration that man both strives for and fears the end of that striving, this latter fear emerging in the destructive rebellion against reason or whatever notion of authority declares that something is the case. To quote the grand inquisitor: "Man was made a rebel, can rebels be happy?"[34] How, then, might we reconcile these statements suggesting the primacy of will with the turn to reconciliation in an ostensibly or potentially final synthesis? Is a final synthesis impossible? Is finality or "peace" as such impossible? Or is the only finality the finality of unending struggle, the finality in which will acts to disturb whatever harmony or balance may have been achieved?

There can be little doubt that the underground man's insistence on the primacy of will, not as the expression of agency that impels us to complete or perfect ourselves but as what ensures that completion or perfection cannot arise, is remarkable. The Platonic mytheme of *erōs* toward beauty seems to be countered by a different *erōs* toward the interruption of beauty, toward destruction, the ugly, the disharmonious—in a word, toward deviation for its own sake.

The possibility of these two diametrically opposed *erōtes* affords us quite a different interpretation of Dostoevsky's heroes of will. For them, we might say, the ideal is simply a pretext or excuse, a form of camouflage for the undiminished exercise of will to counter the possibility of any order. From this perspective, Raskolnikov and Kirillov are heroes of will in a different and perhaps purer sense, since the residue of sense that seems to attach to their expressions of discontent is merely that: a residue, or even a simulacrum. As the narrator remarks in the chapter that introduces Father Ferapont: "For those who renounce Christianity and rebel against it are in their essence of the same image of the same Christ, and such they remain, for until now neither their wisdom nor the ardor of their hearts has been able to create another, higher image of man and his dignity than the image shown of old by Christ. And whatever their attempts, the results have been only monstrosities."[35]

If we return to the notion of strains or lacerations, we may come to identify two radically different kinds of heroes: those who seek to heal the wound and those who seek to keep it open, who live from the wound that they have no desire to heal—rather, they continue to prick it. But this is not masochism in any ordinary sense. Quite the reverse; this is a declaration of vitality as the capacity to suffer, to go against the common accord, to sow discord as the proper way of being human. Man is violence! Long live the underground!

If we take this view seriously, the hesitations of the underground man emerge as acts of will, as results of a decision not to obey, rather than an inability to decide. Indeed, this inability to decide is merely the propaganda of self-pity. The underground man celebrates his imperfection in a way that is utterly opposed to the Platonic model. He is a monster maliciously aware of his monstrosity. He is a Silenus, like Socrates, who hides a more fundamental will to destruction under the guise of a constructive doctrine of self-perfection, whose vitiating irony is of course the obvious, if unspoken, connection between perfection and death.

The divine madness of Plato that seeks freedom from the confusions of our life in this world, from the many indignities and necessities to which we are subject as long as we are beings in this world, finds its opposed mirror image in the hero of will. The core of the hero of will is not the desire to found the New Jerusalem, nor is it the desire to become a god beyond all human restrictions. Rather, the hero of will is a pure rebel, one who seeks to mock and undermine the creation. He is the most aggressive madman or criminal of all, because the hero of will has no other intent but to negate whatever is taken to be authoritative at any given time. The hero of will is the critic who goes beyond words to action—the one who negates but does not necessarily bring about good in doing so.[36] The powerful question that arises is whether this hero of will, focused on personal salvation, on striving to be one with God, on becoming a god vis-à-vis the world and all others, is not the most dangerous and violent of all criminals. The contrast to this remarkable personality is the hero of self-sacrifice and kenotic release, the social hero whose most heroic act is not the highest self-affirmation but its exact opposite: the highest self-abnegation, in something akin to the realization of a responsibility to and for the other, for all.

3

GODMEN

A purely human universe is inconceivable because without nature man is nothingness, pure and simple.

—ALEXANDRE KOJÈVE

W hat is left of madness after Fyodor Dostoevsky? The striving to be like a god or to become God cannot seem to escape its association with crime, the most violent and wholesale rejection of our servitude to others and to nature. Emancipation so understood is essentially asocial and cannot succeed as a social project because all such projects involve restriction, a rootedness in servitude that is not peripheral or accidental but of the very essence of the social compact. The conflict between reason and will emerges in this context as a conflict between the individual and society, between the "vertical" eros of metaphysical emancipation and the "horizontal" eros of social emancipation, the latter being little more than a form of enslavement, or "bad conscience," as Friedrich Nietzsche put it so eloquently in *Towards a Genealogy of Morality*.[1]

In the wake of Dostoevsky, two remarkable attempts to effect reconciliation between reason and will in their various avatars emerge in Russia, generating in no small degree the foundation for the religious renaissance of the late nineteenth and early twentieth centuries. At stake in both is the rescue of the concept of deification from the Dostoevskian polemic, not as a concept authorizing the most extreme emancipation from the social compact but indeed as the necessary *condition* of emancipation as a social project. Rather than affirming the lonely strivings of social outcasts, misfits, and criminals, the rogues' gallery for which Dostoevsky is both celebrated and pilloried, these attempts affirm a much more extreme project of universal deification or of deification as relating to all, not just to the lonely few, a project whose precondition is the emancipation *of*, and not *from*, all.

The two central figures here are Vladimir Soloviev and Nikolai Fedorov. Soloviev is considered the most important Russian philosopher. His concept of the Godman (богочеловек) is an attempt to effect the reconciliation of reason and will in favor of reason. Fedorov is an altogether more unusual figure, whose thought evokes astonishment and disbelief, for he argued that the only task of humanity, the only genuinely human task, is to overcome death, not only by saving all those who are alive but also by resurrecting all those who have ever lived.

Soloviev and Fedorov agree that deification is the proper end of history—that history ends once human beings have become divine. In this respect, they both reject the tension one finds in Dostoevsky regarding finality. Yet they come at finality in wildly diverging ways. Fedorov is quite obviously the more radical of the two. He holds that metaphysical emancipation is the only condition of possibility of emancipation. Any form of emancipation short of complete emancipation from the imperative to physical self-preservation, the fons et origo of sin and fear, is necessarily vitiated by its lack of completeness. Soloviev maintains a more moderate position according to which it is possible to become one with the deity by subordinating one's will to the deity's; by learning the proper lessons of subordination, one liberates oneself from the miseries of death.

VLADIMIR SOLOVIEV: *LECTURES ON DIVINE HUMANITY*

Soloviev's most influential and concentrated exposition of his notion of deification may be found in the famous Lectures on Divine Humanity

(Чтения о богочеловечестве), which he gave to a large audience in Saint Petersburg in 1877–1878.[2] These lectures offer a remarkable synthesis of theology and philosophy, as their title promises, as well as of elements in the Eastern Orthodox tradition and those of the Western intellectual tradition. In both senses, one might claim that Soloviev's lectures present a model for what Kojève was to do with G. W. F. Hegel some fifty years later in Paris. This layer of repetition should not be ignored, since Kojève carries on a polemic with Soloviev that is implicit in the Hegel lectures, though explicit elsewhere in Kojève's writings on Soloviev.[3] Hence, one may regard the Hegel lectures as a response to two masters as well as two different orientations to the singular question of what deification may entail.

Soloviev was a pivotal figure in nineteenth-century Russian thought, both the creator of the first truly comprehensive Russian religious philosophy and one of the principal inspirations behind the Russian religious revival of the so-called silver age of Russian literature, which ended with the revolution. He was born in 1853, in Moscow. His father was a prominent Russian historian. Soloviev attended Moscow University in 1869, first in the physics and mathematical faculty, then in the faculty of history and philology. He was an extraordinary student with very broad interests but an absorbing concern with theological issues. He attended the Moscow Theological Academy for a year after leaving the university, but he ended up studying philosophy at the University of Saint Petersburg, where he wrote his first book, *The Crisis of Western Philosophy (Against the Positivists)*, in 1874. He took a position at Moscow University but went to England on a yearlong grant to study gnosticism and mystical theology. He had the first of his famous visions of wisdom or *"Sophia"* at the British Museum. He returned to Russia in 1876 and produced a second book, *The Philosophical Principles of Integral Knowledge*. He resigned his post at Moscow University and became involved in the Pan-Slavic fervor of the Russian war with Turkey, in 1877. He delivered a speech in 1877 whose content is characteristic. Paul Valliere gives a fine summary:

> His thesis was as simple as it was bold. The world is dominated by two opposed, but equally flawed, religious principles: the Islamic or oriental principle of "the inhuman God," a formula justifying universal servitude, and the modern European principle of "the godless human

individual," a formula validating "universal egoism and anarchy." The conflict between these principles can only end in a vicious circle. Fortunately for humanity there is a country, Russia, where East and West meet and transcend their spiritual division in a higher religious principle: *bogochelovechestvo*, the humanity of God. As history's "third force," Russia is destined to blaze the path not just to Constantinople but to the universal, divine-human cultural synthesis of the future.[4]

It is a short step from this lecture to the series of lectures on divine humanity that we examine below. At roughly the same time, Soloviev produced another significant work, *The Critique of Abstract Principles*, published in 1880. During the last twenty years of his life, Soloviev engaged in an astonishing variety of activities journalistic, artistic (he is a significant poet), and of course philosophical. He wrote three important works: *The Meaning of Love* (1894), *The Justification of the Good* (1897), and *Three Dialogues on War, Progress, and the End of History, with a Brief Tale of the Antichrist* (1899). He died in 1900.

Soloviev's twelve lectures on divine humanity cover an immense range of thought about the proper end of human life, reprising that most traditional of philosophical questions—What is the good life?—in a distinctively modern context in which, with the rise of positivism, the question appears to have lost much of its force.[5] Characteristically, Soloviev opens his lectures with a plea to return not to philosophy but to religion or to a religious attitude to the world that more properly considers what for Soloviev is the crucial issue: the connection of the ostensibly contingent existence of "humanity and the world with the absolute principle and focus of all that exists."[6] The plain task of the lectures is to determine the nature of this connection and the consequences for action which follow from that determination. In this sense, the lectures are expressly political, though by couching their task in the language and conventions of religious discourse, Soloviev is able to mute the political implications of his conclusions.[7]

Before delving into the lectures, I should like to provide a guiding summary of their basic points. By doing so, I hope to make my subsequent discussions of the lectures clearer. Soloviev can be very pointed in his formulations, but he also covers so many issues in the lectures that they can tend to be diffuse at times as well.

Soloviev's central point is an apparently simple one: the striving proper to humanity is to assume the divine identity, to reflect maximally the divinity as the absolute in the contingent and relative circumstances of our everyday existence in the world.[8] We attain to divinity, becoming Godmen to the extent of our success in imitating the divinity, in a world that by definition does not allow for complete imitation. Every particular life is particular, though it may try maximally to express the whole or the universal in its particularity. And, to be sure, this is the final purpose of the striving to be truly human in Soloviev, for the most truly human being is the one who has most effectively made herself absolute, that has dedicated herself to the assumption of divine absoluteness or universality.

Soloviev's interpretation is remarkably—and no doubt self-consciously—triadic. One such triad identifies Plato with Augustine and, finally and more generally, with German idealism as the most modern avatar of the fundamental Platonic model and that which brings out most fully the implications of the Platonic model. German idealism is Platonic-Christian thought coming to its fullest and thus most self-conscious expression. The common element in all three is the identification of divinity with the absolute as necessarily idealist, as proposing a task that may be fulfilled only by the most radical incarnation of the absolute in each human being. Soloviev, as the emphasis on religion suggests, is not after personal salvation but the salvation of humanity as a whole, and nothing less than this total salvation can make a claim to that term.

The emphasis on salvation for all offers a response to the heroes of negation in Dostoevsky. It is also an attempt to explore the ostensibly positive aspects of Dostoevsky's fiction by giving philosophical depth to the seemingly exiguous claims for brotherhood, made most memorably in Zosima's speech in *The Brothers Karamazov*, where Zosima exhorts his listeners to bow down in guilt before each other. While I do not wish to linger on this point, it is interesting to note that Soloviev's turn to the great traditions of discourse about being, whether pagan or Christian, seems itself to betray Dostoevsky's emphasis on mythic representation. Zosima is very much an attempt to represent a good life to be followed or cherished as an example for action that leaves behind the endless talk of the underground man.

THE NEGATIVE ABSOLUTE

Soloviev's text is concerned, from the very beginning, with the negative, with the hero of negation or the human being understood primarily in the negative. If we recall the underground man's concern with the infinite, as leading from one determination to another to yet another and so on, Soloviev's account of the absolute in the second lecture makes abundant sense: "Absoluteness, like the similar concept of infinity, has two meanings, one negative and one positive. Negative absoluteness, which undoubtedly belongs to the human person, consists in the ability to transcend every finite, limited content, not to be limited by it, not to be satisfied with it, but to demand something greater. In the words of a poet, it consists in the ability 'to seek raptures for which there is no name or measure.' "[9]

One may argue that this is a perceptive description of the predicament of the underground man, and to a large extent it is, if one accepts that the underground man is indeed in pursuit of "something greater," a finality or absolution from the miseries of finite human existence in the underground. If this is so, the underground man becomes the archetype of the nonarchetypal being, the being whose identity is not to have an identity, a being defined by what it is not, an apophatic man to mock the notion of an apophatic god and, thus, the notion of man having become God. For, in this case, man having become God is little else than the man of the mystical tradition who engages in an ecstasy of self-annihilation in that precious moment of mystical union, the *unio mystica*, or "night in which all cows are black."

But Soloviev also has another modern type in mind, the active man. To put this in broader terms, Soloviev provides a critique of the modern bourgeois emancipation narrative as well. This narrative may be expressed best through the secularization thesis made popular by Karl Löwith, who claims that the modern enlightenment merely transforms the Christian notion of advancement into the bourgeois myth of progress.[10] Rather than advancing toward spiritual salvation in the afterlife by living a good, Christian life here below, one advances toward the bourgeois variant of salvation: the acquisition of material comfort. Without a unifying ideal— and Soloviev sees in the bourgeois variant of salvation only self-interest writ large—there can be no salvation as an overcoming of our rootedness in selfishness, since my freedom comes at the cost of others and must be defined solely negatively, by my ability not to succumb to limits. The ostensibly positive ideal of comfort is essentially reducible to the negative ideal of unlimited self-assertion.

Soloviev seeks to counter both the "apophatic man," a creature of irony and resignation, and the active man, who seeks only his own comfort, by another man; or, better, Soloviev argues that the negative man conceals a positive demand for "full content" (требование полноты содержания). For "in the possession of all of reality, of the fullness of life, lies positive absoluteness." As to why this positive demand has been abandoned remains muddled. Soloviev seems to claim, quite traditionally, that the modern world has simply lost its way, beguiled, one supposes, by the idols of modern science or capitalism, the possibility of literally becoming a god, which can lead only to dissatisfaction because Western civilization has "asserted infinite striving and the impossibility of its satisfaction" by inculcating a negative ideal of freedom.[11]

THE POSITIVE ABSOLUTE

Having thus expressed the significance of affirming a positive absolute idea or ideal, Soloviev proceeds to develop that idea or ideal by tracing its lineage in both the philosophical and theological traditions. Here Soloviev creates a history of Platonism as a history of the self-revelation of the absolute that reaches its culmination in Soloviev himself as humble prophet of the neglected truth.

The triadic and Trinitarian narrative Soloviev creates is fascinating. Its basic structure belongs to the "golden age" format whereby an eternal and absolute truth, a truth implicit in an origin, slowly becomes unfolded in time.[12] One may identify this narrative with one of its great instantiations in Plato, in which the task of thinking is recollection of the perfection that we have left behind due to our miserable embodiment. The great and epochal difference is the decisive transformation provided by the incarnation of the truth in Christ. In Plato, it is quite clear that return to the hyperouranian realm, the realm of perfection, of absolute truth, is only possible without the body—a most inconvenient fact for the creature whose sad essence is to exist in the material world.[13]

Christ transforms the Platonic narrative from one of impossibility (or negativity) into one of positive acquisition whereby the body is suffused with the absolute. The significance of the Incarnation for Soloviev is difficult to overestimate: the Incarnation is the event that transforms history by making the absolute accessible to the embodied individual, in vivid contrast to the Platonic prohibition. If, in other words, Platonic wisdom is essentially one of tragic futility according to which the striving to glimpse the forms in the hyperouranian realm cannot possibly meet with success because it is quite literally not in the nature of things to allow that success, the Incarnation allows for the most powerful act of transformation. One may literally become an embodied god, as unusual as that may seem—at least at first blush.

What can an embodied absolute possibly be? Soloviev deals with this problem at length. The most technical elements of the lectures originate in his attempt to explain the seemingly contradictory concept of the embodied god or the contingent absolute. His first and most fundamental claim is that revelation is absolutely necessary if one is to be assured of the reality of the absolute principle. Soloviev is surprisingly blunt on this point, claiming that the certainty of the absolute principle's reality, its existence, can be given only by faith and not deduced by pure reason alone.[14] If this is indeed the case, Soloviev's elaborate arguments for delineating the identity and import of the absolute principle seem to be little more than a complicated form of philosophical pedagogy or, in cruder terms, propaganda in the oldest sense of the term as *propaganda fidei.*

These arguments come in a bewildering variety. To keep with Soloviev's own tendency toward triads, I might arrange these arguments in three groups, the first setting out the historical shape of the absolute as it reveals itself in Christianity, the second setting out its theological structure, and the third explaining why that history is necessary in the first place. Thus, Soloviev sets for himself the usual tasks of the Christian apologist, with a particularly interesting focus on why the absolute principle only comes to its fullest self-expression with Soloviev's own writing—the lectures are themselves the final revelation of the absolute principle of what, according to Soloviev, was always already there. Soloviev, not Hegel, proclaims the end of history in the explicitation of its fundamental significance.

Soloviev's historical account is of interest primarily for the way in which it weaves together three stages of religious development with three elements in the Christian tradition:

> This first main stage is represented by polytheism in the broad sense, which comprises all the mythological religions, or the so-called *nature religions*. I call this stage *natural* or *immediate revelation*. In the second stage of religious development, the divine principle is revealed in contradistinction to nature. It is revealed as the negation of nature, the nothing (the absence) of natural being, the negative freedom from it. I call this stage, which has an essentially pessimistic or ascetic character, *negative revelation*. Its purest type is represented by Buddhism. Finally, in the third stage, the divine stage, the divine principle is successively revealed in its own content, in that which it is in itself and for itself (whereas previously it was revealed only in what it is not, that is to say, in its other, or in the simple negation of that other, and therefore still in relation to it, but not as it is in itself). This third stage, which I call, in general, *positive revelation*, consists of several clearly discernible phases, which should be analyzed separately.[15]

The first and second stages are intimately related because they both deal with the will. The first stage describes the discovery of the so-called natural will, which is the "exclusive self-assertion of every entity . . . the inner and outer negation by one entity of all others." The natural will describes the ostensibly natural imperative of self-preservation, the struggle to assert one's existence, which cannot be brought to an end, according to Soloviev, even if the need for food and other "lower passions" is satiated. At this level, what Soloviev calls "natural egoism" still prevails. And, in a move that is fully consonant with the Platonic stance Soloviev develops, nature emerges as a "blind external force, alien to human beings, a force of evil and deceit [силой зла и обмана]."[16]

If the natural religion Soloviev connects with this view of nature cannot overcome nature and in fact represents a coming to terms with nature, the other two kinds of religion he identifies, negative and positive, are both unified by their hostility toward nature, their attempt to overcome nature as the dominant force in our lives. Negative religion denotes a transformation of the will from self-assertion to self-denial. Rather than being the most powerful assertion of one's existence vis-à-vis all other beings, the notion of will that prevails in negative religion is one of denial as liberation from the entrapment in the natural process of self-assertion. This will is thus a will to self-annihilation or self-immolation; it is the will to suicide that liberates one at last from the chains of natural will or material self-assertion.[17]

Like the stage that follows, this negative stage is an attempt to overcome evil, understood precisely as self-assertion and as the inability to overcome self-assertion that seems to be the central claim of natural religion. The crucial element that transforms the situation—and it is well to keep this in mind when we come to Kojève—is negation. The first divinely made act is an act of negation whereby one *counters* nature. The act is divinely mad because it is an act that seems aimed at one's own "natural" interests, and it is divine because it arises from what we may call a yearning for the universal in face of the particular. The universal describes exactly this move to negate the particular, for in the negation of the particular—of my will as such—I cannot help but enter into a realm where the particular structure of my actions comes to undermine itself. To act in favor of not acting in favor of my own interests is indeed to act in the name of no interest whatsoever, and this peculiar interest—an interest whose interest is not to have an interest—is an act of self-effacement or annihilation.

But, as we know, this self-effacement is also an act of liberation from the tyranny of nature, of self-assertion, of what Soloviev calls "evil." Thus, the first step away from evil toward the good is an act of negation: "This absolute rejection of all finite, limited attributes is already a negative determination of the absolute principle itself. For a consciousness that does not yet possess that principle itself, such a negative determination is necessarily the first step toward positive knowledge of it."[18] Soloviev ascribes this purely negative appreciation of the absolute to Buddhism, which can remain only negative. We find ourselves still within the negative absolutes of the great Dostoevskian heroes; the end of life, true emancipation, is death.

To put the matter in Platonic terms, this negative eros is not sufficient. Yet what of positive eros? If the positive eros, the accession to the ideas in themselves, is impossible for Plato, it becomes possible for Soloviev, of course, through the agency of Christ. Soloviev couches the essential import of the positive principle in the language of dominion, arguing that the "actual positive freedom of an entity [существа] presupposes dominion, positive force, or power over that from which the entity is free."[19] Hence, Soloviev identifies negative freedom with servitude and positive freedom with mastery, an identification which we will have occasion to address again in the context of Kojève's major recognition narrative.

The master is the one who assumes the absolute idea in the guise of Christ. But what exactly does this mean? The structure Soloviev develops, the second part of his exposition, is a striking if obvious synthesis of Platonism and Christianity, drawing from masters in both the Eastern and Western traditions. It is perhaps remarkable that this exposition reaches a high point with a discussion of Augustine, the foremost thinker in the Western Christian tradition that Soloviev otherwise decries.

TWO ABSOLUTES?

More triads. Soloviev nests inside his triadic conception of religion a triadic conception of its final element, positive religion. But before I address this triad, I want to return once again (the third time) to the key notion of Christ as the mediating element that allows for an overcoming of Platonic impossibility, the Platonic declaration of the inaccessibility to human understanding of that final view of the hyperouranian realm. From this perspective, it seems quite obvious that negation holds sway in Plato as well, despite the positive doctrine of the forms. For if those forms are, in the final account, not fully accessible to the finite mind, what can they be other than a tantalizing temptation, a variation, indeed, of the predicament of Tantalus, who is capable of perceiving what he cannot possess?

What kind of mediating element can Christ be? Nothing is more controversial, perhaps, in Christian dogmatic theology. An either/or has ruled responses to this question, based on what nature in Christ is more fundamental: the divine or human? This either/or hints at the profoundly difficult question of how one may possibly live a universal life, a life of divinity. Does one live this life as metaphor, as fiction, or as a "reality"?

This question is the nodal point that ties Soloviev to Fedorov and, ultimately, to Kojève; it is *the* question that animates all three. It also allows us to distinguish among them, because their responses are so different: Soloviev retains the notion of a divine absolute and a "divinely human" one (his famous—and problematic—"two absolutes"), whereas Fedorov seeks to create a divine individual no longer subject to death, and Kojève an absolutely finite being that accepts its finitude as an absolute horizon by abandoning the notion of a divine absolute (in Soloviev's terms).

Now Soloviev's response:

It is clear that Divinity must be a willing person, a living God, for the human personal will to be determined positively. But can Divinity in its absolute nature be a person? This question is obscured by misunderstandings resulting from the one-sidedness of two opposing points of view, both of which contradict the original concept of Divinity as absolute. On the one hand, those who affirm the personhood of Divinity usually affirm at the same time that Divinity is *only* a person, a certain personal being with such and such attributes. Pantheists rightfully rebel against this position, demonstrating that it implies a limitation of Divinity, deprives it of infinity and absoluteness, and makes it one thing among many. Indeed, it is clear that Divinity, as the absolute, cannot be *only* a person, only an *I*, that it is more than a person. But those who protest against this limitation fall into the opposite one-sided position of asserting that Divinity is devoid of personal being, that it is merely an impersonal substance of the all. But if Divinity is substance, that which exists from itself, then, since it contains the all in itself, it must differ from the all or assert its own being. Otherwise, there would be no container, and Divinity, devoid of inner independence, would be not a substance but merely an attribute of the all. Thus, as substance, Divinity must necessarily possess self-determination and self-discernment; it must possess personhood, and consciousness.

Thus, the truth clearly is that the divine principle is not a person only in the sense that it is not exhausted by a personal determination; *it is not only one but also all*, not only an individual being but also the all-embracing being, not only existent but also essence. As absolute, the divine principle is subject and substance at the same time.[20]

The crucial phrase is the final one: that "the divine principle is subject and substance at the same time." This phrase originates in the preface to Hegel's *Phenomenology*, and, in the words of Kojève, it describes with all possible concision the central idea animating the Hegelian project.[21] Such overstatement or generalization offends many commentators as being ridiculously or fancifully reductive, and so it should. How else might one speak of the absolute principle, for is this not the essence of reduction itself, that all becomes one? To be sure, the varieties of reduction may be considerable, but the trope—to use a curious term—that comes to the fore here is one of immense reduction, of the transformation of the life of the individual subject into the life of the all, and the reverse.

But is this really the case? What is divine about this reduction? And what is pernicious in this sense about reduction? While I do not wish to spend too much time on this issue here, it might be useful to consider what is at stake in the dogma according to which reduction is to be avoided at all costs as a want of subtlety or discrimination.

For Soloviev, the attachment to multiplicity as such, to sheer variety, is little more than a return to the attitude of natural religion. It is thus the concomitant of self-assertion and the assertion of the particular against all other particulars. The most radical assertion of this kind is that of the absolute individuality of each particular that is, as such, inexhaustible— the particular becomes like an infinite god itself. The grounding impetus of the particular is to differentiate itself from all other particulars; the attachment to individuality must reflect the same impetus. The particular so understood precludes understanding or, at least, precludes full understanding on the assumption or wager that partial understanding is possible as understanding.[22] In other words, we think "provisionally" about things because we cannot think finally about them. But this raises the question of whether partial or provisional thought is any kind of thought at all or is merely a rejection of thought in favor of a useful fiction, that of the hallowed particular in itself. What I mean here is the question—of great moment to Kojève, as we shall see—of whether a partial account can have any sense if it refers to no coherent whole. For if a sense is fleeting or changeable, is it sense or merely pseudo sense? Or, if there is no final standard available, how do we distinguish sense from madness or the utter lack of sense?[23]

Soloviev has to deny this particular because it prevents or blocks the divine principle entirely. There is no escape from mere natural existence if the particular is not overcome as having some ineffable particularity. Why should one escape from natural existence? What is wrong with natural existence? Soloviev refers to it as evil and carries on throughout the lectures a polemic with nature as being the locus of evil. But to what end? The particular is in fact the locus of evil; it is, as Augustine also suggests, a lure that leads one away from the absolute, from the purity and beauty of the absolute, which is nothing other than the fullest freedom from particularity. But Soloviev is not, of course, that dismissive. The particular may become beautiful, too, and it may become so to the extent that it conforms to or reflects the absolute. If the particular is coveted, so to speak, merely in itself as having "value" only in itself, then for Soloviev it is nothing, or, worse, the obstinate attraction to a nonsensical, contradictory thing. For the corollary of the madman who seeks only his own satisfaction is the particular that lives as it were only for itself.

Hence, for Soloviev reduction must be understood in a completely different way. It is in fact the reduction of things to their peculiarity, to their "secret lives," that weakens and corrupts them—they lose touch with the absolute, lose the ostensibly inner connection with the whole that first pulls them out of their abstraction or the contradictory notion of particular cognition. That is to say that if all cognition were in fact particular, there would be no cognition at all. The world in which each makes a demand for its own self at the cost of others—or without regard to others, as if they possessed only a phantasmal existence—would prevail, and no knowledge would be possible. But, again, this notion of knowledge begs the question. As Wittgenstein proved rather convincingly, a private language is not possible; it is indeed a kind of madness, in the terms Kojève employs.[24] Likewise, the notion that particulars can in fact come to possess a kind of knowledge is fraught with difficulties, for the same reason.

For there to be knowledge and mutual cognition (i.e., any cognition at all), there must be something beyond the particular. We may then ask why this something beyond the particular must be absolute. The answer is fairly simple. If one does not have an absolute, all knowing is particular, and if all knowing is particular, there is no knowing at all—at least this is the core of the view that Soloviev defends.

If this is so, then positive assertion of the absolute would seem to be of the utmost urgency, since the negative absolute cannot in fact constitute knowledge other than via a Socratic maxim like the claim, from the *Apology*, that Socrates's wisdom arises from his recognition that he does not and cannot know. The philosopher is then distinguished by his superior knowing only in a negative sense, by the fact that he realizes, unlike the others, that he cannot claim to know—to know absolutely—and, thus, to know anything at all. The philosopher's superior knowledge stems from a constitutional inability to possess positive knowledge of the whole. All claims to knowledge are thus a form of deception.

Soloviev sees fundamental weakness in this essentially skeptical position. The thinker must go beyond it and, guided by faith, come to an assertion of a positive form of knowledge. This positive form of knowledge is to be found in Platonism transformed by the possibility of incarnation of the absolute in the individual, a perfect harmony of one and many, by which the individual becomes one with the deity and, in so doing, deifies herself.

But this deification is not to be confused with a merely individual act whereby some are saved and others are damned. The more searching aspect of Soloviev's interpretation is to suggest, in a way that recalls (and quite consciously) Gottfried Leibniz, that all beings seek to reflect the absolute principle to the extent of their capacity to do so. Of course, as is typical of these approaches to divinity, the creature in which the absolute principle comes to fullest expression is the human being. Soloviev's daring is to suggest that this fullest expression is not a limited one but can be as absolute as the principle it reflects; indeed, it *must* be, or else the promise of the incarnation cannot be fulfilled, for "every determinate being can be, primordially, only an act of self-determination of that which absolutely is" and becomes absolute in the process.[25]

This remarkable claim constitutes the focal point of the lectures in lecture 6. Having declared that the absolute can appear absolutely in a conditioned material form, Soloviev moves on to describe how this form, throughout all differences, masks, and apparent errors, is the fundamental form latent in all of human history—and that he is the first to recognize it as such.

DEIFICATION

This fundamental form is deification. The notion of deification (θέωσις) has deep roots in the Eastern Christian tradition.[26] Soloviev's repetition of that tradition is interesting insofar as it weaves together traditional Neoplatonic aspects of the tradition with Augustine, thereby revealing Soloviev's attempt to uncover the one form latent in all appearance. In this respect, Soloviev's thinking once again takes a triune structure as its basis. His synthesis of different elements in the tradition creates a very intriguing and important central triad: will, reason, and being. He thus brings together not only Platonism and a key thinker of the Christian tradition but also German idealism. Soloviev argues, in effect, that all three kinds of thought can be layered on top of one another like a palimpsest describing an essentially unitary underlying structure. And we may presume that this structure acts as a gloss on the triadic structure Soloviev also applies to his categorization of types of religion, from the natural through the negative to the positive.

Soloviev describes this fundamental structure as follows:

In our spirit, we must differentiate between its simple immediate being (*esse*), its knowledge (*scire*), and its will (*velle*). These three acts are identical not only according to their content, insofar as the one who is knows and wills itself. Their unity goes far deeper. Each of them contains the other two in their distinctive character, and consequently, each inwardly already contains the whole fullness of the triune spirit. In fact in the first place, I am, but not simply "am"—I am the one who knows and wills (*sum sciens et volens*). Consequently, my being as such already contains in itself both knowledge and will. Second, if I know, I know or am conscious of the fact that I am and that I will (*scio me esse et velle*). Thus, here too, in knowledge as such, or under the form of knowledge, both being and will are contained. Third, and last, I will myself, yet not simply myself, but myself as one who is and knows; I will my being and knowledge (*volo me esse et scire*). Consequently, the form of the will also contains both being and knowledge. Each of these three fundamental acts of the spirit is completed in itself by the other two and thus becomes individualized, as it were, into full triune being.[27]

Soloviev claims that this fundamental structure is, however, merely an analogy, just as the Neoplatonic triad, the so-called three hypostases—the one (τὸ ἕν), intellect (ὁ νοῦς), and the soul (ἡ ψυχή)—as well as the "classic" (Fichtean) German idealist triad of the absolute subject (*das absolute Ich*), which contains the empirical I (*das Ich*) and the Not-I (*das Nicht-Ich*). Soloviev seems to align both these triads, with being (*esse*) as the one and the absolute I; knowing (*scire*) as the intellect or the I; and will (*velle*) as the soul or the not-I.

These overlapping conceptual analogies only fit together with some violence, through a fairly extreme deracination of the concepts from their original context. And this may be Soloviev's point—the absolute principle appears throughout history in approximate triads, but the triadic structure is possible and mirrors the other crucial triadic structure, the Trinity. Whatever we may think of Soloviev's exactitude, the point is abundantly clear: the world is constructed in triads that embody and thus can lead one back to the absolute in its fullest form. There is no reason to say that the absolute cannot be realized in the particular, since so many particulars have already found shelter in the absolute.[28]

Still, the qualifying terms and the rough harmony of the comparisons is somewhat jarring. If Soloviev is trying to convince us of this unity in diversity, he leaves the more difficult questions as to the origins of that diversity to the side, at least initially. More striking still is the reference to analogy, the old Aristotelian tool whereby one may speak of things one cannot truly know as they are in themselves. The use of analogy would seem to suggest that the absolute principle cannot be known as it is in itself, and, in fact, we are thrown back to Soloviev's initial declaration of the importance of faith to obtain certainty about the existence of the absolute principle.[29]

One cannot help but surmise that there is something akin to an "als ob," or "as if," principle at work here that leads to a difficult circularity, perhaps an inevitable one. The circle is this: to know the absolute principle, one has to know it exists, but in fact one cannot know that it exists;

one has to assume it in fact does, and so faith anchors thought.[30] And this circle refers us in turn back to the problem of the madman who builds a logical structure over an abyss, claiming all the time that that structure is in the fabric of reality and, thus, that we have to accept it as such. That Soloviev is explaining the necessary consequences of an unnecessary positum is an extraordinary aspect of his enterprise in the lectures, and one that neither Fedorov nor Kojève forgot, for both conceive of the absolute not as a distant "given" to be retrieved but solely as a universal project to complete. On the contrary, Soloviev finds himself in the far more difficult position of exhorting us to achieve what is, as a positum, always already there, thus exhorting us to strive for what we already have. Hence, Soloviev needs to explain why it is that we do not see, or have forgotten, what we possess, why we have come to the forgetfulness of the absolute (what Plato explains through myth).

If we regard Soloviev's project, then, as one that proposes the necessary implications of an unnecessary positum, the lectures tend to become less persuasive after lecture 6. This is the case because Soloviev spends the balance of the lectures attempting to show why the absolute has not hitherto come to light in the way it has for him, as the prophet of its truth. This terribly common difficulty—it appears to afflict all philosophers who claim that their point in time is somehow privileged, allowing for the final or "synoptic" account of the meaning of all that has come before in philosophy (think both Hegel and Martin Heidegger)—pushes Soloviev to create a further narrative, by now quite a conventional one, of decline and return, with his own time being an appropriate one in which to advocate for such a return.

SOPHIA

There is, however, one extremely important concept that Soloviev develops in the subsequent lectures: that of wisdom, or *Sophia*. As Soloviev suggests, "Wisdom is the idea that God has before Him in His work of creation and that He consequently realizes." The divine demiurge is now Christ, now each one of us who is called to realize the same project as the proper *imitatio Christi*. The content of this ideal is ideal or perfect

humanity, "eternally contained in the integral divine being, or Christ."
What is this perfect humanity?

> Although a human being as a phenomenon is a temporary, transitory
> fact, the human being as essence is necessarily eternal and all-embracing.
> What, then, is an ideal human being? To be actual, such a being must be
> both one and many and therefore is not merely the universal common
> essence of all human individuals, taken in abstraction from them. Such
> a being is universal but also individual, an entity that actually contains
> all human individuals within itself. Every one of us, every human being,
> is essentially and actively rooted in and partakes of the universal, or
> absolute, human being.[31]

This is more declaration of a program than it is argument. The problems of "partaking" or "participation" alone are so thorny and dense that
Plato himself devoted an entire, and genuinely aporetic, dialogue to it, the
Parmenides. Here Soloviev solves those problems largely by reference to
Christ. The role of Christ in the lectures—and, of course, in Christianity
as a whole—provides him with a handy dogmatic justification for doing
so. But this is a curious, if not mistaken, move. The most penetrating thesis of the lectures is that one may realize a universal or absolute principle
in a conditioned, relative life; the promise of living infinitely arises from
this move, a promise perhaps as seductive as it seems to be potentially
incoherent.

We return again to this simple question: How does the absolute emerge
as such in the conditioned? While it is no doubt true to argue that the
absolute cannot "appear" in any other way, can the absolute possibly appear
as it is in itself, as absolute? The obvious objections are legion. Does Soloviev push us into a more radical position dependent on faith, that is, a
position in which one takes it as a dogmatic article of faith that the absolute appears and may appear precisely as the unconditioned in itself, as
absolute?

This is indeed the main argument—that there is no real contradiction in claiming that the absolute may appear in its absoluteness within
a thing. The first response is one that Soloviev seems to have anticipated—
that the absolute may appear in the conditioned only as an absence, that
the only way to come to the absolute is through the negative. The most

daring and troubling response given by Soloviev, however, is that the absolute can appear in the conditioned to the extent that the latter attempts to imitate the "being" of the former. Imitation is a *project*, something one must do to become absolute. Here the absolute is employed to generate a project of striving. How does this striving work out, and why is it not asymptotic, unable to reach its goal? How, in other words, can a finite being—or at least one that has to die—imitate or "comprehend" the unlimited, the infinite? According to Soloviev:

> Divine forces constitute the single, integral, absolutely universal, absolutely individual organism of the living Logos. Likewise, all human elements constitute a similarly integral organism, one both universal and individual, which is the necessary actualization and receptacle of the living Logos. They constitute a universally human organism as the eternal body of God and the eternal soul of the world. Since this later organism, that is, Sophia in its eternal being, necessarily consists of a multiplicity of elements, of which she is the real unity, each of the elements, as a necessary component part of eternal Divine-humanity, must be recognized as eternal in the absolute or world order.[32]

Does this passage take us any further? Kojève argues—and it is difficult to counter this argument—that Soloviev does not realize the promise of the Incarnation by creating a divine being that lives in the world. Rather, Soloviev retains the force of imitation, as this passage seems to confirm. The human being is thus always in a secondary position, as imitator, and not really capable of union with the absolute principle on an equal footing.[33] The best the human being can do is to subordinate herself fully to the divine principle. But this subordination can never succeed fully; the human being cannot give up her will completely, even if "held in reserve." Put in simpler, Platonic terms, the human being can do no better that be a simulacrum of the absolute principle, and even an encyclopedic simulacrum remains a simulacrum, liable to succumb to defect or fallible performance.

The performance aspect of the problem needs emphasis, and it presents severe difficulties for Soloviev. How can a creature living in time—acting, in other words—possibly be the same as an absolute principle, which, as such, must be outside of or prior to time? One may press the argument even further to suggest that time must first be created by the absolute principle. The distinction between the atemporal and the temporal merely repeats other distinctions whose basis is similar (infinite/finite, perfect/imperfect, complete/incomplete, and so on). In all these cases the negative is associated with any being that is not absolute—to be not absolute is indeed to be negative, that is, conditioned, limited, to lack.

To live in time—and what other life is possible?—is necessarily to be imperfect, to countenance error in the performance or imitation of the absolute. Indeed, life in time, from the perspective of the absolute, is itself an error if the absolute is truly atemporal or prior to time. Kant recognized this problem and thus considered perfect performance of the moral duty, the categorical imperative, ultimately impossible for an imperfect being, that is, a being still essentially rooted in time, in everyday experience, the being Kant referred to as inalienably heteronomous.[34] Soloviev, on the contrary, refuses to accept this difficulty but does not offer a persuasive alternative response. He must explain time, history, and thus the discovery of an absolute to which we must return. One ends up in an essentially Kantian position, with an ethical imperative that one must and cannot fully follow because complete performance would require complete extirpation of self-interest—or, in Kantian terms, inclination or propensity (*Hang*).[35] Transformation cannot be merely metaphorical, it seems; transformation must dare to be more radical.

NIKOLAI FEDOROV AND UNIVERSAL RESURRECTION

Radical transformation is the solution offered by Nikolai Fedorov, a most unusual thinker whose philosophy of universal resurrection seems completely mad, if not preposterous, to most. The briefest outline invites laughter or disbelief. If philosophy truly is a voyage led by madmen to the *verkehrte Welt*, the world turned upside down, in Hegel's words, then one of its most daring captains must be Fedorov. What is it, after all, to proclaim universal resurrection as the end of human being, to proclaim that human life lived to its end is ridiculous, mad, stupid, unless we try as a collectivity to overcome that end, literally and physically, not only for ourselves but also for all who have ever lived? This latter aspect of the pursuit of eternal life is the most forceful, strange, and distinctive aspect of Fedorov's "project," his "common cause" or "task" (общее дело). For Fedorov, there really is no middle ground, no compromise that is not first a catastrophe, a turning away from the truth—Christ represents the truth in resurrection.

Lest one think Fedorov simply mad, it may be well to note that he attracted the most serious interest from many of the best minds in nineteenth-century Russia, among whom one can count Dostoevsky, Soloviev, Leo Tolstoy, and an illustrious cohort of scientists and adventurers, such as Konstantin Tsiolkovsky, the father of spaceflight.[36]

Fedorov was born on June 9, 1829, in Kliuchi in the Tambov province. He was the illegitimate son of Pavel Gagarin, an aristocrat. Fedorov was allowed a decent education, though he left the equivalent of high school for reasons that are not entirely clear and did not attend university. He became a schoolteacher in southern Russia for about twenty years, moving from town to town until he ended up as the main librarian at the Rumiantsev Library in Moscow, where he remained for the rest of his life.

Fedorov attracted attention immediately. His knowledge of the library's holdings and their contents was legendary, as was his frugal lifestyle and his one obsessive thought, the "common task" (общее дело): universal resurrection. His early admirer N. P. Peterson brought his thought to the attention of Dostoevsky and Soloviev, who grew fascinated with Fedorov's idea. Tolstoy took notice too, and Fedorov and Tolstoy engaged in many conversations during the 1870s and 1880s. While Tolstoy admired Fedorov's simplicity, he disagreed with Fedorov's project of universal resurrection (considering it a *rejection* of our humanity rather than as the highest expression of it).

Fedorov also acquired a series of other admirers, such as Tsiolkovsky. His major work, *The Philosophy of the Common Task* (Философия общего дела), was published in two parts, in 1906 and 1913. It consists largely of comments recorded by Peterson or another disciple, the remarkable polymath Vladimir V. Kozhevnikov.

After the revolution, Fedorovian communities emerged in various places (such as Harbin, China), and his influence can be felt in the communist insistence on the new man and the sometimes very radical hope of abolishing death; the Immortality Commission and the embalmment of Vladimir Lenin is one product of this hope. The great twentieth-century writer Andrei Platonov was an enthusiastic Fedorovian, and the thought of that important rival to Lenin, Alexander Bogdanov, reflects Fedorov's influence as well.

With this in mind, I want to explore Fedorov's "idea" within the confines of several important texts contained in the compendious miscellany that is *Philosophy of the Common Task*. The two primary texts I examine have extraordinary titles: "On the Problem of Brotherhood or Kinship, on the Causes of the Non-brotherly, Non-Kindred, that is, the Non-peaceful State of the World, and of the means for the Restoration of Kinship: A Memorandum from the 'Unlearned' to the 'Learned,' Clergy and Laity, Believers and Non-believers" and "Supramoralism or Universal Synthesis."[37]

THE COMMON TASK

"On the Problem of Brotherhood" is an extraordinary text, the title's inordinate length itself suggestive of the inordinate central propositions that Fedorov advances.[38] Of these, perhaps the easiest to address is the call for a wholly different attitude to human coexistence, the more or less perennially hackneyed call for unity in a common cause. Yet Fedorov transforms this hackneyed call into a call for revolution that is exhilarating, if not mad, in its sustained radicality.

Fedorov's long text (almost three hundred pages in the most recent Russian edition) is divided into four parts.[39] The first begins with a discussion of the terrible Russian famine of 1891. He describes one rather extreme attempt to combat famine: the use of explosives to make rain. Fedorov finds this use of explosives of substantial interest because it is an example of a radically different use of the explosives, as a means not of destroying others but of helping them to sustain themselves. Here a technology developed solely for the ends of conflict is transformed by being employed for a diametrically opposed end. This transformation is a crucial emblem of a different possible future for humanity, one in which the tremendous powers of technology are harnessed not for the purposes of mutual destruction but for the creation of a community that will outlast all other communities that have ever existed.

So far, this sort of thinking seems to move within the sphere of cliché, of endlessly repeated cries to tame the impulse to destroy and negate. But it is important to remember that these cries to tame the impulse to destroy and negate come largely as a result of another epochal transformation by which one of the greatest and most violent empires in recorded history, that of Rome, became an empire devoted to the Christian mission of creating a universal empire of peace, a city of God on earth.

Of course, nothing of the sort happened. Rome collapsed, and the promise of universal empire passed on to Byzantium and thence to Moscow—the third Rome. It is tolerably clear that this claim animates Fedorov's text and his renewed call for transformation of the bellicose impulse into one establishing a universal empire that brings together all human beings in a common cause.

The claim for universal empire is hardly new; indeed, it is one of the most potent tropes of Western thought. Kojève himself fancifully attributes the rise of this trope to philosophy, specifically to the fact that the first truly universal conqueror of the West, Alexander of Macedon, was a student of Aristotle.[40] For Fedorov, however, the claim for universal empire is not Aristotelian: it belongs squarely with the promise of Christ and—here is the radical turn—with the promise of resurrection. To put matters with summary bluntness: universal empire, for Fedorov, does not mean merely the acquisition of empire on earth, the fabled city of God, but acquisition of the greatest possible empire, that which extends beyond the earth to eternity: empire over our greatest foe, death. Human beings will only ever become truly human, truly brothers of the greatest human being, Christ, by accepting his invitation to divinity, by becoming one with God in resurrection.

Fedorov's text is devoted to outlining a plan for achieving this end. The first point of that plan is already somewhat clear. The immense resources made available to us in the prosecution of war now must be channeled into the greatest war of all, against death itself. The second point of Fedorov's plan is of considerable interest: he seeks to eliminate the distinction between theory and practice by eliminating any pursuit of the mind whose end is not the elimination of death, an eminently practical end.

The doctrine of resurrection could also be called positivism, but a positivism of action. According to this doctrine it would not be mythical knowledge that would be replaced by positive knowledge, but mythical, symbolic actions that would be replaced by actual, effective ones. The doctrine of resurrection sets no arbitrary limits to action performed in common, as opposed to action by separate individuals. This positivism of action derives not from mythology, which was a fabrication of pagan priests, but from mythological art forms, popular rituals and sacrifices. Resuscitation changes symbolic acts into reality. The positivism of action is not class-bound but popular positivism. For the people, science will be a method, whereas the positivism of science is merely a philosophy for scholars as a separate class or estate.[41]

Fedorov simply rejects the basic assumptions of Platonic thought that ensure the separation of theory and practice. This is a breathtaking move and merits more careful comment.

For Fedorov, theory is the result of a tacit admission of impossibility. One engages in theoretical work because there is a suspicion that that work may never have any impact at all on how human beings actually live—the mind is left to think in a vacuum because there is no connection between the mind in this respect and our material reality. Fedorov registers this difference by reference to two classes, the "learned" (ученые) and the "unlearned" (неученые). The learned are associated with theoretical, the unlearned with practical activities. Fedorov insists that the learned must leave behind their occupation with questions that do not pertain to practical issues of survival and human well-being. Indeed, by confronting these practical challenges, the learned come to join the unlearned in common agreement about the primacy of the practical so defined. The fusion of the learned and the unlearned in this immense practical task creates a further basis for community.

This is a shrewd move. On the one hand, Fedorov in effect reverses the relation of theory to practice as the precondition for its elimination. He does so by openly encouraging the "learned," or what in the Russian context has typically been referred to as the "intelligentsia," to become practical. Theory does not direct practice but becomes wholly directed to achieving practical ends. Fedorov thus simply reiterates one of the primary implications of modern Western thought, with the same end: technological mastery over nature. On the other hand, Fedorov eliminates what he considers the most pernicious division in society, one that is far more divisive than that between the wealthy and the impoverished. The startling proposition that the division between those who know and those who do not know is the root of inequality and conflict within a society is one of the most distinctive features of Fedorov's thought. By ensuring that all work together on a reasonably equal basis in the production and diffusion of knowledge, for the realization of the ends of the common task, Fedorov seeks to eliminate the central cause of internal dissension in his new community.

The first two sections of Fedorov's text outline thus the development of a community that eliminates dissent externally and internally through an all-absorbing dedication to the singular task of creating technologies that will enable empire over the earth. He refers to nature consistently as the "blind force" (слепая сила) and insists that this blind force be transformed by reason into a regulated force that may be exploited for the proper ends of the nascent brotherhood of humankind. Of course, the most important of these ends is the creation of technologies that eliminate all destructive forces—if the brotherhood in humankind has truly overcome enmity in itself, it seeks to impose the resulting harmony on nature and can only affirm its own harmonious quality by doing so. Nature, once so opposed to humanity, must become its intimate partner in the task of setting up the proper preconditions for the final task: universal resurrection.

It goes without saying that this universal resurrection does not apply to any other creature on earth. Fedorov's common task applies to humankind alone and is not so much a partnership with nature as a massive project of the most radical domestication of nature imaginable—empire, indeed. While Fedorov uses bland bureaucratic terms like "regulation" (регуляция) to describe the project of turning the blind force of nature into a rational one, it is quite evident that this regulation means little more than transforming nature in accordance with the narrowly human end of unlimited self-preservation. What is rational is what serves self-preservation.[42]

This equation is astonishing in light of Fedorov's consistent assertion of the properly Christian nature of the common task. Indeed, one of the most delicate aspects of Fedorov's thought is the question of its orthodoxy. Both the assertion of fundamental enmity with nature and the exhortation to turn that enmity into friendship by actions that turn nature into a servant of human interests—primary among which is the interest in self-preservation—seem at first blush more consistent with diabolical rebellion against God. After all, the common task is tantamount to the correction of nature in accordance with human ends.[43]

Fedorov seems to dismiss this question by insisting that God granted us mastery over the earth so that we might use our freedom to transform it and thereby show our fealty to God. In this respect, there is a far more interesting and penetrating reason for Fedorov's insistence on the Christian nature of the common task: the fact of resurrection itself. For Fedorov, Christ's suffering and resurrection is a model narrative of the overcoming of servitude to nature and, in the final account, death. Fedorov suppresses the nagging question here: that resurrection seems to fulfill the inherently selfish interest in self-preservation that Christ otherwise overcomes by willingly dying. Fedorov clearly sees this problem nonetheless, and he attempts to deal with it rather more subtly (or madly, if you like) by turning the common task of overcoming nature into one devoted not just to the interests of one generation but to those of all generations that have ever lived on earth. This outrageously expanded common task becomes the very essence of morality for Fedorov. Devotion to the project of universal resurrection is evidently supposed to overcome the objection that the concerted effort to master nature reflects satanic pride and monstrous self-assertion rather than properly filial Christian piety.

The filial aspect of Fedorov's common task cuts to the core of these thorny issues. Fedorov's attempt to reconcile human selfishness and self-assertion with Christian self-abnegation comes out perhaps most clearly in his remarkable attempt to reconcile a primary expression of self-preservation, the family, with the notion of a universal community devoted to a task that somehow transcends self-preservation, the final community Fedorov seeks to ground and create.[44]

Fedorov employs two central metaphors, drawn from familial relations, to describe this community: brotherhood and kinship. If we may understand "brotherhood" as expressing the relation we have with our contemporaries in the common task, those with whom we work and live in devotion to the task of transforming nature from a blind force into a rational one, we may understand the term "kinship" as referring to the end of this task: universal resurrection. Fedorov is extremely clear about this. Universal resurrection is the proper expression of kinship because it establishes and affirms an attitude of devotion to one's ancestors that far exceeds mere ancestor worship. The common task has two fundamental aspects in this respect, for the project of mastering nature is the fundamental precondition for the arguably more ambitious project of returning all our ancestors to life, of "becoming mature" or discarding our "immaturity," as Fedorov argues at several spots.

Fedorov's synthesis consists in his use of terms applicable to the family in furtherance of a universal common cause. He thus attempts to transform the family from a particular unit within a community to a universal one. This is of course a bold move, because it attempts to overcome the focus on narrow blood ties that led Plato to suggest that the family, as a necessarily exclusive biological unit, needs to be dissolved because it is potentially detrimental to the project of creating a universal community. As we all know, one of the most radical claims of the *Republic* is its insistence on suppressing ties of blood relation among the guardians, most notably in their holding offspring in common. Fedorov counters this concern by universalizing the family and providing it with a common, "familial" task.[45] Fedorov decides for filial love in the place of divisive erotic love, which shall have no place (and is of course not necessary) in his new community.

Yet the objection I have already mentioned, that this "familial" task does not achieve true universality, cannot be ignored. One has to ascertain in what way communal self-assertion differs from individual self-assertion, and Fedorov does not deal with this issue directly. He seems to assume that selfishness is based essentially in material individuation, in the needs of my body as opposed to those of any other's. Hence, the transition to a common project, if not the end, is in fact a graduated stage whereby the selfishness that hinges on our material, corporeal existence is at least initially projected onto a collectivity dedicated to eliminating the origin of that selfishness in toto. If the task is defined by its end, the initial stage of the common task is merely a stage that leads to a final, momentous transition, the "singularity," whose principle feature—the eradication of death—eliminates the material condition of selfishness and thus selfishness itself, once and for all.[46]

If we may describe Fedorov's project in stages—something Fedorov does not directly do—we arrive at the following:

1. Cessation of hostilities among different nations—the creation of a world state.
2. Cessation of enmity within the world state by eliminating the distinction between the "learned" and the "unlearned."
3. Transformation of the world state into a brotherhood unified as such by two tasks: the regulation of nature and the preservation of ancestors.
4. Achievement of technological mastery over nature—regulation of and empire over the earth.
5. Achievement of perfect recuperation of history, the filial task of memory being the precondition to universal resurrection.
6. With universal resurrection, the establishment of a final community of deathless individuals, full recuperation and abolition of history, empire over death.

We have discussed the content of most of these stages already. It remains to clarify two points: Fedorov's concept of history and the concept of universal resurrection itself. These two concepts are the main subject matter, respectively, of the third and fourth parts of Fedorov's text.

Fedorov's view of history is distinctive and is consistent with his focus on action. History understood as telling stories of the dead, as attempting to preserve their lives in memory—history, in other words, as a form of resurrecting the dead that remains purely *metaphorical* (воскрешение в смысле метафоры)—is history for the learned, those who have withdrawn from action, having succumbed to leaving the process of resurrection at metaphor only. History as a recuperation of the past, as a presencing of the past, as a way of cultivating memory, is little more than an admission of defeat in the face of death. This kind of history must be suppressed in the common task by a new kind of history that prepares the way for the literal resurrection of the dead by preserving as much as it is possible to preserve of them. History is a *project* that looks forward to the time when universal resurrection will be technically possible; history prepares for this moment and is indispensable to it.[47]

History in this new sense is a reflection of filial piety because it preserves the past not as a component of the present or as a way of understanding the present but for the sake of the past in itself. By preserving the past, we demonstrate our dedication to preserving our ancestors, not necessarily as we see them or as our forerunners—both attitudes that reflect the egoism of a generation that thinks its reality is first and foremost—but as it was for our ancestors. In short, we look back lovingly and grant the past equal dignity with our present or, as I have suggested, we imbue the present with the past, we "presence" or reanimate it. Hence Fedorov's peculiar fascination with the museum and the archive as institutions whose genuine value resides in their reminding us of our duty to bring the past back to life, to recuperate the past not merely in memory (though this is itself a necessary beginning) but literally, through the discovery of a technology that can return this ostensibly lost life.

The fourth and final part of Fedorov's text completes the discussion of universal resurrection with an astonishing exhortation to move beyond the confines of our planet by transforming our planet into a sort of space vehicle. By means of this vehicle, we may proceed to distribute the resurrected dead throughout the universe.

GOD OR BEAST?

Let us state the obvious: Fedorov's thought is outlandish, mad—perhaps the dream of a madman whose essential premise is that life makes no sense *unless it can be redeemed by resurrection.* The structure Fedorov builds on this premise may seem absurd, the brainchild of a madman, but one may also counter the immediate dismissal that accompanies such assertions with the fact that his basic premise is not so easily dismissed. Indeed, it is an ostensibly Christian restatement of the Platonic challenge that tries to transform history from a narrative of error and errancy into a positive project seeking to correct that error and to do so in the name of Christ. That is, Fedorov claims that Christ is a redeemer precisely insofar as he shows us the way to redeem our existence on earth by literally, not metaphorically, overcoming death.

The contrast with Soloviev is instructive. While Soloviev showed tremendous sympathy for Fedorov's project, he seems to have been ultimately unable to accept the extreme transition from the realm of metaphorical to literal resurrection. Aside from the obvious, there are more subtle reasons for Soloviev's resistance, and they have to do with the very notion that bodily death is to be overcome. For, if Soloviev is to be consistent, he cannot argue that bodily death is the terminal event that it seems to be for Fedorov. To become a Godman is no longer to fear bodily death; it is to be one with God as what ultimately expresses its perfection in the embodied world.[48] To demonstrate an attachment to the body, such that one should seek to transform the world and the body by technology in order to become immortal, represents for Soloviev, at the very best, an essential confusion that betrays an inability to become God other than by perpetuating our material being. And it is exactly by freeing ourselves from the obsessive concern with the material body, with the particular, that we truly participate in God. For if God appears to us in bodily form in the guise of his son, God himself is ultimately beyond this corporeal appearance. Failure to realize this crucial distinction is failure to realize what becoming God really entails. Rather, the attachment to the material that anchors Fedorov's project suggests—despite Fedorov's attempt to obscure the animal selfishness of his project through its connection to a greater moral project, our duty to our ancestors—that Fedorov's project is a kind of bestializing in which all that matters is the continuation of material existence.[49]

What does one become, then, a god or a beast? Must man be overcome? Is the truly human fate of the human being to overcome or destroy itself? Indeed, is this overcoming or destruction the aim of history? These questions, which emerge directly from the radical speculations of Dostoevsky and his followers, are fundamental to the sprawling philosophical project of Alexandre Kojève, as we shall see in the following chapters.

II

THE HEGEL LECTURES

❖

4

THE LAST REVOLUTION

Kojève's lectures on G. W. F. Hegel, published after World War II by Raymond Queneau, constitute the boldest and most comprehensive introduction to Kojève's revolutionary project. It is now commonplace to dismiss these lectures as philosophically and philologically unsound—as "bad" Hegel. Unfortunately, it is equally commonplace to dismiss these dismissals with the confident declaration that they are beside the point, Kojève being not merely an interpreter of Hegel but also a philosopher himself, who is thereby permitted greater interpretive license.[1] There is a powerful precedent for this defense of Kojève in the interpretive practice of Martin Heidegger.[2] Throughout the 1920s, and perhaps even more aggressively in the 1930s, Heidegger developed a style of interpretation that he himself, not without boasting, referred to as "violent." In the preface to the second edition of his famous book on Immanuel Kant, *Kant and the Problem of Metaphysics*, Heidegger responds to accusations of *Gewaltsamkeit*—violence or even brutality—in his interpretation of Kant:

> The accusation of violence can indeed be supported by this text. Philosophico-historical research is surely correct with this accusation whenever it is directed against attempts to set in motion a thoughtful dialogue between thinkers. In contrast to the methods of historical philology, which has its own task, a thoughtful dialogue is subject to

other laws. These are more easily violated. In a dialogue what comes short is more threatening, the shortcomings more frequent.[3]

Heidegger speaks to two audiences here, the philosophic and the nonphilosophic. He defends interpretive violence as being almost, if not surely, inevitable in genuine philosophy, defined as a "thoughtful dialogue" (*denkerische Zwiesprache*), and he concedes that this violence appears to be a shortcoming only for those who are not philosophic. Heidegger simply closes the door on his critics—presumably even the "violent" ones—since merely to critique his interpretive style shows their unsuitability for philosophy.

Those who defend (or attack) Kojève as something more than an interpreter or commentator repeat a variant of this argument.[4] While I shall not repeat this defense, I do think the question of interpretive violence is vitally important if we are to come to terms with the complicated attitude to Hegel's text that emerges in Kojève's lectures. For Kojève certainly does not seem to engage in a standard academic exposition of the Hegelian text, despite his frequent reliance on academic conventions of interpretation. One might even argue that his reliance on convention tends to do little more than leaven or disguise the sheer outrage of his approach, as if a patina of social grace were enough to conceal a more thoroughgoing affront. One of Kojève's most notorious affronts is his predilection for broad generalization or aphoristic reduction, which so outstrips the limits of careful, reasonable research that it asks to be dismissed as fanciful or extreme.

Kojève's apparent concentration on recognition via the relation of master and slave in *The Phenomenology of Spirit* is a case in point. But one can find many extreme statements strewn throughout Kojève's commentary that seem at once bathetic and contradictory in their exhortation to declare a particular aspect of Hegel's text the most important. For if Kojève emphasizes time and again the centrality of recognition—the volume edited by Raymond Queneau opens with a commentary on this section—there also are countervailing declarations like that found in the book's final lecture: "The key to understanding Hegel's system as a whole" may be found in a short passage in the preface to the *Phenomenology*, whose main contention is that "all depends on explaining and grasping the truth not only as substance but as subject as well."[5] The contrast between the beginning and the end of the book raises a number of fundamental questions about its underlying structure and coherence.

Other startling declarations abound, with Kojève's pronounced epigrammatic talent showing itself to good effect: "Man is absolute dialectical disquiet (*Un-ruhe*)";[6] "Human existence is a mediated suicide";[7] "Language is born of discontent. Man speaks of Nature that kills him and makes him suffer";[8] "*Rameau's Nephew universalized*—that is the *Aufklärung* [Enlightenment]";[9] "Man must be an emptiness, a nothingness, that is not pure nothingness, *reines Nichts*, but something that *is* insofar as it *annihilates* Being";[10] "One could define man as an error that maintains itself in existence, that *endures* in the real";[11] and "Human existence itself is nothing but this Action: it is the death that lives a human life."[12]

These aphoristic phrases are not the common coin of academic discourse; on the contrary, they resemble philosophic bons mots meant to astonish or beguile his French audience, whether with ironic intent or not, and are part of Kojève's "philosophical pedagogy."[13] Kojève would surely be censured for his exuberance and lack of probity—he must explain, not create puzzles or riddles. The task of the interpreter or commentator comes down precisely to this: he or she must explain the enigmatic, must clarify, must bring to light whatever in the text seems recalcitrant—what is, in other words, resistant to explanation. Interpretation begins with what resists access, what holds itself back from immediate comprehension. Kojève seems freely to admit this elsewhere, but he also seems content to leave something for interpretation, with the claim that "one has to leave something for the reader: he should go on to think on his own."[14]

More than that, the published commentary is notoriously unbalanced, with an overwhelming focus on two narratives: that of the master and slave and that of the sage. The master and slave, from section A, chapter 4, of the *Phenomenology*—a mere nine pages in the German edition Kojève used—is discussed in detail throughout Kojève's commentary. Likewise, the narrative of the sage, from the final chapter of the *Phenomenology*, is fifteen pages in the German text but comprises 173 pages of Kojève's commentary—the concluding twelve lectures. In contrast, Kojève's treatment of the first three chapters of the *Phenomenology* is schematic, a mere nine pages in the French edition. The same may be said for his treatment of the long fifth chapter of the *Phenomenology*; Kojève's commentary comprises seventeen pages covering 129 pages of German text. Kojève is more careful with chapters 6 and 7 of the *Phenomenology*, but it is clear, in the end, that Kojève's commentary is almost wholly focused on two short chapters. Kojève's own division of the text confirms this dramatic preference, with emphasis given only to chapters 4, 6, 7, and 8.[15]

In all these respects, Kojève's commentary flaunts its departure from academic propriety, its "eccentricity," and this raises serious issues of interpretation. How are we to approach Kojève? If we approach his work as if he is an academic interpreter or commentator, do we not betray its spirit, the predilection for "violence" or "eccentricity" that seems to course through the text? And if we approach it as Kojève seems to approach Hegel, do we not arrogate to ourselves the title of "philosopher," the one entitled to engage in violent or eccentric interpretation? After all, am I not supposed to interpret Kojève according to the very conventions that Kojève may be mocking, and perhaps nowhere more powerfully so than in regard to the generally unspoken imperative to provide an interpretation of his text that holds together?[16]

KOJÈVE AS THE COMMENTATOR

Stefanos Geroulanos makes the important comment that Kojève's ties to Friedrich Nietzsche have generally been underestimated, and I think he is right.[17] Perhaps the closest analogue for Kojève's treatment of Hegel may be found in a work that has many startling connections with Kojève's commentary, Nietzsche's *Towards a Genealogy of Morality*.[18] In both cases, a specific genre, ostensibly devoted to the painstaking and sober treatment of a topic—the kind of work, we may presume, that occupies the sober English psychologists Nietzsche so delights in mocking—becomes the vehicle for proposals of extraordinary daring. Here we have a Trojan horse that seeks not the edification but the conquest of its audience by means of a dramatic and extreme rhetoric—indeed, an almost apocalyptic rhetoric—that suggests the significance of our current epoch and thus of the actions *we* might take in response to the doctrines contained in these works. This is not a rhetoric of reserve, of cautious consideration, but of revolution, and in both cases the exhortation is to throw off the shackles of the slave in favor of a radical form of emancipation.

The emphasis on emancipation is central to Kojève's commentary, and it invokes an obvious irony because the "ordinary" work of the commentator is not one of liberation from the text but of humble servitude to it. As I have already noted, the commentator is supposed to explain the text using careful principles of explication whose authority has been established by the tradition of commentaries going back to the ancient commentaries on Aristotle, if not further. These commentaries emerged out of the ancient academic milieu and sought to explicate difficult texts of the master—referred to merely as the Philosopher in a later tradition of commentaries, those of the great Arab thinker Averroes, which exerted enormous influence in the medieval West. These commentaries were ways of continuing and refining the tradition, not of bringing it to an end or transforming it. They dealt with each part of the Aristotelian text, and they tended to shy away from the broad statements that pepper Kojève's work. To put a long story into a few words, these commentaries were acts of service to a grand tradition that they sought to preserve.

We seem to find nothing of the sort in Kojève's commentary, in which an ironic and playful self-consciousness reigns supreme, as the very first section of the Hegel lectures indicates. This section, taken from an article Kojève published in 1939, plays the role of commentary, providing both the Hegelian text and Kojève's comments.[19] But, unlike most traditional commentaries, the setting off of the two texts is rather confusing because they are separated only by brackets and italics. Moreover, the commentary freely intrudes on the Hegelian text at many points. One has the impression not of respectful commentary but of an attempt to create a dialogue of equals or, even more radically, a dialogue in which the commentator—who is surely in a superior position in this respect, since the philosopher himself cannot respond—prevails by clarifying what the master was evidently unable or unwilling to say.[20]

Let me be perfectly clear here: Kojève's commentary develops a philosophical theory—specifically that of the origins and ends of identity—that seems to use the Hegelian text as a pretext. To be sure, Kojève shows a basic fidelity to the Hegelian text, but he spins an entire philosophical theory out of it in a way that constitutes much more than a tried-and-true explication of the text. Rather, Kojève takes the text as a basis for an imaginative construction of his own whose story of origins and ends can be connected to the Hegelian text only imprecisely or ambiguously. Kojève pays heed to the master but also departs from the letter of Hegel's teaching to create what seems to be a teaching of his own.

Perhaps I have engaged thus far in what one may consider only a pedantic way of suggesting that Kojève's commentary is not "merely" a commentary but in fact a philosophical construct of its own. One need not debate the issue of correctness or adequacy of the interpretation, because these concerns are largely beside the point. Moreover, this approach to the accuracy of interpretation, under the influence of Heidegger but also of Kojève, has become common coin in contemporary academic discourse. There is now no original text but merely a proliferation of discourses, which is itself supposed to be a kind of "proof" of the absence of an original. Dogma becomes Derridian in the sense of the singular Derridian declaration that the condition of possibility of interpretation—and thus interpretations—is that there is no *one* interpretation of any text.[21] That this condition of possibility becomes Derridian dogma is itself ironic because the dogma is belied or betrayed by its content; if there is no interpretation that can claim to be the final one, no interpretive dogma should be final, provided that the ascription of dogma itself is an interpretation, a story that, like any other, is neither more nor less authoritative.

This complete collapse of the text is one of the outcomes of Kojève's approach to the Hegelian text. Not so obvious is the corollary: that Kojève's text itself collapses as well. There is no final text, no original, merely a proliferation of texts, all of which are ironic "simulacra," copies of an absent original.

Yet this is manifestly *not* what Kojève is after in his commentary. The commentary is designed to lead to a decisive final point that does not engage in the sort of "spinning in the void" that may result from Derridian proliferation. But Derridian proliferation is no doubt a possible outcome of Kojève's approach and, by revealing this possible outcome, Derridian proliferation points to an underlying tension in Kojève's approach, between interpretive license, or philosophical madness, and final constraint, the end of history or final state that is one of the most important dogmas Kojève proclaims throughout his lectures. To put this in terms we have already employed, there is a marked tension in Kojève between what appears to be a purely negative approach and a positive one, between the opposed and perhaps mutually exclusive tasks of destruction and creation.

These arguments require a much more thorough account of Kojève's interpretation than I have given so far. For the moment, suffice it to say that the interpretive license that Kojève seems to allow himself opens up formidable, indeed vertiginous, possibilities, which Kojève himself would later seek to undermine. One of the most powerful aspects of Kojève's later thought is its attempt to show that the kind of proliferation evinced by what I have called (somewhat jocularly) the Derridian dogma is impossible, or not a proliferation, but its opposite: the potentially endless repetition of a simple operation.[22]

What, then, is the significance of Kojève's distortion or parody of the generally accepted approach to commentary? Is it really, as I have noted, an arrogation of authority based on Kojève's philosophical nature, his assumption that he is a philosopher himself and not merely a commentator? Is the commentary on Hegel, then, an example of that *denkerische Zwiesprache* whose radical shortcomings may be excused as the inevitable byproduct of genuine philosophical discourse? Or should we take another tack, that of Kojève's friend Leo Strauss, the rather notorious advocate of the distinction between the exoteric and esoteric aspects of a text?[23] From this point of view, might we say that Kojève is concealing his radicality behind the mask of academic propriety?

There is even another possibility, perhaps the least likely at first blush, but important nonetheless, since it is one that Kojève himself relies on time and again: that he is merely repeating Hegel's text in a manner suitable to a different time. In this respect, the enormous philosophical project that Kojève engaged in, largely in secret, after the war was, in his own words, an attempt to bring the Hegelian system up to date for a new audience. But the question remains: If Hegel's system is the end of history or the end of philosophy, why would it need an update? It is not at all unreasonable to assume that an update is needed precisely because history or philosophy did *not* end—people did not get the point, so it needs to be made again.

If we boil the options down, we get two: either Kojève is an innovator or tendentious simplifier who transforms Hegel for his own revolutionary purpose; or he is a faithful commentator who transforms Hegel, in service to the master, as a contemporary renovator of the truth, as if Kojève were a nineteenth- or twentieth-century Thomist attempting to prove the adequacy of Aquinas to the modern age. Kojève is either master or servant, as the case may be, one who negates or upholds the claims of the master in purporting to explain them. Or perhaps, in a more complex act of extreme fealty and betrayal, Kojève is a modern-day Judas whose betrayal of the master first allows the master to appear in his true role as the culmination of history, and who does so in a way that surpasses even his predecessors among Hegel's earliest students.[24]

We may examine all these options, initially, by exploring the opening text of the *Introduction to the Reading of Hegel*. Accordingly, I intend first to provide a reading of this text in order to set the stage for a careful reading of two other crucial texts from the *Introduction*, the lectures from 1938–1939, which, in my view, are the other centerpiece of the entire book, and the book's dramatic coda, the remarkable lectures on death. In brief, the opening text sets out the basic mytheme of the lectures, the recognition narrative, in a way that offers an implicit account of Kojève's own interpretive procedure, one that has a significant impact on what I am doing myself as an interpreter of this most devious and self-aware interpreter of Hegel.

I might add in passing that, by proceeding in this manner, I am disregarding the advice Queneau gives to the reader in his editor's note (which is not reproduced in the English translation). Queneau asks the reader who does not want to follow the text of the *Phenomenology* to read only the introduction, the two appendixes, and the first three lectures from 1937–1938.[25] While Kojève's English translator and editor seem, in part, to have followed this injunction, which may very well be traced back to Kojève himself, the elimination from the English edition of almost three hundred pages of the French text, including an important appendix on death, all the lectures from 1935–1936 and 1936–1937, and half of the lectures from 1938–1939 seems wholly inappropriate. This radical truncation of the original French text omits a large portion of what Kojève himself wrote, and one wonders whether the argument for Kojève's violence as an interpreter does not unduly benefit from this omission.

DESIRE, THE BIRTH OF THE HUMAN

The opening text of the *Introduction*, "In the Guise of an Introduction," sets out a creation narrative, a story or philosophical myth of origins based on the famed chapter 4 of Hegel's *Phenomenology*, in which Hegel describes in extremely compressed form his notion of self-consciousness. Kojève does not open with a citation from Hegel's text but with his own words: "Man is self-consciousness."[26] The opening text is the creation narrative of self-consciousness and thus of man as well. The equation of man with self-consciousness is not terribly bold within the Hegelian context, nor is the claim that Kojève makes a few paragraphs further along, that self-consciousness presupposes desire, that the *I* which emerges as the first sign of self-consciousness is an *I of* desire: "The (human) *I* is the *I* of a desire or desire itself" (Le Moi [humain] est le Moi d'un—ou du—désir). Far bolder, however, is Kojève's justification of this claim by means of an apparently original creation narrative about the birth of the word *I* (la naissance du mot "Moi"). Kojève provides no further justification or deduction of the claim.[27]

According to Kojève, man initially contemplates or is totally absorbed in what he contemplates. As such, man is not aware of himself. More abstractly stated, the knowing subject simply loses itself in the object it knows. Kojève explicitly makes the connections between man and knowing subject, the thing contemplated and the object. He thus transforms the terms of his initial discussion from something akin to the natural attitude to one that fits within the terminology of subject and object, the terminology of modern philosophy. Kojève makes another connection by referring to the birth of the *I*, of self-consciousness, as the birth of human reality (la réalité humaine). Not only man but also human reality is self-consciousness, a connection that makes perfect sense on its own but also has wider implications, because the term "human reality" seems to be a reference to another definition of the human, Heidegger's "Dasein." One of Kojève's students, Henry Corbin, used the very French term "réalité humaine" as a translation for *Dasein* in the 1930s.[28] Thus, Kojève affirms the equation of being human with self-consciousness not only against the ancient and Christian definitions of man but also against that of

Heidegger or existential philosophy, this being one of the first of many critical asides aimed at Heidegger, whose significance will become increasingly apparent as we move further into the text.[29]

How is self-consciousness "born"? Of course, it is born through desire. Kojève claims that man remains absorbed in what he contemplates only as long as desire does not recall him to himself. I use the unusual English construction "recall him to himself" because Kojève uses the French verb *rappeler* (to recall) to describe how desire reveals the self to the self. The use of this verb is intriguing for two reasons. First, it seems to contain a (largely parodic) reference to the notion of the call (*Ruf*) in Heidegger, whereby Dasein comes to itself. Second, it suggests a waking up or a returning to a self, which is initially quite confusing, for how can man be recalled to himself if he has not yet been constituted as a self? If the moment of desire is the moment of emergence of the *I* as *I*, of the self as self, how can this action possibly be what it claims to be: a founding, a beginning? To put the matter more starkly, how can a self first be revealed to itself if the act of revealing presupposes the very identity (of the self, the *I*) it is supposed to establish? Do we not enter here into an infinite regress or vicious circle?

The issues raised by this question at the very beginning are momentous. If the self-founding of the *I* is flawed or not possible, then we must take Kojève's account as flawed in a crucial respect, or grossly mythic, merely giving an impression of logical development that cannot withstand closer inspection. One might argue that this flaw simply points to the rhetorical nature of the Kojèvian enterprise, its reliance on narratives that *seem* convincing but are not worthy of rigorous inspection, and we have Kojève's own admission in a letter to Tran Duc Thao that the lectures were a kind of philosophical propaganda.[30] To put the matter with less decorum, must we come to the conclusion that Kojève lies to us in order to convince us to accept a philosophical construct that is nothing else than a lie or fiction carefully wrought? This would seem to be a paltry result, or an assertion of Kojève's weakness as a propagandist, since it is surely no hallmark of propaganda to make arguments that may be so quickly and easily pulled apart and fail to compel assent from the outset. I do not think it wise to take Kojève so lightly.

How then can the self reveal itself to itself for the first time? The properly Kojèvian answer, I think, comes only with the definition of desire.

Kojève initially defines desire in terms of purely biological needs, like the need to eat, for example, and he maintains that self-consciousness cannot emerge in any other way than within the context of a "biological reality" (une réalité biologique). Kojève further identifies that reality with animality—the first appearance of desire is in the form of pure animal necessity, such as food, sex, protection, and so on. But this appearance of desire, while necessary, is not yet a sufficient condition for the emergence of self-consciousness, which first emerges with a different kind of desire, the object of which is not immediately found within the biological world. Still, Kojève has given us only the *kinds* of desire. He has not yet told us what desire *is*.

Desire is negation. What sort of equation is this? Kojève introduces negation by identifying it first with disquiet or restlessness and then with action. Desire is disquiet, restlessness that leads to action. Once completed, action returns us to a state of quiescence, a state that we may identify with satisfaction. Now Kojève makes a crucial move in describing the action of satisfying desire as negation, as the "destruction or at the very least the transformation of the desired object." He provides an example by referring once again to eating, his metaphor of choice for describing animal desire. To satisfy hunger, one must destroy or transform the food. In a typically sweeping gesture, Kojève indicates that "all action is negative" in this sense: "Far from leaving the given as it is, action destroys it; if not in its being, in its given form." Desire is action that negates or transforms the given so as to become satisfied or "full"—complete in such a sense that desire dissipates in contentment or satisfaction. The emphasis on transformation rather than destruction leads to Kojève's next point. Desire as negating action transforms the given into a new reality, a subjective one: "For if the action born of desire destroys an objective reality in order to attain satisfaction, it creates in its place and by means of the destructive act itself, a subjective reality."[31]

Desire creates by negating. The first thing it creates is a subject. Every action brings—or recalls—the subject to itself as the negating actor, as negation in process. Thus, Kojève's claim that the *I* of desire is a void (*un vide*) that only receives positive content by its negative actions seems now to make better sense as an origin that does not presuppose the very identity it is supposed to create. Rather, Kojève describes a dynamic process of construction of the self, the first step of which is a negative relation of the self to the self as the void of desire. It thus is not identity that is presupposed but rather the *absence* of identity, a beginning point from which to proceed to acquire identity through actions that negate or transform the given.

Kojève creates what seems initially to be a productionist model of the subject, including the idea that truth is itself a "product." He then sketches out the plan of production. But this is a radically simplified productionist model that reduces the apparatus of mediation to negation itself. One imagines a negating machine that transforms its inputs into outputs according to a program that determines the production process from the outset—that is, the production process merely repeats a production pattern that functions a priori. According to Kojève, the difference between a negating machine and an animal (whose instinct presumably plays the role of program) is the "sentiment of self" possessed by the animal—curiously enough, a sentiment of self that is, strictly speaking, impossible to prove definitively. The difference between a negating machine and the human being must be somewhat more complicated, since the human being apparently negates without a prior program. The human being becomes itself in a process of negation not foreordained in advance. There is no a priori, no plan to be repeated; the "plan" (if one may still call it that) first emerges from the process of production itself. This is *in nuce* a distinction between nature and history, where the former is the realm of necessity, the latter of freedom.[32]

To characterize human action as a process of production not dictated a priori is perhaps unfair to Kojève. I say this because human production is distinguished from that of animals not only by its non-aprioristic character but also by its object, the given that is supposed to be the target of negation. What is the distinctively human given, the "food" that the human being "negates" by ingesting it or by transforming it so that it may be ingested? For what does the human actor hunger?

Kojève's answer is clear: desire. The object of human desire is desire. Now, this may sound estranging, even arbitrary. Kojève has not even bothered to cite the relevant Hegelian text yet.[33] We are still in the beginning. While the simple productionist metaphor may adequately describe Kojève's basic approach to animal desire, whereby "raw material," the given, is physically transformed into something else by the activity of the animal, it seems to fail, at least at first blush, when loaded with this second object, whose givenness is unmistakably different because it relates to an object that in turn describes a relation to the given. Thus, the desire for a desire is a relation not to an object as concrete given but to another relation.

So we have a relation relating to another relation that relates in turn to something else. What is this something else? Is it the raw material, the given or "object" of animal desire, or yet another relation? The distinction here is of some importance, since the one relation is "grounded" in a given that offers a starting point for the hierarchy of desire, whereas the other, the relation to yet another relation, may end up deferring that starting point endlessly. In the first case, there is a sort of ground, a fixed originating referent, whereas in the second case such a ground is absent or infinitely deferred. Since the second case would undermine the model of desire that Kojève creates (and lead perhaps to the kind of Derridian proliferation I mentioned above), it is quite unlikely that human desire may relate only to other human desires. We must in fact accept what Kojève has indicated earlier, that desire as negation is not purely ideal but presupposes a biological starting point. The origin story only makes sense, it would seem, if the origin is biological, rooted firmly in the material world. But one wonders all the same if it has to be so. There is, in other words, an ambiguity about the given, whether that given is in fact already a product itself or is raw material, something akin to nature.

This is important because Kojève justifies his claim that desire for desire is distinctively human on the basis that it is *not* natural, that its object is not the raw material of nature that the animal transforms but, rather, already another desire. This other desire is not natural insofar as it transcends (*dépasse*) the given reality: "For Desire taken as Desire— i.e., before its satisfaction—is but a revealed nothingness, an emptiness that is unreal. Desire, being the revelation of an emptiness, the presence of the absence of a reality, is something essentially different from the desired thing, something other than a thing, than a static and real being that stays eternally identical to itself."[34]

Human desire presupposes animal desire, which is the condition of possibility of any notion of desire, but also surpasses it. Since human desire surpasses animal desire, it must also surpass the concrete (or "immediate") materiality of animal desire, and the way to denote this surpassing is by identifying human desire with nonidentity or negation as Kojève uses the term. But there is nothing self-evident about this conclusion. It warrants careful consideration.

On the one hand, it is hardly clear how animal desire can generate human desire. The genesis of human desire from animal desire shows no necessity whatsoever. So why does it come about? On the other hand, it is also unclear why the content of human desire must be emptiness or nothingness, a paradoxical content, since it seems to turn what cannot be an object into an object. Perhaps these two objections are merely two different ways of approaching the central dilemma of Kojève's definition of human desire: the creation of an object that cannot truly be an object, an object whose content undermines its form, an object afflicted by paradox or inconsistency.[35]

Kojève seems to hold that this paradox or inconsistency is the "wound" that desire seeks to heal. Human desire is born of dissatisfaction with natural ends, though it cannot fully free itself from natural ends (as origin of this dissatisfaction). Nonetheless, it is this very desire for freedom from natural ends that characterizes human desire, which, in this precise sense, must be understood *in itself* as negation or emptiness because there is no natural object or given that can possibly correspond to it. To put this in different terms, Kojève appears to describe human desire as dissatisfaction with natural ends—human desire emerges with dissatisfaction, with some kind of breakdown in the functioning of the natural order. Human desire emerges from animal desire because something breaks down in the latter.

Where does one find this claim in the text? Is this an inference one must make? And if so, is it a fair inference? The clearest anticipation of this characterization of desire is Kojève's identification of desire with disquiet or restlessness. Note Kojève's piquant observation that "Man is absolute dialectical disquiet (*Un-ruhe*)."[36] Of course, dialectical restlessness is associated with the "monstrous power of the negative," the engine of dialectical movement in the *Phenomenology* that emerges in the three chapters that precede the chapter on self-consciousness.[37] So there is nothing extraordinary about this claim, from the perspective of the movement forward, other than its obstinate focus on man as the dialectical agent. This focus brings up several thorny issues with regard to the dialectic and reveals one of Kojève's most distinctive assumptions: that the dialectic does not necessarily describe a structure immanent in the world itself, in mind and nature, but in the form of the human response to nature, a response that can only be coherent as negation insofar as it is a sign of dissatisfaction, of enmity, of conflict.[38] Kojève's utter disregard for Hegel's philosophy of nature becomes quite comprehensible when viewed from this perspective—there can be no positive philosophy of what, for us, is little more than an object to be negated or transformed, regardless of its specific contours.[39]

Before taking the account of desire a bit further, I should like to pause on this point, because there seems to be a tension between Kojève's insistence on the importance of our biological reality and the hostility to this biological reality revealed by the concept of desire we are developing. To put the issue somewhat differently, there seems to be a tension in Kojève between reconciliation with nature, a recognition of ourselves in the natural world, and the suppression of nature in a project of negation that does not seek harmony or reconciliation but conquest. As we will see, this same tension emerges in Kojève's account of recognition, in the sense that there are at least two possible ways of interpreting Kojève's programmatic assertion that human desire is the desire of desire.

On the one hand, this assertion may entail that one negates the desire of the other in a radical and absolute fashion, such that I only guarantee my *I* at the cost of all others, who must conform their desires to my own. We all become one as imitations of my *I*, through the pure, undifferentiated imposition of one identity on all others, a task that must end in failure, for the elimination of the other, just like the elimination of our biological reality, involves my own elimination. On the other hand, the further possible outcome of this "assimilation" of desire is a universal and homogeneous identity in which we all freely accept the same identity.[40] While these questions get far ahead of the present task of interpretation, I hope they help clarify the significance of understanding exactly what Kojève means by identifying desire with disquiet and dissatisfaction, not only in terms of the relation to nature that is implied by dissatisfaction but also by the relation to other human beings as desiring beings, which is superimposed upon this first relation as its necessary double.

To return to the initial question: Is the inference that human desire originates in dissatisfaction with natural desire, and thus with natural ends, an inference that one must make? Do restlessness and disquiet reveal dissatisfaction that in turn reveals to us an essential enmity with nature? I think that we may grant the first inference without having to grant the second, or at least without having to grant the second unqualifiedly. As I have noted, what is at stake here is something very important: whether negation is after reconciliation or conquest or, more precisely, a dialectical combination of the two whereby reconciliation and conquest are one and the same or mutually opposed. In this sense, the identification of negation with the action of an agent, a human agent, is a provocative move that may well undermine the notion of reconciliation and shows again Kojève's hostility to considering nature as a proper object of philosophy.[41]

Let us now proceed to the next steps in Kojève's opening commentary. Kojève makes the crucial statement that "the Desire that relates to a natural object is not human unless it is 'mediated' by the Desire of another relating to the same object: it is human to desire what others desire because they desire it."[42] Here we have perhaps a clearer reason for the emergence of dissatisfaction, for Kojève notes that the precondition for the competition of desires, for the rise of distinctively human desire, is that there is a plurality of natural or animal desires. The unspoken assumption is that this plurality in itself gives rise to conflict because it reveals the fragility of natural desire as arising from the absence of a single natural desire. But difference itself is not enough. The possibility of different "natural" desires is indeed merely harmless or undifferentiated until these desires come into conflict with each other. Conflict of desires raises the question of the naturalness of nature and, thus, of identity. We come to ourselves as selves when we confront others who are markedly different from us—the negation of our own identity implied by other manifestations of desire, by other "natures," compels a breakdown in our identity. We either acquiesce in this breakdown or aggressively seek to overcome it by transforming the natural desire of the other so that it conforms to ours. We desire the desire of the other in order to assure ourselves of our own identity or, more precisely, to eliminate the challenge to our own identity presented by that of the other.

We may say, then, that the enmity against nature as such has its ground in the disharmony revealed by different "natures," by the plurality of natural desire itself. The "wound" revealed by desire has to do with the radical incommensurability of different arrangements of desire; that is, in Nietzsche's fateful words, "Man is the unfinished animal" (der Mensch ist das noch nicht festgestellte Tier).[43] Or, as we might say, man is the radically *imperfect* animal, ugly and needy, the erotic animal.

Beasts and gods are perfect because they know no difference, no defect, no absence.

Our imperfection leads to community, of which beasts and gods, as perfect beings, have no need. Community presupposes plurality and conflict. Thus, it presupposes human desire and a dawning consciousness of self. Human desire attempts to overcome its dissatisfaction or disharmony with nature in the formation of community; the city or state is the completion of nature—or its overcoming.

RECOGNITION

This narrative, pioneered by Jean-Jacques Rousseau and Hegel, is the heart of the celebrated "recognition thesis" that completes Kojève's opening interpretation of Hegel.[44] In fairness to Kojève—and as a counter to those who argue that Kojève takes a fanciful approach to Hegel—he seems fully justified in granting primary significance to this portion of chapter 4 in the *Phenomenology*, which, in the words of the eminently sensible and careful Hegel scholar Robert Pippin, is "the most important chapter in all of Hegel."[45] The key point of this chapter is that my identity as a self-conscious being, as human, relies on another self-conscious being. My desire relates to the desire of an other; there is no formation of human identity that is not thoroughly social. Radically individual human identity is madness or incoherence. Thus, Kojève's notion of madness, the argument he sets out in "Tyranny and Wisdom," finds its proper origins in the Hegelian insistence on the primacy of sociality as the origin of any human identity. In this respect, Kojève strikes a decisive blow to the Dostoevskian heroes we examined earlier, insofar as their attempt to escape limitation, to be like gods in some fashion, confines them to defeat in paradox. They seek personal salvation, whereas—and this is the crucial distinction that aligns Kojève with Vladimir Soloviev and Nikolai Fedorov—Kojève seeks collective salvation, which, indeed, is the only form of salvation that is not tinged with madness.

Human desire is mediated by otherness. As we have noted, this mediation is precisely the desire of another in relation to a certain thing. If similarity is presupposed—the thing is recognized as desirable from two perspectives—the difference of perspective is decisive because it must involve conflict if it is to lead to the formation of identity, a particular consciousness of self. Kojève moves this argument along by indicating that perspective involves valuation: "All desire is desire of a value."[46] This is, again, an estranging move: What exactly does "desire of a value" mean? We may be justified in our surprise. Kojève has defined desire as desire of desire of an other and has indicated that this desire is truly human because its object is not to be found in the natural world. If we grant the latter point, we come to a new equation: human desire as nonnatural is the desire of a value; the concept of value distinguishes what is human from what is not. To ascribe value is human because this value is ascribed merely on the basis that some common X is desired differently by different subjects. That is, conflict or competition about a natural object supplies the raw material for a valuation, and valuation is little more than a way of recording the relation of the different desires, the one to the other.[47]

The crucial distinction here is that all animal desire comes down to one overwhelming "value," self-preservation. A question of value as such can never come up because the ultimate value is always the same. Human beings are different. They ascribe value to things merely because others desire them, no matter what their utility for survival is. This disregard for utility, for subsuming all things under a regime of self-preservation, is the sign of a distinctively human reality.[48] It follows, then, that the most purely human reality involves the most complete disregard for self-preservation. To deviate from the regime of self-preservation is the clearest expression of distinctively human desire.

> Differently put, man "proves himself" human only if he risks his life (animal) as a function of his human Desire. It is in and by this risk that human reality creates and reveals itself as reality; it is in and by this risk that human reality "proves itself," that is, shows, demonstrates, verifies itself and gives evidence of itself as essentially different from animal, natural reality. And this is why to speak of an "origin" of Self-consciousness is necessarily to speak of risking one's life (toward an end that is essentially nonvital).[49]

Human desire is the desire of the desire of an other (le désir du désir d'un autre).[50] Merely to desire the desire of an other, though a necessary condition, is evidently not a sufficient one. More is needed. One not only must desire the desire of an other to be human but also must be prepared to risk one's life to "win" that desire. If, as Kojève argues, human desire is still analogous with animal desire, to win the desire of another can only mean that the desired "object" must be negated or otherwise ingested or assimilated, analogies whose precise meaning is not so clear when the object is the non-object, human desire itself.

To begin to grasp what Kojève is after, we must look at what negation is, namely, action. Kojève is not talking about moves in some conceptual game that never escapes the realm of theory; he is clearly talking about action in the world—this is another way of appreciating his insistence on the importance of our biological reality. For Kojève, it evidently makes no sense to talk about desire if the analogy between human and animal is completely severed—the animal remains. In this respect, Kojève is genuinely Hegelian in suggesting that the overcoming of a given reality does not entail its eradication but rather its inclusion in a new reality that assumes it in decisively moving beyond it.[51]

So, if desire is action, then the acquisition or assimilation of this action can only take the form of orienting that action to harmonize with my own actions. In terms of the notion of value, Kojève notes that the desire of the desire of an other is, in the final account, a desire fulfilled by substituting my value for that of the other. The relevant passage from the text is very curious. Rather than saying that I desire to substitute my "values" for those of an other, the text says that I desire to substitute my value, that "value that I am or that I represent," for the value of the other.[52] I want the other to recognize my value in place of his or her value—recognition is in this sense conquest.

This conquest involves a struggle to the death. My value may only prevail if I am unafraid of negating the desire of the other by risking my life to do so. In this competition over value, there is no middle range, no peaceful agreement not to disagree, no reconciliation that leaves both sides as they were before they came into conflict. There is only one outcome to the conflict, and that outcome can be assured only if the struggle is to the death. Kojève holds that, without conflict, there would never have been any humans on earth.

This kind of notion offends the democratic sensibility whereby disagreements may be resolved not by death but by careful discussion. But we must be very careful here. Kojève is talking about origins, and his account of these origins will ultimately imply a proper place for democratic discussion.

Struggles to the death are of three kinds: both parties die or one lives or both live. There is only an origin in the third case. This is important, because it emphasizes the social imperative: a lone victor does not create a society because the lone victor is alone. A consciousness fully alone cannot come to full self-consciousness because there is no other, and without the other, there is no self—the mutual implication here is fundamental. The third case, then, is the proper case for the origin or foundation of society. In this case, the two parties survive only because one chooses not to fight or, at least, not to fight to the death.

> In order that human reality come into being as "recognized" reality, both adversaries must remain alive after the fight. Now, this is possible only on the condition that they behave differently in this fight. By irreducible, or better, by unforeseeable or "non-deducible" acts of freedom, they must constitute themselves as unequal in and by this struggle itself. Without being "predestined" to it in any way, the one must fear the other, must give in to the other, must refuse to risk his life for the satisfaction of his desire for "recognition." He must abandon his desire and satisfy the desire of the other: he must "recognize" the other without being "recognized" by him. Now, "to recognize" him thus is "to recognize" him as his Master and to recognize himself and to be recognized as the Master's Slave.
>
> Differently put, in his nascent state, man is never just man. He is always, necessarily and essentially, either Master or Slave. If human reality can only come into being as social reality, society is human—at least in its origin—only on the condition of implying an element of Mastery and an element of Slavery, of "autonomous" existences and "dependent" existences.[53]

The two basic propositions here are that there can be no human reality that is not recognized and that the original form of this recognition features a radical asymmetry or disharmony.

Why does human reality have to be recognized? If we turn again to Kojève's own madness argument from "Tyranny and Wisdom," we may perhaps obtain a clearer understanding of what recognition means.

Kojève essentially equates madness with the refusal to admit the primacy of the social constitution of reality and, in a sharply ironic gesture, claims that the philosopher who attempts to live "outside" or "above" social reality cannot distinguish his life from that of a madman. But, of course, this madness is madness because it thrives on a basic inconsistency: as madness, it must in some way affirm the very social reality it otherwise denies—its rejection of the social reality presupposes that reality. Whether one likes it or not, the human or social reality is the only reality that we may safely refer to as such. Any other is an inconsistent projection, a kind of madness, a detour, a dream or hallucination, a seeing of devils with Father Ferapont.

Thus, to argue that human reality is "recognized" reality is merely to argue that it is constituted and mediated by social relations. By "mediated," I mean to refer to one of Kojève's most interesting claims, that what one values is a creation of a social reality having no "intrinsic" value of its own, if that value is understood to be in the nature of the thing itself or due to another, similar ascription of value that in effect denies the social constitution of value by suggesting that the value is somehow prior to or outside sociality. There is no such thing for Kojève as a "natural" or "self-evident" value.

Perhaps the most wide-ranging impact of this view—one that Kojève emphasizes when he claims with dogged persistence that Hegel is radically atheist—is that desire turns out to be wholly horizontal in orientation. The primary form of desire is oriented to another self-consciousness, to another human being, and not to God (as it is in Dostoevsky's Christian hero, Zosima). The Platonic order whereby eros is directed upwards to the hyperouranian realm is in fact a move in the social, that is, political, struggle for recognition. Put more bluntly, Kojève's emphasis on the social origin of human reality creates a radically new narrative of origins that *subordinates* other origin or creation narratives, like those of Plato, which do not claim that the social relation is fundamental. We are not created by a God but rather create that God as a move in the overwhelming social conflict emerging from an initial conflict whose conclusion creates the grounds for more conflict. While this view is decisively different from those of Fedorov and Soloviev insofar as God is placed within the social relation and not as the external guarantor of it, the impetus to create a final society is nonetheless the same. What has been eradicated is the temptation to the eternal, atemporal (and very personal) salvation that always remains when God is creator and not our creation.

Kojève affirms his own claim that the "only" mistake of Christianity is resurrection.[54]

The conclusion creates these further grounds for conflict because it expresses an essential inequality: the relation of master and slave. Kojève begins his proper commentary on the Hegelian text with this notion as Hegel unfolds it in part A of chapter 4 in the *Phenomenology*, the celebrated—and very brief—discussion of master and slave.[55] This is of course a provocative and intriguing move in itself, for it seems that Kojève has substituted his own account of the origins of desire for that of Hegel.

Kojève may well be justified in doing so, since Hegel's introduction of desire at this point in the *Phenomenology* has occasioned puzzlement among Hegel scholars.[56] Two main questions seem to come to the fore. First, what relation does chapter 4 have to the chapters that precede it? And second, how does one fit desire into a rational account of sociality? The second question returns us to the tension between reason and will (or theory and practice) in an extraordinarily complicated way but with the same essential implications. These may be expressed as formulating a question about Kojève's account of Hegel, in itself, as either establishing the primacy of reason or of will. Here the implications of Kojève's account of the origins of human reality are momentous, for they suggest that the legislative rules of social reality have no grounding in any other reality. They are not "in" God or Nature or Truth, for all of these are "moves" in social struggle—artifacts or, indeed, weapons of conflict. If that is so, however, what can Kojève's own account of these origins be? What authority can it exercise? Is it not an artifact or a weapon too?[57]

These possibilities emerge from Kojève's account of the origins of human reality, and the questions they pose are of crucial importance. But we are not in a position to deal with them adequately yet. We still have to complete our account of Kojève's opening commentary by examining the master-and-slave relation itself.

SELF-CERTAINTY

Kojève follows Hegel's text much more closely in this part of his opening commentary, though he retains many of the same emphases as in his initial narrative of origins.[58] He begins with a variant of the madness argument discussed above and then turns to a central emphasis of this portion of the commentary: the need to address the other as a way of securing one's own certainty of oneself as an objective truth, not merely a subjective certainty.

> The "first" man who meets another man for the first time already attributes an autonomous, absolute value to himself: one can say that he believes himself to be a man, that he has the "subjective certainty" of being a man. But his certainty is not yet knowledge. The value that he attributes to himself could be illusory; the idea that he has of himself could be false or mad. For that idea to be a truth, it must reveal an objective reality, that is, an entity that is valid and exists not only for itself, but also for realities other than itself. In the case in question, man, to be really, truly "man," and to know that he is such, must, therefore, impose the idea that he has of himself on beings other than himself: he must be recognized by others (in the ideal, extreme case: by all others). Or again: he must transform the (natural and human) world in which he is not recognized into a world in which this recognition takes place. This transformation of the world that is hostile to a human project into a world in harmony with this project is called "action," "activity." This action—essentially human, because humanizing and anthropogenic—will begin with the act of imposing oneself on the "first" other man one will meet.[59]

Subjective certainty is epistemically suspect. I may suppose myself the king of Spain or a god or a pane of glass, but these are merely wind eggs of the imagination until another accepts my characterization of myself as such. My self-interpretation is merely a fancy until someone accepts it as true, as a reality. The upshot of this is obvious and troubling: objectivity has no ground outside this relation of one consciousness to another.[60] Objectivity is not simply immanent in the world, is not something to which we all must jointly bow down. Rather, objectivity is the product of *action*, whereby I transform subjective certainty into objective truth by successfully imposing my self-interpretation on others as something they *must* accept themselves—indeed, this process of self-assertion constitutes my identity. I can only impose this, as we know, by showing my resolve to fight to the death for my subjective certainty, and provided I find others who prefer to accept enslavement rather than death. And the "first" enslavement is indeed the acceptance of the value imposed by another as being one's own.

This acceptance as voluntary is the crucial beginning of the master-slave relation. But it is not its end. We must ask: What then is the end of this relation? Or, indeed, does this relation end? We may cite the cliché that all that begins must end, but it is hardly evident that this must be so.

Kojève insists, however, on an end. The slave is not content to remain a slave. Nor is the master content. The relation between master and slave is inherently unstable because it is not a relation that fully satisfies either. The reason for dissatisfaction lies in the fundamental inequality of the relation. The slave is not recognized as of equal worth, as being human, and the master is not recognized because the slave, not being human, is incapable of recognizing the master as equal. If the master seeks to secure his own sense of self by eliminating the other, he fails to the degree that the other is not fully capable of recognizing him except as a slave who is not human. The slave is not human precisely on account of his refusal to risk his life by fighting the master. As a result, the slave shows himself to be more concerned with self-preservation, or with the preservation of his animal existence, than with becoming truly human. In other words, the slave is unable or unwilling to recognize his identity as "pure negation" by engaging in the restless negation of the desire of the other and, thus, of his own animal desire (for self-preservation). As Kojève says, "Man is human only to the extent that he wants to impose himself on another man."[61]

Yet it is one thing to say that the slave is not human and quite another to say that he seeks to be human, to be recognized. Why, after having surrendered to the master, does the slave not simply acquiesce in his servitude? How can the slave voluntarily accept a fate that he does not *truly* want?

There seems to be a conflict in the slave that does not have a correlate in the master, and one might argue that the disequilibrium in the relation between slave and master is reflected in the slave himself as a conflict between different kinds of desire with different objects. We have already identified two kinds of desire, animal and human, which are related to each other analogically, though their ends could not be more different— they are in fact essentially opposed. Animal desire may be boiled down to the desire to stay alive, the celebrated *conatus* that Spinoza defines as the essence of all living things.[62]

Human desire is not nearly so simple. Kojève first considers human desire as the desire to assimilate the desire of an other. This mildly pedantic way of expressing the essence of human desire allows us to bypass the simpler point: human desire is the desire to transform otherness into a reflection of itself, by substituting itself for all variant desires of any and all kinds. That is, human desire seeks to transform every otherness (both natural and human) into a reflection of itself, into a chorus in which all voices sing the same song or all plurality resolves itself in replication of the one. Human desire is at bottom the desire to be in a position vis-à-vis nature and other human beings that is equivalent to that of a god or God itself, since, as Kojève suggests, monotheism is the purification of polytheism.

Ultimately, to have the position of a god vis-à-vis all others means that all others must be slaves; that is, they must not be ready to become God themselves. The desire that is truly human eliminates all impediments to its hegemony, but it cannot be fulfilled by slaves. And here is the remarkable logic that Kojève begins to develop. The master must himself in some sense desire that his slaves become completely like him so that he may receive full recognition as an autonomous consciousness of which he is worthy. The master can, of course, only receive this recognition from another master, a recognition that is tantamount to the fullest self-consciousness because it is one that is absolutely pure, since both masters recognize themselves in the other—what is *I* is other, and what is other is *I*. Otherness per se has not been simply abolished; rather, it has been brought to a point of full self-reflection. To employ the metaphor of reflection again, we can say that the relation of God to his manifestations, as sought by the master in relation to his slaves, cannot be one of perfect reflection. There remains an otherness that is necessarily recalcitrant, that emerges as imperfect reflection of the master in any given slave. But this relation can be transformed to the extent the slave overcomes his attachment to animal desire, the blemish that impedes perfect reflection. It is only by overcoming this blemish, the slave in himself, that the slave may properly recognize the master for what he is.

This process occupies the final third of Kojève's commentary, for, as Kojève repeatedly insists, the slave is dynamic, changing, the genuine motive force that creates history.[63] In contrast to the slave, the master is an impasse. The master's willingness to risk death to impose his value on the slave leaves the master with nothing to do. He cannot be properly recognized by the slave, to be sure, and he cannot directly bring about that recognition. The master is left in splendid repose, or languor (this being a deft parody of the Nietzschean master, who is all natural ferocity, a "bird of prey" among lambs). Only his involuntary influence brings about the end of his condition as not fully recognized—his "tragedy," in Kojève's words—by imposing servitude on the slave such that the slave seeks to free himself from that servitude. One is in fact not at all sure what this master can be. This master is a necessarily enigmatic being because he has no further desire to negate, no content for his negation, and thus no positive content, either. In the Kojèvian account, the master acts merely as a trigger or "catalyst" for the beginning of a history that would not otherwise begin at all. But if the master is responsible for beginning history, he plays no further positive part in it. The master's presence is negative, an absence to be overcome—the absence of freedom for the slave.[64]

The notion of freedom here should be quite concrete. The slave wants to enjoy the same freedoms as the master. It is important in this connection to recall that desire, for Kojève, is always mediated. But the slave, by definition, is the one who substitutes the desire of an other for his desire. The servant recognizes the master's desire by negating his own, but the reverse is not the case. This reversal is the primary characteristic of the slave, who seeks recognition from the master by negating the negation of his own desire. The process of the negation of the master's desire is what Kojève calls history. The slave makes history, not the master, who is essentially inert.

The negation of the master's desire, however, is also an *assumption* of it. In other words, the negation of the master's desire ends up preserving it as well, in a transformed desire.[65] Here we need only recall the endlessly repeated caution about the German term *Aufheben* that Hegel employs to describe properly dialectical negation as both negation and preservation of what is negated. This movement of negation and preservation merely expresses the commonsense notion that negation bears the identity, if only in the negative, of the thing it negates. Thus, if the slave negates the master's desire to substitute his value for that of the slave, the negation can only follow as a reversal of that substitution—if the master sought to assimilate the slave's desire, the slave now seeks to assimilate the master's desire.

The slave assimilates the master's desire initially through *work*, the negation of nature. The slave works to transform the environment in order to feed the master. By doing so, the slave transforms not only nature but also his relation to the master, since the master becomes dependent on the work of the slave. The slave learns to plan, to organize, to calculate, to negate apparent natural immediacy or the connection to nature that made the slave into a slave in the first place. One could argue that the slave's work, as such, is a negation of his origin, that the history created by the slave erases his history *as* a slave.

> Therefore, by freeing the Slave from Nature, work frees him from himself as well, from his Slave's nature: it frees him from the Master. In the raw, natural, given World, the Slave is slave of the Master. In the technical world transformed by his work, he rules—or, at least, will one day rule—as absolute Master. And this Mastery that arises from work, from the progressive transformation of the given World and of man given in this World, will be an entirely different thing from the "immediate" Mastery of the Master. The future and History hence belong not to the warrior-Master, who either dies or preserves himself indefinitely in identity with himself, but to the working Slave. The Slave, in transforming the given World by his work, transcends the given and what is given by that given in himself; hence, he goes beyond himself, and also goes beyond the Master who is tied to the given which, as one who is not working, he leaves intact. If the anguish of death, incarnated for the Slave in the person of the warrior-Master, is the sine qua non of historical progress, it is solely the Slave's work that realizes and brings that progress to completion.[66]

Moreover, the slave learns to delay his own satisfaction—time first comes into being in the delay of satisfaction imposed by work. As such, there is a potential end to time as well, an end that seems to result from the achievement of final satisfaction.

Kojève confronts the issue of final satisfaction, appropriately enough, at the end of his commentary. Remarkable here is the focus on death, specifically on the anguish or fear of death. In the final account it is precisely this fear of death that makes the slave a slave and from which the slave seeks to free himself through work, through overthrowing the master, who represents for the slave the attachment to a world that the slave, in contrast to the master, cannot accept. Work is the emblem of nonacceptance, of the slave's desire to overcome his status by overcoming the world ruled by the master—by transcending it.

> The Master can never detach himself from the World in which he lives, and if this World perishes, he perishes with it. Only the Slave can transcend the given World (which is subjugated by the Master) and not perish. Only the Slave can transform the World that forms him and fixes him in slavery and create a World that he has formed in which he will be free. And the Slave achieves this through the forced and anguishing work carried out in the service of the Master. To be sure, this work by itself does not free him. But in transforming the World by his work, the Slave transforms himself, too, and thus creates the new objective conditions that permit him to take up once more the liberating Fight for recognition that he refused in the beginning for fear of death. And thus in the long run, all the work of servitude realizes not the Master's will, but the will—at first unconscious—of the Slave, who—finally—succeeds where the Master—necessarily—fails.[67]

This is a very intriguing paragraph, as we shall see. One might expect that the work of the slave would in fact bring the slave into a relation of mutual recognition, the reciprocal recognition that would seem to be the proper resolution to the conflict opened by the slave's initial acquiescence to the master, as is suggested by Kojève in other parts of the Hegel lectures. But Kojève does not say this here, at the beginning. Rather, the work of the slave transforms the world so completely that the master disappears, and the master disappears because death seems to disappear as well. For what, other than the conquest of death itself, might free the slave from the fears that made him a slave?

Kojève makes it clear that the slave transforms the "given world" into an artifact, becoming in that process a being that frees itself from its attachment to nature. As we know, the master cannot free himself from this attachment because the master, by definition, has no interest in changing the world. Strictly speaking, the master is utterly inscrutable for us because the master, as a contrast to the slave—that is, as one who is tied to the world he does not fear—cannot know growth, change, transformation. The master is free in this respect, and thus also nontemporal.

How could we imagine the master other than in a negative way? For we, as creations of the work of the slave, are now hard pressed to understand what mastery can mean other than in terms of our own technical mastery, the various modes by which we transform the world into one that no longer terrifies and estranges us. We become, to bend Novalis's famous phrase, "everywhere at home." If the threat of a fight to the death generates the emotion and the object, the potent fear of death, it also generates the radical overcoming of that fear, the creation of a being for which there is no fear at all, thus resembling the master by having transformed his forbidding world into one that offers us a home.

5

TIME NO MORE

Time shall be no more.

—REVELATION 10:6

The philosopher is the slave par excellence.[1] The philosopher is the being whose essence is change. The philosopher seeks to overcome the limitations that he encounters, that prescribe the situation in which he finds himself. The philosopher seeks not to remain a lover of wisdom, as the word *philo-sophia* indicates, but to become a *sophos* (ὁ σοφός), a wise being, one who transcends limitations in complete, unblemished self-awareness, capable of answering with perfect coherence all basic questions relating to his actions.[2] The philosopher represents a bridge, a transition, to a different kind of being for whom nothing is unfamiliar, strange, novel. The philosopher, having become wise, has achieved what Novalis refers to in his romantic idiom—he has learned to be at home everywhere—and for him there is no more time because the philosopher has become at home in time. Even death no longer enthralls the philosopher. The nagging caution from *Antigone* that so exercised Martin Heidegger falls silent.[3]

Here in a nutshell is a description of central propositions that Kojève develops in the most extensive series of lectures reproduced in *Introduction to the Reading of Hegel*. This series comprises twelve lectures from the fateful years 1938–1939, the last years of Kojève's seminar, which did not continue during the occupation of France. The lectures take up roughly a third of the French text of the *Introduction*. They are its centerpiece, the fullest unfolding of its central doctrines, and the most distinctively original aspect of Kojève's reading of G. W. F. Hegel, weaving together the Hegelian narrative of struggle with a complex recasting of Vladimir Soloviev's idea of divine humanity, or *Sophia*. Unfortunately, less than half of this particular lecture series is included in the English translation, an omission that seriously impedes access to the complicated core of Kojève's thought for those who do not have French. It is no exaggeration to argue that this Kojève remains, in important respects, largely unknown in English.

My purpose in this chapter is to give an account of Kojève's overriding concern with the sage, the wise man, or *sophos*, the guiding figure of the second major narrative developed in Kojève's commentary. Philosophy comes to its end in the figure of the sage, who gives definition and thus sense to philosophy as a way of being or, put more simply, as a way of life. Kojève's concern with the identity of the sage, then, is also a concern with the identity of philosophy; the two go together, and neither can be defined without reference to the other. Hence, to grasp Kojève's understanding of philosophy, one has also to grasp his understanding of the sage. Moreover, Kojève's concern with defining the sage unfolds in another context, that of the relation between master and slave that we examined in chapter 4. Kojève in effect superimposes two narratives, the master-and-slave narrative that he extracts from chapter 4 of Hegel's *Phenomenology of Spirit* and the narrative of the sage, which he extracts from chapter 8, the final chapter of the work.

Kojève does not tie the two narratives together explicitly, though it is clear that the philosopher is a slave. Since the interrelation of these two primary narratives is a central facet of Kojève's thought in the *Introduction*, I want to give a brief account of how the philosopher fits into the master-and-slave narrative, as a preliminary step on the way to a fuller understanding of the significance of Kojève's concern with the sage.

PHILOSOPHY AND SERVITUDE

As we have seen, Kojève conceives of the master as being at an impasse. A master can do literally nothing of fundamental importance, as we understand it, because the essence of the master is to remain the same, that is, *not* to change. The master has shown us, through his willingness to die, that he has no attachment to change. The willingness to die in order to impose his desire on the slave is the starkest expression of his unwillingness to change.

The moment when the slave refuses to fight, the pivotal moment that defines the slave as such, is also the moment when the slave opens himself to change. The slave cannot remain the same and live. The two propositions find themselves in contradiction, and it is precisely this contradiction that the slave seeks to overcome. For the slave is never "himself" until he is capable of assuming an identity that is no longer an identity defined by what amounts to a lack of identity. As long as the slave must change to adapt to the desire of the master, the slave is, strictly speaking, only identifiable as a nullity.

This may seem to be too strong a term. What can "nullity" mean? It means that the master does not recognize the slave. The master only recognizes the slave to the extent that the slave adapts to the desires of the master and substitutes those desires for his own. In this sense, the slave is nothing more than a cipher or a tool whose identity is defined by the master in relation to the tasks the slave is asked to perform by the master. The slave may remain as such, a tool without identity, but as we know, the slave is not content or satisfied to remain in that position. The slave's refusal to die leads to a life of combating nonidentity.

Kojève insists that the relation of master and slave itself changes in proportion to the master's increasing dependence on the slave. This insistence warrants closer examination for the assumptions it reveals. These assumptions boil down to one basic proposition, not stated openly, but inferable from the structure of recognition itself: that inequality cannot maintain itself indefinitely. The corollary is to assert that harmony or equilibrium must rule in the end. This certainly does seem to be the basic import of the recognition thesis, that the initial disequilibrium—in which neither party to the fight that does not take place receives the recognition it seeks—must lead to the establishment of an equilibrium—mutual recognition.

Another way to express this is through a simple formula, now practically a commonplace: lack breeds desire, which seeks to overcome that lack. If we regard disequilibrium as a kind of lack, then it follows that disequilibrium invites its own refutation. But is there any reason that we must accept this "logic"? Is this, indeed, a logic? Can we not conceive of a permanent instability, a permanent inequality? Can we not agree with the underground man that, in some cases, our desire does not obey the "logic" of equilibrium, the imperative of equilibrium to overcome the lack?

We must be very precise here. What lack is at issue? What is the slave's lack? Is it merely identity? What dominates the slave, what creates his identity as such, is the initial fear that created him: the fear of death. The lack that initiates the slave's life is a profound lack, the lack of permanence expressed by death. The slave is indeed the being that recognizes impermanence, and in this sense the slave's transitory, temporal being is the expression par excellence of finitude, of the being that cannot maintain its own being, that cannot transform it from the transitory to the permanent.

If we map the patterns onto each other, we see that the fundamental lack of identity is defined by an equally fundamental lack, the lack of being. Here we may be tempted to apply a sweeping statement to the slave: that desire is essentially oriented to maintaining one's own being. Baruch Spinoza's simple proposition triumphs—self-preservation is the primary rule. But is this really so? One could just as easily come to the point that self-preservation is precisely what the slave seeks to overcome, that a more complicated or subtle kind of desire is at work in the slave.

This more complicated desire is to be *freed* from the desire for self-preservation in order to be *recognized* by the master. Freedom and recognition go hand in hand; the one is not possible without the other. The slave's work for the master becomes in this respect a task of overcoming the fear that created the slave relationship in the first place; it is an immense task of reversal and transformation. The parable of the slave is not one of mere contentment with servitude, with self-preservation on the condition of denial of recognition or identity. On the contrary, the parable of the slave is eminently human in the sense that it describes a desire to be recognized, which reverses the slave's initial "mistake"—his refusal to fight, based on the fear of death—by transforming the world of the master into a world that belongs to the slave, not only with regard to the master of this initial fight for recognition but also with regard to the other masters that stand within that struggle, as moves in the game created by that struggle: God and death.

If death is the "absolute master," in Hegel's words, Kojève situates mastery *within* the social struggle that opens up history. This struggle can only come to an end with the overcoming of the social master and the fear that initiated the slave's position of social inferiority or nonrecognition. It is important to keep in mind here, then, that the slave's project is not one of personal salvation in some "beyond" but of salvation through recognition in this world, as it is created by the slave. Indeed, the world created by the slave, the state freed of all constraints on recognition, the essentially egalitarian state or, as Kojève calls it, the "universal and homogeneous state," is first and foremost a vehicle of salvation through mutual recognition.

What remains murky here is the relation of this universal recognition to death. Kojève admits that the slave transforms the world through technology, and it seems clear that the slave's work must eliminate anything that may serve to impede full recognition—like the slave's initial fear of death—but Kojève is not so clear about whether transformation of the world entails the most radical possibility in the overcoming of death or not. We will return to this theme explicitly when we come to discuss the final lectures recorded in the *Introduction*, which address the issue of death directly. Suffice it to say for the moment that Kojève's attitude toward death is strangely ambiguous in this respect. This is a matter of no small importance, because there is a substantial difference, to put it mildly, between a Fedorovian account of emancipation that insists on the literal emancipation from death as a necessary condition of emancipation and one that does not go that far. In the first case, emancipation affirms the importance of the individual—the fear of death evinces an overwhelming attachment to individuality—whereas in the second case this is not clearly so, for collective identity seems to prevail.

To put this important point with all possible simplicity: to argue that literal emancipation from death is the precondition of any political emancipation is to insist on the primacy of the individual, of the body. The only other mode of emancipation from death is figurative, and the central model here is Christ, whose death is indeed a parable for the death of the self that gives birth to a community based on the primacy of communal, not personal, identity. We might infer from this distinction Kojève's inclination to view the overcoming of the fear of death as a basic commitment to community, to the creation of a collective identity, since the notion of personal identity that one may connect with literal emancipation from death seems to be largely incoherent, as we shall see.[4]

While Kojève recommends overcoming the fear of death through work and community, in the introduction to the Hegel lectures, he also describes what appears to be another, quite different approach in the lectures from the fateful years 1936–1937: the overcoming of the fear of death through terror.[5] Kojève is blunt:

> One more time: it is by Terror that Slavery ceases, even the relation of Master and Slave and thus Christianity. From henceforth Man will seek *Befriedigung* [Satisfaction] on this earth and within a State (where there will no longer be absolute freedom—except for the leader who is Napoleon; however, one could say that even this freedom is limited by reality; nonetheless the head of the post-revolutionary State is fully "satisfied" by his action, since this reality that limits him is his own creation.[6]

The embrace of terror as demonstrating the slave's willingness to die, and thus to accept death as a revolutionary soldier, does not initially appear to fit well with the notion of overcoming death through work. Are these indeed alternative presentations of the end of servitude and therewith the end of history or do they have a complementary relation to each other, the peace ushered in by the universal and homogeneous state being the necessary condition for the final overcoming of nature, a structure very reminiscent of Nikolai Fedorov's thought? In most cases, Kojève simply combines the two by suggesting that it is struggle *and* work that go together in the creation of final emancipation.

These differing versions or stages of emancipation reflect the dual nature of the slave, who is both animal and human, both a product of the assertion of self-preservation—the refusal to fight to the death—and of the human capacity to negate that refusal. As a product of self-preservation, the slave should not seek to change. But the fact that the slave does change is clear evidence of his essential "humanity," in Kojève's terms. To change, even if at the behest of the master, is to take the risk of creating (a human) identity and, through the work of transformation of the world, to take the risks necessary to tame and master nature by transforming it into an artifact.

Yet, while the transformation of the world may bring substantial risks, the result of this transformation is not to face death voluntarily in a violent uprising (the terror) but to obliterate it; the slave's "revenge" against death is the technological world. So, despite the humanizing appearance, it is just as likely that the conquest of nature through work may resemble a kind of bestialization. The other possibility, that the slave obliterates the master in the terror accompanying the universalist revolution, comes far closer to avoiding this sort of bestialization.

At play in both these examples is self-preservation. Emancipation, according to Kojève, can only result from overcoming self-preservation. Yet the mere fact that the slave continues to live calls his emancipation into question—full emancipation leaves one with the impasse of the master, an unlivable life. Thus, we may infer that the slave does not achieve full emancipation, that full emancipation is not compatible with continued existence, since every moment of continued existence implies at least a very basic adherence to self-preservation, whether individual or collective. At the very minimum, then, we nourish ourselves and protect ourselves from basic dangers—our fear of death is maintained.

The emancipated slave, which Kojève refers to as the "citizen" (citoyen), both warrior and worker, god and beast, is thus a curious hybrid, and it is not clear that Kojève resolves the tensions inherent in this hybrid even in the universal and homogeneous state where conflict has been eradicated though the imperative to self-preservation has not been, at least to the extent that the citizens of the universal and homogeneous state continue to live. There seems to be no way to reconcile complete emancipation (or "absolution") from servitude with the servitude to the body that is the necessary result of respecting the imperative to self-preservation (if only in the form of continued living). Even if we argue that the slave's emancipation is effected through the humanizing process of revolution and work, whereby the world is transformed into an artifact, the slave becoming thus a fusion of worker and warrior, the problem of continued existence does not simply cease unless that continued existence takes on a radically different form, showing no servitude to physical need whatsoever. And this possibility may indeed be what Kojève has in mind, though he never definitively clarifies the issue. He looks at the post-historical being as a beast or a god or neither.[7] For that matter, as a fusion of worker and warrior, the citizen should be beyond both.

To return to the main thread of our account: the slave's "project" of transforming the world and his master is thus the essence of history as Kojève understands it; namely, as the social struggle to establish equality of recognition, whereby master and slave overcome that relation in the new—and final—relation of mutual recognition denoted by the term "citizen." The various shapes of the slave's evolving relation to the world are indeed the shapes of social consciousness, whose description and integration are, for Kojève, the primary ends of the *Phenomenology*.[8] The *Phenomenology* announces the self-consciousness of the slave and, in so doing, leads to the overcoming of the slave's dependence on a world that is external to him by showing that the external world is a creation of the slave— that it is in fact as much dependent on the slave as the slave is dependent on it. Here, once again, the assumption of equilibrium shows itself as essential to the *Phenomenology* understood as analysis and project—that is, as a project of dissemination of the final truth, harmonious plenitude.

As we have just seen, however, Kojève is hardly sanguine about the possibility of this final harmonious plenitude. The tension in the slave between self-preservation and self-abnegation or immolation admits of no easy resolution. If Kojève promotes the universal and homogeneous state precisely as the locus of this resolution, he also denies that that state is capable of the full freedom that he otherwise associates with suicide or coming to accept one's essential emptiness or identity with death.[9] We are left with a tension that comes to the surface, in the lectures on absolute knowing, in different terms: as visions of the post-historical state that seem to diverge from Kojève's generally positive accounts of the universal and homogeneous state, the final "superstate" created by the man of action and described by the philosopher.

Given the foregoing, it may well be that the Fedorovian reading is most attractive and consistent, the universal and homogeneous state constituting the transitional postrevolutionary political structure on the way to the attainment of the complete negation of nature through work. Nonetheless, Kojève shows tremendous ambivalence about this final goal, an ambivalence that has to do with what is left after the end has been achieved. The citizen of the fully realized universal and homogeneous state, the warrior-worker, seems to be nothing more than an automaton, a living death, neither animal nor human but the product of the apparent disappearance of both at the end of history.

Where does the philosopher fit in this narrative? The first and perhaps most obvious inference is that philosophy is the expression of the consciousness of the slave. The grand movement of the *Phenomenology* is the record of the slave's conscious discovery of himself as slave and of the transformation of that slave being into a being that is beyond both master and slave: the sage. The *Phenomenology* is thus a very special kind of book, both philosophical and beyond the limits of philosophy. In this sense, one can say that the *Phenomenology* brings an end to philosophy as a temporal discourse by seeing, from a view no longer temporally limited, beyond what philosophy has hitherto seen, because it is finished, complete and absolute, "absolved" of all unrealized possibility. And one of Kojève's probing concerns is to ascertain just what such a view might be.

These are sweeping claims. All too often, Kojève has been accused of making sweeping claims without grounding them sufficiently in the text or a web of argument. For this reason, I want to address these claims by a careful examination of Kojève's account of the sage, which emerges in his reading of the final and "most cryptic" chapter of the *Phenomenology*.[10]

THE AUTOBIOGRAPHY OF THE SAGE

We may express Kojève's fundamental point quite simply: the *Phenomenology* is the "autobiography" of the sage who is all and none; it is the book the sage creates as "proof" of his wisdom and as a fundamental constitutive document of the state created by and for the sage, the universal and homogeneous state.[11] Hence, the account of the master-and-slave relation is the slave's account of his own origins—the beginning of his journey to the overcoming of his slave being in the figure of the sage. The philosopher is the intermediary figure that describes the various stages of the slave's self-overcoming as different ways of taking account of his situation, culminating in the complete self-awareness of the sage.[12] Kojève uses the term "conscience de soi," literally "awareness of oneself," or self-consciousness. "Self-consciousness" is in fact preferable because it foregrounds the collective aspect of awareness, evidenced by the etymology of the term (the Latin *cum*, "with," and *scientia*, "knowledge"), an aspect of the term not available in the German (*Selbstbewußtsein*). Hence, the translation of the German into French here has philosophical significance because it exposes the public aspect of consciousness, that consciousness is in fact the expression of an awareness that is not some essentially inchoate sense of self but rather is a cultural artifact "produced" by the slave in his struggle with the master.

This clarification may in turn serve to put in bold relief one of the most distinctive aspects of Kojève's account of the sage: that the sage is not a lonely individual but a public (and political) figure to the very highest degree. Kojève stresses time and again that the sage cannot come into being without the establishment of the universal and homogeneous state. By doing so, Kojève eviscerates a long tradition according to which the sage walls himself off from the world in lonely self-contemplation or meditation. This wisdom figure is, for Kojève, only one station on the way to the full unfolding of wisdom, and it is inadequate precisely because it fails to take action to transform the world into a proper place for the sage to live openly with other human beings rather than hidden away from them in isolation or in the kind of cloistered community that is unable to defend itself from accusations of madness.[13] For Kojève, the very universality of the sage requires a universal state in which all citizens are effectively sages—the sage, as such, is the final figure of human existence, the figure that establishes the very equilibrium that I have already mentioned as the decisive assumption of Kojève's interpretation of Hegel.

I mention this central point now because it is properly preliminary to any discussion of the sage. It is all too easy to impute to Kojève's discussion of the sage traditional notions of the wisdom figure as being alone, apart, above—in short, as having failed to extend his perfect self-consciousness to all. But, of course, this failure is fundamental. One of Kojève's principal insights is to assert that there is no private wisdom that deserves the name of wisdom. He argues that such wisdom cannot really be wisdom because it cannot successfully distinguish itself from madness. The sage's apartness, his isolation from the many, is indeed a kind of madness to the degree that the many simply cannot understand or grasp what the sage has to tell them.[14] Kojève quite astutely infers that this notion of the sage requires the creation of a source of wisdom away and apart from the world that acts as a bastion of authority, which may justify the sage's failure to convince others of his wisdom.

This aspect of Kojève's lectures—that they attempt to persuade—should not be underestimated.[15] There is unquestionably a mirror effect at work here, for the comments that Kojève makes about the sage apply to his own declaration (albeit derived from Hegel) that he has achieved wisdom. Kojève's autobiography of the sage is one that he assumes in propagating it, and his resulting philosophical pedagogy is an effort to persuade his listeners to accept this model of the sage, for it is only this acceptance that will give it the value of a full and final truth—a point that is worth underscoring again and again in the context of Kojève's lectures. Kojève's famous comment to the effect that his lectures were a form of philosophical propaganda can all too easily serve to dismiss the more comprehensive and interesting philosophical point he makes about the nature of the sage and the truth, that they are not, so to speak, purely theoretical creations but rather require action to become realized. As Kojève notes in his postwar epitome "Hegel, Marx and Christianity," Hegel's is the only philosophy that has not yet been refuted, because the nature of his philosophical project is precisely that it is a project to put into effect. The slogan here—an estranging one, to be sure—is that one must act or work to create the truth; the task of philosophy is the work of truth, to *produce* the truth.[16]

Reading the *Introduction* is a work of philosophical pedagogy meant to bring about wisdom, not to discover it as if it were always already there. Wisdom is thus a discursive creation of the philosopher, an end that the philosopher sets for himself. In this respect, we may return to the discussion of Kojève's approach to the task of commentary in a new light. If Kojève is arguably not as fanciful or arbitrary a commentator as some of his critics would have us believe, there can be little doubt that his purpose appears to be different from that typically associated with commentaries or scholarly literature in general. Kojève's commentary has an openly political task: to bring about the conditions allowing for the establishment of a political reality that would permit the completion of the philosophical endeavor in the figure of the sage. Kojève is thus not revealing to us a correct reading of what is there in the text; rather, he is reading the text in such a way as to offer it as guidance for a project of completion to be undertaken by those who are willing to listen and follow, to undergo "conversion" to the truth.

This intent is clear from the very outset of the lectures. Kojève makes an interesting point when he indicates that the sage is not the *necessary* end of history. Kojève first indicates that the notion of the sage is "only valid for the philosopher." He supports this claim by noting that it is only the philosopher who "wishes at all costs to *know* where he is, *to take account* of what he is, who does not go further without first having taken account of what he is."[17] The upshot of this is that the philosopher is the one who acts, only after having taken account of where and what he is. In other words, the philosopher is the one who is self-conscious and, accordingly, the only one likely to accept the challenge of wisdom grasped as complete self-consciousness. The philosopher is thus the one who seeks to account fully for all actions in which he is involved, who seeks to be in this sense omniscient, satisfied, and morally perfect, as Kojève notes.

If the philosopher is the only one likely to be interested in the ideal of the sage, then it is not clear what happens to others who are not concerned with becoming completely self-conscious. Kojève specifically addresses the distinction between the philosopher and the believer (*le religieux*). He does so because he finds that there is a structural similarity in the assumption of completeness or absoluteness that both philosopher and believer express in their adherence to perfection, either that of the perfect human being (the sage) or that of the perfect being (God). Kojève claims, however, that no one can convince the believer that it is necessary to become a philosopher. The believer is in fact not in the "space of reasons" because the believer does not base his adherence to the perfect being on argument but rather on revelation. The philosopher can no more argue about revelation than can anyone else, since the effect of revelation is to exclude the content of that revelation from the space of argument. One believes because one believes. To argue about belief is in effect to undermine the authority of belief—it is already to be outside of belief, a position that should not be possible other than as a mistake or sin. The same goes for other regions of human activity that accept a set of fixed foundations as the very condition of their possibility—one may refer to examples from mathematics. In these cases, one cannot argue "outside" of the axioms without calling into question the generality or applicability of those axioms.

In all these cases, where there is acceptance of grounding principles, there is something "unthought" that is the basis of all thought that proceeds from it. The philosopher is the one who cannot tolerate this unthought.[18] But, as Kojève notes, this refusal to accept an unthought—though it is an affirmation of the ideal of the sage for whom nothing, not even nothing, is unthought—does not necessarily result in the affirmation of wisdom. Kojève identifies two possibilities: the Platonic and the Hegelian. The Platonic tradition denies the possibility of attaining final wisdom. That is, Plato denies that the philosopher can become wise by overcoming the unthought; *Sophia* is unattainable. The best the philosopher can do is recognize that wisdom is impossibly remote. The philosopher is thus the most aggressive form of gadfly, unable to become wise and equally unable to become content with that inability. The philosopher is in this respect a figure of discontent who is aware of his discontent.[19] For Kojève, Hegel overturns Plato and makes the astonishingly daring claim that a human being can become wise, such that there is no fundamental unthought, no fundamental question to which there is and can be no response. A human being may return to the beginning, thereby completing the circle of knowing and, in so doing, becoming a sage.[20]

This may sound like a preposterous response. Is Kojève not advocating omniscience for human beings? Who can answer perfectly all questions, no matter how arcane, that relate to his or her actions? But here the difference between the Platonic ideal and that of Kojève's Hegel comes out most clearly. Omniscience as we commonly understand it assumes that one can have complete knowledge of what is, was, and will be—all in one swoop. The model is visual, as Heidegger notes in his course on Gottfried Leibniz from the summer of 1928; there is a *visio Dei* or *intuitus* that grasps all "at once."[21] Obviously this kind of knowing is not discursive because it dispenses with time. But if knowing is "in" time, how can it possibly be complete? The Humean argument, to name just one, comes to mind, according to which the necessity (or unquestioned and unquestionable stability) of one relation, X, throughout time cannot be absolutely guaranteed. Variation remains possible until one has passed through all possible iterations of this relation—in other words, until time has ended.

The Platonic answer is obvious: one cannot know completely in time what is outside of time. One ends up with a model of more or less adequate imitation in time of a model that is outside of time, so much so that it is difficult even to grasp how the one can relate to the other, the Platonic notion of "participation" (μέθεξις) not being fully satisfactory. The burden of argument lies on the one who seeks to assert the completeness of knowledge in time without having to end time (sending us back out of time) to do so. This burden is one Kojève takes on in the second major section of his lectures, comprising lectures 6 to 9.[22]

Before I take up the main points Kojève develops in these lectures, I want to return to another aspect of Kojève's figuration of the sage that will loom ever larger as the lectures proceed to their end: that Kojève develops a homology between the philosopher coming to wisdom and the assumption of the role of God by the philosopher understood as the exemplary citizen in the universal and homogeneous state. Consider this remarkable passage from the fourth lecture:

> It suffices to read a manual of Christian theology (I emphasize: Christian), where God is in fact a total and infinite Being, and to say after having read the manual: the being in question—that's me. This is simple, of course. Yet, even today, this seems to us to be an absurdity, an "enormity" without equal. And we label as mad anyone who openly makes the affirmation. This means that it is extremely difficult to affirm (that is, seriously). And it is a fact that millennia of philosophical thought have passed before a Hegel came in order to dare to say it. It's simply that it was not at first easy to come to the concept of a Christian God. And, then, having come to it, it was not easy to identify oneself with this concept, to apply it to oneself. Hegel tells us that this is possible only for the Citizen of the universal and homogeneous State. For it is only this Citizen, that is, Man having effectively realized the triune whole of existence through the circularity of movement which, starting from the Particular, returns to it after having raised itself to the Universal by way of the Specific. It is only this Citizen who may affirm the identity with God without being mad, who may affirm it by being a Sage, who may affirm it in revealing thus a reality, that is by proclaiming an absolute Truth.[23]

Though laced with a certain irony, this passage brings together several of the main strands of Kojève's argument as it leads into a more detailed account of the possibility of finite omniscience. The sage is not merely the end of philosophy; the sage must also bring to an end the theological position, and this is only possible if the sage assumes the identity of God.

While this argument does sound unusual and certainly challenged Kojève's admirers, it is hardly as outlandish as it might seem when it comes to Kojève's daring—and very Russian—account of Christ as the preeminently Christian figuration of the "God, the Christian one, that suppresses itself as God by becoming Man." In other words, Kojève exploits the figure of Christ for an argument holding that atheism, understood as the assumption of God's identity by the human being, is a *necessary* outcome of Christianity: "In brief, the atheism of the Sage does not establish itself in accord with any Theology: it is born from Christian Theology, and can only be born from it. (More exactly, it is not a matter of atheism, but of anthropotheism; now, this Hegelian anthropo-theism presupposes *Christian* Theology, since it applies to Man the *Christian* idea of God.)"[24]

This is of course not an argument that follows from either Soloviev or Fedorov. But it twists their willingness to explore the unity of God and man in Christ to an unexpected result that achieves, through the death of God, the birth of the human being as the sage. The human being as the sage finally comes into being as such, freed from its servitude—in the sage, the Godman, though hardly in the sense of Soloviev, much less that of Fedorov. Here Kojève—in a characteristic move—transforms the notion of deification explicit in Soloviev and implicit in Fedorov by reversing its sense. Man does not become God, thereby letting go of his limitations; on the contrary, man becomes God by assuming finitude as absolute.

Moreover, the human being becomes the sage by assuming the identity not only of God but also of all preceding philosophies. This melding of the Christian and philosophic traditions might strike many critics as fanciful, if not basically unsound, from a number of points of view. After all, one of the firm modern dogmas in philosophy is that intermingling Christianity and philosophy does damage to both, for there is no equilibrium to be achieved between the two—as Kojève seems to affirm himself when he suggests that only philosophy is capable of full self-consciousness.[25] Thus, it is perhaps somewhat surprising that Kojève emphasizes simultaneously the integration of Christianity into the history of the sage and of philosophy; the autobiography of wisdom is in this sense profoundly integrative. But on what basis? Is it possible to integrate these two disparate and mutually exclusive traditions? What is Kojève's justification?

Like Friedrich Nietzsche, Kojève seems to justify this integration—at least initially—by claiming that Christian thinking is merely a version of Platonism.[26] Insofar as Christianity thinks, it thinks in a distinctively Platonic way. To put this more starkly, Kojève seems to argue that, to the extent Christianity seeks to take account of itself, to come to terms with itself, to become conscious of itself, it must rely on the conceptual armature of the Platonic tradition to do so. If we consider Kojève's seemingly bold—and very modern—claim that philosophy is self-consciousness, then Christianity, like any other area of discourse, needs to turn to philosophy or "become philosophical" in order to give an account of itself. In this respect, Christian theology is a veiled or limited form of philosophy that cannot but return to philosophy in the end if it is to become fully aware of itself. Kojève exploits the Christ figure in this respect to authorize his suggestion that theology is in fact not the basis of human identity but merely a stage in human self-recognition, governed, as all the other stages in this narrative, by the struggle to overcome the master that marks the life of the slave. Moreover, in contrast to Plato, Kojève insists that Hegel's triumph is to overcome theistic philosophy by the assimilation of God into man and, in this sense, Kojève regards Hegel as having grasped the truly revolutionary core of Christianity as well as having overcome theology in favor of anthropology.

In this respect, while Kojève does not add that Christianity is "Platonism for the people" (Platonismus für das Volk), the notion that the figure of Christ acts as a figuration for the democratization of God certainly seems to follow the basic lines of Nietzsche's thought. Here it is important to keep in mind that the revolutionary, absurd phrase "I am God" is also, in the context of Kojève's notion of the sage, a statement having revolutionary democratic impact. The sage is the figure of the "citizen soldier," the final product of the French Revolution and, as we shall see, the final product to be achieved by and in history. If Nietzsche's claim about Christianity seems little more than a sneer at the rabble, Kojève transforms that sneer into a rallying cry for the most radical political project: the "deification" of the masses in the figure of the sage, a sort of universal and homogeneous subject populating the universal and homogeneous state. Kojève thus pursues the cherished aim of his Russian predecessors in a new and theologically radical Christian form insofar as the essence of Christianity, for Kojève, is that it brings about atheism by transforming man or the human being into the absolute.[27]

Of course, this deification is somewhat unusual as well because it is the deity who becomes man and not the reverse; thus, one might argue that this is no deity at all, a point Kojève freely acknowledges when he refers to deification in this sense as anthropotheism—what results is a radical-ization and reversal of Soloviev, who, as Kojève notes repeatedly in his various works on Soloviev, does not succeed in suppressing the primacy of God in the relation of Godmanhood. The Solovievian Godman, for Kojève, remains primarily a man under the yoke of God, a secondary fig-ure akin to the Kantian moral actor who attempts to become a member of the kingdom of ends (*Reich der Zwecke*).[28] In this sense, the Solovie-vian God never really becomes man; the hierarchy maintains itself.

Kojève's notion of deification is, if anything, almost a parody. The Pla-tonic challenge with which we began in the first chapter is met by a thor-ough transformation whereby the primacy of the vertical and hierarchi-cal erotic relation—the distant progenitor of the notion of desire essential to recognition—is eradicated in favor of a horizontal and egalitarian erotic relation—the relation of mutual recognition that provides the foun-dation for the universal and homogeneous state. The assumption of equi-librium appears here again as *the* guiding assumption of the Kojèvian philosophic enterprise. The constitutive lack of equilibrium characteris-tic of the Platonic challenge, a lack of equilibrium that can only spawn endless conflict, is finally abolished.

THE TEMPORALIZING OF THE CONCEPT AS A FIGURATION OF DIVINE HUMANITY

Kojève realizes, however, that one may not merely abolish or "complete" a tradition by fiat. His philosophical pedagogy is just that—a pedagogy, albeit a revolutionary one. If the general lines of Kojève's notion of deifi-cation in the figure of the philosophic sage are set out in the first five of the 1938–1939 lectures, the next three lectures offer, as I have noted, a cru-cial, original, and far more detailed philosophical account of how one might realize the ideal of the sage in a finite individual.

Kojève confronts the basic issue of how perfection or completion, as embodied by the sage, can possibly emerge in time, which, as flow or motion—evanescence itself—would seem to be fundamentally opposed to completion. The stakes of Kojève's account are extremely high, for he takes it upon himself to explain how the final figure of history, understood as essentially temporal, can appear in history. How might one reconcile rest and motion, being and nothing (das reine Sein und das reine Nichts) in a "final" totality?

Of course, Hegel has a famous response to this: becoming (das Werden) offers the reconciliation of rest and motion, being and nothing, eternity and time.[29] While Kojève begins with the final two terms, he in effect refers them back to another venerable relation, between space and time. The spatial is self-sufficient; it is complete, at rest. What is in time is not self-sufficient; it is incomplete and in motion. Kojève refers to eternity as space and to time as the transformation of space, thus recasting Hegelian becoming as a spatiotemporal relation, an evolution in the relation of space and time.

Kojève nests his account of the problem within the context of omniscience as the full and final truth; one is reminded of the famous phrase from the preface of the Phenomenology: "The truth is the whole" (das Wahre ist das Ganze). There is good reason for Kojève to do so, since it is possible to think of a sage as being satisfied or morally perfect—both qualities being applicable to the Stoic sage, as Kojève admits—but not omniscient.[30] Omniscience is a "quality" that no one before Hegel has dared to apply to a being living in time, a finite individual. Kojève notes that the truth—and there is no truth for Hegel until it is complete and, in this sense, eternally static—has not for that reason been taken to coincide with time. As a result, Kojève's account examines the relation of the various oppositions associated with eternity and time in relation to the concept as the vehicle of knowing, of acquisition of the truth. By proceeding this way—with the concept—Kojève anticipates the correlate claim that one need not rely on something akin to intuition in order to claim a total grasp of existence. Kojève wants to insist that it is Hegel's daring innovation to maintain that a complete discursive account of the whole—that is, an inherently temporal account—is possible. Kojève lists four primary possibilities of relation between the concept and time:

1. The concept (C) is eternity (E). As Kojève shows it: $C = E$ (as in Parmenides/Spinoza).
2. The concept is eternal (E'). $C = E'$, with two variants: either C relates to E' outside of time (T) (as in Plato) or in T (as in Aristotle); or C relates to T (as in Immanuel Kant).

3. The concept is time. $C = T$ (as in Hegel).
4. The concept is temporal (T'). Kojève sets this off in square brackets as impossible: $[C = T']$.[31]

Kojève brackets the last relation as rendering knowledge impossible—pure or nonrepeating flow being somewhat like an irrational number—and focuses his attention on the others. He notes that the relations set out in (1) and (3) are relations of the concept to itself, the first being characteristic of Parmenides and Spinoza, the second of Hegel. Relation (2) has two subgroups that describe the relation of the concept to another, either eternity or time. In the first subgroup, the concept relates either to an eternity outside of time, this relation being characteristic of Plato, or to an eternity inside of time, this relation being Aristotelian. In the second subgroup, the concept relates to time itself, a relation Kojève attributes to Kant's philosophy.

With typical concision, Kojève reduces all possible relations of the concept to time to these five possibilities, and this is an important move, since it thereby reduces the basic shapes of consciousness down to this limited group of possibilities, it being simply impossible to conceive of consciousness without concepts. To attempt to do so would force us into reliance on the kind of intuition that Heidegger describes in connection with the divinity, and the requirement of such intuition is that it have no relation to time at all, thus no language, no conceptuality, nothing but "pure" being—that is, nothing.[32]

If the delimitation of the possible forms of the concept's relation to time is an extremely important move, suggesting as it does that the possible shapes of consciousness are necessarily finite, the exact interpretation of each is far less clear. One can readily imagine complaints about the stunning reductiveness of Kojève's account and the simplification that goes along with it.[33]

Kojève meets this concern by providing two complex sets of diagrams that purport to describe all possible forms of the five relations to time, first in the context of temporality itself and then as a taxonomy of the forms of consciousness that result from these temporal relations. This is classic Kojève—even his students made sport of his penchant for diagrammatic explanations. And when one casts a glance at some of the extraordinarily complex diagrams in the manuscripts—both the third

volume of *Attempt at a Rational History of Pagan Philosophy* and the book
on Kant stand out—one can certainly sympathize with the bewilderment
they seem to have felt, at least initially. There is also a peculiar irony at
play in the first set of diagrams (set out in lecture 6), which purport to
translate temporal relations into spatial ones as a means of clarification.
Yet, for Kojève, a spatial grasp of things avoids or flattens the temporal
effect of incompleteness. Indeed, this is one of the interesting aspects of
Kojève's diagrammatic approach—that he seeks to find an appropriate
pedagogic means to convey the completion of time in time, thus mirror-
ing the basic problem at issue in the explanation itself. While this may
seem far-fetched to some, or an example of an overly heightened sensi-
tivity to rather minor points, it is well to keep in mind that Kojève's entire
enterprise is an exercise in self-consciousness. Thus, even the most pica-
yune points cannot be accidental; they can only be wrong due to inter-
pretational misprision or incompetence.

The combined effect of the two sets of diagrams is to provide a compact visual account of the only possible shapes of consciousness. As such,
they are a pictorial representation of the *Phenomenology* itself, tracing the
movement of the concept from an essentially theological relation to an
external point of reference to the complete self-referentiality of the concept in Hegel. They thus describe the same anthropotheistic movement
that Kojève has already asserted in the preceding lectures. That is, if one
were to superimpose the first set of diagrams (eleven in all) on the second (merely seven), one would have a complete picture of the governing
relations of the concept to time, and a translation of those relations into
theological or anthropological terms, for the movement they describe, as
I have already suggested, coordinates the transformation of the essential
referent of the concept from an external to an internal one, with the
assumption by the human being of the identity associated with God.

Let me quickly note a few important details of Kojève's graphic portrayal of the anthropotheistic narrative. The graphic portrayal emphasizes the distinguishing problem of relation (1), between the concept (C)
and eternity (E). Although Kojève identifies this equation with Parmenides
and Spinoza, he prefers to use Spinoza's system to illustrate what he
refers to as the absurdity of this equation. The most illuminating term
Kojève uses is "acosmism," and it suggests that the central flaw in Spinoza's system is that it is impossible to relate it to human minds because

the system by definition excludes time. Human minds need to think, and thinking takes place in time. Thus, as Kojève remarks, to attempt to grasp Spinoza's system is to betray it in that very attempt—or, better, it reveals the impossibility of grasping a system that excludes time discursively, that is, *in* time. Kojève stresses here one of his fundamental claims: that we need time to think, that we are discursive beings whose horizon of understanding is decisively shaped by a temporal dimension. All the other examples Kojève adduces respect this basic claim, and as I have noted, the assumption of God by man that is the basic narrative thread of Kojève's lecture series as a whole is most evident in the increasing temporalizing of the concept.[34]

The next two examples, in relation (2), relate the concept to the eternal (E'). They do not equate the concept with eternity; rather, they suggest that the concept as such relates to the eternal, to something fixed and unchanging. The primary difference between these two relations is in the corresponding relation of the eternal to time (T). For the variant Kojève associates with Plato, the eternal is outside of time—the Platonic idea or ideas do not include time. Thus, we encounter another variant of the problem encountered with regard to Parmenides and Spinoza insofar as the relation of the concept to an atemporal standard is very problematic, for it is of course not clear how thinking that unfolds in time can convey what is not in time but outside it. While it is problematic as such, however, it is not precluded from the outset, and this is a significant step. One might say that this step coincides with philosophy's venture into the marketplace where "the existence of man becomes important for knowledge."[35] The Aristotelian variant in (2) places the eternal in time as a way of avoiding the Platonic impasse—the eternal works out as the fixed structure of forms, which substances realize as their proper end or perfection in time a fixed structure that repeats itself in various determinable ways.

Kojève then moves to Kant—thereby avoiding an enormous chunk of the history of philosophy—and this dramatic move underscores the revolutionary importance Kojève ascribes to Kant as the one who begins the decisive transformation that ends with Hegel. In Kant, Kojève identifies the relation of the concept not to the eternal but to time. What exactly does this mean?

Rather than making the eternal the condition of the possibility of the concept as the vehicle of discursive understanding, Kant takes the dramatic step of attributing this role to time. Kojève cautions that this does not mean that the concept "becomes" temporal. He claims that, for Kant as for all "true philosophers," the concept remains eternal, that is, it is itself unchanging. But unlike Plato and Aristotle, Kant relates the concept openly not to the unchanging but to what changes; the concept becomes the fixed or unchanging structuration of change itself whereby Kant seeks to reconcile the concept with movement. While Kojève does not state this directly, the significance of this change is to remove the external standard for conceptual understanding from an essentially theological identification of the concept with the eternal to an essentially atheistic or anthropotheistic standard, that of everyday life: time (and history). The second set of diagrams makes this point quite clear.

In relation (3), the extraordinary equation of the concept and time ($C = T$) that is, for Kojève, the hallmark of Hegel's thought takes this movement from eternity or the eternal to time one step further by eliminating any external standard and establishing the temporality of the concept itself as an identity. The concept is not a relation to time but is time itself. This is no doubt a difficult identification, because it seems to undermine the notion that the concept is somehow a fixed mark that either avoids or transforms the flow of time into a fixed pattern, the former being the Platonic, the latter the Aristotelian position, according to Kojève. If the concept is time, how can one avoid the conclusion that the concept as movement is no longer capable of being the basic vehicle of knowledge or truth?

But, according to Kojève, equating the concept with time is the only way to account for change, action, the only way to account for an understanding of the human being as an individual emancipating itself in history *as* history. Otherwise, the relation of the concept to eternity or the eternal cannot help but assimilate the human to a truth that has little to do with human existence in time, in a world. When Kojève argues, for example, that the Spinozist system is acosmic, he means to suggest that the equation of the truth with eternity precludes the possibility of human involvement in knowledge or truth—the language of mathematics is the equivalent of silence.[36] The other options open the door for human involvement in knowledge and truth—"passively," so to speak, in both Plato and Aristotle, and actively in Kant. This transformation from passive or theoretical to active participation in knowledge and truth is recorded by Kojève as the emphasis on time that is crucial to Kant and Hegel.

According to Kojève, the equation of the concept with time entails the becoming human of the concept as the becoming of the slave. Indeed, that the concept is time implies a further equation, made explicit in Hegel's thought: the concept is history and history is the concept. Now, it may seem here that I am merely adding one puzzling statement onto another by way of "clarification." What I mean to emphasize is the assertion that the concept is history, a narrative, and, as may be obvious, that the history that is the concept is the *Phenomenology* itself as well as Kojève's account of it. In other words, the narrative set out in Kojève's discussion of the "descent" of the concept from eternity to time is the concept itself that finally and only comes to itself in the completion of that history through the philosophical process of assuming that history as its own; the completion of the process of understanding is in the understanding of that process itself.

Kojève makes several crucial identifications that subtend this primary identification. He equates time with desire and negation, and, in a crucial gesture, he equates the human with all three—time, desire, and negation—and, finally, with the concept itself. He identifies the concept, in turn, with discourse and work—the work of the slave. Thus, we have a string of remarkable identifications that we need to unpack.

Kojève denies that there is "natural," "cosmic" or "deep" time.[37] He declares that there is only time to the extent that there is history; that is, human existence (and there is only this existence, for Kojève) is the result of the fight that begins history as the story of the slave. The "man who, in the course of History, reveals Being in his Discourse is the 'empirically existing Concept,'" the term Kojève uses to translate Hegel's "der daseiende Begriff," in the Hegelian identity Kojève claims between time and this "empirically existing concept."[38] Only man is in time—"indeed, man *is* time, and time *is* man." Without man, "nature would be *Space*, and Space *only*." These statements lead to the conclusion that time is associated only with man, and space only with nature. Kojève underscores this distinction when he refers to man, merely a few pages later, as a "hole" (*trou*) in space, "a void, a nothingness" in the present.[39] This hole in space is the presence of an absence. It is desire understood as dissatisfaction with the present, as a desire precisely to negate the present in favor of a reality to be realized in the future.

If we bring time, desire, and negation together here, we may discern an intense interaction between all three. Time is desire and desire is negation and thus time is negation (of eternity, pure presence, the "nunc stans").[40] Time describes the movement of negation of the static present in favor of the future, this negation of the present becoming a past. Time describes the movement of negation that transforms the present into the past of a new present that may in turn be negated in another new present, depending on the orientation of desire to what is not yet. "Thus, in a general manner: *historical* movement is born of the Future and passes through the Past in order to *realize* itself in the Present as the temporal Present. The Time Hegel has in view is thus human or historic Time: this is the Time of conscious and voluntary Action that realizes in the *present* a Project for the future, which Project is shaped on the basis of acquaintance with the *past*."[41]

This triune entity—time, desire, negation—constitutes the very essence of human historicity as the dialectical concept. We are this concept, and this concept describes a specific history as the negation of a given reality— the fixed or eternal reality of the master—in favor of an idea of the future that we have for ourselves. "Thus, man creates and destroys essentially as a function of the idea he conceives of the Future."[42] Accordingly, time describes the way of man-in-the-world as negating the spatial reality of the "given." In this respect, time as negation is equivalent to work. Time is the work of the slave as he liberates himself from eternity, the impasse of the master, into time itself. In more abstract terms, history is the story of the temporalizing of the concept.

By equating the concept with time, Kojève develops a remarkable account of history as the work of negating a given—the spatial or, in temporal terms, the eternal—which in turn expresses the desire for the realization of a future, an ideal. What, then, is this ideal? If the negation of the given is in turn the creation of an artificial or technical reality, a human or historical reality, as Kojève maintains, then the exact contours of this reality in terms of its content seem rather more elusive, unless we take the *Phenomenology* itself as that history. And this is exactly what we should do. The complicated enterprise of the *Phenomenology* is circular in the sense that the history it describes is its own—it is, as I have noted, an autobiography of sorts, the autobiography of the concept that gives us the concept of autobiography. Put in different terms that bring out the same distinction, the *Phenomenology* is the history of the concept that gives us the concept of history, and it gives us this latter concept as an equation that history is the concept and the concept is history. The ideal of the slave is the eradication of eternity in favor of time.

Of the many objections one might have to this equation—which seems to create a vicious historicism—is that the notion that there is a paradigmatic or theoretical reality somehow beyond time lies utterly in ruins. Theory, understood as such, loses all sense and authority. Hence, Kojève's statements about the master-and-slave relation, the concept, negation, and so on are to be understood as applying not to a theory applicable to different situations and circumstances but only to the one history that they help to unfold to the point where that history recognizes itself as such—as complete and, in this sense, as omniscient. They are immanent not transcendent.

Now, the question that occupies us here is this: Is Kojève's account of the coming into being of omniscience convincing (or Hegelian)? The question reveals the difficulties: How can perfection come into being as time? As we know from Plato, perfection cannot come into being. Perfection does not lend itself to becoming; it is always already there. This is a way of describing Plato's notion of the concept as Kojève sees it: the definitive relation is to an external standard—the eternal—that cannot possibly be realized in time, that belongs to the impasse of the master, not the slave. Aristotle's version of this, according to Kojève, is to affirm that perfection can come into being insofar as each being comes to be what it is (its form or essence, the "what it was to be," or τὸ τί ἦν εἶναι) in time. The Kantian variation is to assert that the coming into being of the thing is that thing itself, time being essential to the unfolding of the thing as one of the constitutive conditions of any possible experience. Yet, since time is the horizon of all possible experience, it is evident that experience is essentially incomplete. For Kant, perfection, whether in knowledge or comportment, is not attainable because it is essentially incompatible with time, as the ineluctable limitation of experience by its temporal character attests.

But what of Hegel? How is the concept time itself? How, indeed, can Hegel assert the equivalence of the concept and time, if the former depends on a degree of fixity inimical to the latter? Put most simply, how can there be complete, fixed knowledge—omniscience—in time?

As we have seen, Kojève's answer is straightforward. Omniscience is possible not "in" time but as the immanent articulation of the very shape of time itself that comes to its completion in the recognition of its own completion, of its own coming aware of itself as time, the central and final narrative. This recognition is not separate or different from the history it describes; rather, it is the final moment in that history, when the concept has come to itself completely by recognizing itself completely as itself *as* its own history. The equation of history and time describes the final equilibrium of the Hegelian system, according to Kojève. It is in this respect another way of describing the equilibrium that the slave seeks to establish by becoming equal to the master, and it assumes the fateful significance of the slave's work in realizing this final equilibrium. The slave at the end of history is the slave having liberated himself fully from eternity into history itself, the slave having come to himself precisely as the work (or "product") of history, which ends with this complete realization. The advent of the slave as time is the final liberation from the eternal as the deepest desire for self-preservation. History ends with the complete acceptance of the human being as historical, temporal, finite— and finished.[43]

Kojève's sage becomes free by giving up the Fedorovian "common task" as an expression of the essentially servile desire (and is there any other?) to avoid death. Yet, once again, this position is fraught with difficulty because the ambiguity incumbent at the end returns. Like the slave, the sage cannot but find himself in the tension of having come to accept human being as historical, temporal, and finite while remaining alive and writing the "Book" (as I will explain in the next chapter). If the end of history leaves nothing for the sage to do, then the sage who continues to live deceives himself and is never at the end, or simply repeats. Still, the sage cannot give an explanation of his choice or repetition; to do so would imply that one is not at an end, that there is something still unfinished. Circularity, Hegel's "innovation," cannot be compromised—to return to the beginning is to return to silence or "repetition" (both of which are virtually the same for Kojève).[44]

Whatever the ambiguities, omniscience, then, is the result of reading the narrative of the *Phenomenology* itself. One joins oneself to the autobiography of the concept as the autobiography of all. But, as Kojève notes earlier in the lectures, the omniscience that results from taking the position advocated by the Book, a position of complete transparency vis-à-vis one's own way of thinking, which emerges only by assuming the same patterns of thought as all those who read the *Phenomenology*, is fragile, the final result of a *decision*. Kojève writes of the difference between the sage and the religious person:

> The opposition is clear. And it is evident that there is *nothing* between these two extreme points. From the moment the Slave worker divided up the World between his Master and himself, annulling by his Work the autonomous reality of inhuman Nature; or, in other words, from the moment the Judeo-Christian man divided up the sphere of Parmenides between himself and his God (who, for us, is made in his own image, and who, for him is the image according to which he was made); from the moment of this total division, man has been unable to project his Knowledge onto a *natural* reality and call it true as did the pagan Philosopher, via the circular motion of the stars. He must relate his knowledge to himself or to God, being unable to relate it to the one and the other at the same time since only one absolute is possible.
>
> And the two extreme attitudes *are* realized: the one by Hegelian anthropo-logy, the other by the elaboration of Christian theo-logy. The two are evidently irreconcilable. And neither can be simply overcome. And if one can pass from the one to the other, it's only by a sudden jump; for there is no *transition* possible since there is nothing between the two. To be in the one is to decide against the other; to reject the one, is to stand in the other. The decision is absolutely unique, and as simple as possible—the matter is one of deciding for oneself (that is, against God) or for God (that is, against oneself). And there is no "reason" or rationale for the decision other than the decision itself.[45]

One decides to know oneself or not; the former is the essence of philosophy, the latter the essence of theology. The former is discursive, the latter ends up in silence, a sort of speechlessness or silent *unio mystica* or, indeed, in infinite conversation (or endless chatter) about an essentially unknowable "other.". The former is the most radical assertion of human sovereignty, the latter a wholesale rejection of that sovereignty in favor of the authority of mystery or the unknown.[46] The former pursues freedom as full self-knowledge, the latter as the permanent absence of that self-knowledge. The former pursues an end, the latter the absence of an end. A blunter way of putting the basic import of these distinctions into their proper context returns us to the question of the relation between Christianity and Platonism. To the extent that one decides to think, one ends up following the philosophical path right up to its culmination in Hegel; to the extent that one decides not to think, one takes the other path, and one can do so because there is no argument that can best faith, whose final response to all rational contestation is "credo quia absurdum est" (I believe it because it is absurd).[47]

Consequently, Kojève seems to be aware that his project of exposition is very much a project but that he is also speaking to those inclined to hear what he has to say—those who have already decided to think. Most important of all, Kojève clearly indicates that one chooses to think, that a necessarily irrational decision lies at the heart of the acceptance of rationality or discourse as such, and this emphasis on decision takes one of the major points of persuasion away from the rational tradition. Reason can no longer direct someone to itself based on its superior insight into the reality of things; on the contrary, one cannot say ultimately why it is better to be rational than nonrational, and this is a very profound problem for Kojève's thought. Kojève relies on arguments whose coercive core is to insist that a decision against rationality and full self-knowledge is equivalent to madness or isolation, but he cannot otherwise give an account of why it is better to be rational. Madness or isolation or sheer willful action like that of the underground man needs no reasons and offers none.[48]

Perhaps Kojève is only admitting the obvious, for if the authority of philosophy were necessary, it would be hard to understand why any philosophical pedagogy would be needed in the first place. Philosophy would already be universal, and no task of creating a proper audience for philosophy would ever arise. Contrary to the view that Kojève simply declares history at an end, it does not hurt to recall once again that, for Kojève, ending history is a *project* to be carried out as the proper completion of philosophy. This project has one end: to produce the sage, full self-consciousness. And, as we know, full self-consciousness can only emerge where struggle is complete; the universal and homogeneous state is the result of the final triumph of the slave.

Kojève's doubts about the realization of this project are far greater than his disciples or detractors are willing to admit.[49] Kojève suggests that even Hegel, despite his formidable audacity, may not have achieved the complete self-consciousness necessary for the sage.

This problem comes into sharper focus in the lectures that follow, on Kojève's account of time. It is in fact remarkable that Kojève expresses these doubts after having set out a description of what I consider one of his most unusual ideas: the Book.

What is the Book? The Book is what the sage creates, the final result of his activity. It contains the truth of the sage, the way to absolute knowledge. The Book is not human in the sense Kojève attaches to the human—that is, the Book is not time, not action, not desire; it has no future. The Book is both the grave marker and autobiography of the sage as the citizen who reflects all others at the end of time.

6

THE BOOK OF THE DEAD

Human existence is a mediated suicide.
The human collective (humanity) should die just as an individual person dies; universal history must have a definitive end.

—ALEXANDRE KOJÈVE

he Book is the wisdom of the sage, a philosophical bible.[1] It is no living wisdom, but the "exteriorization" or "objectification" of the sage in a material artifact. There is a curious irony at work here, given the signal fact that the sage is the fulfillment of a circular process of interiorization (*Er-innerung*) whereby the other that was God becomes man in the figure of the sage.[2] Being a sage is evidently not quite enough. The sage leaves behind evidence of his wisdom, and according to Kojève, this evidence is not merely secondary but a necessary element of the sage. There is no sage without the Book. What is more—and even more puzzling—is that the Book is the death of the sage. In this respect, the Book not only has the role of evidencing the sage's wisdom; it also evidences the finite character of the sage's wisdom, since the sage is not enough. He must leave something behind because he is unable in and of himself to preserve his wisdom. The sage is always and necessarily finite. He dies, and the Book of the sage is the living—indeed, eternal—monument to his death.

The Action of the Sage, that is, of Knowledge, detaches itself from Man and passes into the Book. The "dialectical movement," by ceasing to be the movement of the *World* or History, becomes the movement of the *Word-concept* or "Dialectic" in the current sense. And this detachment from Man, or this passage of "the movement" to the word-concept, takes place because, being exempt from contradictions, the World and Man cannot "move" themselves any more. Put differently, the World is *dead*; it has *passed*, with all that that implies, Man included. And, being *dead*, the World and Man-in-the-World can no longer serve as material support for the "dialectical" Concept that continues to "live" or to "move." The material support of the perpetual "movement" of the Concept is from now on in the *Book* called "Logik": it is this Book ("Bible") that is the incarnation of the eternal Logos.

The Sage does not then act as a Man. But he does not so act for the sole reason that Man no longer *can* act at the moment the sage becomes possible. And, inversely, wisdom becomes possible only when *all* possible human objectives have already been *attained*.[3]

Coming at the very end of the tenth lecture, these two paragraphs provide an arresting summary of some of Kojève's most unusual and challenging ideas about the sage and the Book he leaves behind. If, for example, Kojève labors to explain how omniscience may find expression in a finite individual, he seems to qualify this claim by asserting that, at the very moment omniscience finally becomes actual in an individual, time—which he equated with the concept—ends in historical fulfillment. The sage is what we might now call the first posthuman being, and while he is omniscient, he is no longer human in the special sense that Kojève applies to the human as the being that is desire, negation, time. Moreover, the action or praxis whereby the sage is realized comes to an end as well. It is preserved purely in discourse as the Book, which transforms the action of negation, the ostensibly dialectical movement whereby the world comes into being and is completed, into the Logos of the Book. Man and history come to an end in the sage and the Book: the apotheosis of the human is also the end of the human.[4]

Not surprisingly, more than a little controversy surrounding Kojève's interpretation of G. W. F. Hegel arises from these unusual propositions.[5] Not only do these propositions emerge at the end of an almost 200-page lecture on sixteen cryptic pages in *The Phenomenology of Spirit* but also the notion of the sage and the Book seems more obviously "read into" Hegel's text as a peculiar, reflexive, speculative move than almost any other portion of Kojève's commentary. No matter how carefully one scans the final sixteen pages of the *Phenomenology*, one is very hard pressed indeed to find mention of the Book, let alone the sage. Of course, it may seem obvious that the *Phenomenology* itself is the Book and Hegel the sage.[6] However, it is equally obvious that in this context Kojève finally discards any claim to philological scruple; he becomes the prophet of the Book. This is a troubling role for several reasons, as we shall see, for, as prophet, Kojève appears to claim that he is not himself a sage, and if he is not, how can he claim to explain the sage? But one may also make the harsher judgment that this final interpretation, the conclusions of which are both so crucial to and characteristic of Kojève's position, is simply willful, an imposition of a foreign doctrine onto Hegel's text that rivals the most violent interventions of Martin Heidegger.[7]

I say "foreign doctrine" intentionally, since one cannot avoid the suspicion that Kojève emphasizes a way of reading Hegel that has much more to do with the distinctively Russian concern with divine humanity, or with overcoming humanity, as we have examined these tendencies in several other chapters. There is nothing really new to this claim; other commentators have suspected it, at least as far as Kojève's obvious relation to the thought of Soloviev is concerned.[8] Perhaps less obvious has been the powerful Russian connection of the end of man and the world with a most peculiar—and particular—universalism, the celebrated connection of the end of time with the establishment of Moscow as the "Third Rome," itself akin to the new community of the resurrected dead that Nikolai Fedorov seeks to create.[9] While the claim is perhaps recklessly speculative, one wonders to what degree Kojève's Stalinism affirms this sense of the apparently impossible: that the locus of the world revolution leading to the end of history and of man, as we understand both, is Moscow. And Moscow is the final point and culmination of the tradition begun in Rome, the *translatio imperii* taken to its most extreme point as empire over nature itself. In this respect, Kojève's intervention in European thought takes on a distinctively different hue and allows yet another reading of the lectures—as an allegory for the overtaking of the erstwhile European master by the colonized slave, a bringing up to date of the declaration that Moscow will be the Third Rome, that the slave shall become equal to the master in an apocalyptic end of time.[10]

Kojève thus succeeds where his predecessors, from Fyodor Dostoevsky to Fedorov, not to mention others, have largely failed. He not only has appropriated the very fulfillment of the European intellectual tradition, Hegel, to his own ends but also has done so in the ostensive capital of European culture, Paris.

I mention these extraordinary points here to give a sense of what exactly may be at stake for Kojève in this final part of the 1938–1939 lectures. But this is only one aspect of the final part, and it seems to me of the utmost importance to examine Kojève's notion of the sage and the Book in greater detail before returning to these points in earnest. If the notion of the sage, together with the complementary notions of the end of man and history, have occasioned more controversy (and acrimony) than perhaps any other dimension of Kojève's thought, some of that controversy seems to arise from the largely polemic intentions of Kojève's interlocutors. Some of the most vocal and influential of these seek to argue that he is antihumanist or postmodern or apocalyptic without bringing out the full implications of Kojève's arguments.[11] Hence, I propose a detailed account of the sage and the figures of finality associated with the appearance of the sage as a counterbalance to these polemics.

THE SAGE

An extensive discussion of the figure of the sage occupies the final third of Kojève's lectures of 1938–1939. While we have examined in considerable detail the possibility of the sage as an omniscient figure, we have not yet examined the actuality of the sage; that is, we have not considered what the actual appearance of the sage as a living being might entail. Here we enter upon one of the most openly speculative areas in Kojève's thought, since it is not even clear that the one who has declared himself a sage, Hegel, has correctly done so. Contrary to what some of Kojève's critics seem to argue, the evidence supporting the assertion that history has indeed come to an end is equivocal. At one point, Kojève associates the end of history with Joseph Stalin, at another with Napoleon.[12] Regardless of the identification of the final point, Kojève's declaration that history has come to an end serves as an exhortation to engage in a philosophical project of completion that is obviously not complete. If it were, there would be no need for Kojève's exhortative commentary.

The crucial point is this: the end of history describes an outstanding *project*, not a fait accompli dating back some two hundred years. Moreover, as befits a project, there is no necessity attaching to its success.

> In our time, as in the time of Marx, Hegelian philosophy is not a truth in the proper sense of the term: it is less the adequate discursive revelation of a reality than an idea or an ideal, that is to say, a "project" which is to be realized, and therefore proved true, through action. However, what is remarkable is that it is precisely because it is not yet true that this philosophy alone is capable of becoming true one day. For it alone says that truth is created in time out of error and that there are no "transcendent" criteria (whereas a theistic theory of necessity either has always been true, or is forever false). And that is why history will never refute Hegelianism but will limit itself to choosing between its two opposed interpretations.[13]

Even Hegel cannot claim to be fully self-conscious, to be a sage, since, as Kojève remarks in the tenth lecture, he cannot explain why it is in him, and not in another, that wisdom first appears.[14] This is surely an extraordinary admission on Kojève's part. It leads immediately to an even more extraordinary surmise: that Kojève is taking it upon himself to complete Hegel's work, not merely to repeat it (as he suggests in later writings), and that Kojève's task of completion is part of an eminently practical project. Kojève thus finds himself in the uncomfortable, perhaps untenable, position of declaring himself the sage in the Book that will introduce us to his "Book"—presumably including the vast archipelago of unpublished and unfinished writings that began to appear only after Kojève's death. In this respect, we find ourselves, as readers of Kojève, in an immense self-reflexive text in which what we read in the text describes that text itself.[15]

Moreover, Kojève's criticism of Hegel is in fact possible only if Hegel was deficient, not yet the sage. Thus, we have to accept that Kojève, otherwise so ostentatiously deferential to Hegel, knows *more* than Hegel, that not Hegel but Kojève is the genuine sage. But, as I have noted, it is one thing to claim to know more and quite another thing to claim to know everything that can possibly be known. While Kojève seems to assume this latter role, the fact that his own commentary is a form of philosophical pedagogy, or an exhortation to complete history, and not the completion of history itself, suggests that this may not be the case. And if this is not the case, then the book we are reading is not the Book but merely another installment in the history of error that is philosophy as Kojève himself conceives it.

It is no secret that there are serious obstacles to the realization of Kojève's radical philosophical project of completion. We have already discussed Kojève's reservations about one key notion: that it is in the "nature" of self-consciousness to extend itself. Kojève counters this assertion by observing that not all people seek to extend their self-consciousness to such a degree. Not all people *want* to be philosophers, regardless of whether they *can* be philosophers. The extension of self-consciousness as characteristic—in fact, as definitive—of the philosophical "nature" does not, for Kojève, seem to be a necessary or "natural" aspect of human beings. In this respect, Kojève keeps his distance from the view, ultimately traceable to Aristotle, that "all humans by nature desire to know."[16] The ostensibly Hegelian version of this is that all humans (as social beings) desire to be fully conscious of themselves, to be omniscient, but Kojève expresses a skepticism about this, the origins of which, as we shall see, reach to the foundations of Hegel's philosophy.

By not subscribing to the claim that the expansion of self-consciousness is necessary, Kojève thus affirms, as we have noted, that his work is a practical project whose chances of success are by no means assured. If, as Kojève suggests at one point, history came to an end in 1806, it is clear that not everyone has grasped that fact—history seems to move on as it did before. Indeed, the absurdity that one may find in this declaration, the sheer eccentricity it seems to express, is the most powerful sign that it not only has failed to come to pass but also has failed to capture the imagination of those who could have helped to make the declaration a reality.

The practical aspect of the end-of-history claim is itself estranging because it completely rejects the notion that the truth is somehow "there" for us to discover. Rather, Kojève makes the still radical point that the truth is something that we make, and the challenge he puts to his audience is to make the declaration that history is at an end true. While the association of the end of history with the work of the slave is quite obviously predicated upon the equation of work with truth, as we noted earlier, the simple statement that we make the truth leads to accusations of solipsism, subjectivity, or madness.

Kojève anticipated these objections, and that is why he insists that the way to the objective truth is paved with a philosophical pedagogy that convinces others to join in the project of bringing about the truth. The truth as project loses its solipsistic or subjective flavor, its association with madness, the moment it becomes accepted as the truth. Moreover, this truth comes to itself as a truth when it is accepted not only by many but by *all*. The truth becomes truth *only* when it becomes universal; we seem to trade individual for collective madness, though Kojève thoroughly denies the possibility of the latter.

This is perhaps still a shocking doctrine, especially in its universalist form. It estranges us not only from the venerable doctrine that truth is discovered, not made, but also from the view that there is no final truth. (Here the claim that Kojève is somehow postmodernist—in the clichéd sense—is flawed.) It estranges us from the doctrine, in other words, that we are limited by a power or absence of power that we can never over-come and which we refer to as nature or God or language and so on. For Kojève, the claim that we are beings that are *necessarily* subject to these "external" limitations is a doctrine that plays a role *inside* of the master-slave relation.[17] The upshot is that it is not nature or God or some other external limitation that shapes us but our relation to other human beings. The human relation is the foundational relation by which we come to know anything, including ourselves. To declare, then, that nature or God limits us is to create a specific structure of authority within the human relationship, a structure of authority that reinforces social or political servitude by anchoring that servitude in an unchangeable external authority. One may fight the master, but one may not fight the absolute master—nature or God (in the guise of death). But this admonition, Kojève suggests, is merely another move in a social or political contest for domination that, in the end, provides powerful reinforcement for the hegemony of nature or God—and, in particular, of death—over human affairs. By reinforcing the authority of death, the master reinforces his own authority as the one who, in contrast to the slave, is not afraid of death.

Accordingly, the notion that truth is anchored in external limitation is yet another position in an overall politics of domination that reinforces the division between master and slave. Those who accept the authority of nature, death, and truth understood in this way condemn themselves to servitude.

Here is a fascinating point: Kojève's reservations about the triumph of philosophy indicate that the slave does not have to triumph. When Kojève suggests that not all people will seek to become philosophers, to become fully conscious of themselves, he means that they will not want to confront the fact that their servitude may be merely a fiction, an illusion behind which lies a structure of political domination. And they will not want to come to full self-consciousness because they will also have to confront death. By confronting death they will in this sense lose their fear of it. But if they lose their fear of death, then they will no longer be slaves, if not *in actu* (for they may still find themselves in the position of the slave) but *in potentia*. The essence of the slave revolt that Friedrich Nietzsche fears and Kojève welcomes is the loss of the fear of death.

For Kojève, no other character in occidental history shows this loss more convincingly than Christ. In this respect, Kojève's claim that Christ shows the way for overcoming the distance between man and God is the paradigmatic expression of the slave losing his fear. The greatest of all slave rebellions is that formulated by Christ as the rebellion against the fear of death, which shows the way to the conquest of nature, God, and death. As Kojève says, in his lecture on death in Hegel from the year 1933–1934:

> It is by resigning himself to death, by revealing it through his discourse, that Man arrives finally at absolute Knowledge or Wisdom, in thus completing History. For it is by starting out from the idea of death that Hegel works out his Science of "absolute" philosophy, which alone is capable of philosophically rendering an account of the fact of the existence in the world of a finite being conscious of its finitude and disposing of it at times as it likes.
>
> Thus, Hegel's absolute Knowledge or Wisdom and the conscious acceptance of death are but one and the same.[18]

The challenge of Kojève's thought as set out here, as a philosophical pedagogy that seeks to liberate all from the fear of death by following a model of emancipation created within Christianity itself—a religion, we may recall, that, in offering the example of Christ, suppresses itself, according to Kojève, and thus brings about its own refutation to the degree that it enshrines not the acceptance of death but rather the fear thereof (in the image of God)—is to eliminate all avatars of the master constructed to impair our acceptance of death by reinforcing our fear of it.

Kojève's thought, in this respect, seems to be an astonishing, apocalyptic account of kenosis. The more I incorporate God, the more universal I become, the more complete, the less I fear death, and the more I come to recognize my essential kinship with death. The journey captured in the *Phenomenology* is an emptying out (*Entäußern*) whereby my *I* becomes one with what was hitherto other than my *I*, where I become one with all, and all becomes one with my *I*. This is, I caution, not a moment of "oceanic feeling" that Sigmund Freud mentions in his *Civilization and Its Discontents*,[19] nor is it a variant of "silent" communion or the *unio mystica*. On the contrary, this is an expression of the highest self-consciousness and thus a conscious recognition of myself in what is other to me, whose correlates are several: the universal recognition with which the master-and-slave relation comes to an end, as well as the fabled union of subject and object in Hegel that Kojève puts aside for yet another unity—that between time and space, understood as the final spatialization of time and the temporalizing of space. Unlike the oceanic feeling, the sage describes this process of emptying out—it is by definition a discursive process—and leaves behind this description in the Book.

There is a great deal to elaborate here. But I want to address first, even if only in a preliminary manner, two positions that express a critique of Kojève's interpretation, one from the right, the other from the left. I will then situate Kojève's response to that critique within an extended discussion of the kenotic aspect of the last lectures of 1938–1939.

NATURE AND THE GIVEN

The lines of engagement pertinent to the first position emerge as an attack on Kojève's disregard for the concept of nature, understood as supplying a sort of "given." From this perspective, the social relation is not essentially a rejection of nature, as it is for Kojève, but rather a specific response to nature whose most basic tenet is that nature cannot be overcome—thus, nature, however it is identified, provides the ultimate limit to the social. While this can sound quite egalitarian—we are all "children" of nature—it is not, since there is a caveat insofar as nature is employed as a means of justifying inegalitarian norms. The doctrine of nature as a fiction, a noble lie, as it is in Plato, provides an order for the many so that the few who have the requisite virtues may flourish without interference from the many. If anything, Kojève's "arbitrary" focus on the master-slave relation merely reveals his astute appraisal of the alternatives. The preferred alternative of those who defend natural law is a "sober" recognition of the necessity of maintaining inequality; the unattractive side of this may be neatly expressed as advocacy for the continuance of servitude for all those unsuited to the "rigors" of freedom.

The other face of this argument is the compliment paid to Kojève by those of the natural law persuasion, who note that Kojève, by taking the logic of the Enlightenment to its furthest limit, shows his clear and sober vision of the "dehumanizing" truth of that logic. "Sobriety" is the word of choice for describing that "austere" attitude toward reality which does not flinch when confronted with the "dangerous" truth. Of course the most dangerous truth, the unlovely truth (*schlechthin*), is that we die.[20] And as we may glean from the *Republic*, death is the greatest injustice, if not the origin of all that is ugly and dangerous in our social relations, which themselves can offer but a palliative.[21]

The most dangerous of these palliatives is the promise of paradise on earth, something very much like the universal and homogeneous state that is the necessary precondition of the arrival of the sage. As if its adherents were all quoting Friedrich Hölderlin's warning in *Hyperion*, the conservative view might be reduced to a claim that to bring paradise to earth will create a hell, not heaven.[22] So when Kojève talks with apparently mordant delight about the death of man and the end of history, he seems to fall into the hands of his critics, and not only those from the right. From the left, the argument is that Kojève hands the conservatives a prize when he describes the ostensibly utopian state as a posthuman state of erotic play in which discourse becomes the " 'language' of the bees."[23] Or, worse:

> The end of History is, properly speaking, the *death* of Man. After this
> death, there remain (1) living bodies with human form, but emptied of

Spirit, that is, of Time or creative power; (2) a Spirit that empirically-exists but in the form of an inorganic reality, one that is not living, as a Book that, being not even animal life, has nothing to do with Time. The relation between the Sage and his Book is thus rigorously analogous to that between Man and his *death*. My death is indeed mine; it is not the death of another. But it is mine only in the future; for one may *say*: "I am going to die" but not "I am dead." The same for the Book. It is my work, and not that of another; and it is there a question of myself and not of another thing. But I am not in the Book, nor am I this Book, except as I write or publish it, that is, as long as it is still a future (or a project). Once the Book has come out, it detaches itself from me. It ceases to be me, just as my body ceases to be me after my death. Death is just as impersonal and eternal, that is, inhuman, as is the impersonal, eternal, and inhuman Spirit fully realized in and by the Book.[24]

This remarkable passage paints a bleak portrait of the post-historical state, establishing an equivalence between the emptying out of the human being that becomes its fulfillment as a universal being and the emptying out of the human into the Book. In both cases, the kenotic act of universalization is equivalent to death. To become a citizen of the universal and homogeneous state seems to be akin to dying—wisdom is not merely the acceptance of death, it is death's enactment. The sage arises ghostlike from the corpse of the once vibrant human being, as a momentary transition to the Book. If sobriety were ever required, it would seem to be required in this case, in the exceedingly sober reflection over the prospect of emancipation that seems to lead the slave in his struggle with the master. Having won this struggle, the slave slips into oblivion, leaving behind only the record of his victory, in the Book that the philosophical slave writes. What is more, the emancipated slave is little more than an animal, a creature of "bodies and pleasures" who has been deserted by the labor that emancipated him. His emancipation recalls the impasse of the master, who also seems to live on in some sort of vegetative limbo as he becomes more and more dependent on the slave for the necessities of his material existence—and indeed, becomes more like the slave.

From the perspective of the left, of those who hold to narratives of emancipation, this narrative of self-annihilation, of the "mediated suicide," can hardly seem attractive. It must fail, not only as a rhetorical effort, if it ever were that, but also as a cold conceptual possibility. The victory of the slave at the end of history is not Pyrrhic—that would give it a far more enticing look. In fact, it is a victory that seems indistinguishable from defeat, since there is nothing left for the slave after the end of history but aimless and unconscious pleasures.

From the perspective of the right, Kojève's post-historical scenario makes for pointed propaganda. No wonder the acolytes of natural law praise Kojève for his sobriety; for them, he envisions the "gray" death of utopianism without illusions, what one might view as the victory of the Nietzschean "last man." There is thus a reason—we are to suppose—for the absence of detailed portraits of the final state in the greatest of the utopian social theorists, Karl Marx (whom Kojève claims to follow): the horrific nature of the final state ensures that it shall never attract many adherents. At the very least, Kojève, that peculiar master of philosophical propaganda grasped as philosophical pedagogy, either stumbles, which is highly unlucky, or decides to paint the cruelest possible view of what realization of utopian hopes must entail.

Is Kojève's post-historical state, then, not a warning to those who would pursue the utopian striving for the final, best state, for the state that establishes at last the rule of the egalitarian principle in all facets of life? Is Kojève a leftist of the right or, as Stefanos Geroulanos argues, is he not a leftist or Marxist at all but an entirely different kind of thinker, a sort of pre-postmodern nihilist?[25]

How are we to take these somber final words of the 1938–1939 lectures? He begins by quoting a passage from Hegel:

> "The entire sphere of finitude, by the fact that it is itself something, of the senses, collapses into the true-or-truthful Faith before the thought and Intuition (Anschauung) of the Eternal [thought and intuition], becoming here one and the same thing. All the gnats of Subjectivity are burned up in this devouring fire; and *even the consciousness* of this giving of oneself (Hingebens) and of this annihilation (Vernichtens) is annihilated (vernichtet)."

Then he goes on:

> Hegel knows it and says it. But he also says in one of his letters that this knowledge cost him dearly. He speaks of a period of total depression that

he lived through between the twenty-fifth and thirtieth years of his life: a "Hypochondria" that went "bis zur Erlähmung aller Kräfte," "to the point of a paralysis of all his forces," and which arose precisely from the fact that he could not accept the necessary abandonment of *Individuality*, that is in fact of humanity, that the idea of absolute Knowledge demands. But, finally, he overcame this "Hypochondria." And, becoming a Sage through this last acceptance of death, he published, a few years later, the first Part of the "System of Knowledge," entitled, "Science of the Phenomenology of the Spirit," where he reconciles himself definitively with all that is and has been, by declaring that there will never again be anything new on earth.[26]

The main point is clear: the left cannot accept the notion that utopia corresponds with the overcoming of individuality. But neither can the right accept this notion, though they are forced to do so if they hold up Kojève as having proven how contrary to humanity the final cherished goal of total emancipation is, for total emancipation in the Kojèvian sense is the emancipation from the individual self. All that is left behind at the end of history is the "animal" body and the spiritual Book.

Kojève forces his critics into a defense of individuality over collectivity, and the thrust of the critical approaches from left and right do tend to focus on the free historical individual as the atomic unit of political action. The primary difference between them concerns the degree to which all individuals can share in freedom, but not the desirability of individual freedom itself. While one may assail the claim as exaggerated, it seems that Kojève's central emphasis on overcoming individuality goes against the single most cherished modern value: individual freedom. The singular cliché of modern bourgeois life—the free, self-creating, or self-fashioning individual—seems to be put at issue in Kojève's thought. One must die so that the whole may live, or, as the famed epigraph to *The Brothers Karamazov* has it, quoting John 12:24: "Verily, verily I say unto you, except a corn of wheat fall into the ground and die, it abideth alone: but if it die, it bringeth forth much fruit."[27]

If anything, the two possible opposing views I have briefly examined show the central challenge of Kojève's own emancipation narrative. One may view this narrative either as a merciless parody of the emancipation narratives associated with the free, self-fashioning individual—a narrative of emancipation suggesting that these other narratives are in some way incoherent—or Kojève may indeed be quite serious in creating an emancipation narrative with a concept of freedom and individuality that is completely inimical to that which animates other such narratives.

Let me explain this final point briefly before returning to a closer reading of Kojève's text. The two notions of freedom at issue here may be defined as pertaining to, respectively, individual and collective freedom. The usual way of describing the relation between the two emphasizes that they are in fact at odds with each other—individual freedom comes at the cost of the collective, and collective freedom comes at the cost of the individual. There is a tension here that may be more abstractly identified as a tension between the particular and the universal. Probably few other tensions in the Western tradition have garnered more attention; in the guise of the relation of the one and the many, this tension appears to be, as Theodor Adorno affirms, the constitutive tension of metaphysics.[28]

While a thorough engagement with this tension would take us too far afield, I do want to attempt a characterization of it that permits us to grasp exactly what is at stake for Kojève in his apparent advocacy of a kind of freedom that seems to be beyond the tension or which represents a definitive dissolution of it—perhaps a final freedom. Kojève seems to impute an essentially corrupt notion of freedom to both the individualist and collectivist notions of freedom, which appears to animate the critics of his view. When I say "corrupt," I mean to emphasize that individualist and collectivist variants of freedom have at their core a similar account of freedom as the freedom to do as one wishes—to dispose of plant, mineral, man, and God as one sees fit, without restriction of any kind. The ultimate form of this kind of freedom is that which we might associate with the creator, who may do as he or she desires, creating hitherto unprecedented combinations in concept and in reality. The essentially negative cast of this conception of freedom is expressed by its necessary precondition: that there are no durable limits that cannot be overcome by something akin to will or *voluntas*, which, as Hannah Arendt explains, is far more than the freedom to choose among given options but is also the freedom to create the given.[29]

Now, this sort of freedom seems to be very similar to the freedom Kojève advocates as negation. The human being is human or free insofar as he or she negates the given, whatever that given might be at any time. This freedom to transcend what one is, at any time, denotes for Kojève a properly human possibility which is necessarily creative because it relates not directly to the given in the way of the animal but to the giving of the given, as it were—to the given as defined in accordance with a set of human desires. One may recall here Kojève's dogmatic insistence that human desire is differentiated from animal desire because it is not a desire for the object "in itself" but for the object as given within another structure of desire. If I may put this less bureaucratically, objects take on significance for human beings as "nodes" of interest. I want X only because others are interested in it and, in the end, it is not the combat against nature that takes precedence but the combat against other human beings. And this desire is only free to the extent that I am willing to die to impose it on other human beings. Any other kind of desire, to the extent it is tied to self-preservation and to not risking self-preservation, is not a free, human desire but an animal desire that holds to the signal imperative to avoid death.

For Kojève, a human being only becomes free when the desire that holds us to preserve ourselves at all costs has been *overcome*. The most purely human desire is the desire that expresses no fear of death, a desire whose freedom arises from its complete absence of fear of death. It is, in this sense, the most truly selfless desire, because it expresses no attachment to the very self of which it is also an expression, if perhaps only in the negative. The bedrock point is that animal desire, the model and precondition of desire itself, seems to be incapable of detachment from the animal self, the body, of which it is the foremost expression. Only the necessarily strange creature we refer to as human desire can overcome this limitation, and Kojève suggests that this desire is itself only overcome in the sage, who becomes most fully human in the combination of the sage and the Book.

Be that as it may, the implicit critique is clear: freedom, when attached to individual or collective animality, is not freedom. Rather, it is the expression of the purely animal fear of death, as we saw in the ambivalence of Alexei Kirillov. Indeed, freedom is not defined as the overcoming of that fear of death but as its highest, if most covert, expression. The freedom that one associates with self-creation, novelty, and so on is not freedom at all but a profound servitude to the animal will to live at all costs, this being, for Kojève, the very definition of servitude.[30]

Kojève thus locates the emancipatory projects of modernity within the fundamental failure to deal with a greater servitude to the fear of death. Both kinds of freedom, then—that of the individual and that of the collective—are, for Kojève, essentially the same. They are kinds of freedom pertaining to the slave, who not only is unable to overcome his servitude but also has made it into the very essence of his life, transforming the potentially human actor into the animal with a human face. Hence, it is surely unsurprising that Kojève would later identify both the United States and the Soviet Union as being of essentially the same underlying orientation, with an accent on the individual in the United States and on the collective in the Soviet Union. Rather than being merely a "fashionable" repetition of Heidegger's notorious assertion that the United States and the Soviet Union were metaphysically the same and, as such, a threat to Germany,[31] Kojève's comparison is fully justified on the basis of his own thought, which, in this respect, may well be a good deal more precise than Heidegger's. Yet the same principle applies to both: the attachment to detachment from material or natural need as the precondition for the possibility of emancipation, any other kind of emancipation being in fact a veiled form of servitude.

Once again. Kojève's reductiveness calls into question the validity of his distinctions. Even if we accept the persuasive force of the basic distinction between a notion of freedom that is tied to bodily fulfillment and one that is diametrically opposed to that notion of freedom, the sweeping quality of these distinctions, which aim to define "modernity" as exemplified by the divergent "twins," the United States and the Soviet Union, is bound to unsettle, and this once again raises the question about the purpose of the lectures as philosophical pedagogy or "serious" philosophical work. Kojève's demeanor, his irony and playful insouciance coupled with his penchant for the diverting phrase, do nothing to upset the image of a somewhat superficial gadfly who, in denouncing one notion of freedom, praises a notion that places demands on human beings so outrageous as to be ridiculous. What is one to say when faced with a doctrine that insists on the need for what appears to be mass self-immolation, the death of the (still animal) human, so that the Book may live? What sort of triumph is this, if indeed it is a triumph at all? The vaunted irony of Kojève takes on a monstrous quality here when the final end of history, the true point of final emancipation for the toiling, oppressed human being, seems to be indistinguishable from suicide. Is Kojève really a progressive thinker, a Marxist, or is he a jocular misanthropist, a sort of Mephistopheles? Or is he both?

PROGRESSIVE OR MISANTHROPE?

To respond to these questions, I want to return to the final set of lectures from 1938–1939, but I also want to examine another pertinent text, the final text in the French original of *Introduction to the Reading of Hegel*, which, appropriately enough, deals with the Hegelian concept of death. I thus bring the lectures that elaborate the concept of the sage and his wisdom together with a text dealing with death, which seems to be the proper element of the sage in the sense that the arrival of the sage signals the collective death of the human as slave, as retaining animality, in favor of the perfectly human. To begin, I cite two important passages from the ninth lecture of 1938–1939:

> Now, Time—it's Man himself. To suppress Time is thus also to suppress Man. Indeed: "the true being of Man is in his Action," meaning action that *succeeds*. This is to say that Man is the objective *result* of his Action. Now, the result of the action of the Sage, that is, of the total perfect Man who completes the process of becoming of human reality is Knowledge [la Science]. But the empirical-existence (Dasein) of Knowledge is not Man; it is the *Book*. This is not Man, not the Sage in flesh and bone, it is the Book that is the appearance (*Erscheinung*) of Knowledge in the World, this appearance being absolute Knowledge [Savoir].
>
> . . . .
>
> To be sure, this existence [of Knowledge] is "empirical," and as such it has a duration: the Book endures as well; it deteriorates and is reprinted, etc. But the nth edition does not differ in any way from the first: one cannot modify anything; one cannot add anything. Even in changing, the Book thus remains *identical* to itself. The Time in which it endures is thus cosmic or natural, but not historical or human. To be sure, the Book, in order to be a Book and not bound and darkened paper, has to be read and understood by men. But the successive readers change

nothing in the Book. And if, in order to read the Book, Man must *live*, that is, be born, grow and die, his life reduced in its essence to this reading (for, let us not forget, that with the advent of the universal and homogeneous State, with desire being thus fully satisfied, there is no further struggle nor work; History is ended, there is nothing left to *do*, and Man is only to the extent that one reads and understands the Book that reveals all that has been and could have been done)—he creates nothing new: the future of Paul who has not yet read the Book is not the past of Peter who has already read it. The Time of the Man-reader-of-the-Book is thus the cyclical (or biological) Time of Aristotle, but not linear, historical, Hegelian Time.[32]

Kojève links together three central aspects of his thought: the sage, the Book, and the universal and homogeneous state. They all describe different facets of the end of history, and they all seem to dispense with time as we have understood it thus far as the characteristically human time of history, in which to be human is to be history, that is, desire, negation, and change. As Kojève notes, time may arise in cycles; this is characteristic, as the second quoted passage shows, of the Aristotelian or "biologic" notion of time, which applies to those who read the Book. But this time does not apply to those who make the Book—they live in Hegelian time that, though circular, only runs through the circle *once*.[33] Kojève thus seems to argue that human history may run its course to completion only once. Thereafter, it can only be repeated, literally as a repetition of the Book that is the lasting result—the only lasting result—of that human history which, otherwise, cancels itself. Yet it is equally obvious that this repetition is nothing like the action that gave rise to the Book, since the Book permits only repetition. If history has indeed come to an end, after all, no action other than repetition is possible.

As we have noted, then, the picture Kojève creates of the end of history, of the human's successful accession to wisdom, deeply challenges the assumptions that we typically associate with the success of that final state. But Kojève also seems to justify the assumptions of those who express hostility to that final state, who see in the final state the loss of nobility and greatness in humans. Even in regard to the latter, however, Kojève is not easily brought into the fold as a Right Hegelian or conservative figure because he also cannot be said to be one who advocates incompleteness or permanent struggle as an end in itself.[34]

In this respect, Kojève makes a remarkable statement in the eleventh lecture, to the effect that the action of the human being corrects an error—the error of human being itself. This statement can in turn be connected with a similar statement in earlier lectures, to the effect that man is an error or that man is a defective or sick animal.[35] From this perspective, human action is devoted to this correction, which involves the elimination of the animal actor as such by transforming the human being into the Book, by restoring, in this sense, the natural balance that the human being has disturbed by his defective actions, his errancy. The final human artifact, the Book, cannot by definition change anything more but refers to the restoration of balance and order—equilibrium again—as a return to cosmic or natural time undisturbed by human action.

The key passage in the eleventh lecture is clear:

> The history of Man, that is, Time, will last as long as there remains a *difference* between (subjective) "Knowledge" and the (objective) "Truth" or the Reality-revealed-by-Knowledge. That is to say that History will last as long as there will be in the World a being that *errs* and, bit by bit, eliminates its errors on its own. Now, this being is Man, and only Man. For, in general, animals and Nature do not err. Or, granted, if you like, Nature errs too. But, if it errs, its error (a monster, for example, or a living being not adapted to its environment) is *immediately* eliminated: it dies or annihilates itself without being able to keep itself alive even temporarily. Only Man can *keep* error in the world by making it *last* in the form of an erroneous discourse. And History is the History of the erroneous Discourses of Man which bit by bit become truths. And this not only because they change to conform to a given Reality but because Man, by work and struggle, transforms Reality itself in order to make it conform to his Discourses that, initially, departed from Reality. And at the moment when the conformity of Reality and Discourse is perfectly realized, at the moment, thus, when Man can no longer *err* because he no longer transcends the given having no further desire—at this moment History stops. Then, subjective knowledge is at once objective; that is, it is *true*, definitively and completely. And this "absolute" Knowledge [Savoir] *is* Knowledge [La Science].[36]

Kojève conceives of truth as narrative. So it is time to ask a basic question: What sort of narrative does Kojève's interpretation of the end of history project? We have hitherto responded to this question by identifying Kojève's narrative as essentially an emancipation narrative whereby the human being understood as slave liberates itself from two separate yokes: that of the master and that of nature. The liberation from both yokes seems to take place simultaneously; the one presupposes the other. This narrative of emancipation presupposes yet another whereby the human being assumes the role previously vouchsafed to God alone. The liberation of the slave from the master and from nature is thus also a liberation from God.

But there is more. All of these forms of liberation in turn describe a more comprehensive movement from a relation to an external agency that defines the slave to the slave's internalization of that relation whereby the slave assimilates the definition of others into his own self-definition. The slave no longer evaluates himself by reference to an external agency but by reference to himself as having created his own standard of evaluation through the struggle and work that allowed him to overcome his own servitude. That is, the reality the slave creates is itself his form of mastery—by creating in response to necessity, the slave overcomes necessity—or so we may be led to believe.

And here is the difficulty we have examined from several perspectives already: the overcoming of necessity by the slave terminates his being as such. When Kojève remarks that the human being cannot survive without nature (other than as nothingness), he seems to mean that the overcoming of necessity in the guise of nature eliminates the human at the very moment of the highest expression of the distinctively human freedom from nature, from the animal. In this connection, Kojève deploys one of the governing images of his commentary as well as of his treatise on right, that of the ring. For Kojève, the ring expresses the materiality of nature, which is the ring itself, and the negativity of the human, which is the empty space within the ring. The human struggle is a paradoxical one, since genuine freedom, as opposed to animal desire, emerges in the human overcoming of nature, the final success of which arises with the advent of the sage and the Book. The paradox inheres in the fact that the truly human expression of freedom eliminates the human as a natural being: it is self-cancellation or suicide.

The simple (for Kojève, dialectical) narrative form, then, is the self-canceling narrative. The truly human end of the human being is to eradicate itself, suicide writ large. The truth of the human is error, but the human being is an error that may correct itself. Note that there is no necessity in this self-correction. If there were, the human being would not be human in the Kojèvian sense but rather a natural being whose essence is to eliminate itself, a most peculiar natural being that would reinforce Kojève's claim that nature eliminates its errors as quickly as it can. Thus, for Kojève, to be truly human is to undertake one's suicide voluntarily, since there is no necessity to it. One must freely choose to eradicate oneself. Not to do so, to retain the error, is what Kojève refers to in one spot as "crime."

We seem to find ourselves in a welter of confusions. Kojève uses the language of emancipation to an end that seems utterly preposterous: the elimination of the human being. His highest form of individuality and freedom seems to explode both notions. The sage, having acceded to the status of a finite god, cannot be referred to as free or individual in any "ordinary" sense. Indeed, it seems that the freedom of the sage presupposes emancipation from the effort to achieve freedom through struggle and work that defines the slave. To be free in this sense is to be free of the desire for freedom—to be freed of any desire at all insofar as that desire exceeds the animal desire for self-preservation. The final freedom, then, is the freedom from self-consciousness, that "disease" about which the underground man complains so bitterly.[37] The universal and homogeneous state must be a state akin to Jean-Jacques Rousseau's state of nature, in which sociality in fact collapses because self-consciousness has been eliminated. All that can possibly remain is unconscious activity.

And yet Kojève wavers, and in many different ways, as we have already seen. We find additional evidence of this wavering in the final lectures themselves, most famously in a note he added to the original second edition of the French text of the *Introduction*, which came out in 1962. While Kojève describes the post-historical state as one of bestialization, of the becoming animal that coincides with the loss of the human or its preservation in the form of the Book, he also seems to grant it some human qualities—he suggests that the Book will have readers. But he also suggests that language will disappear in the post-historical era. Presumably the Book would disappear along with it. Further, Kojève differentiates between human time and natural time. As we have seen, human time is circular, but it completes itself only once, whereas animal time resembles the biological time of Aristotle.[38] This animal time seems to apply also to the Book, which can be reread infinitely without change; each reading of the Book is identical. But what animal can read, and what being deprived of self-consciousness can read? What kind of reading can be mere imitation?[39]

Difficulties accumulate, because the universal and homogeneous state is the precondition for the advent of the sage—it is the state where all are sages—but its exact nature outside of this role is not consistently fleshed out by Kojève in the Hegel lectures. On the one hand, Kojève describes a state populated by beings that seem barely distinguishable from animals, the human having died with the advent of this new state. On the other hand, Kojève seems to grant some level of humanity to these posthistorical creatures, who may have a language like that of bees or engage in erotic play. What seems to count here is a ritualization of life that is the human equivalent to the instinct that we attribute to animals. The human disappears because the chance event that gave rise to the human has been reversed in a return to something akin to the natural state.

Now, as we know, Kojève has raised the issue of the possibility of achieving wisdom and the only state appropriate to it, the universal and homogeneous state. But he has to some degree suppressed another issue: whether the achievement of that state is desirable. Kojève no doubt seems to condemn the notion of error and "errancy" as being essentially antiphilosophical states, and this condemnation reveals, on yet another level, the problem of the Kojèvian project as a form of philosophical pedagogy. The doubts Kojève addresses with regard to philosophy—that self-consciousness must of necessity extend itself to include all things—render philosophy itself vulnerable on its own terms.

In other words, if it is not necessary to become philosophical—and Kojève cannot claim that it is—then how can a philosophical pedagogy have any persuasive power, especially if it forces one into the structure that Kojève describes? Not only is the acceptance of philosophy the acceptance of the role of a slave but also its final destination is one whose subtraction from the world is so extreme that it resembles death itself, for the sage is in this respect the posthumous man, a ghostly presence who merely describes what he has seen in the Book.

The argument that Kojève can bring against this view is that it cannot assert itself consistently. To argue against philosophy, as Aristotle noted, is to engage in philosophy. One can thus argue that there is no discourse that can wholly reject philosophical discourse, since that rejection involves an acceptance of the conventions of philosophical discourse as a condition of the rejection itself. The best way to reject philosophical discourse is through silence or action that need not explain itself. Otherwise, as soon as one seeks to provide an account of one's resistance to philosophy, one finds oneself already implicated in what one seeks to overcome.

But implication does not mean that one cannot still reject philosophy, and Kojève's thought offers counterarguments, both by indicating that there is no necessity involved in taking up philosophy—that is, in the project of coming to full consciousness of oneself—and by setting up another tension—that between negation and completion. This tension between negation and completion comes clear in the potential clash between the notion that to be human is to negate the given and the notion that this act of negation is necessarily finite insofar as it must end, at some point, in final satisfaction.

This necessity is the most obscure. It seems to be predicated on an assumption that negation can only be determinate and that it can only be determinate if it is finite, if at one point or another the negation is complete. Otherwise, the identity of negation itself has to come into question, for if negation is not essentially finite, it can have no identity at all. But if it can have no identity at all, how can we know that there is a nonfinite negation? Simply put, we cannot; infinite negation is not negation as we understand it. Hence, Kojève seems to conceive of negation as relating to a concrete given and developing from there in a series of concrete acts of negation. But if that is so, then another problem emerges, because we can describe abstractly this concrete case. Concrete negation is already an abstract theoretical entity—it transcends the concrete, finite context in every case, and must do so.

The—dare we say?—theory of negation presented by Kojève threatens to call into question not only his notion that negation must come to an end but also—and maybe more significantly—the identity between time and the concept that is supposed to be the linchpin of Hegel's radical novelty. If the concept and time are indeed one, then the conceptual horizon governing all thought has to be temporal as well. The upshot is that what *is* comes to be as narrative, and most fully comes to be what it is at the end of that narrative, when no further changes are possible. To describe negation as Kojève does, to describe the concept as Kojève does, to speak about the nature of reality as Kojève does—all of these possibilities are inherently reflexive, immanent in the overall narrative Kojève unfolds in his commentary. They clarify the origins of how we think the way we do, and they cannot by definition describe or refer to any other kind of thinking, because to do so would be to take them out of the temporal fabric that made them what they are and to suggest that such abstraction is in fact possible. In other words, abstraction of this kind derives, from rules applicable to one narrative, general rules applicable to all possible narratives. This is a problematic inference, unless one argues that one cannot transcend the horizon of one's own understanding—and it would seem that Kojève does argue this way. If that is the case, whatever I find that is other to my thinking must be assimilated to my thinking as the condition of my being able to make sense of the other. This is simply a different way of describing exactly the process that the Hegelian subject goes through as it assimilates what was other to itself, as it internalizes what was hitherto exterior, thus absorbing anything defined as outside of its proper sphere.[40]

The Hegelian approach transforms contingency into necessity, by holding that the Hegelian approach can conceive of difference or the other only within its own terms. Thus, to the extent that it encounters anything other, it transforms that other into itself—it is a machine of internalization (*Er-innerung*).[41] Still, even if this is so, we have no reason to assert that this process of assimilation must come to an end. If we can argue that the Hegelian notion of self-consciousness tends to absorb into its own terms anything it encounters, that is not to say that this process is necessarily finite.

NEGATION AND FINALITY

This tension between negation and finality dominates the final set of lectures in the *Introduction*, entitled "The Idea of Death in the Philosophy of Hegel." Though these lectures come from the first year of Kojève's seminar (1933–1934), they reflect the same basic attitude that one finds in the very last set of lectures. The degree to which Kojève's thought seems to have coalesced early on, despite a certain degree of variation, is quite remarkable in itself. Kojève opens these lectures with a discussion of a variant of this tension—the relation of substance to subject that Kojève identifies as giving us the "essential and unabridged content of his [Hegel's] philosophy."[42] Kojève characterizes Hegel's thought as essentially a process whereby substance becomes subject, recognizing of course the importance of providing an account not of one or the other but of their interrelation, of how substance relates to the subject and vice versa.[43]

This might seem to be a peculiar beginning for a set of lectures that seek to explain the idea of death in Hegel. What does this dualism of substance and subject have to do with mortality, if anything?

Kojève maintains that the definition of totality as a relation between substance and subject implicates negativity. The basics here are familiar. The subject as human creates itself through action, through negation of the given. The relation between subject and substance, whereby substance becomes subject, is thus a description of the process of negation, whereby what was other to the subject becomes one with it, a determinate negation that preserves the identity of the other in negating or incorporating it. By including the subject in the totality, Kojève suggests that Hegel brings together two radically opposed traditions, the Greek and the Christian. First, the Greek:

> Now, the Man which Hegel has in view is not the one the Greeks believed they had identified (*apercevoir*) and which they left to philosophical posterity. This supposed Man of the ancient tradition is in fact a purely natural being (= identical) which has neither liberty (= Negativity) nor history, nor, properly speaking, individuality. Just like an animal he does nothing more than "represent," in and by his real and active existence, an eternal "idea" or "essence," given once and for all and remaining identical to itself.

Then the Christian:

> The Man which Hegel analyzes is, on the contrary, the Man who appears in the pre-philosophic Judeo-Christian tradition, the only truly anthropological one. This tradition has maintained itself in the course of

"modern times" in the form of "faith" or "theology," incompatible with ancient and traditional science and philosophy. And it is this tradition that has transmitted to Hegel the notion of the *free historical individual* (or of the "Person") that Hegel was the first to analyze *philosophically*, by attempting to reconcile it with the fundamental notions of ancient philosophy and the philosophy of Nature. According to this Judeo-Christian tradition, Man differs *essentially* from Nature, and he differs from it not only by his thinking alone, but by his activity as well. Nature is a "sin" in Man and for Man: he can and must *oppose* it and *deny* [*nier*] it in itself.[44]

The tensions in Kojève's own account of the advent of wisdom appear to reflect the tension between what Kojève identifies as two radically opposed traditions, one seeking to subordinate the human being to nature, the other seeking to subordinate nature to the human being. Surely the bleak and peculiar imagery Kojève associates with the post-historical human being, shorn of all resemblance to the human being whose actions brought forth the post-historical state, is a rather shocking reflection on the Christian paradise. In this connection it may be helpful to recall an earlier comment by Kojève, to the effect that the great mistake of Christian thought is to offer resurrection, an otherworldly reward. If we examine this statement a little more closely, we may well come to a better understanding of Kojève's unusual interpretation of Christianity.

Why is the resurrection a mistake? Pace Fedorov, the most obvious reason is that the resurrection appeals not to what Kojève considers truly human in the human being—the capacity to suppress the animal imperative of self-preservation—but precisely to that imperative. The obedient Christian is the one who offers up obedience—servitude—because he or she wants to extend earthly life. The brutish, selfish urge to preserve one's bodily self above all other things rules one's life such that one never becomes human in Kojève's sense. One remains essentially animal.

To be truly human, to be the "free, historical individual" that Kojève identifies as the essence of Judeo-Christian anthropology, requires one fundamental act of self-abnegation or, in Kojève's parlance, negation—the overcoming of the fear of death that dominates the animal. The "free, historical individual" is only free because he accepts his mortality. The fundamentally free act that enables all other free actions is the acceptance of death, and this acceptance is impossible without the renunciation of any and all afterlives. Kojève takes this somewhat further: to renounce the afterlife is to renounce God. It is the first step in radical atheism, and the import of atheism from this point of view is that it evinces the courage to face death as it is, without any palliative myths of return.

Kojève puts the matter bluntly in this early lecture: "Thus, Hegelian absolute Knowledge or Wisdom and the conscience acceptance of death, understood as complete and definitive annihilation, are one and the same." But he goes further again and declares an identity between Man and death: "But, if Man is Action, and if Action is Negativity 'appearing' as Death, Man is, in his human or spoken existence, but a *death*, more or less deferred and aware of itself." Even more pointedly, he says, "That is to say, therefore, that human existence itself is nothing but this Action [of negation]; it is the death that lives a human life." And finally, Kojève adds that this capacity to risk one's life, to allow oneself to die consciously without any "valid" biological reason, makes man a "fatal *disease* of the animal."[45]

These citations support the inference that to be human is, above all, to negate the vestiges of nature in us, the stubborn hold of self-preservation. Subjectivity and negation are thus connected intimately with death because they flourish at the cost of the animal. Given that the path to wisdom is marked by an ever-increasing self-awareness, it also is not surprising that, to the extent the subject internalizes the given reality through continued action, it comes to recognize that death is not some strange external entity but the subject itself; the very possibility of freedom, for Kojève, is connected with death. Only a mortal being can be free because only a mortal being can choose to overcome the most crushing necessity of its mortality, the fear of death that attaches to the imperative of self-preservation.

The narrative we have associated with the slave is in this respect a narrative of liberation from nature. The slave takes measures that are, in the end, much more radical than any the master might take. The slave suppresses nature. He is not merely content to live with nature, to come to terms with nature, or to risk his life. On the contrary, the slave transforms

nature in order to eradicate its capacity to threaten human being; ultimately, the slave comes to accept death by eradicating it and himself
along with it. This is an inference one may draw from the text, though
Kojève does not say this directly.

But is this eradication of nature not precisely evidence of the rule of
self-preservation? Is the kind of technological mastery over nature that
Kojève imputes to the work of the slave not the expression of a servile
concern for self-preservation? Does the slave truly liberate himself? Is the
universal and homogeneous state a state of masters or of slaves?

The obvious immediate answer is that it is a state of neither masters
nor slaves. Kojève affirms this in various spots and in an important passage from his work on legal theory, from 1943, which we will discuss in
chapter 8. But this answer does nothing to resolve the guiding question.
Kojève is in fact surprisingly enigmatic when it comes to an understanding of the dialectical fusion of master and slave, which can appear either
in the guise of the grotesque animal or corpse without spirit or in the
somewhat more banal "citizen," the fusion of warrior and slave, Caesar
with the soul of Christ. If the universal and homogeneous state is a utopia in which human errancy is finally corrected, it does not seem to be an
inviting utopia—Kojève's own descriptions, with their ironic insouciance,
hint unsubtly at the utter strangeness of this final state.

As I have suggested, Kojève may well be provoking his audience with
the example of the universal and homogeneous state in order to reveal the
problematic notion of the "free, historical individual," which seems to be
the basic political unit assumed by both right and left in the modern era
that has followed upon the French Revolution. If we take up this discussion again, we can see quite clearly now that Kojève's conception of freedom and individuality seems to have very little to do with the conceptions of both that are usually advanced in support of the "free, historical
individual." At the risk of some repetition, let me review the basic positions one more time.

For Kojève, freedom comes down to freedom from our animal nature,
a freedom that he readily admits can never be fully achieved because
we cannot, in the very end, simply eradicate the beginning point. On
the contrary, the beginning point determines the entire course of the movement away from it. Our freedom is thus based on the extinguishment of

our animal nature, and the final mark of that freedom is the sage and, in particular, the Book, which has nothing more to do with our animal nature since it is itself pure discourse. To put this differently, our freedom consists in an act of suppression of our animal nature, which means that we bring our death upon ourselves so that the achievement of our freedom, the Book, may live on, unlimited by animality.

Likewise, our uniquely human task consists in eradicating the individuality of the animal, the radical separation among members of a species that results from their corporeal individuation. The correlate of freedom as a distinctively human or free creation is the suppression of individuality whereby the differences that emerge from our corporeal separation are overcome. Once again, the most pertinent figuration of this overcoming is the Book, the uniqueness of which arises from the distinctiveness of the story it tells and then retells in the form of pure abstraction. The individual—or transindividual subject—that emerges in the Book at the end of history is a perfect fusion of the one and the many, each individual a mirror reflecting all others, each being all and all being in each, the perfectly Hegelian "we" that is "I" and "I" that is "we" from chapter 4 of the *Phenomenology*. Indeed, we might say that each individual is a perfect replica of the other, differentiated only by homogeneous space, and that each individual conveys all.

Needless to say, these notions of individuality and freedom have little to do with the "free, historical, individual" as typically conceived, and Kojève's challenge is precisely leveled at the difficulties that seem to coalesce around the figure of the "free, historical individual." These difficulties might be expressed as stemming from the central claim to self-determination that seems quite explicit: the free individual is free only to the extent he is not restricted by others, and the central freedom afforded to the free individual is freedom from the fear of violent death. But the significance of this central freedom is of course that it makes self-preservation into the governing principle of political community and action.

Hence, as I have already suggested, Kojève's seemingly outlandish radicality is in fact a challenging affront to the conception of man as "free, historical individual," which assumes more or less explicitly that self-preservation, or perhaps even self-interest, is the highest value—a very precarious value, to be sure. The ghastly visions of the end of history that Kojève provides strike at the desire for self-preservation that animates most utopian visions, as if one could simply live on in one's present form forever, or for a very long time, undisturbed by fear or boredom. These visions express the same sense of ridicule that one finds in Kojève's claim that resurrection is the only "theist" mistake of Christianity.[46]

III

THE LATER WRITINGS

7

NOBODIES

Taken in itself, negation is pure nothingness: it is not, it does not exist, it does not appear. It is only as negation of identity, that is, only as Difference. It can thus exist only as a real negation of Nature.

—ALEXANDRE KOJÈVE

Kojève's equation of time and concept, arguably the guiding equation of his thought, leads to seemingly insuperable difficulties.[1] One may be pardoned for assuming that the pattern of self-immolation asserted so regularly in *Introduction to the Reading of Hegel* has general application, possessing the authority of an irreducible truth. Kojève does nothing to dispel this identification. And yet, if we take the connection between time and concept seriously, the notion of truth as we understand it—as a fixed standard having application to various "cases"—can no longer be sustained, at least as a transcendent truth applicable to all possible worlds and not just to our own, unless of course our own contains *all* possible worlds.

To get a sense of the difference of Kojève's thought, we have to come to terms with the fact that the identification of time and concept suggests not only that the concept is narrative but also that this narrative relates only to itself. The narrative cannot have "general" application as a truth outside of itself, for the atemporal or eternal dimension in which that truth resides is denied from the outset by the equation of time and concept. Simply put, the truth achieved by equating concept and time can only relate to that equation itself immanently; thus, it cannot be said to be a general or eternal truth applying to all possible narratives in the traditional sense. On the contrary, the holism of this equation can result only from its comprehensiveness—all possible narratives play but a part in this greater, singular narrative, the "Book," the final end of which is to liberate them from their particularity by demonstrating their subservient role in the construction of precisely this final narrative and no other, since at the end of history no other is possible: "Absolute philosophy has no object that might be exterior to it."[2]

"The truth is the whole"—yet again. This famous Hegelian phrase seems also to govern Kojève's work. But we might just as well reformulate this phrase as "The truth is death." For the progress of truth toward itself is a process of universalization that undermines the particular in its inexorable movement to completion. Indeed, universalization may be described as a process of negation of all attachments to a particular context, and all attachments are particular attachments, even to the extent that they are abstract.

Kojève explicitly connects this movement to negation and death in his comparison of G. W. F. Hegel with Martin Heidegger, which appeared in a book review from 1936 that remained unpublished during Kojève's lifetime.[3] There, Kojève quotes Hegel as affirming the proposition that negation in its complete or absolute form is death: "The absolute of negation, pure freedom, is—in its appearance (Erscheinung)—death." This may seem to be logical enough; surely death is an absolute of sorts, since it negates completely the particular life whose final end it is. Our "growth" is a movement toward an end that cancels out that growth by bringing it to its terminal point. In this respect, one's life is indeed a self-canceling narrative, or a narrative whose end is its own elimination. As Sigmund Freud laconically put it, the end of life is death.

Has Kojève simply generalized this narrative to history as a whole? Is the end of history the eradication of history? This latter point initially seems a plausible argument because human action negates, and what it negates is its relation to a given. To employ a perhaps questionable metaphor, negation is motion that burns up the fuel of the given in coming to a final stop. Kojève uses a similar metaphor, of the ingestion of food, in describing the basic arc of negation that he associates with desire: the animal negates a given in order to continue to move. Movement stops either when the given is exhausted or the animal's capacity for ingestion has collapsed, along with its other functions.

Of course, there is a significant distinction here, for Kojève is careful to indicate that, unlike the animal, the truly human human being embraces his death by negating first and foremost the animal imperative to self-preservation. The human being freely brings about his own end. He does not acquiesce in his end but he freely brings it on by becoming a different kind of being, to the extent that he can eradicate his attachment to self-preservation. The master does this immediately, while the slave, through work and struggle, comes to the same conclusion, having transformed himself and the world into an artifact that overcomes his fear of death and thus negates the imperative of self-preservation.[4]

The upshot is that the slave recognizes that he is negation and, as such, death. His identity is the eradication of identity, and he learns to free himself by freeing himself of identity. He overcomes individuality by becoming universal, and thus comes to pass the final state, when all individual lives match the universal narrative, when there is complete harmony between part and whole, a harmony that signals the end of history in the universal and homogeneous state.[5]

Thus, if we return to our opening point, the truth only emerges in the complete harmony of the universal and homogeneous state, the state in which the individual life, the animal life, has been completely eradicated—we all become nobody or something akin to nobody, each is all and all is each. What one has, in effect, is a state of replicas, different from one another only in position but otherwise exactly alike. The final negation of the given produces absolute identity as the negation of any given identity.[6] Absolute negation leads to the kind of death Kojève describes in the context of the sage, who ceases to be human (and animal) the moment he has become wise and left behind his life as the life of everyman in the reified Book.

Kojève seems to regard this basic structure as having final authority. If that is so, it cannot apply to any other circumstances, since other circumstances cannot come into play. If they did, finality would not have been achieved. No other circumstances would be possible; all that one could contemplate would be repetition of what has already been. Nothing new would be possible, as Kojève indicates in his startling end to the 1938–1939 lectures.

Yet what kind of repetition could this possibly be? Or more pertinently, how can we be sure that we have reached an end point? How can negation come to an end? The fundamental question is of course that of equilibrium: Is it ever possible to create an equilibrium or harmony between negation and finality? How can we ever become nobodies, eliminating our own individuality, our own attachment to the world, without being dead? And how can we experience our own death, know that we are in fact dead?

If we know we are dead, death is not the end, and death is not complete or absolute. But if we cannot know our own death, then how can we identify with death or the end while still alive in some sense?[7] This problem is no minor one. It threatens to mock Kojève's claims for finality at every step, because the declaration of an end, of having come to the end of history or time, presupposes what it must otherwise deny—that there is a position somehow beyond the end that allows one to claim that end. But if the notion of an end cannot allow for that position, one comes into insuperable difficulties that align themselves with the difficulties with which we began. If Kojève declares that only the truth is the whole, and the whole must be complete for there to be truth, then he must make that claim either immanently, from within the "logic" of the whole itself, or from without—and, of course, to make the latter claim undermines the claim to finality.

Does this logic apply to negation as well? If it does, then negation would be interminable—every "final" point would in fact imply another, and so on ad infinitum. If no final point may be reached, then the entire structure of negation comes into question. Kojève is well aware of the difficulty, and his response seems to amount to a claim that negation comes to a final point that is in fact its starting point. Kojève considers this aspect of Hegel's logic its circularity and insists that circularity is necessary to any logic at all. Thus, negation persists until it reaches a point that resembles a return to its beginning—absolute negation leads to the complete negation of the given, a negation that may in turn be negated by a new beginning itself. Negation negates itself in the positing of a new beginning, and negation only negates itself when there is nothing more than itself as the given. We end up with a circular version of history in which the end of history designates that point at which history begins again. What Kojève describes is a variant of eternal return in which a finite series repeats itself exactly and infinitely, or at least potentially infinitely. The alternative, the infinite repetition of an infinite series, is outside the range of cognition, at least of nonmathematical cognition.[8]

Let me explain more carefully. Kojève insists that negation as difference depends on a given that is transformed over the course of time such that it appears only as the distant antecedent of a reality that is created wholly by negation. The narrative of negation that Kojève gives is essentially that set out in his commentary on chapter 4 of *The Phenomenology of Spirit*, the famous narrative of master and slave. There are two crucial elements in this narrative with regard to negation: struggle and work. Struggle is the political operation of overcoming the rule of the master over the slave; work is the operation whereby the slave transforms nature itself so as to become, in Kojève's blunt terms, "master of the world." While the relation of the two is not without ambiguity, Kojève seems to imply that each is in fact the necessary condition of the final realization of the other. (As we noted in chapter 5, the political revolution of the terror may well be the necessary condition for completion of the technological revolution permitting final liberation from the world of the master or the world suitable to the master and vice versa.) The entire narrative, in its extreme abstraction, describes a process whereby one world is negated in favor of another; in this sense, the negation carried on by the slave is the precondition of a new beginning. But it is not immediately evident from this narrative that the narrative will in fact repeat itself. Indeed, the final state achieved by the slave, the universal and homogeneous state, seems to be a permanent end in itself. There is, in this case, no apparent negation of the slave's negation, no new beginning; rather, there is a kind of stasis.

Is this an inconsistency in Kojève's account? Is Kojève's apparently circular logic not in fact linear? Moreover, if Kojève's logic is linear, then how is it possible for Kojève ever to claim finality, that a truly final state has been achieved? As I have already noted, the mere existence of a description of this final state suggests that it is not final or that there is some perspective that is not wholly assimilated in the final state. But if this perspective has not been wholly assimilated into the final state, then the final state is certainly not final, and so on. Kojève may counter that his account of the final state is merely descriptive, an articulation of the Logos of the Book, but one wonders to what extent such an articulation as articulation can really take place after history has ended and the need for articulation of the Book must seem superfluous.

To put the problem in different terms, if the end of history is the complete overcoming of individuality, the emptying out of the individual in the "trans-individual" universal and homogeneous state, why would anyone need to articulate that process? To be sure, there is the Book, but why would anyone read it? Would there be any "one" to read it? If, as Kojève acknowledges in a manuscript not published until 1990, "philosophy eliminates bit by bit all reflection to the extent that it transforms itself into Knowledge or Wisdom,"[9] then what would this reading be? Can one read "unreflectively"? By this I mean to question the possibility or, indeed, coherence of a reading that is not aware of itself as such. If it is aware of itself as such, then wisdom has not yet been achieved, since wisdom brings about the end of self-awareness, understood as a gap of sorts, the very gap that creates the reflexivity wisdom is supposed to overcome.

This is a complicated point worth considering. The achievement of complete self-consciousness is the extirpation of difference—there is nothing left to negate, nothing that is not known discursively. This is the day in which all cows are transparent white, a brilliant day that is not really even day anymore because night has been overcome: it is pure immanence. If the Book records the struggle and retains the memory of the struggle, such that one sees the dialectical tension that led to its own overcoming/sublating (*Aufhebung/suppression*)[10] or completion or consummation (*Vollendung*), then there can be no one left to read it because there can be no one left who is not fully transparent to himself—no one is left at all. We have absolute identity as the absolute negation of identity, at once positive and negative, pure being and pure nothingness, an "is" that "is not" insofar as determinateness itself has been overcome; identity and nonidentity are one.

Is this not the same state that Kojève critiques in the case of Parmenides and Baruch Spinoza? Once time and the concept are one and that relation has come to its fulfillment in a given narrative of narratives, how may one discuss that fulfillment without calling it into question? How may one speak after the end of history? Kojève seems to hold that one may speak only as Pierre Menard speaks, by repeating the words of the Book.[11] But is this speech? Of course, we have the problems I have already mentioned: Who speaks? And what does this "one" do in speaking? What is it to repeat syllables on a page—is that speech?

To declare the end of history is simply ironic; the declaration itself seems to belie the end declared. There is a stubborn homology with death here, to the extent that it is equally impossible to speak about the end of one's own history. Of course, there is the attractive dodge—that the end describes the state where all possibilities of life or historical action have been explored, the rest being "mere" repetition. But is there any such thing as mere repetition?

AUTOMATIC LIFE

Here we come to a governing issue in Kojève's later thought, that attractive dodge of repetition. If history comes completely to an end, then it seems quite obvious that any post-historical speech is nonsense, or "mindless" repetition, or ironic to the degree it is not mindless. If history comes to an end as the discovery of the new and turns into repetition of what has already come before, then repetition has a different function. In this sense, repetition returns us to the Greek concept of nature as Kojève characterizes it. We read and live the Book without exception or deviation or awareness that we are doing so.

We either negate so as to be free of negation—we become free by freeing ourselves of ourselves—or we negate so as to continue negating, the only difference being that subsequent negations are repetitions of the "first" negation and can only be repetitions of that first negation because it has already run through all possible forms of negation. If we are unable to do either, we find ourselves in a state of inveterate incompletion or indecision—in irony.

While Kojève entertains all three possibilities, the main thrust of the large corpus of writings that followed the *Introduction* is to elucidate the possibility and meaning of repetition in the post-historical state. In this respect, Kojève's later writings may be divided into essentially two groups, one setting out the actual shape of the post-historical order and the other attempting to prove conclusively that this order is already upon us, thus extending the course of arguments advanced in the *Introduction*. The second group of writings predominates, and it is reasonable to suppose that they dominate because of the difficulties I have described. The first group is, however, of enduring interest because it provides a detailed sketch of what the post-historical order may look like if it is ever achieved.

Another way of defining the relation between these two kinds of writings raises intriguing questions. It is quite possible to define their relation in terms of their proper "jurisdiction," since these writings are just as easily classifiable into writings applicable to thought and writings applicable to action. The writings that provide a sketch of the post-historical order seem to belong to the writings applicable to action, whereas those applicable to the process of thought and, above all, to providing a final account of thought seem to belong to the former group.

The division here between thinking and action is interesting, first and foremost, because it affirms a distinction that must itself be overcome in the end of history, where thought is action and action thought. Indeed, this equation of thought and action is a crucial precondition of finality, signaling the final consummation or overcoming of cognate tensions such as that between finality and negation. These various forms of tension as I have introduced them thus far—theory and practice, reason and will, sociality and individuality, and others—are all implicated in this comprehensive division between thought and action.

The overcoming of this division is a crucial element of the assertion that the concept is time. Hence the striking irony of Kojève's pursuit of two lines of finality, one in thought and one in action, an irony that is the correlate to the difficulties we have just addressed with regard to the relation between finality and negation. If history has truly ended, these tensions must be overcome—there can be no thought that is not action and no action that is not thought. This overcoming has to be the most startling consequence of the achievement of Kojève's philosophical project, and, to express my previous arguments with reference to the vocabulary of the relation between thought to action, there can be no further thought *about* action, no reading that is merely a reading. Everything becomes, strictly speaking, performative, or a performance that cannot be thought about or viewed as such, because nothing is thought about or viewed in the post-historical world.

But what sort of existence does this extraordinary unity describe? We seem to move within the circle of Eastern conceptions of mindless or intentionless action, *wu wei*.[12] Or we move within the circle of the notion of discourse promoted by Boris Groys, a careful student of Kojève, who views communism as the realization of the unity of thought and action in discourse.[13] In either case, we come to a point where thought can no longer be aware of itself, a lack of awareness that must also apply to language. The advent of the sage is the complete termination of the self-conscious actor, and the beings that are left seem to be no more than automatons that do not even know they are following patterns of thought or action. Another word for this kind of automation is "instinct," and here another reading of Kojève becomes available, to the extent that one can argue that the aim of history is to correct the error that is human being by giving human beings instinct.

What exactly does "giving instinct" mean? The Nietzschean phrase we have already cited once—that man is the incomplete animal—may allow the surmise that it is precisely the want of instinct that distinguishes the human being from the animal and that this want of instinct is a sign of incompletion. There is nothing terribly surprising about a claim such as this, given the relative values established in our tradition with regard to perfection and imperfection. It almost goes without saying that imperfection is to be eliminated, and the conventional link between desire and absence or a lack—a link Kojève of course affirms—merely underscores this attitude toward imperfection. Hence, the human being understood as an incomplete animal is imperfect and even defective; we are, in Kojève's memorable words, the "deadly sickness of the animal."[14] One would think, then, that the way to free the animal of this sickness would be to direct desire, and thus human action, toward eradicating it.

This is surely one of the tart ironies of Kojève's assertion that the most genuine expression of our humanity is to risk our lives in an attempt to attain completion, for is it not the fundamental import of recognition that one be recognized as complete, self-sufficient, fully worthy, like a god, and that this recognition itself be complete in every way? "Man can only be *satisfied* by being *recognized universally*; that is . . . man can only be satisfied by being perfect."[15] This perfection entails complete self-sufficiency. The perfect man needs nothing, depends on nothing—the perfect man is in both these senses truly universal.

One could identify sickness with dissatisfaction, with imperfection, with fear of death, and all the other limitations that impede our being complete and finished, in and of ourselves. There is good reason that Kojève equates individuality with crime.[16] The individual, as such, is a failure to overcome itself, a failure of perfection, for man achieves perfection only by transcending individuality, by self-annihilation as an individual. Individuality is a kind of defect for Kojève because individuality can arise only from a difference that cannot be resolved or understood in the accustomed language of the larger community in which that individual finds himself. To the extent that the individual is not fully clear to himself he cannot be fully clear to others, and therefore his proper worth cannot be universally recognized because that proper worth cannot be clarified to all.

The individual cannot thus free himself of his particularity, which is a particularity of imperfection or incompletion. The urge to finality overcomes these defects. Each individual recognizes the other and can recognize the other because this mutual and universal recognition is predicated on complete transparency, such that every individual is an exact replica, in all essential respects, of every other individual. The differences that one may attribute to the physical or animal being of the individual are thereby effaced. Moreover, every individual thinks according to the same principles and in the same way—error itself has been abolished. This similarity of thought is also a similarity of action, since thought and action are one in the truly universal and homogeneous state. We may thus finally argue that this uniformity of thought and action functions in a way that is an exact correlate to instinct, or even to a kind of computer program. In either case, the basic motive patterns of the individual are in every way the same; we may assume that every individual, when confronted in the same way with the same difficulty, is likely to react in the same way.

If this sounds something like what the underground man railed against in *Notes from Underground*, there is good reason for this similarity, because the underground man mocks and fumes at the enactment of a final system of rationality as represented by the Crystal Palace.[17] This fallen prince of nonsense cannot free himself of his own attachment to error, a certain kind of freedom, which is pitted against the sort of freedom possible for those who delight in the Crystal Palace. He cannot go gently into that good night; he cannot become nobody or an animal body that repeats the same actions when confronted with the same circumstances, the animal that is complete unto itself in its dealings with its surroundings. In the end, becoming nobody means becoming a creature of ritual, repetition—and bureaucracy.

Yet, as should now be clear, Kojève's attitude toward the post-historical state seems to be very ambivalent, as ambivalent as his varying descriptions of the slave's path to the post-historical state. On the one hand, he describes the post-historical state in terms of what appears to be a horrendous apocalypse, or the end of the human, with nothing attractive or salvific about it; better to remain in the confusion of history without a certain end than at the end of history. On the other hand, the achievement of a post-historical state seems to be the highest end of genuinely human striving, an end to be brought about and perfected at the cost of a comprehensive, final revolution, without which human life would not make any sense at all. Kojève offers, it seems, two radically opposed alternatives: a continuation of the nonsense of history that heads nowhere, achieves nothing, and speaks of itself in the plaintive tones of the underground man; or a history whose aim is to cancel itself out in a final end that frees human beings from the otherwise nonsensical muddle that history must be in absence of a definitive end.[18]

If we may put it so, the governing irony in Kojève's work is related not only to the practical task of achieving this final state but also to the question of how we can *know* it has come to be realized at last if one of the results of the institution of the final state is to eliminate the very consciousness that could recognize it as such. In fact, irony also extends to the desirability of the final state. Do we truly wish to become free by eliminating our animal existence? Do we truly wish to become universal through the most radical plan of de-individualization imaginable, one akin to death—if not literal, then metaphoric?

SENTIENT, NOT SAPIENT

If the expansive treatises Kojève wrote after the *Introduction* tend to deal with the issue of achieving the final state, the comments strewn throughout the *Introduction* itself bring up concerns about its desirability. The most famous of these is the note Kojève added to the original second edition of the *Introduction*, which came out in 1962.[19] This long note has occasioned a great deal of comment, to put it mildly, because it is proffered as a self-correction with regard to the date of the end of history and to the consequences of that end. As we have seen, the notes to the final lectures of 1939 are unusual insofar as their depiction of the final state, the universal and homogeneous state, does not fit well with the overall account of the advent of the sage and the Book. If the advent of the sage and the Book should be a welcome final event, the overcoming of history in the acquisition of final truth, the notes attached to these sections provide a very different account.

The added note of 1962 does nothing to dispel this impression. The note is appended to the twelfth lecture of the 1938–1939 series, and its playful tone belies its rather disturbing content. The note is connected not to the text but, in a typical Kojèvian gesture, to another note to the text, thus creating a comment on a comment on the original text. The first note discusses the consequences of the disappearance of man after the end of history. The disappearance of man is not a "cosmic catastrophe," nor is it a biological catastrophe. Indeed, Kojève suggests that the disappearance of man might be a boon for nature since, after the end of history, man is in accord with nature or the given. Kojève can say this because the end of history is nothing else than the establishment of a final accord or truce with nature, signaling that man has no more demands to make of nature, is indeed satisfied with nature, having overcome the deficiencies of nature and himself.

Keep in mind that Kojève identifies man's continued existence with error, if man does not seek to overcome that error by ending history. We also know that the elimination of error thus renders man in harmony with nature, even if that harmony has been achieved through the most thorough plan of domination over nature, that of the slave. Having come to this point of dominance, when there is literally nothing more to do, one finally succumbs to repetition. We might say that man, in having mastered nature or become "master of the world,"[20] has given himself instinct, so that he need no longer think or wonder, and wisdom describes precisely this instinct, a λόγος that writes human life once and for all.

The note from 1962 takes these conclusions a good deal further. Kojève recognizes, in part, the problem of repetition that we have just mentioned—if the human has departed with the advent of wisdom, then only those beings with instinct remain, beings that are satisfied, who have no human desires. How can beings such as these be the ideal celebrants of ritual or be those who might read the Book? As we noted, Kojève questions what language may mean for being such as these; after all, what understanding can mere repetition allow? The only kind of language suitable to the post-historical being is something like the language of the bees, a language that is not self-conscious, that is merely a set of signals that produce accustomed responses.

The stress is on instinct again, on the fact that the λόγος that governs these post-historical beings acts like a computer command or a basic code furnishing all possible reactions to a given stimuli. To repeat an example presented by Robert Brandom in *Making It Explicit*, one must distinguish between sentience, which describes the capacity to respond to certain stimuli in delimited ways, and sapience, which describes a relation whereby the stimuli themselves may be transformed or reoriented, where the being in question does not merely respond but transforms. For Brandom, only the latter attitude applies to human beings, and it hints at the gulf that divides humans as potentially creative actors from other beings whose possibilities for response are strictly delimited.[21]

The post-historical being has to incline to mere sentience, a point Kojève canvases with considerable humor when he discusses the similarities between the Soviet Union and the United States. Kojève insists that history ends with the 1806 Battle of Jena, and he attempts to bolster this point by suggesting that nothing significant has occurred since Jena and that both the Soviet Union and the United States are realizing the bestialization of humanity in states created purely to foster the physical well-being of their respective citizens.

But this darkly humorous view of sentience is complicated by the peculiar account of snobbery that Kojève introduces toward the end of the note:

It was following a recent trip to Japan (1959) that I had a radical change of opinion on this point. There I was able to observe a Society that is one of a kind, because it alone has for almost three centuries experienced life at the "end of History"—that is, in the absence of all civil or external war (following the liquidation of feudalism by the commoner Hideyoshi and the artificial isolation of the country conceived and realized by the noble successor Ieyasu). Now, the existence of the Japanese nobles, who ceased to risk their lives (even in duel) and yet did not for that begin to work, was anything but animal.

"Post-historical" Japanese civilization undertook ways diametrically opposed to the "American way." No doubt, there were no longer in Japan any Religion, Morals, or Politics in the "European" or "historical" sense of these words. But *Snobbery* in its pure form created disciplines negating the "natural" or "animal" given which in effectiveness far surpassed those that arose, in Japan or elsewhere, from "historical" Action—that is, from warlike and Revolutionary Struggles or from forced Work. To be sure, the peaks (equaled nowhere else) of specifically Japanese snobbery—the Noh Theater, the ceremony of tea, and the art of flower arrangement—were and still remain the exclusive prerogative of the nobles and the rich. But in spite of persistent economic and political inequalities, all Japanese without exception are currently in a position to live according to totally *formalized* values—that is, values completely empty of all "human" content in the "historical" sense. Thus, in the extreme, every Japanese is in principle capable of committing, from pure snobbery, a perfectly "gratuitous" *suicide* (the classical samurai sword can be replaced by an airplane or torpedo), which has nothing to do with the *risk* of life in a Fight waged for the sake of "historical" values that have social or political content. This seems to allow one to believe that the interaction recently begun between Japan and the Western World will finally lead not to a rebarbarization of the Japanese but to a "Japanization" of the Westerners (including the Russians).

Now, given that no animal can be a snob, every "Japanized" post-historical period would be specifically human. Hence there would be no "definitive annihilation of Man properly so-called," as long as there were animals of the species *Homo sapiens* that could serve as the "natural" support for what is human in men. But, as I said in the above Note, an "animal that is *in harmony* with Nature or given Being" is a *living* being that is in no way human. To remain human, Man must remain a "Subject *opposed* to the Object," even if "Action negating the given and Error" disappears. This means that, while henceforth speaking in an *adequate* fashion of everything that is given to him, post-historical Man must continue to *detach* "forms" from their "contents," doing so no longer in order actively to transform the latter, but so that he may *oppose* himself as a pure "form" to himself and to others taken as "content" of any sort.[22]

I have reproduced a large portion of the note because of its intrinsic interest to the issue of the post-historical epoch. The note first sets out the possibility of bestialization that might characterize the post-historical epoch and seems to follow from the various problems we have discussed above in regard to the period after the end of history. Against this train of thought, Kojève introduces here a basic notion of ritual: human beings may repeat actions that were once filled with the immediate force of struggle or desire without possessing anything close to the magnitude of that original force or desire. Put slightly differently, one can identify a marked difference between those who make history, who forge the essential pattern of history, that λόγος that ends up preserved in the Book, and those who merely repeat that λόγος. Among those who repeat, the original sense of the actions they imitate may be very remote indeed, but the actions remain as pure forms to retrace and imitate. What was once the creation of spontaneous human action, the negation of the given, now recurs as purely formal repetition.[23]

There are a number of interesting examples that may be adduced here, especially in terms of art, where the connection of Kojève's thought with the notion of the postmodern that appeared in architecture in the 1980s and 1990s is astonishing.[24] According to that notion of the postmodern, architecture and art become increasingly devoted to the rearrangement of forms that have already emerged, the possibility of new forms having become exhausted. All that is left to the architect or artist is the art of combining forms already at hand. What might have once been referred to as mere eclecticism is now all that is left to art, as an *ars combinatoria*. While Kojève does not go this far, it is evident that he also affirms something similar insofar as all that is left to human beings in the post-historical epoch is repetition of forms that were created in another time. The situation must be so, since by definition the end of history means that all possible forms of human action have been realized. Unlike the post-modern architect, then, the post-historical human being Kojève projects does not seem capable of new combinations of forms torn out of their original historical context—this implies a certain negation of the given that suggests that history has not ended. By contrast, Kojève's post-historical human being would simply repeat, without being aware of that repetition as having any other significance other than as repetition.

Here one might be tempted to compare post-historical life to a play or drama repeated endlessly in the post-historical epoch. The post-historical being is an actor who follows the guidelines of a role created once and repeated potentially infinitely afterwards. Since the post-historical human being could have no sense of self, even to confer a consciousness of his own position as an actor in a play would have to be impossible.

The obvious model for this kind of attitude is to be found in Martin Heidegger's distinction between inauthentic and authentic modes of existence for what Heidegger refers to as "Dasein." The inauthentic life, for Heidegger, is the life that does not become aware of itself as such. This is the life that is lived according to whatever conventions govern that particular life. The conventions are never called into question, never contravened (except as purely "mechanical" error to be corrected instantly); rather, they are followed, as we might say, "mindlessly," or more precisely, "unconsciously." That is, inauthentic Dasein lives in a kind of oblivion of his own life; he merely repeats the same patterns without even recognizing them as such. In this sense, we may say that the inauthentic Dasein is very much like an animal, having instinct, even if this instinct has been acquired through a struggle that had no model or template. What was first created in a conscious relation of struggle is now repeated without any notion of creation or struggle.

We say "unconscious" because Kojève is also getting at a central aspect of the kind of repetition that attends ritual—that it is not the object of thought. We seem to engage in a variety of these kinds of activities every day. They mimic, so to speak, our involuntary functions so effectively that it takes a considerable effort of thought even to recognize that these activities are acquired through human action. To the extent that we live without taking account of these activities, we live oblivious to them, and, if we are the post-historical beings of Kojève, we cannot help but live oblivious to them—if not, indeed, to all activities.

"Oblivion" is perhaps the best word to describe the post-historical state. It is a state of oblivious or blind action; it is the state in which human beings exist in a manner of total oblivion, as if they had managed to return to that inchoate beginning from which they came with the advent of the first act of human desire. But Kojève does not give us this kind of account, which is more in line with Jean-Jacques Rousseau, in any case. Though he may allude to Rousseau—how could he not, in dealing with Hegel's description of the master-and-slave relation?—he never directly refers to Rousseau. And this is curious, since Kojève's final state seems to seek to achieve the kind of completion that Rousseau identifies with the state of nature and tries to recreate in the notion of the general will.[25]

ERADICATING HISTORY AS BREAKDOWN

If we put this squarely within Kojève's own terms we arrive at a most unusual result. The aim of Kojève's account of history is to eradicate history; the aim of history is to overcome whatever gave birth to history in the first place. As we already know, history is associated with error, an error of nature, the correction of which we might describe as history. History, as a movement from an initial breakdown in the natural order to the reestablishment of an order that is no longer natural but created by the work of the human being, is nonetheless a correction in that breakdown in the natural order.

Kojève's thinking is in this sense a philosophy of breakdown or crisis. History is the overcoming or correction of that breakdown. To be human, to negate, is to negate the error that created the human in the first place. This surely has to be one of the most intriguing aspects of Kojève's thinking, since it is a thinking that seeks to eliminate thinking as error. In other words, Kojève tacitly reconceives the project of emancipation from nature as a project whereby the equilibrium of nature is reestablished through the action of human beings. If we indeed become masters of nature or of the world in a certain sense through the work of the slave, the final result of that mastery is the extirpation of the error that led to the human being in the first place. Our mastery is, from this perspective as well, a termination of the human or, better, the full expression of the human as coming to itself in self-termination.

To get a better sense of what Kojève is after, let us take the presumably contrary position. Human being is not an error but, rather, human beings are creatures of nature who either have a natural purpose or whose purpose is to design their own purposes; human being is a free, creative being—almost like a god.

If we take the first alternative, that human beings have a natural purpose, then we of course rob human beings of their freedom. There is no way to differentiate human beings from animals in this respect. All we might do is indicate that human beings are in the peculiar position of being able to grasp their own want of freedom. Error for the human being, in this scenario, is to not grasp one's proper place in nature, to offend against nature such that nature returns with a vengeance. Here we have an essentially tragic model of human errancy. The tragedy inheres in that we are conscious of ourselves as beings, that we sense in some fundamental way that we have a freedom or power to dispose of our own fate, but that in the end we find out that we are terribly deceived. Our efforts to overcome our destiny can only meet with failure and show us to be a being most unkindly disposed to be aware of its own limitations without being able to overcome or change them in any substantial way.

If we take the second alternative, that human beings design their own purposes, then we grant to human beings the most radical freedom imaginable. The human being is the self-creating being par excellence. Human being, in this respect, has no essence; indeed, the essence of the human being is to have no essence. All origins—and, finally, death itself—may be completely overcome. Now, one has to ask exactly what this notion of self-creation can concretely mean. What is it to be a being that is in a continual process of creating itself? Is such a being even thinkable? Moreover, is there a point at which self-creation becomes a possibility, the point of overcoming the mortality or death that seems to limit self-creation? Or is it indeed the very condition of possibility of self-creation?

The latter point seems prior. One may argue that only a limited being can possibly be creative and that the aim of creativity must be to overcome the limits of that limited being. What sense, after all, may one apply to the notion of an immortal or unconditioned being as a creative being? There are perhaps too many difficulties here, because the notion of an immortal or unconditioned being is itself so problematic. While our imaginary abounds in immortal beings, most of them bear a strong resemblance to mortal beings whose lives do not end. To imagine a being that does not live in time as a real limit, that has no fears for its own security, no needs to secure itself—to imagine such a being must be almost impossible, because it would be so utterly different from what we can possibly know, we who live within limits at any and every given moment. If we cannot imagine the immortal self-creating being, then we have to return to the first alternative, that human beings have a natural purpose. And if we do so, we give to creativity a necessary condition: that it overcome mortality. Our creative power has first a simple purpose that it must overcome in order to exercise itself with utter freedom.

The problem is that, once this is overcome, the being that might emerge is likely outside the powers of our imagination. If it has no need to create, why does it create? If there is no need prompting creation, what can creation even be? Does it coalesce in a form? Why would it ever choose to coalesce into a finite form, thus restricting its own freedom or returning, tacitly, to the finite world it has left behind? If the self-creating being cannot overcome mortality, then to what extent can it be self-creating? Surely it cannot be fully self-creating, because to be fully self-creating is of course to banish death as a limit, to banish any limits whatsoever. Thus the difficulty of imaging a being whose essence is to not take any one form or any form at all—pure self-creating sounds suspiciously like pure spontaneity and thus cannot be anything other than essentially inscrutable if it is to retain its curious identity. If it is not, therefore, fully self-creating, then to what extent, if any, can it create?

What can be the meaning of finite creativity? The finite in this combination refers back to a context, and creation, which is necessarily based in that context, can only realize itself as a negation of that context. But even that negation affirms the context. There is no absolute self-creation but rather a relative one, and is relative creation really creation? A relative creating is nothing like an absolute creation. A relative creation has to be an unfolding of the possibilities inherent in the original context. In overcoming the origin by negating it, one also realizes the possibilities inherent in it, since the negation always relates back to a conditioned starting point. Is this creation?

We end up with two very different models of creation—one infinite, the other finite. We can perhaps dispense with the first model fairly quickly, since infinite or unconditioned creation, the *creatio ex nihilo*, can only be an abstract supposition for human beings, who never find themselves capable of unconditioned creation because they themselves are conditioned, most fundamentally, by death itself. If *creatio ex nihilo* proves to be entirely impossible for human beings, radical self-creation can be little more than a deception or handy myth that flatters us with powers we cannot possibly possess. The second model seems to be the only one pertinent to human beings, and it proves to be far less flattering to human beings because it emphasizes that creation is not bringing something literally out of nowhere but only enumerating possibilities that must somehow be inherent in whatever context we are in. The origin dictates the possibilities of creation; the origin dictates the end.

If this is so, we come quite close to Kojève. Far from disproving Kojève's model of ostensibly creative development, we seem to be close to affirming it. Indeed, if we return to the opening discussion of this chapter, we see that Kojève's equation of the concept and time is a way of describing the complete unfolding of the possibilities inherent in a given situation. The key point to keep in mind is that all situations turn out to be the unfolding of an original situation; we can know no other beginnings than our own. The creative journey of Kojève's history turns out to be nothing more than the discovery of ourselves as created out of a certain historical context. But this creation is manifestly not a creation from nothing, merely the enumeration or expression of the possibilities inherent in the beginning. It is a self-unfolding of the individual that is concomitant with the self-unfolding of the whole to which the individual belongs—again the "I" that is "we" and the "we" that is "I."

THE FINITE GOD

Kojève finally rejects any homology between God and man that transforms man into God, capable of infinite self-creation or transformation. On the contrary, Kojève creates a finite God. That he does so is an accepted interpretation in Kojève scholarship.[26] But, of course, a finite God is not really a god at all. If anything, a finite God is a parody of God, since a finite God can free itself of its finitude only through an absolute act: suicide. The finite God may choose suicide freely—the master—or may choose the mediated suicide of the slave who works to liberate himself from himself in the end. In either case, the only truly Godlike act the finite God can take is to eliminate himself, to cancel himself out, to become nobody, either with the dramatic flourish of Alexei Kirillov or in the innocuous acquiescence of the bureaucrat, whether Stalinist or the architect of a universal bureaucratic state.

8

ROADS OR RUINS?

A work of poetry is never finished, only abandoned.
—PAUL VALÉRY

The extent to which Kojève's final works are themselves attempts
to complete the "Book" that the sage leaves behind is likely a question with no simple response. Although it is a well-known biographical tidbit that Kojève referred to himself as a "god"—perhaps ironically, perhaps not—it is also fair to say that Kojève's doubts about G. W. F.
Hegel's own achievement of this status apply equally to Kojève, who is no
better than Hegel at explaining why the end of history in the figure of the
sage is necessary. Indeed, a less generous mind might assert that Kojève's
own work, as philosophical propaganda ushering in the end of history,
makes no sense unless that end is *not* necessary; Kojève's ambiguous
admission that the end of history is a project merely confirms this want
of necessity.[1]

If this is so, then the works Kojève produced as attempts to "update"
or repeat Hegel's own have no greater right than Hegel's to be considered
the Book, within the terms Kojève himself employs. One has to conclude,
then, that the large corpus Kojève wrote after *Introduction to the Reading
of Hegel* amounts to an attempt to complete the Book from the precarious position of a project whose chances for completion are by no means

certain. The grand enterprise of philosophical propaganda that Kojève attempted to complete after the *Introduction* remained for the most part incomplete or unpublished, and this itself tends only to affirm once again the central difficulty of declaring finality.

If the end of history is the finite god or the sage, then the danger is that the point of absolute proof of this status—self-immolation—cannot come to pass, for the reasons I have already set out in some detail. While Kojève may deride Alexei Kirillov, it is by no means obvious that Kojève's finite God does not find himself in the same sardonically ironic position: to declare definitively the end of history is to kill oneself or become unconscious. If one does neither, however, one is in the uncomfortable position of writing tracts, of continually contemplating final status in a way that betrays finality. The act of betrayal, which I have already referred to as the act of Judas, is the ultimate acknowledgment of the comic pathos attendant on the finite God, who, in the end, is no god at all.

Kojève's immense corpus of post-historical writings attests to this pathos. They do so most spectacularly in the often strained, ironic jocularity that accompanies an evident delight in ornate complexity, which Kojève himself refers to as "preciosity."[2] Kojève's final writings proclaim a finality that they cannot seem to endure, or they address this finality by elaborating it obsessively, by digression, indirection, and, especially, an increasingly involved mode of presentation in which the proliferation of distinctions, terms, and introductions seems to belie the finality they all declare with studious monotony.

Yet this view is arguably unfair to Kojève. While we have abundant evidence of the ironic Kojève, this later work is also an impressively detailed and serious attempt to address the problem of declaring finality (and of *not* declaring it), a problem of which Kojève was perhaps only too keenly aware. More than that, the two most important strands in this later work, the juridical and the historical-philosophical, reveal the originality of Kojève to an extent that is simply not available in the Hegel lectures. Both *Outline of a Phenomenology of Right* and *Attempt at a Rational History of Pagan Philosophy* are intensely original works, even when we accept the pervasive influence of two fundamental narratives of Hegelian provenance: that of master and slave and that of the ascent to wisdom.

While Kojève generally claims merely to follow Hegel, both of these major works are heterodox. His exploration of right has little in common with Hegel's *Elements of a Philosophy of Right*, even while developing an entire theory of the final state on the basis of the master-and-slave narrative. Moreover, his capacious study of pagan philosophy has no direct equivalent in Hegel and creates its own interpretation of dialectical logic as part of a distinctive theory of discourse intended to negotiate a final narrative situated between silence and infinite conversation. In this instance, Kojève provides an enormously expanded version of his somewhat cryptic argument, featured in lectures 6, 7, and 8, from 1939, that the history of philosophy is essentially the story of the temporalizing of the concept, of its (and our) discursive liberation from silent eternity. The idea that distinctively human life is a liberation from eternity shows, without a doubt, the influence of existentialism, but, given its end in an ending, it might also be viewed as a critique or parody of existentialism.

Although many of Kojève's later writings have now been published, with the conspicuous exception of a large (900-page) manuscript written in Russian in late 1940 and the spring of 1941, it is by no means clear that Kojève wanted them to be published. The only major text he prepared for publication in his lifetime was the first volume of the *Attempt*. Hence, it seems important to confront the question of the authority to be granted these later, largely unpublished texts.

Kojève died suddenly. He did not leave extensive instruction about the publication of these texts, and it is difficult, if not impossible, to discern any firm intention on Kojève's part to have them published. Given the derisive attitude expressed by Kojève in regard to Raymond Queneau's interest in the publication of the *Attempt*, one might assume that Kojève preferred that his writings not see the light of day.[3] If this is indeed the case, then it should behoove us to exercise caution in examining those works that remained unpublished at the time of Kojève's death— with the exception of the *Attempt*, where we at least have a clearer intention to publish.

We certainly do not want to affirm Martin Heidegger's extraordinary attitude toward Friedrich Nietzsche, in his view of the *Nachlass* as the repository of Nietzsche's genuine thought.[4] Heidegger indicates, in a highly self-referential way, that the thinker holds back his genuine thoughts, merely permitting a glimpse of them (at best) in the published works. Heidegger suggests that a thinker's genuine thought should be reserved for the few capable of grasping that thought in the appropriate manner, a claim that also seems important to one of Kojève's friends, Leo Strauss. The so-called Straussian school is notorious for its open embrace of a "closed" or "hidden" teaching, an irony only some of Strauss's acolytes address directly. For Strauss, every philosopher worthy of the name has a hidden or esoteric teaching. The reason for hiding this teaching is that it is inherently dangerous to the city or society, since the philosopher is the one who thinks beyond the city.

Kojève is hardly sanguine about these kinds of philosophical fantasies, a point he clarifies both in his essay "Tyranny and Wisdom" and in his short essay on Emperor Julian.[5] Kojève is refreshingly free of the philosophical cant one finds in Heidegger and Strauss. On the contrary, Kojève pokes fun at both by suggesting that the cloistered philosopher is more a madman than a threat to the city, more ridiculous than dangerous.[6] The truly dangerous philosopher is the one who advocates action and does so with an open pedagogy that attracts not merely the few but also the many. For Kojève, all teaching for the few has the signal defect of its exclusivity. Instead, the philosopher reaches out to the many, seeking to universalize his teaching as the *only* confirmation of its merit. A teaching incapable of support from the many, if not from all, is simply ridiculous, a private teaching that prefers to consider itself superior, or for the few, rather than to recognize that its lack of success as a teaching for the many may signify nothing more dramatic than its fundamental inadequacy.

As a result, it seems to me wholly inappropriate to regard Kojève's unpublished work as a privileged esoteric teaching. Indeed, the fact that Kojève published so little in his lifetime points to a far more ambiguous attitude toward philosophy than either Heidegger or Strauss could ever have countenanced. As Kojève notes in his letter to Strauss about Queneau's proposal, he is careful lest he take himself too seriously. One might even argue, as another of Kojève's students does, that Kojève was essentially dissatisfied with his philosophic efforts and failed to publish them on that account alone. According to this view, Kojève was aware that he was not on the same level as the philosopher whom he aspired to supplant, Hegel, and despaired of his role as commentator.[7] This sounds like dubious speculation, and I would suggest that Kojève's reticence about publication has much more to do with his ambiguous relation to philosophy than with any lack of ability.

This ambiguity emerges in Kojève's notorious irony. While this irony certainly has to do with Kojève's claim that we are at the end of history, it seems to have as much to do with Kojève's general misgivings about philosophy. Those misgivings appear in his attack against philosophical esotericism, but they also are evident in his radical change in career. In the only interview he ever gave, to the journalist Gilles Lapouge, in 1968, Kojève delights in mocking the philosopher, claiming that bureaucracy is the more noble game. As we noted in the introduction, the notion of a radical change in thinking has been associated with no less than three major philosophers of the twentieth century, Martin Heidegger, Georg Lukács, and Ludwig Wittgenstein. But none of those thinkers took the radically different course that Kojève took. Kojève's transformation recalls—ironically, of course—the most famous nineteenth-century Russian transformation—that of Leo Tolstoy. Kojève's transformation resembles Tolstoy's insofar as Kojève could not cease to engage in philosophy while mocking philosophy. Moreover, Kojève turns to bureaucracy as the proper way to bring about a new society and therewith an end to philosophy.

Though it is prima facie outlandish to think of Kojève's becoming a bureaucrat as a sort of conversion comparable to Tolstoy's, there seems to me little question that Kojève viewed his turn to bureaucracy as an ironic or parodic conversion narrative with the same intent as most conversion narratives: to bring about a new (and final) world. In this respect—and typically—Kojève's ironic response to Lapouge reveals what seems also a serious project, for the end of philosophy resembles the bureaucratic state to the extent that all fundamental puzzles have been resolved; what remains is to promulgate and compel compliance with rules.

Given the complexity and ambiguity of Kojève's attitude toward philosophy in the postwar period, it seems wise to regard the unpublished writings with caution, not as containing a genuine or secret teaching but, on the contrary, as revealing both the necessity of and the difficulty inherent in attempting to say that final or last word. These writings, then, are an ambiguous coda riven with tensions that Kojève seems to have been unable to resolve to his satisfaction. They may thus be construed as works that, in declaring it, undercut his claim for finality and, in this respect, reflect the ambivalent attitude to the end that we have already discussed at length.

The following examination of these works focuses for the most part on two primary writings: *Outline of a Phenomenology of Right* (1943/1981) and *Attempt at a Rational History of Pagan Philosophy* (1968–1973; including Kojève's book on Immanuel Kant, which supposedly belongs to the *Attempt*). While I give an account of some other unpublished writings, I am of the view that these two works present the clearest and most original development of the Hegel lectures insofar as the *Outline* describes the order of the universal and homogenous state and the *Attempt* articulates in immense detail the central discussion of the relation of the concept to time that we have already recognized as a key aspect of the Hegel lectures.

While these two works seem to complement each other, one providing a "phenomenological" account of the postpolitical order in the postrevolutionary final state, the other setting out in great detail the philosophical basis for the achievement of that final state, there seems to be an odd tension between them as well. The tension is interesting precisely with regard to the prospect for finality. The *Outline* describes the basis for a final order that admits that the universal and homogeneous state is a "limit case," something akin to a regulative ideal in the Kantian sense.[8] The *Attempt*, on the contrary, seems at pains to assure us that the final state has already been reached. In this respect, the *Attempt* seems merely to extend a given set of arguments from the Hegel lectures, specifically those dealing with the equation of time and the concept, while the *Outline* stakes out its own territory and, as such, is an unusual work in the context of the Kojèvian corpus as a whole.

As I have already suggested, the very uncertainty about finality that the existence of these two volumes reveals points to a remarkable oscillation in Kojève's thought. Kojève offers a radical view of finality in the Hegel lectures that seems to be controverted by the *Outline* and ironized by the *Attempt*. If the underlying conviction in Kojève's thinking is the overcoming of the animal in the Aristotelian *animal rationale*, the ways of reaching this final end seem more plural than one might assume from a reading of the Hegel lectures alone. Indeed, as Kojève famously remarks in a letter to Leo Strauss:

Historical action necessarily leads to a specific result (hence: deduction), but the ways that lead to this result, are varied (all roads lead to Rome!). The choice between these ways is free, and this choice determines the content of the speeches about the action and the meaning of the result. In other words: materially <i.e., factually> history is unique, but the spoken <i.e., narrated> story can be extremely varied, depending on the free choice of how to act. For example: if the Westerners remain capitalist (that is to say, also nationalist), they will be defeated by Russia, and *that* is how the End-State will come about. If, however, they "integrate" their economies and policies (they are on the way to doing so), then *they* can defeat Russia. And *that* is how the End-State will be reached (the *same* universal and homogeneous State). But in the first case it will be spoken about in "Russian" (with Lysenko, etc.), and in the second case—in "European."[9]

This extraordinary comment makes two fundamental suggestions. First, that the end is not in question—"All roads lead to Rome!"—which, as we know, is hardly an innocent phrase but rather one that carries with it the entire semantic content of the final state, that "eternal state" or "city of God," which it is the essence of human history to achieve and for which the precondition to achievement has been met in the philosophy of Hegel. Second, that the way to this end state is not yet certain in the sense that the particular narrative has not yet become fully clear.

Let me explain this latter notion somewhat more carefully. Kojève indicates not that the road, as a factual matter, will be different but that the account of that road may be different depending on whether the United States or the Soviet Union ends up as the victorious entity that will submerge itself in the end state. In this respect, as I have noted before, the United States and the Soviet Union are, for Kojève, "metaphysically the same," though the language that each side uses is different. Both envision an essentially hegemonic bourgeois freedom that the end state will somehow transform into the profound freedom from the animal that remains the deepest postulate of Kojève's antibourgeois notion of freedom.

In this light, we may suggest that both the *Outline* and the *Attempt* represent different roads to the end state and that the tension between them has more to do with the modality of presentation than with the ultimate consequences they both presuppose. The greater difference, then, is between these later presentations of the final or end state and that presented in the Hegel lectures, including, of course, the note added in 1962, discussed in chapter 7. For the dire apocalyptic visions outlined in the Hegel lectures and the vision of the ritualized state are not at all evident in either the *Outline* or the *Attempt*. There may be a number of reasons for this difference, some of which I will discuss in chapter 9. It may suffice for the moment to argue that the Hegel lectures present a uniquely radical vision—perhaps the most comprehensive vision Kojève provided—whereas the later works, with all hesitation and irony taken into account, present those roads to the final Rome in a manner that shows itself to be yet another rhetorical road to the final state, avoiding the extremity of the Hegel lectures while hewing to their basic intent: the eventual overcoming of the individual, the animal self. In this sense, both these later works act as introductions to the final state.

THE UNIVERSAL AND HOMOGENEOUS STATE

Kojève's most significant work addressing the universal and homogeneous state, the proper post-historical society, is *Outline of a Phenomenology of Right*, written in 1943 but published only in 1981, at the insistence of Raymond Aron. If one sticks with the Hegelian model, as Kojève bids us to, by the title alone, this long text (586 pages in the current French edition) assumes a function for Kojève similar to Hegel's *Elements of a Philosophy of Right* as the most explicitly political of Kojève's texts. In it, Kojève offers an overview of the basic structures that pertain to the universal and homogeneous state as legal structures or as structures of what Kojève refers to as *droit* or *Recht* (right). Still, though the function and main concerns may be similar, this treatise, as I have noted, has relatively little else in common with Hegel's in terms of its specific content and structure.

Now, the first question that may come to mind is hardly superfluous: Why would one need a text such as this in the post-historical state, the universal and homogenous state? If the human being, meaning the "free, historical individual," is to disappear in the new trans-individual reality of the post-historical state, why take the pains Kojève does to sketch out what amounts to a basic set of constitutional guidelines for this state?

Would not the end of history lead to the abolition of the legal regime as such? If we have truly overcome individuality, then what sorts of offenses would even be possible? To put the issue more bluntly, if the post-historical state corrects the error that is the human on its way to overcoming itself, why would one need a regulatory system whose primary task is to maintain standards of correctness?

The obvious (but not necessarily correct) answer has to be that the *Outline* performs a function that is similar or complementary to that performed by the lectures included in the *Introduction* (whose publication was not even contemplated in 1943, when Kojève was writing the *Outline*). The *Outline* is in this sense another introduction to the final state or a *transitional* vision of the final state that must be implemented by political action. Like the *Introduction*, the *Outline* appears to be a work of philosophical propaganda or pedagogy, though of a more immediately practical order than the *Introduction*. Perhaps for this reason—and this reason alone—Perry Anderson refers to it as a more important work than the *Introduction*.[10]

This surmise is supported by the structure of the book itself, in which the second of its three main parts lays out a deft summary of the master-slave relation that is so central to the *Introduction*.[11] Unlike the later published version of the *Introduction*, however, this summary comes only in the middle of the text, after Kojève has completed an elaborate discussion of the basic components of what he calls "right." The emphasis in the *Outline* is clearly on elaborating a system of right, with the development narrative having a less fundamental role.

This system of right resembles a calculus or "logic" of action. It is the correlate or companion, as I have noted, to the *Attempt*, which develops the Hegelian notion of the concept to its fullest extent. Like that treatise, we may assume that the *Outline* plays the role of an introduction to the universal and homogeneous state, made necessary by the fact that this state has not yet been fully realized (or may indeed not be capable of full realization). While I do not intend to examine the *Outline* in detail as a major legal work in its own right, it is at least important, as an introduction to Kojève's later work, to present an account of the main features of it as a significant component of Kojève's philosophical enterprise, for the *Outline* is concerned with right in a very interesting way, as the essential calculus of action promoting the postpolitical, super-, or end state.[12]

The juridical system proposed by Kojève is thus explicitly hegemonic. It permits no remainder of custom or justice external to the system of right it proposes. It is universalist and final or, at the very least, points to a final system of regulation in the universal and homogeneous state.[13] Hence, the system of right that undergirds this state will no longer be merely one system of right among others but almost a sort of surrogate "instinct" or "program" regulating all individuals completely and finally.

To this end, the central thrust of the treatise is its establishment of an extensive adjudicative apparatus, akin to what Carl Schmitt describes in his major text on Thomas Hobbes's *Leviathan*.[14] We might say that Kojève writes the formal, legal groundwork for the Stalinist state, or for a state that considerably exceeds the Stalinist state in its totalizing tendency, since no one person can take a position of primacy.

The first section of the treatise sets out a very abstract formal or "phe-nomenological" account of the basic structural unit that ties the entire treatise together: the "juridical situation," which is a strictly formal rela-tion between three parties—two agents in potential conflict with each other (A and B), and a third, intervening figure (C) that seeks both to police and to adjudicate any possible conflicts. Kojève indicates clearly that this relation is not an abstraction, but he refers to it nonetheless as the simplest possible relation that may give rise to intervention or adjudi-cation by the third, C. The essential details of the juridical situation are fairly straightforward. For a juridical situation to arise, A must have a right vis-à-vis another, represented by B. "Right" describes the authority or responsibility to do or to refrain from doing an action. A has a right; B infringes that right. A acts or does not act; B reacts so as to cancel A's act or omission. C intervenes the moment that A's right has been infringed. C either simply stops the infringement or adjudicates or both.

There is no juridical situation when there are only two parties involved (the minimum for any relation whatsoever), simply because there is no possibility for adjudication.[15] This apparently straightforward point merits more careful consideration.

Adjudication is the crucial notion underlying the entire treatise. Adju-dication presupposes a conflict with an assumed procedure for its resolu-tion, the essence of right. In a conflict with only two parties, there can be no assumed procedure of resolution; indeed, the assumed procedure for resolution is, according to Kojève, the trajectory of history itself as the history of the master-slave dialectic. Therefore, a resolution procedure or right is only possible at or near the end of history, when the basically dyadic conflict between master and slave has come to a conclusion. Hitherto there is no genuine adjudication, only conflict, and a necessarily partial approach to the question of adjudication in the sense that the criteria for adjudication reflect the interests of one or the other of the parties to the conflict, either A or B.

Politics gives way to right, to the juridical situation. Kojève addresses the distinction between the political and the juridical relation by arguing that the former presupposes conflict between friend and enemy whereas the latter presupposes a more general amity.[16] In other words, the juridical relation presupposes general agreement among the parties as to the procedures and institutions of conflict resolution; it thus assumes that the desire for recognition, which gives rise to such conflicts, has been satisfied. If that desire has been satisfied conclusively, we have the advent of the universal and homogeneous state and thus a final perspective from which to judge differences, which themselves must be errors or the persistence in error, a persistence which may be incorrigible.

The treatise admits this difficulty somewhat by suggesting that the universal and homogeneous state in its "purity" is a "limit case," as noted earlier. Nonetheless, the comprehensive teaching of the treatise makes no sense without a firm presupposition that the juridical signals the end of the political. The end of the political, as Carl Schmitt feared, is precisely the universal state. Where the political finally ends, the juridical truly comes into its own as the authoritative ordering of action in the universal and homogeneous state in which the relation of master and slave has *begun* to dissolve.[17]

EQUALITY, EQUIVALENCE, EQUITY

Kojève devotes the second major part of the treatise to a discussion of this relation, which in many respects follows the discussion Kojève set out in the Hegel lectures. But there are some telling differences. Kojève develops the master-slave relation in the context of justice or the search for justice that underlies the development of a system of right. He grounds the concept of justice in equality, as we might expect, given the general tendency of Kojève's thinking, his persistent emphasis on equilibrium, balance, and harmony as the proper ends of truly human striving. He develops two different notions of equality that ground a justice of the master and of the slave. The justice of the master is based on an equality of recognition; a master recognizes other masters as equals insofar as they, like the master, show no fear of death. The justice of the slave is based on equivalence—it is a calculative understanding—whereby others have a position equivalent to that of the slave. Thus, the justice of the master is based on an equality of risk, that of the slave on an equivalence of position or circumstances.[18]

Kojève sees these two different relations as emerging from a deeper equality, that of the initial combat between master and slave, in which, at least at the beginning, both parties are equal.[19] It is the slave who forfeits this equality by voluntarily acceding to the master in return for his life. By forfeiting this equality, the slave voluntarily submits to the inequality between himself and the master, which distinguishes his status as slave. Yet there is also an equivalence here, albeit an inverse one: the master is equivalent to the slave insofar as the master values death above servitude and the slave values servitude above death.[20] Most interesting here is that the relation of equivalence is based on interests. The slave imputes an interest to the master that, as interest, is similar to what the slave expresses in refusing to risk his life. That this equivalence does not properly express the reason for the master's risk, or expresses it in terms of the notion of interest, merely indicates the radicality of the qualitative difference between the two, notwithstanding their ostensive underlying equivalence.

The striving of the slave, the work that creates society and thus a juridical polity, attempts to regain the slave's original position of equality in the sense that the rights of the slave will come to be equivalent to the rights of the master. The slave will come to enjoy the freedom of the master, though, to be sure, this freedom will still be marked by interest; the slave's interest in self-preservation leads to a desire to overcome the master not by facing risk but by eradicating it. The ultimate end of the slave's striving is to create a state in which equivalence reigns, in which all citizens are equivalent on the basis of the equitable management of what amounts to self-interest. Nonetheless, Kojève insists that the slave's regaining of equality leads not to a return to the original position but to its fullest unfolding as a historical development, which is equivalent to the development of the slave's interest in overcoming his fear of death by transforming the world through work and transforming his relation to the master through struggle.

Kojève refers to the two models of equality in the sense of historical struggle, as aristocratic right against bourgeois right. Kojève calls the final relation of these two equalities the "right of equity" (*droit d'équité*) and claims that it is in fact a synthesis of the different kinds of justice applicable to the master and the slave in the person of the citizen, who fuses both.[21] What exactly this fusion means is somewhat more delicate. How may one fuse a right of risk with a right of conservation or self-preservation?

This is perhaps the most delicate question in the treatise because it brings out the difficulty of the end of history. If equity is the final mode of justice reflected in the final system of law, what exactly does this mean? Does this final satisfaction entail a freedom from self-preservation, its elimination? The distinction between the two forms of right gives rise to concern; if the master has no regard for self-preservation, the slave's entire being is defined by it. The end, for the slave, is final satisfaction, the vanquishing of death. This is the slave's version of suicide. The slave comes to be like the master in a radically different way, while the result, a kind of self-immolation, is clear. The animal fear the slave overcomes by the conquest of nature is utterly different from that of the master. Hence the question: How can the two possibly be reconciled? What can equity mean?

In the Hegel lectures, Kojève wavers in a very significant way. On the one hand, Kojève asserts that the slave transforms his servitude in the final revolution by making revolution, thus risking his life for an ideal.[22] On the other hand, Kojève holds that the animal triumphs because that is all that remains—the new being created by the slave is essentially like an animal, since it is "programmed" and, consequently, no longer conscious of death. The slave does not kill the animal in order to overcome it; rather, the slave becomes fully animal. If the first case is somewhat murky—what brings the slave to conquer servitude through risk so late in the game?—the second certainly does not seem to be an *Aufhebung* (overcoming/sublating) in the Hegelian sense, in which both master and slave are preserved in a harmonious balance. Rather, the master *as* master disappears and does not reappear in the slave, other than as that which drove the slave to most fully express his animality.

Equity would seem beset by similar difficulties. If the slave's work aims at annulling risk, then the slave overcomes the master by refuting his position. Hence, as in the previous case, that position is only incorporated in the slave's equity as a position to be overcome; it is preserved or conserved as overcome or discarded. As a result, the slave's equity emerges as a system of mutually beneficial exchange that sounds a lot like an idealized form of capitalism. The "bourgeois" in bourgeois right comes to dominate the notion of right as a system of equivalences that seems little different from the economic system Karl Marx describes so brilliantly in the first few chapters of *Capital* or, for that matter, from the reified social relations that emerge within that system.[23]

Perhaps Kojève's irony lies in the fact that the system in effect reduces the slave to taking up positions of equivalence. All are equivalent, and particularity or individuality thus disappears. In attempting to overcome servitude, the slave only most perfectly expresses servitude to a regulatory system that seems to be the precursor of the type of ritualized structure Kojève famously describes in his 1962 note to the Hegel lectures. The remarkable aspect of this account is its similarity to the accounts of reification, in Georg Lukács, and technology (*Machenschaft*), provided by Martin Heidegger.[24] The de-individualizing final state is the machine state or the state of complete reification. The victory of the slave ends up transforming the interest of the slave into a nullity or an interest that describes the self and the whole because what has taken place in this final juridical order is the perfect reconciliation of whole and part.

The corollary to this elimination of interest in the name of interest is the elimination of thought in the name of thought, which is at the core of the later presentations of Hegel's philosophy, when Kojève reprises, with obsessive attention to detail, his discussion of the reconciliation of time and the concept. Hence, we might make an argument to counter our previous claim about the radicality of the Hegel lectures, for it may now be evident that Kojève's later works pursue the notion of de-individualization, of reification, with superbly consistent logic. That is, these works are just as radical in intent as the Hegel lectures, but they differ in that they provide a more subtly nuanced picture of the various kinds of possible movement toward the end state. The roads to the end are indeed varied.

SOPHIA, PHILOSOPHIA, PHENOMENOLOGIA

Kojève seemed to have worked on a methodical presentation of his interpretation of Hegel's philosophy from the end of the 1930s until the mid-
1960s, when he seems to have abandoned further attempts at this presentation. The appearance of the *Introduction*, in 1947, may seem to have
rendered additional writings irrelevant. But Kojève obviously did not
hold this view, because he wrote thousands of pages after the appearance
of the *Introduction*.[25] One may identify two general projects that remained
mostly unpublished until after Kojève's death. The first is the remarkable
manuscript that Kojève seems to have completed at lightning speed in
1940–1941. The second is the series of texts that, taken together, constitute an enormous text of 1,292 pages that develops in prodigious detail the
crucial insight about the evolution of the identity of the concept that
Kojève sketched out in the 1938–1939 lectures.

The 1940–1941 manuscript, *Sophia, Philo-sophy and Phenomeno-logy*,
was discovered in 2003 in the archives of Georges Bataille, to whom
Kojève had entrusted it before fleeing Paris in 1941. This large manuscript, some nine hundred pages of handwritten text in Russian, remains
unpublished, except for two fairly short excerpts (81 pages in all) culled
from the introductory sections and published in Russian in 2007 and
2014.[26] The excerpts reprise aspects of the 1938–1939 lectures, particularly the focus on the notion of wisdom as perfect self-knowledge, at least
in regard to the decisive questions one may pose to oneself. Kojève once
again points out that the conclusion that wisdom cannot be achieved is
an essentially theist position implying the existence of a reality which by
its very nature is not accessible to philosophy. In this same vein, he
argues that genuine philosophy must insist on the attainability of wisdom through human thought, a position that brooks no gods of any kind
and is thus atheistic. Kojève goes on to attempt to prove that wisdom
may be achieved, that thought may bring closure to itself consistently.

He works through this point with an argument that he attributes to
Hegel: to know one thing really as it is, one must know everything connected with it, and since everything is interconnected, one must end up by
knowing all connections of any kind in order to know the one thing truly as
it is, without omission, in its fullness. Kojève gives the example of his desk:

The circumstance that it is impossible to know my chair if this knowledge does not include knowledge of the universe may be explained by
the fact that every real material thing is in reality connected with the
entire remaining material world and is factically inseparable from it.
Someone expressed this circumstance very perspicuously, saying that
the match I light affects even the sun. Every real thing interacts with all
remaining things, and they all form, in this way, a unified whole [одно-
единственное целое].[27]

Now Kojève turns this argument back to the beginning: if I am to know
myself, then I must know all these things and the interrelations among
these things and myself. For Kojève, this means knowledge of the things
as they are and the multiple relations we might have with them, because
"it is often forgotten that the real universe includes not only all real, material things, but also all people actually living with their consciousness,
knowledge, thoughts, conversations, etc." Kojève's notion of totality is
vertiginous, comprising not only the things "themselves" but also every
possible relation among them and among those who encounter them in
the course of history. Indeed, one might argue that the course of history
is nothing else but an exhaustive account of this encounter.

Jorge Luis Borges comes to mind. "Funes the Memorious" is an experiment in totality. The eponymous main character, after being injured by
a horse, acquires a most unusual trait: an unlimited memory. He remembers not only things but his relation to the things and, indeed, any number of other relations to the things.

We, at one glance, can perceive three glasses on a table; Funes, all the
leaves and tendrils and fruit that make up a grape vine. He knew by
heart the forms of the southern clouds at dawn on the 30th of April, 1882,
and could compare them in his memory with the mottled streaks on a
book in Spanish binding he had only seen once and with the outlines of
the foam raised by an oar in the Río Negro the night before the Quebra-
cho uprising. These memories were not simple ones; each visual image
was linked to muscular sensations, thermal sensations, etc. He could
reconstruct all his dreams, all his half-dreams.

Funes remembers everything connected with any given moment, and
everything is connected with any given moment, so his memory expands

exponentially. It expands so vastly that Funes gradually finds himself incapable of functioning in any way, much less remembering the past. As the narrator notes, "I suspect, however, that he was not very capable of thought. To think is to forget differences, generalize, make abstractions. In the teeming world of Funes, there were only details, almost immediate in their presence."[28]

The dissolution of Funes's memory into grasping things in their particularity points to a dreadful problem: that the specific historical recovery of things renders them so complicated that they cease to be the things they were. Their generality dissolves as they are placed within an expanded set of particular relations, the result being that one would have to narrate the story of every thing and of everything possible thought about that thing. Since each impression grasps an aspect of the thing and of its interrelation with other things, any number of combinations is possible.

While Borges insists on the infinite here, Kojève seems to take the opposite position, insisting that the whole must be delimitable in the end or it is not a whole. And if it is not a whole, then it can contain no consistent parts, because they cannot clearly be understood until their final determination within the whole.[29]

Kojève's argument for the comprehensibility of the whole as such arises from the comprehensibility of the basic formative principle of that whole. Kojève maintains that this principle is the dialectic. The dialectic organizes all relations to the thing through a process whereby things are posited, negated, and combined in a form that in its turn will be posited, negated, and combined, until the process can continue no more and returns to its beginning. This circular pattern, which Kojève stresses time and again, organizes the process of giving and taking answers to the questions one may ask of oneself, so that at some point all answers may be given and one comes back to the beginning.

How does one know when this point has been reached? When is it no longer possible to go further without returning to the beginning? We come up against the same difficulties we encountered earlier in this connection, because it must be difficult to know with certainty when one is stuck in a loop of repetition, when the possibility of something new occurring has been reduced to zero.

In this respect, we might examine a thinker of the opposite tendency, Kojève's favored foil, Martin Heidegger. In the 1930s, Heidegger began writing a series of remarkable texts, the so-called Ereignis manuscripts. Heidegger's stated purpose in the first of these texts, *Contributions to Philosophy* (1936–1938), is to get beyond an impasse—that philosophy has become routine, its foundational terms "used up" or "exhausted."[30] Heidegger seeks to overcome the impasse of an exhausted mode of thinking with a wholly new way of thinking. As many have noted, however, the *Contributions* are striking for their repetitiousness, a point Heidegger himself seems to stress, perhaps to mark subtle differences. Yet Heidegger's attempt to overcome an exhausted tradition nonetheless ends up in an extraordinary litany of repetitions as he tries to express what has hitherto been incapable of expression in the tradition.

Heidegger's experiments in the Ereignis manuscripts may be taken as evidence of Kojève's thinking, that the tradition is indeed at an end because the attempt to break new ground shows itself to be impossible. There is nothing more to unfold in the tradition, novelty ending up identical to nonsense—one surrenders to the "madness" cultivated by the underground man.

Still, Kojève's arguments are haunted by their internal inconsistency. How may one speak of completion without implying the opposite? The mere act of speaking about completion as completion seems to imply that there is a position beyond that completion or one that has not been assimilated to the completed position yet. Despite the ingenuity and power of Kojève's unpublished manuscript, the problem remains unresolved. On the contrary, Kojève seems to have expended a great deal of effort on overcoming this fundamental difficulty, as his subsequent works, most of which remained unpublished at his death, show. When does repetition become otiose, a sign of failure (as in this very chapter itself)?

THE SYSTEM OF KNOWLEDGE
(*LE SYSTÈME DU SAVOIR*)

The later series of manuscripts constitutes a somewhat fractured whole consisting of three introductions to Hegel's "system of knowledge" (*le système du savoir*). The first two introductions are contained in a volume that was abandoned in 1953 and first published in 1990, called *The*

Concept, Time, and Discourse, while the third is the first part of the enormous *Attempt at a Rational History of Pagan Philosophy*, ultimately comprising three volumes, the first of which was published in 1968.

This immense work is an incredibly, obsessively involved elaboration of the suite of three lectures (8, 9, and 10) from the *Introduction* dealing with the relation of the concept to time, which I discussed in some detail in chapter 5. Indeed, it seems that Kojève dedicated the rest of his philosophical career to developing the basic schema he discussed in the Hegel lectures, a fact that attests to the significance Kojève attached to this analysis as the cornerstone of his interpretation of Hegel, if not of his entire philosophical career.

The Concept, Time, and Discourse consists of two separate introductions to the Hegelian system of knowledge. Kojève indicates that three introductions to the Hegelian system are in fact required to allow the contemporary reader access to it as a phenomenological account (in the Hegelian sense) of the relations of the concept to time, which culminates in the identification between the two declared by Hegel. This temporalizing of the concept, or the introduction of time into the concept, is the primary event that creates the history of philosophy as the history of the concept included in the identity of the concept itself. The concept is history and history is the concept.

I am not going to discuss *The Concept, Time, and Discourse* in any detail.[31] Suffice it to note that the first two introductions describe the concept and time, respectively, as mediated by the philosophical tradition—by Aristotle, in the case of the concept, and by Plato, in the case of time. The third introduction, which we will discuss in detail below, deals with the interrelation between the two, which Kojève then proceeds to describe in laborious detail in the history of philosophy that follows upon that introduction. These introductions are all a concerted and detailed defense of Kojève's interpretation of 1938–1939. Perhaps their most distinctive departure from these lectures is the heightened emphasis on the centrality of discourse. These introductions contain none of the pathos of the 1938–1939 lectures. Gone are the disturbing accounts of the post-historical state in favor of an enhanced account of repetition, both in the sense that the introductions themselves are intended to prepare the reader for an updated repetition of the Hegelian system and in the sense that repetition is the consequence of the end of history.

THE UNFINISHED END: *ATTEMPT AT A RATIONAL HISTORY OF PAGAN PHILOSOPHY*

The crowning work of Kojève's philosophical career, and the only book he published himself, is indeed the third introduction, the unfinished *Attempt at a Rational History of Pagan Philosophy*, the first volume of which appeared shortly after Kojève's sudden death in 1968. Two subsequent volumes appeared in 1971 and 1973, for a total of 1,292 pages of text. According to some accounts, Kojève planned to add a history of Christian philosophy as well, but it may well be that the volume on Kant discovered among Kojève's papers after his death was the final volume in the series, since Kojève almost never speaks of Christian philosophy.[32] Whatever the case may be, the scope of the work is forbiddingly monumental, a philosophical opus whose size matches or surpasses that of the great Russian novelists Kojève so admired.

The *Attempt* has not received anything near the attention of the Hegel lectures of the 1930s, and even allowing for the historical significance of the latter, it is not hard to see why.[33] Whereas the Hegel lectures are, for the most part, luminously clear and sharply formulated (in marked contrast to Hegel's *Phenomenology of Spirit* itself), the *Attempt* is a wholly different text that makes very few concessions to its readers. The detailed descriptions of the Hegel lectures simply pale in comparison to the elaborate, playful, and precious constructions of the *Attempt*. This preciosity is in evidence in the florid title itself, which, like many other aspects of the *Attempt*, is at once comprehensive *and* tentative.

The word *essai* comes from the French verb *essayer*, "to try" or "to attempt," and is most celebrated in French literature because of Michel de Montaigne's *Essais*, itself a large and involved text. In Montaigne's hands, the essay is truly tentative, unsure, an exploration that does not come to certain, final conclusions, an exploration that does not cancel itself. But a "rational history" (*histoire raisonnée*) is quite a different genre that has a far stronger identification with totality, though not to the extent of an encyclopedia. Indeed, the *histoire raisonnée* could be quite an eclectic compendium—even an eccentric one. This combination of differing generic identities seems to be singularly ill-suited to the task the *Attempt* undertakes—a complete history of Western thought, showing that it has and must come to an end. The first formal signpost in the text is itself a sign of a differing or opposed intention that seems to be a wry comment on the ambition of the text.[34]

Nothing in the first few pages of the text dissuades us from this irony. The opening paragraphs develop a set of related problems. To begin with, Kojève notes that the history of the evolution of philosophy is also at the same time a philosophical comprehension of history that includes itself in that comprehension. This latter assertion is the troubling one, because it assumes that the philosophical comprehension of history can include itself in itself.[35] The nerve of the problem here is this: How can my comprehension of X be also a comprehension of my comprehension of X? There seems to be an illicit doubling, for how can I comprehend one thing and my comprehension of that thing without suggesting that I am comprehending from yet another perspective, which is itself not comprehended? In other words, if the doubling is illicit, we have the makings of an infinite regress that from the outset undermines the very possibility of completion and finality held out by the history itself.

We may draw on a mathematical analogy: the problem of the biggest set, the set holding all sets. If there is a set of all sets, it cannot belong to itself. For if it did belong to itself, then it would not be the set of all sets but rather a subset of itself. A similar concern seems to apply to Kojève's philosophical comprehension—if it includes all aspects of the history of philosophy, should it not include itself as well? But if it includes itself, the inclusion indicates that that history is not over.

Thus, Kojève immediately raises a red flag about his project, and a fairly serious one, because it suggests that the totality sought in the work itself may not be achieved. Still, Kojève may respond that the repetitive lack of closure is itself a closing move that can only repeat itself continuously, thus serving as a signal of finality in that sense, as a finite pattern repeating itself continuously.

If we look back at our other comments about this problem, we see that it raises the issue of perspective we discussed in chapter 7. And it does so fairly obviously at the very beginning of the work. But Kojève does not leave it at that. He brings up, immediately thereafter, in the second paragraph, another problem that is possible only because of an underlying difficulty in identifying the whole.[36] This problem is a variant of the hermeneutic circle that asks whether it is possible to examine anything in a way that does not merely reinforce the approach one takes in that examination. The hermeneutic circle suggests that the process of interpretation is essentially shaped by the initial approach, though the reason for interpretation is to get beyond that perspective or to understand its origins in a way that transforms or at least illuminates that original approach.

Kojève is much more teasing with this second problem. He notes that it is not prudent, at the beginning of one's work, to discuss why that work is not going to succeed. But he also says that he puts this potentially vitiating critique up front out of honesty, so that we may appreciate the scope of the problem and its impact on how we are to deal with it. He calls this an introduction to his introduction—yet another doubling effect. But if one thinks a bit more carefully, the irony of Kojève's declaration begins to emerge. How can one discuss the failure of one's work as a work of sense? Here the venerable problem emerges, the classic critique of a certain notion of skepticism: How is it that the skeptical critique that suggests, say, that sense is in the end indeterminable or fluid makes sense itself? Is it not the case that the skeptical argument contradicts itself insofar as we may understand it, as it is indeed cogent and persuasive? The very fact that the argument is coherent or can be understood seems to work against what it seeks to say. To say "I am not making sense right now" is of course problematic, because the phrase itself makes sense.

SENSE, NONSENSE, AND PSEUDO SENSE

The problem of sense becomes the central problem of this exceedingly complicated essay. Kojève's extravagant beginning emphasizes the problem by the very fact that the essay communicates effectively, or at least purports to do so, a concern that by its very nature puts that communicability at issue. If sense can never really become transparent to itself, if its contours are not capable of being defined once and for all, then what sense we have is either essentially false or misleading, because it is merely a fiction of sense that hides its own fragility or precariousness. This seems to be a central claim of Kojève's, that sense, if not defined with reference to finality, is either merely an illusion of sense, because the final identity of that sense cannot be attained, or, in this respect, is a kind of fiction or "pseudo sense" that we create. Indeed, we cannot but create fictions if there is no final or ultimate standard.[37]

Of course, one may counter that the absence of a final standard does not necessarily entail that what we hold to be the case at a given time is a fiction. If there is no final standard, then there is no standard from which to derive the correctness of a given point of view, but also none from which to derive its falseness. Where there is no falseness, there is no correctness—there is neither the one nor the other. We merely hold certain things "to be the case." Yet it is difficult to maintain such a position, because any assertion that something is the case seems to carry with it an implicit assertion that we may rely on that assertion, that it may hold for more than one example of that case. Indeed, if the case is not a hapax legomenon, an isolated instance, this shows us that a larger claim is inevitable.

Kojève argues thus that we cannot help but make broader claims if we make any claims at all. If these claims are merely provisional, claims made without any assurance of reliability, then they essentially undermine themselves as claims. One begins to speak nonsense or "pseudo sense" because sense is not possible; no sense we give to a term can prove itself to be anything but temporary or provisional.[38] We return to the beginning with the renewed question about sense, since the problems can be very effectively conveyed to us. Although the problems call the possibility of sense into question, the fact that they may do so effectively, that we can communicate these problems effectively, tends to be at odds with the problems themselves. Kojève's basic argument is that sense must be fully determinable to be determinable at all. Finality is the crucial precondition of sense; without the possibility of a final judgment that shows us where all things lie, there is no possibility of judgment at all, no possibility of sense.

Kojève reprises here the madness argument in a much more sophisticated form, though the essential point is the same. If we are unable to ascertain a full and final discourse that by definition binds all, then we have not eradicated subjective certainty, the root element in madness. To put this in different terms: if we cannot eradicate subjective self-certainty, it is not clear how any regime of understanding is possible among differing kinds of subjective self-certainty. The assumption of a generality whereby different discourses can be reasonably brought together cannot be maintained. In its stead, one has a series of differing views, each of which denies any connection with the other. The only way to open that connection is by compulsion, whereby one party forces the other to accept its subjective self-certainty.

The balance of the introduction to the essay is devoted to an exposition of the possibility of sense as the possibility of philosophy itself. By putting the question so, Kojève sets the main issue as not merely one of finality but also as one of finality that allows us to be free of skepticism and the otherwise wretched tissue of error that comes from not knowing where or what one is. Kojève puts the issue in the simplest of terms: if there is no possibility of attaining to wisdom, then philosophy can be only the study of error. But, indeed, it cannot be even that, because without a final standard, philosophy cannot be a meaningful discourse—or, as Kojève says, it can be only a discourse of pseudo meanings, essentially mendacious or misleading, and indeed infinitely so.[39]

Kojève's discussion here echoes discussions of the identity of philosophy in other works that he left unpublished at the time of his death. Kojève is always concerned to differentiate philosophy from theology and, still further, to distinguish theistic philosophy from atheistic. Both theology and theistic philosophy reach some point where reason alone must falter. Philosophy that is skeptical about the attainment of wisdom is, for Kojève, largely theistic if it still posits truth, because it must locate wisdom not in human reason but in the superior "mind" of another, namely in God. Atheistic philosophy either fails completely, there being no final point at all, or it locates that final point within reach of human intelligence—the final point is available to human reason. Human beings can become wise without a God holding their wisdom for them.

Kojève sets out to do nothing less than prove that philosophy can attain wisdom and complete itself, that there is no need for theology or theistic philosophy, both of which are expressions of skepticism.[40] Kojève seems to go further than this to the degree that he claims that philosophy cannot make sense of itself unless it can be completed, if only in principle. If philosophy cannot be completed, if the whole cannot be made explicable in toto by reason, then we remain enslaved by powers that we can neither understand nor combat. We can never become free of an unclear existence; we can never overcome our lack of instinct by negating the confusions of animal existence through the construction of a self-contained reason. We cannot become masters of ourselves, no matter what ironies may finally accompany such mastery.

The central difficulty we have discussed, the impossibility of declaring finality consistently, is the central concern of the *Attempt*, which labors to dispel the doubts occasioned by Kojève's extravagant claim that Hegel has brought history to an end. Kojève's approach insists on demonstrating that a final end not only is necessary for any ultimate assertion of sense but also may be achieved through a logic that, if owing a lot to Hegel, seems to go beyond him decisively in its attempt to assert that a final view of history is possible. Thus, the problem brought about in the *Introduction* emerges once again in the *Attempt*: How can one reconcile negation with finality? Is there a way in which negation comes to an end "naturally"?

IS PHILOSOPHY (SENSE) POSSIBLE?

Kojève's arguments are extremely involved and possess an almost scholastic technicity which I do not have the space to reproduce in full here, though, according to Kojève, full reproduction may be the only way to communicate these arguments effectively. As a consequence, I confine my account of this immense work to two crucial aspects of it: first, the account of the temporalizing of the concept, the principal "subnarrative" of Kojève's wisdom narrative; and second, the division of philosophy into three basic elements—ontology, phenomenology, and what Kojève refers to as "energology."

The main thrust of the arguments contained in the 162-page introduction to the *Attempt* should not surprise. Kojève reprises the principal argument of his 1938–1939 lecture course with regard to the relation of the concept to time. He does so, however, by accentuating the dialectic quality of the evolution he sought to outline in the earlier lecture course. The continued focus on the evolution of the concept that Kojève first developed in the Hegel lectures affirms both the importance of that scheme and the inference that Kojève in some fashion sought to write a final account of his account of finality. Before proceeding to that argument, I want to canvas briefly several other arguments that set the scene for

Kojève's much more comprehensive treatment of the evolution of the concept.

The first of these has to do with the identity of philosophy itself. Kojève identifies philosophy with discourse and the concept. The primary philosophic entity is the concept, and Kojève works to confer a sense on the concept. As he says himself, the task of philosophy is to grasp the sense of the concept, regardless of its appearance—what Kojève refers to as its morpheme.[41] A beginning step in this process is determining the distinctness of the philosophic concept, and Kojève does so by reference to discourse, specifically to the self-consciousness of discourse as a combination of all discourses into a comprehensive whole. Kojève holds that philosophy is, above all, the discourse that asserts the concept and then proceeds to define the concept—to confer *sense* on it, in Kojève's definition of "sense" as a complete explicitation of all discursive possibilities constituting the concept.[42]

The explicitation of this sense is indeed the history of philosophy itself. All knowledge, insofar as it is discursive, is philosophical and subject to examination in the process of reflection that is the essential movement in the explicitation of sense.[43] In a way that recalls Heidegger, Kojève comes very close to suggesting that the various kinds of discourse, from astronomy to literature, are incapable of asking questions about themselves. Indeed, Kojève presents a view of philosophy as the discourse that examines the questions that arise from particular discourses about themselves.[44] Unlike Heidegger, however, Kojève insists that this process of questioning is inherently reflective and governed by a specific logic of reflection, which Kojève unfolds in the introduction. This way of approaching philosophy is, Kojève affirms, distinctively Kantian and an immense extension of the authority of philosophy as the governing discourse of all discourses; philosophy is discourse having become conscious of itself as such. Philosophy thus becomes the discourse that clarifies the sense of discourse, no matter what subject matter a specific discourse governs. Philosophy, while no longer queen of the sciences, retains an immense authority as the articulation of what discourse is—insofar as discourse has sense. Philosophy sets the parameters for sense through the concept.

Kojève then sets out two further arguments before taking up the evolution of the concept in earnest. The first of these arguments is largely negative and seeks to question the validity of three important kinds of discourse—sociology, historicism, and psychology—all of which are "antiphilosophical" in suggesting that philosophy, as the overriding discourse of sense, is impossible. Kojève seeks to show that these discourses are flawed to such an extent that they cannot make sense of themselves as discourses.[45]

Kojève's main target is sociology, which he accuses of permitting a vicious relativism because of the ostensibly neutral position it takes toward different truths, in the way we commonly say that there are "different truths for different people." Kojève notes that history aids sociology in asserting this point: different peoples may have different histories that are all quite acceptable on their own; there is neither a singular truth nor a singular history to which we must adhere.

Kojève questions the sense of this proposition and the sense one may make of the assertion that the truth can be several, even contradictory or essentially partial, for if the truth is essentially several and partial, is there really any truth at all? And if there is no truth, then what enduring sense can sense have? For Kojève, it comes down to a replacement of philosophy with ideology.[46] The universalist claim that Kojève associates with philosophy has to dissipate, as does the authority of universalism—or, for Kojève, any authority at all. To make the point more sharply, the notion that one may retain an opinion without need for further reflection because all is "opinion" or "self-interest" or "the way I think" must itself become antiphilosophical precisely because it denies the reflective, synthetic role of philosophy as an organizing discourse about discourse, the task of which is to integrate various discourses into a final harmonious whole. Without this possibility of integration—as long as one totally ungrounded and ungroundable or dogmatic phrase is uttered—philosophy becomes impossible.[47]

Sociology as such assumes the impossibility of philosophy. The sociologist knows only different practices and ways and does not claim to be able to know anything more. Kojève seems to view the sociologist merely as one who assumes the impossibility of philosophy; he remains silent as to whether that impossibility is desirable or not. For Kojève, as I have noted, the more salient point, at least initially, is not the desirability of philosophy but its possibility. Kojève's concern, however, cannot simply be reduced to a defense of philosophy as a significant discourse. On the contrary, at issue for Kojève is the possibility of sense itself. This is Kojève's "plea" that the sociologist is a kind of sophist selling whatever wares he can without regard to their quality. Like the sophists, the sociologist has no criterion of truth. Discourses may come and go, and the more "learned" one is, the less concerned one is with engaging in the foolhardy insistence on the superiority or correctness of one discourse as opposed to another. One faces multiplicity—history tells us so, our experience of sheer variety tells us so. Why should we insist on limiting that variety? Dare we? Can we?

Kojève is clear: without philosophy, all we have are false or pseudo discourses. If we cannot defend or assert them on any basis, they literally are just positions we *might* take—we know not what and cannot know why. It is not merely that political authority might dissolve but also that any orientation of any kind might dissolve into non- or pseudo sense. The consequence Kojève draws from this is the obvious one: the condition of retaining a partial view is that one not think about it vis-à-vis other views. One merely holds on to the view, which is a kind of given whose meaning and authority are never subject to question.

Sociology is thus a refusal to think in any way other than the accustomed one. Sociology may in fact offer multiple kinds of thinking, might allow one to become more "well rounded"—traveling does one good, according to the old adage; "Tout comprendre et tout pardonner" (To understand all is to forgive all); and so on. One does better not to think, and one ends up in dogmatism the moment a question arises.

Kojève next approaches psychology, and his main target in this section of the text seems to be Sigmund Freud.[48] The specific bone of contention is the notion of the unconscious. Kojève's objections should be fairly clear by now. Since Kojève argues that it is the singular duty of philosophy to assert the ultimate accessibility of wisdom, to claim that one can become fully self-conscious, the notion of an ultimately inscrutable unconscious is completely vexing. Modern psychology not only creates an unconscious but also turns that unconscious into a virtually inexhaustible resistance to the transparent self-knowledge that Kojève sees as the ultimate form of wisdom, of adherence to the philosophic maxim "Know thyself" (γνῶθι σεατόν). What is more, psychology creates a virtually infinite market for itself by demanding that analysis clarify the unconscious—clarifying what, by its very nature, must always resist clarification. Psychology does not talk about an unconscious that can be eradicated or completely recovered but rather about an unconscious that becomes less threatening, understood in its resistance to understanding, a sort of perverse *lux ex tenebris*.

Kojève proceeds from acquiescence to the impossibility of knowledge about history and society to acquiescence to an equal impossibility embedded in the individual. In both cases, the underlying concern is with an acquiescence to authority—either that of the given or that of mystery, the unknowable—that has a great deal in common with a vitiating fatalism or pessimism about the capacity of human beings to do anything but act in error. Human beings simply collapse in a muddle that both promises and defies description, that promises openness and freedom at the cost of our being able to know where and what we are. Here we rely on what we do *not* know.

Nietzsche, for one, seems quite amenable to this idea. Nietzsche praises the Greeks for their "learned ignorance"—their superficiality that comes from profundity, from suffering, from recognizing that there are "dangerous" truths that it would be better for us not to know.[49] Nietzsche may not turn ignorance into a virtue with ease, but he does call into question, with great severity and ingenuity, the insistence on clarity and openness that seems so crucial to Kojève.

Still, it is all too easy to be deceived. Kojève's position is not necessarily a moral one or about what one ought to do in a moral sense. Kojève's position is about sense, period. How can we possibly make sense of ourselves if we are convinced that we cannot even know these selves, if we remain in some mysterious, chthonic way estranged from ourselves? Our claim to rationality—to the extent that rationality remains restricted—is purely spurious for Kojève. To insist that there are things we simply cannot know or can know only in part is, for Kojève, if not nonsense, then what he calls pseudo sense. If we cannot know that what we know is indeed what we know, without the agency of a God or an ideology of some kind, then we are simply condemned to endless chatter that is, in Kojève's memorable phrase, equal to silence.[50]

If speech is equal to silence, we have effectively suppressed what makes us distinct from other animals. The thought that may permit us to move beyond the sort of animal desire Kojève describes in the Hegel lectures proves to be nothing more than the dupe of that desire. We end up in the world of instrumental reason, of reason as tool of the desire not to be liberated from, but to serve, animal desire.

SELF-REFERENCE AND SELF-INCLUSION

The polemic is familiar. Kojève proceeds with two arguments in support of philosophy, one new, one an extension of older arguments. It should be obvious by now that, for Kojève, philosophy demands sense, demands achievement of complete knowledge as a condition of distinguishing itself from these other self-defeating and deluding discourses. Philosophy must become complete. If it cannot do so, then the human being is nothing but a comic and tragic creation, condemned to endless muddle and struggle, suffering without purpose.

Kojève's new argument, if it is indeed so new, takes aim once again at the problem of complete self-consciousness as a reductio ad absurdum. Let us take the classic example of a person looking at the wall.[51] Who is looking at the wall? We may say that X is looking at the wall. But we soon recognize that X cannot be simply silently looking at the wall. If X were simply silently looking at the wall, he could not communicate that action. X can only communicate that action by discourse, and X can only employ discourse if he recognizes himself as looking at the wall.

The basic point is that communication requires awareness, and awareness involves a doubling of X, whom we might call the subject, with the wall as object. X is in effect aware of himself as looking at the wall. But we have not yet answered the initial question: Who is looking at the wall?

Let us call nonverbal X, X^1 and verbal X, X^2. X^2 describes X^1 looking at the wall. How does X^2 know this? Or, again, who is X^2? We know who X^2 is because X^3 describes X^2, who describes X^1. For Kojève, everything comes down to this X^3. If the explanation does not end with X^3 but has to have recourse to an X^4 to explain X^3, then there is no way to call a halt to the progression, which becomes infinite or endlessly indefinite—in going on without end, it goes nowhere.[52]

The argument that posits a progression ensures that no matter how far along we get, there will always be another X, unknowable in itself, that gives us the preceding X. This puzzle of self-consciousness is a major problem for the post-Kantian tradition—is the self essentially unknowable or not convincingly knowable or not? For Kojève, as we might expect, self-consciousness comes to complete self-transparency only when the concept is fully unfolded in history; the concept is nothing other than this history itself, as we have seen. Hence, Kojève attempts to get around the difficulty of an indefinite chain of (non)-identification by arguing that history must come to an end. Not only does this coming to an end create the basic contour of identity, but also the identity itself must appear, because in no other way is coherence possible.

This latter argument is difficult. Why must identity appear? For Kojève, coherence is a *project*. Thus, if we speak Kojèvian, we argue that identity must appear in the end because it is the final result of the continued process of negation that must in the end come to an end at the cost of being considered negation, a process—indeed, anything at all. The vaunted negation Kojève describes must be determinate and can only be so if the process of negation is finite. Kojève essentially denies that any process that is not finite can deserve the name. To make this claim, it is noteworthy that Kojève simply dismisses mathematical examples out of hand. He argues that mathematics is not discourse, not conceptual, but rather a form of silence, and thus one can only infer that Kojève denies the availability of the linguistic analogy to mathematics.[53]

Discourse, to be discourse, must therefore have a sense, and a clearly definable sense. If this sense is not clearly definable, the discourse is either nonsense or pseudo sense; that is, it is a discourse that is not immediately absurd, like "It flatly lookout cheese," which is nonsense, but something more like "Birds fly upside down," a phrase that does make sense though it may be shown to be only partially or incidentally true. Kojève goes against the tradition of "trans-sense" (заум) discourse in Russian poetry and, it seems, would be very circumspect about so-called poetic license. He essentially denies the validity of discourses that seem to be untranslatable or not interpretable. He is refreshingly honest in this respect, claiming that a discourse whose meaning cannot be placed within a definite framework is inadequate.

The key point Kojève makes in this section of the text is to defend the possibility of closing interpretation of an action off at the level of X^3. His claim is based, as should not surprise, on the dialectic logic he develops at length in the first volume of the *Attempt* and which may already be somewhat familiar from the previous chapters of this book. To reiterate: Kojève argues that discourse must have sense to be discourse. Further, the sense cannot be indefinite or infinite and still be considered sense. Hence, any discourse must at some point or another come to an end; it must be capable of finite development. Indeed, the end of this finite development of discourse is, for Kojève, the end of history, the complete discourse, which can no longer change but can only be repeated. In our example, then, Kojève admits the relation between X^1 and X^2 but claims that this relation must be finite if it is to be properly discursive. And if it is finite, it can be run through completely by X^3, who can do little more than ensure that a complete account is available such that the only possibility of continued description has to be realized as repetition.

Why is there no need for a further party? Why no need for X^4 or X^n or X^{n+1}? This will become more obvious when we come to a discussion of the logic Kojève develops to bolster this account. However, there should be no surprise about this logic, since it is the same dialectic logic one sees everywhere in Kojève's work. This logic involves only three positions, with X^3 being something like the synthesizing agency who describes the progress of the dialectic movement immanently, as it were, since to describe the logic is to understand it completely. Let me move on to this logic.

DIALECTIC

The account Kojève presents in the *Attempt* sets out dialectic logic in a different way, which in itself is an interesting move for one who claims, as Kojève does, merely to be repeating the thought of the master to fit it to the needs of a different time. Kojève uses the clichéd division of the Hegelian dialectic into thesis, antithesis, and synthesis, with a new element that Kojève calls the "parathesis."[54] The thesis performs its accustomed role as the positive statement, as does the antithesis, the negation of this positive statement. This positive statement is of the utmost importance and is preceded by what Kojève refers to as a "hypo-thesis," "being the intention to speak in order to say whatever might nevertheless have a sense."[55] This leads to a sort of "first" discourse—or, indeed, any discourse—that acts as a starting point, the positive statement that is the thesis generating its antithesis and preparing the way for a final synthesis, achieved after (perhaps many) parathetic interventions.

While the possibility of having a starting point in any discourse seeking to make sense is certainly an innovation, the fundamental difference in Kojève's treatment lies in his interposing a parathesis whose logical functioning is prior to the synthesis; the parathesis is an expression and elaboration of the introduction of time into logic via the dialectic. The parathesis plays a dynamic temporal role, for it too may be divided up into the triad of thesis, antithesis, and synthesis; thus, one has a parathetic thesis, a parathetic antithesis, and finally, a parathetic synthesis. The parathetic differs from all the other thetic positions by its partiality. The parathesis draws on the thesis, antithesis, and synthesis only partially—a parathetic thesis is thus a partial assertion of the thesis. The same holds for the antithesis and for the synthesis, which can only be a synthesis including differential proportions of the thesis and antithesis.[56]

The essence of the parathesis is to permit blends of the antagonistic elements in the thesis and antithesis. These blends represent attempts to attain a synthesis of thesis and antithesis in order to avoid an immediate contradiction leading to a synthesis that simply cancels itself out. In this respect, Kojève offers his famous example: I walk into a restaurant and tell the waiter that I want a beer and don't want a beer. Evidently the waiter turns away without knowing what to do because, strictly speaking, there is nothing to do, no guidance for thought or action, until the two contradictory positions have been worked out.[57] To avoid this state of affairs, Kojève invents the parathesis as a way to finesse the obvious contradiction. So I want a beer, but I want a beer in ten minutes. Kojève's example deliberately introduces the element of time, to suggest that the contradiction presented by the thesis and antithesis if both are asserted at the same time may be averted by differentiating them in time, by introducing time into the logic of the concept as a parathesis.

The basic idea is that the parathesis cancels itself out by going through all the possible combinations of declaring thesis and antithesis, until one is finally ready to arrive at a final synthesis. This final synthesis is nothing other than the result of the interplay of the parathetic. The possible combinations—the contradiction between thesis and antithesis that at one point led only to mutual canceling of each other or to a full contradiction—may now unfold as the *temporal* movement from the thesis through to the synthesis. Kojève insists that it is only by reference to time that one can come to a solution to the problem of immediate contradiction that emerges with the assertion of thesis and antithesis without regard to time.

The parathesis is therefore Kojève's way of describing the various combinations of thesis and antithesis that lead in the end to a synthesis, which is the fulfillment of the concept and history as concept. Perhaps the most unusual aspect of this part of the *Attempt* is that it returns so dogmatically to the schema developed in the Hegel lectures from 1938–1939. The original thesis is that the concept is eternity. The original antithesis is that the concept is non-eternity. The paratheses are of course three: that the concept is eternal, relating to the eternal outside of time; that the concept is eternal, relating to the eternal inside time; and, finally, that the concept is eternal, relating to time itself. The final result of this structure, the totalizing synthesis, is the expected equation of the concept and time—Hegel's basic achievement, according to Kojève.

Again, as we might expect, Kojève matches up this dialectical structure with the same philosophers he names in the 1938–1939 lecture—excluding Baruch Spinoza, whose prominent role in those lectures has been eliminated. The rest of the *Attempt* is an enormously detailed history of the various philosophers, with the expected end in Hegel, an end that returns Kojève to his beginning with the Hegel lectures of the 1930s.

This result may seem a meager reward for wading through the many discussions of the Introduction to the *Attempt* and to its numerous expositions of important philosophers. Yet the *Attempt* cannot be overlooked. It is a sophisticated development of the central idea of the lectures from 1938–1939, with two important differences that need to be emphasized: Kojève drops the language of negation so prominent in the *Introduction*, and he places strong emphasis on repetition. Gone as well are the striking, if horrific or apocalyptic, descriptions of post-historical humanity. In their stead is an insistence on repetition, the notion that, no matter what we might think, we are in a time of repetition from which we cannot easily escape, if we can escape it at all. Moreover—and most importantly—the purported logical innovation of the *Attempt* sheds light on a fundamental aspect of the principal narratives of the Hegel lectures, that of master and slave and the ascent of the sage to final wisdom. Both these narratives are distilled by the logic Kojève outlines in the *Attempt* into an underlying narrative of the temporalizing of the concept.

The temporalizing of the concept is the complete articulation or explicitation of sense. In different terms, the concept is its own history, and the primary movement of that history is to turn away from two "eternities": the initial silence from which the concept liberates us and the endless chatter that is equivalent to silence, which afflicts us if we find ourselves unable to accept the basic promise of philosophy—the ascent to wisdom or final truth. Within the terms of the master-slave narrative, the temporalizing of the concept is a description of the work the slave takes on and a response to the impasse of the master. Yet for this work to be truly emancipatory it must come to an end; otherwise, the incomplete character of the work imposes a slavery without end, the kind of slavery to dogma or mystery that Kojève identifies as a key aspect of the skeptical demeanor. This latter characterization of slavery puts the problem of incompletion in a new light, since incompletion is for Kojève an acquiescence to perpetual slavery. Of course, one may respond—and this response is practically a continuous refrain of the present study—that the alternative is hardly encouraging. For to end history in repetition demands the fortitude Nietzsche associates with the eternal return. It demands that we see our lives as wholly temporal and passing and welcome that aspect of life, without remorse or revenge, as true liberation. The earnest ambivalence of Kirillov returns to haunt Kojève's project *as a project*.

One well-disposed critic put the matter succinctly: the *Attempt* is a suffocating work. Time and again it tells us there is nothing left for us but repetition, that reason has no creative force whatsoever but is to be defined precisely as noncreative.[58] Yet this is not the only caution. One begins to wonder whether creation was ever possible in the first place. This is a much more aggressive point that reveals one of the consequences of the a priori–a posteriori structure of Kojève's logic, for if the a priori structure determines its shape as we see it at the very end of that development—so that we can fairly say that in my beginning is my end, and the reverse— how can there be any room for creativity? The development in history, if it is to prove to have a Logos, and precisely the self-reflective Logos that sees itself finally and fully reflected in its own history, could never have been otherwise. What might have seemed to be a free choice turns out to have been necessitated by the Logos that allows us to understand that act as such. Thus, the act could not have been free, could not have been creative in that sense, but only disclosive of a possibility that was "always already there" in the logic itself. No creativity, in terms we might normally associate with the modern artist, is available in Kojève, and, for that matter, an art unavailable to rational critique would be nothing more than non- or pseudo sense. Hence, the free modern individual of the Hegel lectures can be nothing other than an error corrected at the end of time.

ENERGOLOGY

In the remainder of the *Attempt*, Kojève offers an expansive context for the unfolding of this temporal (or spatiotemporal) logic in his division of philosophy into three principal parts: ontology, "energology," and phenomenology.[59] These parts ostensibly correspond, in Hegelian terms, to the logic, the philosophy of nature, and the phenomenology. To complete my brief account of the *Attempt*, I outline the fundamental components of this division as constituting yet another innovation that complicates the ostensibly faithful relation to Hegel's thought that Kojève never tires of affirming.

The most unusual term Kojève uses in this division is of course "energology." He grants to energology an important systemic function as a mediating element between ontology and phenomenology in determining the truth of the discourse of philosophy on its way to wisdom, the final truth.

Kojève first clarifies the relation among these three different elements of philosophy in his account of Democritus's thought, contained in the opening volume of the *Attempt*. He relies on the simple metaphor of a house with three floors. On the ground floor, we encounter "empirical existence," the "subjective," or "phenomenal reality," which phenomenology considers as its proper subject matter. On the main floor (*bel étage*), we encounter what Kojève refers to as the "objective reality" that corresponds to the subjective, phenomenal reality. On the second floor, we encounter "Being-given" (*l'Être-donné*) as such, the proper concern of ontology, according to Kojève.[60]

If *phenomenology* and *ontology* are terms that have a ready history beyond Kojève's description of them, *energology* does not. Kojève describes it in the following terms:

> Democritus projects an *energo*-metry [which, in any case, remains for him in the state of an "implicit" project since he only makes explicit an energo-*graphy*] that in fact demands as a philosophical "complement" an *Energo*-logy that no philosopher had hitherto made explicit as such and which will be made explicit only to the extent philosophers will try to take into account (discursively) the Physics founded by the atomists insofar as it is Energo-*graphy* and -*metry*.[61]

Kojève distinguishes here between accounts of phenomena that are rooted essentially in measurement and a philosophical account of physics or "nature" that is discursive, rooted in the concept and its dialectical structure. What is he getting at?

Kojève denies that there can be a direct philosophical account of nature or natural processes.[62] He makes this point clear in the Hegel lectures, where he is radical enough to claim that there can be no philosophical knowledge of nature, for if philosophical knowledge is based in the concept, and the concept is the product that arises from the negation of nature, it follows that there can be no direct conceptual, and thus no philosophical, knowledge of nature. Kojève goes so far as to say that to make such a claim—that there can be a conceptual account of nature—was Hegel's principal error, one that undercut his otherwise epoch-making equation of time and the concept.[63] As we have noted previously, nature, as what is negated, has no positive identity in itself other than as the product of negation; nature is understood only as relative to the humanizing work of the concept. Hence, Hegel's claim that there can be a conceptual understanding of nature as it is in itself is, for Kojève, tantamount to making the claim that Hegel, like God, has created nature. In short, Kojève completely rejects Hegel's monism.[64]

Kojève's concern illustrates in the bluntest possible terms a fundamental postulate of his thinking: we know only what we make through the work preserved in the concept.[65] If this is so, then any claim to conceptual access to nature puts us in the position of the creator of nature, a veritable God, rather than of the one who negates nature, the finite God that Kojève has us become at the end of history.

Still, if this is so, then one might be tempted to ask why Kojève bothers with energology at all. To grasp what Kojève is after, it is important to consider why Kojève deems it necessary to interpose energology as a mediating element between ontology and phenomenology. For the purposes of his account of energology, Kojève defines ontology as the branch of philosophy that seeks to give an account of being as given (*l'Être-donné*) and insists that ontology deals with what is common to all phenomena— that they *are*, as opposed to not being. Kojève defines phenomenology simply as dealing with empirical experience (*existence-empirique*) inhabited by different things or "monads." If ontology concerns what is common to all things, their homogeneity, phenomenology concerns their difference, their heterogeneity, and for Kojève the question that arises is how the homogeneous can possibly relate to the heterogeneous. How does undifferentiated being appear as differentiated in beings?[66] Energology deals with "irreducibly opposed" elements, whatever they are in differing conceptions of physical process.

Energology, in this context, has to be something like a discursive account of the many attempts to clarify this relation and its completion: "By observing physicists, philosophers become discursively aware of the Objective-reality with which they are concerned and they see it at once directly 'in the light' of Being-given and in the reflected light of empirical-existence which are the phenomena."[67] The light imagery here may be slightly deceptive insofar as, for Kojève, philosophy represents a project of completing the discursive account of reality, but it is otherwise quite clear: a discursive account of energology articulates the changes in the mediating element, from Platonic idea onward.[68] Energology is a mediation that finally consumes itself as such, along with the difference it mediates, this consummation being the completion of history.

By "discursive account," I want to emphasize another important aspect of Kojève's energology. As I have noted, Kojève holds that there is no properly discursive account of nature itself. The only discursive account of nature is one that presupposes nature as negated—as unavailable in itself—and this is how Kojève describes the understanding of nature as "energography" and "energometry." Both of these terms refer to scientific accounts of nature as physics. For Kojève, the science of nature, physics, is concerned with the measurement and management of nature, and he associates energometry with quantum physics and energography with classical mechanics.[69] Natural phenomena are reduced to mathematical models that turn away from the phenomena in order to grasp what is common to all of them. Yet these attempts, understood discursively, are essential components in the creation of a durable (indeed seamless) relation between the one and the many that overcomes all possible contradictions.

To put the matter differently, the relation of the three elements of philosophy bears a more than passing resemblance to the dialectical and parathetic logic Kojève unfolds in the *Attempt*, with ontology and phenomenology taking the role of thesis and antithesis and the various forms of energology offering a parathesis seeking to bind the other two into a durable synthesis. Thus, when Kojève proceeds to detailed accounts of Plato and Aristotle in the second volume of the *Attempt*, he divides each into three sections: ontology, energology, and phenomenology. He proceeds in the same manner in the final volume of the *Attempt*. Hence, it seems reasonable to suggest that the energological moment in these various accounts describes the mode whereby what is ostensibly indeterminate and eternal, being itself, is linked to what is inherently temporal and differential, the phenomena that inhabit what Kojève refers to as empirical existence. In other words, there is a homology between the framework Kojève outlines in the introduction to the *Attempt*, that of the temporalizing of the concept, which takes place through many different combinations, though the most important of these are only five. In this respect, it is intriguing that the third volume of the *Attempt*, aside from its astonishingly baroque account of Proclus (among others),[70] directs so much attention to a school of thought that he tends typically to pass over in silence.

With Kant, the supposedly final volume of the *Attempt* returns us to the list of six thinkers that Kojève considers most important (Parmenides, Heraclitus, Plato, Aristotle, Kant, and Hegel). We do not know whether Kojève really planned to write an extensive account of Christian philosophy. All we have left of that project is his book on Kant, which dates from the same period as the *Attempt*. Still, Kojève insists in this book that Kant is the *first* genuinely Christian philosopher. To complete my sketch of the *Attempt*, I want to address briefly this most provocative statement about Kant, as a way of returning to what constitutes for Kojève's Hegel's decisive move. Kojève makes his case on the first page of his Kant book:

> On the one hand, Kantian "empiricism," which is at once a complete reiteration of anti-Platonic Aristotelianism and an anticipation of authentic Hegelianism, in fact determines the radically *atheistic* character of Kant's System. By the same token, his identification of the human in man with "pure Volition," that is, with creative Freedom or, to use Hegelian language, negating Action (active Negativity), makes of the Kantian System the authentic philosophical expression of *Judeo-Christian* anthropology which culminates in Hegel.[71]

This thought takes us all the way back to Kojève's statement cited at the beginning of the present study: "The pagan way: become what you are (as idea = ideal). The Christian way: become what you are not (yet): the way of conversion."[72] The pagan belongs more properly to the "natural" world of the master, the Christian to the "artificial" world of the slave. The pagan world is marked by necessity and an impasse: one reaches a final point and repeats, a whole monistic system of repeating phenomena constituting the cosmos in which man is included. The Christian is radically dualistic and presupposes both combat with the master and the creation of work as an emancipatory activity recorded by, and finalized in, the full discourse of the concept—the full discourse of history itself as the account of the slave's emancipation in the figure of the citizen of the universal and homogeneous state.

For Kojève, Kant's contribution is crucial because he introduces this radically new idea of volition.[73] Where Kant does not go far enough for Kojève, however, is that he retains the notion of the "thing-in-itself" that ensures the impossibility of the complete transformation of the natural world into a human artifact. By retaining the thing-in-itself, then, Kant remains essentially unable to make the fundamental Hegelian move toward finality; for Kant, according to Kojève, history cannot come to an end. One is thus left with an unending struggle to end that is dangerously close to skepticism. Perhaps even worse, Kant's prescriptions for action function on the basis of an "as if." One acts "as if" that action could have a decisive impact on the natural world, whereas in truth it cannot because the thing-in-itself ensures the infinite distance between the activity and its goal.[74]

Kant leaves one at an impasse and, in this sense, anticipates revolution from a position that precludes its possibility.

TERMINAL TRANSITION

Kojève's postwar works refine and emphasize with exhaustive thoroughness the impossibility of novelty, of change that is not repetition, for all those living in the post-Hegelian age. The effect of this view, as one can glean from the *Outline*, is a society where nothing is open to chance, where all action is regulated and nothing outside the ordinary can happen other than as an error that must be corrected immediately. In this sense, Kojève makes good on his claim that the end of human life should be to correct the error that is human life when it has not turned toward the end. As creatures of this regulated society, we lose our individuality, as we must if we are going to submit to the machinery of legislation that eliminates all that our animal being has bequeathed to us in the way of individuality and the fearsome urge for self-preservation. Kojève manages to create a true (a)theocracy in which the individual finally submits to the universal command, having no other choice—a rather Stalinist (a) theocracy, if one may risk the expression.

This is a society that aims to complete the suicide of the individual. This is a society that eliminates the error of individuality. This is the society that, in Kojève's hands, Hegel bids us to create, a modern society that offers a total state of a kind never before imagined. If we truly emancipate ourselves in the way Kojève advises us to, we will bring forth this new universal and homogeneous state without question. If we fail to emancipate ourselves, choosing the virtual nonsense of animal survival of the one state, we will likely suffer in endless error.

Yet the structure of the state itself expresses a fundamental misgiving about the possibility of the realization of the final state. As Kojève says in the first section of the *Outline*:

> To be sure, in the limit case of a perfectly homogeneous society where all conflict among its members is by definition excluded, one would have no need of Right. But one may ask oneself whether a homogeneous society will still be a society, whether it will maintain itself as a society. For in the societies we know the social link is conditioned by the diversity of its members, one giving to the other what the other does not have. (This point has been has been illuminated very well by Durkheim in his book on the Division of social work.) But no matter, for the real societies we know are never homogeneous.[75]

More than a complement to this final state, which now seems to admit a terminal transition that never achieves its supposed end, the *Attempt* advances a powerful variant of the central emancipation narrative in Kojève's work: the liberation from eternity. This narrative fits with the two other principal narratives, that of the freedom from nature (the master) and the ascent to wisdom; it is their temporal and discursive equivalent. Hence, the three principal narratives in Kojève's philosophical thought converge as a flight from the eternal and unchanging, nature, space, the master, silence, and so forth. All of these are original figures that the work of history, the work of the concept, seeks to overcome by humanization or anthropogenic desire that insists on the temporal, the changing, and the discursive. Yet the final achievement of such overcoming cannot be other than a return to those initial figures, this being a mark of the circularity of the "system of knowledge" so dear to Kojève.

This circularity raises many more questions than it answers. Kojève offers us a series of narratives of emancipation that bring us, in our end, back to our beginning. Is this emancipation? Is this truly becoming free of slavery? Kojève was clearly aware of the problematic nature of the final end, the suicide, the end of history. None of these seem attractive as ends, simply because they mock our entrenchment in interest—above all, our interest in living longer at virtually any cost. Mockery cannot offer, however, a particularly rich philosophical pedagogy, and one wonders whether Kojève's studiously unfinalized approach to finality does not itself offer another way. If one becomes finally aware of the impossibility of finality—awareness being itself a sign of the absence of finality—one may come to terms with a terminal lack of an ending that is itself an ending because it is completely determinate. In short, one repeats. Every action repeats self-interest, which, once aware of itself as such, as the only final directive in our lives, may be played out in the wretched Beckettian sense of "I can't go, I'll go on," an admission of courage and cowardice at the same time and a powerful echo of the terminal situation of the underground man with which we began.[76]

And yet this "solution" can be only unsatisfactory, a return to the terminal dissatisfaction of Christianity—of the religious philosopher, in Kojève's terms. Kojève then seems to go no further than Kant, admitting the impossibility of his own self-refuting project. Kojève's revolution proves itself to be vulnerable to the very counterrevolutionary propaganda that it sought to overcome, and he certainly seems to betray the revolutionary forces he sought to encourage (if one is to trust his own characterization of his work from the 1930s). Hence, it is hardly surprising that questions have arisen about his possible loyalty to Marxism, or to Stalin himself.[77] Moreover, Kojève calls his own status into question with this nagging inconsistency. If he is only the prophet of the sage, and not the sage, how is it that he can possibly bring us to understand what the sage understands? And if he does understand, if he is the sage or *a* sage, why does he take the stance of the prophet, of an actor not simply describing the end of history but attempting assiduously to bring it about? After all, the sage is content, need not act any further—indeed, can have no further interest in action.

Most damning of all is precisely the *achievement* of Kojève's extreme vision—a final utopia entailing the complete termination of the human being and a darkly ironical "return to nature" that frees the latter of the human aberration, even if it is indeed an artifact or product of that aberration. As a variant of Marxism, this result is of course invidious, since the "end state" is manifestly an affront to the emancipatory hopes invested in Marx's thought. Kojève's genuine radicality overturns the utopian hopes one may associate with Vladimir Soloviev, Marx, and perhaps even Hegel himself. The turn to deification as the absolutization of finitude is almost certainly a parody of these thinkers, and indeed of Heidegger as well, for the turn to absolute finitude terminates any hope for the transcendence of death by overcoming the selfish attachment to life that has created the various narratives Kojève undermines. If there is irony or laughter in this conclusion, it is that of either the Buddhist sage or the Swiftian misanthrope. After all, the fruition of humanity is to end humanity as an inherently unstable combination of human and animal. Kojève's emancipation narrative thus emerges as a sober brand of philosophical "black humor" directed against the fecund and deviously selfish human imagination that tries at every turn to justify an ignoble desire to live at any cost.[78]

9

WHY FINALITY?

The raging desire to come to a final conclusion is one of the most deadly and sterile obsessions that belong to humanity. Every religion and philosophy has made claim to its own God, to have touched the infinite, to have discovered the recipe for happiness. What pride and what emptiness! To the contrary, I see that the greatest geniuses and the greatest works don't come to final conclusions.

—GUSTAVE FLAUBERT

Whether he succeeded or not, whether ironic or merely seriously playful, Kojève's thought is preoccupied with bringing an end to thought. If this is indeed a philosophy of emancipation, it is no doubt a most curious one—the final emancipation appears to be indistinguishable from what we may perceive as suicide, the death or extirpation of the self. We may point to the obvious affiliations with Buddhism, with crucial currents in Christian thought, with crucial currents in the burgeoning Russian intellectual tradition of the nineteenth century, which shows itself to be a complex synthesis driven by concerns about the proper ends of human life. We may suggest that this suicide is the ultimate *imitatio Christi*, a triumphant declaration of the "inner truth and greatness" of Christianity in the guise of a thoroughgoing atheism. Or we may comfort ourselves with the notion that this suicide is merely a metaphor describing how one may subordinate oneself to the creation of a greater community where no one is everyone.

Whatever approach we take, whatever guise we choose to identify as the real Kojève, we still find ourselves faced with a singular challenge: to be truly human is to be free, and to be free is to eradicate one's attachment to life. We are thus truly human, truly free, only in becoming freed of our servitude to self-preservation. The truly human life is very much a "mediated suicide," in Kojève's provocative phrase, these mediations being points of resistance to a final truth, our proclivity for error that must, in the end, be overcome.

If ever a philosophy were untimely, it would have to be that of Kojève. For error or, in Heideggerian parlance, "errancy," is in its own inconsistent way the dominant surface dogma of our time. But Kojève's is not simply a conservative voice railing against the apparent nihilism of our time in any of its various forms, from the supposed nihilism of the collective straw man known as "postmodernism" to that of the modern consumer society that turns everything into a product for consumption. Few conservative voices recommend a turn to collective deification by immolation of the self. This sort of thinking is rather too exotic or extreme to play well in what remains of the conservative tradition, though it would likely do well among those traditionalists on the left influenced by Alain Badiou, whose grand vision of a new kind of communal subjectivity bears more than a little resemblance to Kojève's thought. Indeed, Badiou's "aleatory rationalism" attempts to attain evacuation of the individual self in favor of a collective subject in a way quite similar to what one finds in Kojève.[1]

But even Badiou is careful to avoid what is most objectionable in Kojève's thought: the obsessive focus on finality, an end of ends. The apocalyptic aspect of Kojève's thought is repellent to our modern or "late modern" or "postmodern" sensibility. Perhaps it is also important precisely for this reason, since the immanence of apocalypse, long a feature of Western thought, is perhaps more convincing now than ever before. Given the rapid advance of technologies that may achieve the self-immolation Kojève describes, we may be closer to an end of history than we imagine.[2]

This is a standard argument insofar as it relies on the long-held cliché that we most stubbornly flee something unwanted or terrifying when it faces us most directly. It is a way of talking about the first stage of the recognition that we are dying—denial—and may nonetheless hold some truth. But it seems to me that the untimeliness of Kojève's thought has more to do with the profound rejection of finality that emerged in the twentieth century in conjunction with an equally profound commitment to freedom as what cannot be defined, made final, reified, or turned into inventory (*Bestand*), as an object for use in processes that transcend that object. From the perspective of those many thinkers who associate freedom with the evasion of an end, Kojève's thought is nothing more than an evocation of tyranny, the death of the human, an apocalyptic invitation to realize the very finality, reification, or objectification that these thinkers seek to combat in a final universal tyranny. Kojève really is a Stalinist, one far more radical than Stalin himself.[3]

How can it be, then, that Kojève's thought may also claim to be emancipatory? What is at work here that we may say that Kojève's thought is at once emancipatory and tyrannical? Do we not find ourselves enmeshed in contradictions or coruscating irony? Is Kojève's account of emancipation in reality a parody of emancipatory movements? Does it reveal something deeply problematic about the way freedom has been understood as the final and ultimate goal of human striving? These questions and arguments hinge on an understanding of freedom. The untimeliness of Kojève's thought consists, in the final account, in its exploration of freedom, and ultimately in its apparent insistence that we may free ourselves only by freeing ourselves from ourselves, a suggestion that sounds closer to the grand inquisitor in Ivan Karamazov's famous poem than it perhaps should.

FREEDOM AND ERROR: *VOLUNTAS*

Freedom is not an immaculate concept; it too has a history. To get a sense of what is at issue in Kojève's untimeliness vis-à-vis the dominant notions of freedom as essentially a kind of inexhaustibility, we must take a brief look at how freedom emerges as a concept. The astonishing thing about freedom is that it seems to emerge first in conjunction with evil. A number of studies come to this conclusion, and it seems to agree with Kojève's own understanding of the matter, which places emphasis on the dramatic difference between the pagan and the Christian view of human agency.[4] As the opening epigraph of this book demonstrates, Kojève characterizes the Greek understanding of human action as a discovery of what one already is—one comes to discover the necessity hidden in the apparent disorder of appearances, one's fate that lies "before" time as what expresses itself in time. According to Kojève, the Christian view is radically different because it sets out no specific fate; rather, the Christian view asserts the fundamental openness of experience and the responsibility that individuals have for their acts, based on this openness.[5] If, for the Greeks, freedom is essentially a kind of vanity to be punished by the realization of the superior role of necessity in our lives, the Christian may be punished not for mere vanity but also for evil, defined as the will to persist in error, to perpetuate error as self-assertion at all costs.

This will to persist in error is what Augustine refers to as *voluntas*. Our abbreviated history of freedom is a history of this unusual, revolutionary notion. Augustine first introduces this notion of the will as *voluntas* in his dialogue *On Free Choice of the Will* (De libero arbitrio voluntatis).[6] It is of course no accident that the dialogue's primary topic is evil and, in particular, the question of God's responsibility for or relation to evil. No more difficult question can arise for the Christian apologist. The underlying problem is to reconcile the three primary attributes of God—his omnipotence, omniscience, and benevolence—with the reality of suffering. How is it possible that God allows suffering if God is truly good and truly powerful? The famous characterization of the problem by Lactantius (citing Epicurus) is worth repeating here:

> God, he [Epicurus] says, either wants to get rid of evil and cannot; or he can but does not want to; or he neither wants to nor can; or he wants to and can. If he wants to and cannot, he is feeble, which is not fitting for God. If he can and does not want to, he is wicked, which is equally foreign to God. If he neither can nor wants to, he is wicked and feeble, and thus, not God. If he wants to and can, the only combination suitable to God, whence evil? Or: Why does he not get rid of it?[7]

Lactantius puts the problem starkly: God is either feeble or wicked, impotent or evil. At least these characterizations of God are a possible consequence of the problem of evil, if an answer to that problem is not forthcoming.

Augustine tackles the problem by directing the responsibility for evil to human beings. If God is incapable of erring, human beings are quite capable of erring, and they often do. One hears in this respect another echo of Augustine's remarkable phrase from the *Confessions*: "si fallor, sum" (If I err, I am).[8] This phrase is more radical because it identifies the human with error, and thus with evil, for evil is precisely error, the unwillingness to live in accordance with the way set for us by God. It is not merely to err as a result of mistaken apprehension; rather, it is the far more interesting and aggressive case where one errs willingly, where one deliberately contravenes God's will. The deliberate contravention of God's will is accomplished by a different will that becomes distinctively human to the extent that it struggles against God. The human will thus describes the capacity or power to contravene God's will and to persist in contravention of God's will. As Kojève puts it, the human being is the only being that may persist in error.[9]

Attributing to human beings the capacity to err is an astonishing move that grants to human beings a power that the Greeks did not see fit to give them.[10] Indeed, the Greek tradition puts tremendous emphasis on the limitations that extend to human beings, limitations that simply cannot be overcome. Any attempt to overcome these limits is both heroic and tragic—the epic and tragic traditions in classical Greek literature attest to this emphasis, according to which the attempt to transgress both fails and warrants the most terrible punishments. The case of Oedipus is paradigmatic (and perhaps falsely so) because it is such a clear case of noble striving—in this case, for knowledge—that turns against the heroic figure, who, in the end, tears his eyes out so as not to see, not to know (both verbs are closely related in classical Greek). The lesson is unmistakable: there are borders that one cannot and dare not cross.

In Augustine's hands, Greek restrictions on the capacity to overcome limitation are largely eliminated. Human beings can and do transgress, and the capacity that fundamentally enables this transgression is will. They also dare to transgress, though in this respect their punishment is supposed to be certain. Nonetheless, the key move is to attribute to human beings a capacity for disobedience that must be very considerable indeed, since it is the origin of evil in the world, the very evil that has such a violent and harrowing effect on other human beings and on natural creatures. It is the ultimate capacity for self-assertion at the cost of all others; it is what Augustine identifies with original sin.

Augustine places the responsibility for evil squarely on the shoulders of human beings. This transfer of responsibility from God to human beings has invited derision. Friedrich Nietzsche said that "the entire doctrine of the Will, the most fateful *falsification* in psychology hitherto, was essentially invented for the sake of punishment." And Hans Blumenberg, in his magisterial study of the modern age, makes a similar point, emphasizing the manifest utility of the Augustinian notion of will as a defense of the deity.[11]

Though Blumenberg and Nietzsche focus on the creation of a will capable of transgressing and transforming limits as the precondition for the proper attribution to human beings of punishment for evil, they tend to stress the incredible increase in human possibility opened up by this new notion of will. Human beings no longer must choose between strictly denominated choices; they can transform those choices, creating new possibilities of exploration (indeed, Robert Brandom's "sapience" is unthinkable outside this concept of will). The vast expansion of human responsibility is accompanied by an equally vast expansion of possibility, expressed in all cases as disobedience or negation, the ultimate disobedience or negation being the negation of God himself.

The negative relation to freedom as freedom to be responsible for disobedience offers another side: the freedom to overthrow the very framework in which that disobedience is possible. Augustine's notion of *voluntas* incites deeply impious hopes for a revolution in which the order that imposes obedience is finally and fully overcome. As much as Augustine's notion of freedom lays a great responsibility on human beings, it also permits them the most expansive freedom, provided they are daring or reckless enough to accept it.

The aftermath of Augustine's notion of will suggests that such daring was not at hand. It is not until far later that the assertion of a capacity not merely to obey but also to master nature was declared. But even in the more radical philosophical projects of the early part of the modern age, the expression and expansion of human will still refers to a fixed structure or system. The human will may expand to cover more areas, but it cannot, in the final account, overcome God himself.

The most important modern apology for God in the face of evil, Gott-fried Leibniz's *Theodicy* (1710), indicates that we cannot do better than realize our similarity with God as well as our distance from him. This distance expresses itself indelibly with the claim that evil is primarily deficiency, defect, or want of being. God, as the ultimate being, sees all at once without shadow or defect. But we, as creatures, as creations of God, and thus as contingent, are unable to see in exactly this way. Our free-dom is located not in our willful disobedience but rather in our sheer inability to be obedient. We are constitutionally unable to see the final ends to which we owe obedience, as God does, but we may make efforts to see in a way that is analogous to God, through logic or mathematics, such that we may free ourselves from our defect—or, at least, this seems to be our task, the perfection of the creation through our proper self-direction toward God. The contrary is of course persistence in error, but unlike in Augustine, this persistence in error, for Leibniz, is not neces-sarily willful—it is much more likely that it is due to our (perhaps) cor-rigible tendency to defect and error.

Leibniz thus stresses the positive aspect of human freedom at the same moment that he reveals its negative aspect. The more difficult question in this latter respect is whether Leibniz ascribes to human beings the same kind of responsibility Augustine does. For there is a very significant dif-ference between responsibility accruing to willful disobedience, when one turns against God's will in full knowledge of the right way, and dis-obedience arising from misrecognition, misprision, misunderstanding. The distinction is hard to clarify. Ignorance in Leibniz seems to flow from the same essential refusal as in Augustine, the refusal to overcome one's selfish or immediate interests in favor of the interests of the whole. Igno-rance is a result of this refusal, since ignorance of the whole is the result of considering only the part or of interpreting the whole from the per-spective of the part. There is, in other words, no fully innocent ignorance, but ignorance is the result of an underlying disregard, which we are free to either maintain or correct.

In these cases and in others, like those of Friedrich Schelling and Vladi-mir Soloviev, the primary move is an identification of evil with the unwillingness to overcome a predominating concern with oneself, with what amounts to one's embodied "animal" interest in the here and now. One is so attached to one's particularity that whatever is other to that particularity takes on importance or interest only to the extent it can benefit that particularity. My individual existence trumps all other considerations.

It is perhaps easy to see the connection between these notions of evil and the immolation of the self that takes place in Kojève's end of history. For the persistence of error is the inability to overcome the self. It is, in Kojève's terms, the slave's inability to free himself from the imperative to self-preservation that is the most powerful expression of the devotion to the particular, to "my" one life, my individuality. The slave remains a slave as long as he refuses to overcome his own attachment to his own life as "my" life. As long as the slave considers his life unique, unrepeatable, and especially worthy on those counts alone, the slave must remain a slave, unable and unwilling to enter into any other contexts, for to do so requires the kind of astonishing journey provided in G. W. F. Hegel's *Phenomenology of Spirit* or Kojève's commentary.

Every step in the *Phenomenology* and in Kojève's commentary requires that one relinquish one's attachment to one's particular perspective. As Kojève suggests, merely reading the *Phenomenology* and understanding it compels a profound self-transformation from the isolated and contradictory individual to the totalizing subject that has become one with substance by letting go of itself.[12] Only by letting go of oneself, in the sense of taking on the kind of universal identity possible for the citizen of the universal and homogeneous state, may the individual open herself to the whole, to a vision that corrects every partial vision by running through all of them. In this respect, the *Phenomenology* is a parable of the emptying of the self, of de-individualization, of death, that brings one to a perspective utterly beyond the partial views that it both incorporates and overcomes. The reader of the *Phenomenology* who reads and understands becomes every reader of the *Phenomenology*, a universal subject that is fearfully abstract, perhaps, but is the combination of all particular individuals (subjects), combined in the process of its own self-constitution.

The only way to overcome evil is by willing oneself free of oneself, a most ironic enterprise whereby the particular or individual will empties itself in the communal identity which no longer is will or intellect. This emptying of the particular will into the communal identity is a description of the process and final end of negation.

ERROR AND ERRANCY

To persist in error, however, is a governing dogma of our time. We do not celebrate finality but rather the plenitude of the future, infinite possibility, the never-ending play of inexhaustible possibility. This way of thinking has its roots in Nietzsche and its greatest flowering in the thought of Martin Heidegger, who raises error or errancy to an exalted status as *die Irre* (or *die Irrnis*).[13] Let me examine, then, the foundations of this propensity to dispense with finality in favor of error in both Nietzsche and Heidegger.

Nietzsche's most direct statements of this position may be found in *Beyond Good and Evil*, which he published, at his own expense, in 1886. The first of the eight main sections of the text, entitled "On the Prejudices of the Philosophers," provides a critique of the "will to truth" that seeks to grasp the function or value of truth. Nietzsche, rather than simply accepting the commitment to truth as unquestionably correct and good, engages in what he considers a more fundamental questioning about what truth means for us in the first place. This in itself is a very interesting move because Nietzsche in effect calls into question the apparent need for finality, of which the striving for truth is merely one manifestation. "Truth" is a term for finality. To the extent one does not have the truth, one does not have the final account, the final view of whatever it is to which the truth relates. If the central issue turns on how one is to live or act, then the acquisition of the final view is an acquisition of the truth, immutable and irrefutable. One may only reject this truth by insisting on error, by sticking one's tongue out at the Crystal Palace, like Fyodor Dostoevsky's underground man.

So Nietzsche is interested in discovering why finality in the guise of truth is significant. He divulges his guiding concerns in the fourth subsection of the first main section:

> The falsehood of a judgment is for us no objection to a judgment; here our new language sounds perhaps strangest. The question is: to what extent is the judgment life-promoting, life-sustaining, perhaps even species-cultivating; and we are fundamentally inclined to claim that the falsest judgments (to which belong synthetic a priori judgments) are the most indispensable, that without accepting the fictions of logic, without measuring reality against the purely invented world of the

unconditioned, self-identical, without a constant falsification of the world through number, human beings would be unable to live—that renouncing false judgments would be renouncing life. To admit untruth as a condition of life: that is to resist conventional feelings about value in an admittedly dangerous way; and a philosophy that dares to do so, for that reason alone, places itself beyond good and evil.[14]

Here in condensed form is the core of Nietzsche's own contribution to the discussion about evil. Nietzsche explains that those judgments which delimit, define, and thus orient us in an otherwise inscrutable world are necessary because it would be impossible to live without them. Truth is important not because it is true itself or a final account of things but rather because that finality fulfills a vital function; it allows one to live, to negotiate the world, to find one's way. Persistence in this error of truth is life-giving because it hides from us what is least acceptable about our existence, that any judgment we make can only be finally false—or, better, no more true than false—because no judgment can be true in the sense of correspondence to a final or ultimate order. The revelation of the fiction of the eternal leads to a potentially horrific loss of bearings that may only be averted by another fiction or myth of the eternal. Truth is an error without which it would be literally impossible to live.

This reading of Nietzsche as exposing the conventional or fictional nature of what we take for the truth or reality itself merely expresses one of the modern commonplaces about Nietzsche's philosophy. The irony is precisely that the truth Nietzsche claims we must conceal for our own good—the ultimately inscrutable nature of the whole—has become a salubrious truth, transformed by Nietzsche's many acolytes into an essential condition of the properly free existence, the existence not fettered by the illusions of order foisted on us by those who would exploit us or deceive us for their own profit.

Heidegger's transformation of philosophy is even more radical than Nietzsche's. Nietzsche still seems to have held that the truth of the impossibility of finality in human affairs was a truth so dangerous that it had to be veiled in various fictions or falsehoods. He is utterly clear on the elitism inherent in his assumption that the many wish nothing so much as certainty, that they seek nothing more avidly than to be liberated from their freedom. In the words of Dostoevsky's grand inquisitor, who shares so many traits with Nietzsche, "Nothing has ever been more insufferable for man and for human society than freedom."[15] Nietzsche realizes this statement and reserves freedom to the few.

While Heidegger also holds to an inveterate elitism, his expression of the inevitability of freedom, of the fundamental incompletion of the whole, is much more far reaching than that of Nietzsche. Heidegger too admits that one of the possibilities inherent in Dasein, in existence, is inauthenticity—put crudely, the possibility of foreclosing possibility based on blind adherence to convention—but he also asserts in this way the more fundamental possibility that is openness to possibility itself. Put differently, Dasein may choose not to exercise its essential freedom, but Dasein cannot thereby discard its freedom once and for all, finally. Dasein cannot be final in any way other than by hiding from itself. Dasein's lack of finality, however, does not consist in a declaration, such as Nietzsche's, of the absolute openness of the whole; rather, Heidegger takes an utterly ingenious course by focusing on death. Dasein cannot know finality in itself—as long as I am alive, I am not at a final point. I may see others that have reached their final point, but I cannot live their final point myself, nor can I live my own final point itself. The one thing that resists finalization, that is not transferrable, not capable of being shared communally, is my death.[16]

Heidegger claims, then, that we simply cannot know an end for ourselves. Neither individuals nor societies can claim finality as long as that final point has not been met, and that final point can never be met. In the case both of individuals and societies, finality must be declared from "outside." As long as I am alive or my society continues, it cannot declare itself complete or finished, other than by a fiction of completion that, in the end, cannot but fall into perplexities and contradictions.

Nowhere does Heidegger make this point more clearly, succinctly, and suggestively than in the short essay "On the Essence of Truth." This essay is of fundamental significance not only because it showcases Heidegger's reinterpretation of finitude but also because it sharply formulates a definition of truth that is radically different from that which we have discussed so far. Heidegger decisively rejects the notion of truth as a standard—a final standard, or *Richtmaß*—against which phenomena should be judged. In its place he develops a notion of truth that emphasizes incompletion, invention. Heidegger creates a notion of truth that encourages creation and discourages finality, absolute limits.

He does so by calling into question the model of truth typically referred to as the correspondence model. An object is truly what it is when it correctly corresponds to a mental picture (*idea*, *Vorstellung*) or image (*eidos*, *Bild*) one may have of it. This picture may be grounded in the mind of God or in one's own mind; the point is that there exists a final picture that dictates what that object is and can be. The final truth of that picture (its ultimate finality) is guaranteed, thus, either by the deity or by another agency whose final authority is not questioned. Heidegger's strategy is precisely to call this picture into question by examining the origin of its authority. Like Nietzsche and his many followers, Heidegger engages in a sort of genealogy, and he does so in order to suggest that the truth associated with the picture is not absolute, not in the order of things, but rather the result of an operation that Heidegger refers to as "disclosure."

As soon as one asks *Whence this idea?*, a problem emerges. If an idea comes into being, then it is not eternal, and if it is not eternal, it must be in some way contingent. If it is contingent, then it could have been different or it could have not been. In either case, one can at least imagine a different outcome. And if one can consistently imagine a different outcome, then the outcome that became canonical loses its authority as the sole outcome. In other words, the outcome that has become canonical has to conceal its contingency at the risk of not giving the complete story that is necessary for a full and final assertion of the truth. Yet a full and final assertion of the truth is not at hand; all assertions of truth rely on a notional moment of disclosure.[17] The more primordial truth then has more in common with error than truth; the essence of truth is error, *die Irre*, or errancy. Error is, however, not merely the result of one operation or another— errancy is what is. We live in errancy or error, just as Nietzsche showed.

FINALLY UNFINISHED?

Heidegger's is arguably the boldest attempt to argue for the unfinished quality of experience—not as leading to a destructive skepticism but as an affirmative impetus to creation, which masters that skepticism by transforming it into transformative action. But what does this notion of transformation entail? What does it mean to be finally unfinished? The contemporary dogma that praises the incomplete and unfinished as the proper precondition of the human being, arguing that to be human is to embrace one's unfinishedness both as a sign of humility and as a task to be fruitfully engaged in, must itself be questioned, if for no other reason than as an example of that openness itself.

If unfinishedness does not take its bearing from some finite point or set of criteria, then the notion of the unfinished itself comes into question as not being capable of describing itself as such. If there are no full final ends to meet or by which one may orient oneself, then one has to ask what it means to be at all—one becomes completely unknown to oneself other than as a fiction that calls on minimal fixed standards so as to avoid the incoherence that attends the alternative.

But here we appear to return to Nietzsche, not Heidegger. For here we contemplate a picture of human being as reliant on fictions in order to make any sense of itself. Otherwise, we risk the predicament of the underground man, who talks endlessly, acts furtively, and can do nothing more and nothing less because there are no restrictions at all that he can convincingly apply to himself or steer himself by. The underground man is perhaps the foremost ahistorical or post-historical figure, because he uses a language fashioned in the conventions of finite discourse to pull that discourse apart. He thus engages in the activity that Hannah Arendt associates positively with thinking: he unravels whatever cloth of talk or action he wove the night before.[18] But one may compare this, and the numbing repetition it implies, more to Sisyphus than to the liberating hero of the intellect, the philosopher who never ceases to think.

This philosopher, like the underground man, cannot know himself or his world. He is the reductio ad absurdum of the ancient philosophic identification of knowledge with self-knowledge, as we noted in chapter 1. Surely, as a political doctrine, this fundamental ignorance cannot seem very persuasive—we bind ourselves together in a community based on a communal failure of identity that we may refer to as cosmopolitan. Or we end up arguing for a "provisional" identity that seems correct or is at least as comprehensive as we can make it at a given time. But the problem remains that we are fully aware that we are provisional, that we have no access to a real or final story. We are in this sense no different from the madmen Kojève describes, for there is no fully convincing reason to adapt oneself to one identity or another. There are no convincing reasons at all, and discourse thus loses one of its signal advantages over force as a mode of creating a community. We might say, then, that we have returned to a condition where there is no alternative to force, discourse having proven singularly unhelpful.

Still, the central argument that underscores this open attitude to identity is that the humility of thought and action imposed by our not having access to a final truth has to lead to a willingness to cooperate, to fashion meaning together, to create a semblance of wholeness that knows it is delicate and fraught with imperfection—like all human things. Two basic alternatives threaten this open attitude that derives an assumption of equality from the impossibility of finality: violence and bureaucracy.

As I have noted, the failure of discourse to orient us in the world otherwise than through fictions leads to the possibility that the authority of discourse is itself a fiction, that all attempts to establish authority in another world or by reference to hidden or unseen powers are essentially forms of deception. Nietzsche's famous argument in this respect suggests that the otherworld is the creation of the slave who seeks final power over his master by convincing the master that there is a fount of authority not based in the threat of force.[19] The ancient argument between Socrates and Thrasymachus about the origin of justice is thus reprised and decided in favor of Thrasymachus, though not without irony, since Nietzsche makes his argument in the guise of an authoritative discourse, a treatise, that itself reinforces the authority of discourse. There is thus, here as elsewhere, a formative irony in Nietzsche's writings, since they point to their own fictional quality and, in that respect, to the fictional quality of all discursive constructions to the extent that they persuade one to lay down one's arms without having to use force to do so. Nonetheless, the absence of discursive authority opens the possibility for affirmation of the most simple and strenuous form of authority, force, to which Kojeve otherwise denies authority.[20]

The other response to this openness is the closure provided by bureaucracy or the tools of bureaucratic management that most contribute to the imposition of a sole system of regulation of life that completely submerges questioning, especially to the extent that questioning addresses the bureaucratic regulatory mechanisms themselves. Heidegger's tenacious argument against technology, against the closure of apparently open human possibility in one overwhelming system of regulation of the human, is in this sense an argument against the deepest tendency of bureaucracy and bureaucratization of human life. Heidegger shares this concern with his most dogged critics on the left, like Georg Lukács and Theodor Adorno, who make a similar argument against bureaucracy as being the full and final reification of the human being that emerges with the victory of capitalism.[21] Reification, of course, has to do with the transformation of all human relations into commodity relations that may be fixed, once and for all, in a calculus of exchange, in which the fundamental unit of exchange is monetary. The market becomes a bureaucracy regulating all aspects of human life.

The critique that I have associated with Nietzsche and Heidegger finds its correlate on the Marxist side with the essential difference that Marxism is still imbued with a teleology, with an end point at which certain fundamental issues will be resolved so that human beings may be free to do as they like, to create freely, as opposed to the basic resistance to material necessity that is the essential bar to human self-creation. In this sense, the final Marxist state, as ill-defined as it has always been, seems to bear some resemblance to the community created in absence of finality that I discussed above. In both cases, the final end is a freedom from all ends, a freedom to self-creation that seems not to be limited by nature or history.[22]

Errancy becomes the supreme expression of the human, thus transforming the association of error with evil. For evil disappears once the notion of a final normative end has also been obliterated. Indeed, the only evil that exists, for these modern thinkers of unfinishedness, is precisely the desire to conclude, to finish, to meet that fixed point from which no deviation is possible other than as error meriting punishment. The final defeat of these ends is the victory of the free historical individual capable of expressing himself as he sees fit, almost as a god, or indeed as a god on earth, free to do as he chooses, without regard to any overarching standard. Perhaps the only standard left, albeit a vexing one, is the standard imposed by the concern for the freedom of others, the essentially liberal notion that the exercise of my freedom is not noxious to the extent that it does not impede the freedom of others to express themselves.

This standard is of course deeply problematic because it enshrines self-interest, discarding the association of evil with self-interest, a relic of Christian concerns with evil and original sin, in order to make self-interest the grounding principle of action and modern political action. The question is whether self-interest can assume the role of grounding principle. Indeed, the horror before technology or reification can quite easily be read as a horror before limitation of self-interest of any kind, even in its ostensibly more benign appearance as collective self-interest.

Heidegger attempts to overcome self-interest by assigning us a responsibility to Being as a whole. Lukács seeks to overcome self-interest by the imperative of community creation based on the promotion of the welfare of all and the assertion of equality.[23] The central struggle in much of twentieth-century thought is in this sense axiological, an attempt to reconcile the interest of individuals with each other and, thus, with the attempt to create a community in which all may be able to express themselves without the threat of sanction. The freedom that seems to be at the center of these concerns is the freedom of self-interest, the very interest, of course, whose expression was understood as evil in itself during the Christian era.

It is therefore not surprising that the concept of evil has suffered an eclipse in the modern age, since the original identification of evil with self-interest and self-will has been transformed into an identification of evil with limitation on self-interest, this transformation being one of the most radical, and perhaps least discussed, aspects of modernity. One may argue that Hegel plays a decisive role in this development. His theodicy—at least for Kojève—is predicated upon the reshaping of reality in the human image, not the proper location of our humanity within a specific framework. In this respect, Hegel brings collective self-interest to its highest expression as the hegemony of the subject over all that is, subject having finally become substance and vice versa.

The apparent terror created by Hegel is that he establishes once and for all the hegemony of the subject, that he is the one who brings the long history of Western philosophy to a close, not in the announcement of the victory of freedom but rather in the victory of a singular way of thought from which no deviation is possible. Indeed, this system of thought is tyrannical, reducing the possibility of new modes of thought or experience to nothing. We are all familiar with this caricature of Hegel, which is promoted in differing ways by Nietzsche and Heidegger as well as by their French descendants, who, almost as a chorus in unison, reject what they see as the monstrous desire to end philosophy, to promote finality, to leave nothing more to the human imagination than an abstract "science of logic" sufficing to settle all possible disputes.

We are again reminded of the underground man, whose hostility to this finality has so many traits in common, even if distantly so, with that of the rebels of the twentieth century who sought to recast Hegel's theodicy as the ultimate expression of evil, the complete and cheerful eradication of human freedom, in favor of a permanent self-perpetuating order. So many crucial figures in the twentieth century, from Heidegger to Gilles Deleuze, stuck their tongues out at this Crystal Palace, mocked it, and tried to undermine or overcome it as an unacceptable image of finality. Some of these acts of rebellion aimed at the Hegelian edifice as an attempt to create a final model of reason; some attacked the Hegelian edifice as denying any place for human creativity and identified philosophy with creativity; some simply mocked history's apparent refusal to prove Hegel right.

One wonders about the foundation of these rejections of Hegel. What prompts them? What is it about finality that seems so unacceptable? If philosophy has for such a long time aimed for finality, sought to find the truth, the final account, why does that enormous effort change so quickly over to its reverse? Is Dostoevsky again right when he claims that we love to build things, to create, but we also very much love to destroy, to frustrate finality, if nothing else? Is Dostoevsky's fundamental point—that we are more deeply attached to our freedom than to any one position, however salubrious it might seem—correct? Let us recall Dostoevsky's words:

> But I repeat to you for the hundredth time, there is only one case, one only, when man may purposely, consciously wish for himself even the harmful, the stupid, even what is stupidest of all: namely, so as *to have the right to* wish for himself even what is stupidest of all and not be bound by an obligation to wish for himself only what is intelligent. For this stupidest of all, this caprice of ours, gentlemen, may in fact be the most profitable of anything on earth for our sort, especially in certain cases. And in particular it may be more profitable than all other profits even in the case when it is obviously harmful and contradicts the

most sensible conclusions of our reason concerning profits—because in any event it preserves for us the chiefest and dearest thing, that is, our personality and our individuality.[24]

ERROR AND EGOISM

Kojève's basic response to errancy and error: error is the refusal to relinquish the individual self, and its self-interest, chiefly in preserving itself. Error is thus servitude and the persistence in servitude. The claim of unfinishedness is seductive. It may appear to offer the possibility of relinquishing the individual self, but in reality it allows the individual self to retain its prerogative—indeed, it must retain its prerogative, because there is no superior point of view that can possibly controvert it, to which it must subordinate itself in the end. If we argue that there is a powerful element of self-negation in Heidegger as well, an attempt to overcome the modern hegemonic subject (or collective egoism) in a surrender of all hegemonic projects to Being as that which both precedes and always exceeds them, we may also argue that Heidegger's self-negation, never complete, never finished, cannot ultimately avoid retraction into the very individual self or modern hegemonic subject it seeks to overcome. The human being may become Dasein, a rather abstract "being-there" or "there-being," which for Heidegger lives in the peculiarly numinous realm of "the between" (*das Zwischen*) or is "appropriated over to the appropriating event" (*dem Er-eignis übereignet zu werden*), the fact is that this "placeholder" of the nothing persists precisely as such, or as an entity of some kind, whose definition remains the basis for an absence of final definition, a pretext for continued affirmation of intrinsically selfish self-preservation.[25]

The human being or Dasein now acts, in a way analogous to Being itself, as a term for a determinate indeterminacy, an identity whose identity is precisely not to have an identity. This definition has long applied to evil, whose being is not-being, the one thing defined by absence of definition. To be sure, we may become strangers to ourselves, but is this enough? Are we truly freed from the necessity of having some identity so as to function with other human beings? Not at all. Rather, we retain an identity that is sort of a parody of identity. We are a conduit of God's mocking humor, neither strong enough to disappear entirely nor so weak as to become wholly convinced of a divine destiny that we are powerless to influence; we are indeed the "between."

Kojève is much more radical than this. We *must* transcend ourselves, our individuality or collective subjectivity, to the extent that it is merely the vehicle of collective self-interest (such as nationalism). This is the imperative and end of history. The only truly human destiny is to overcome the human, to cancel the human out definitively. This is Kojève's genuine madness. Any other destiny, partial or otherwise, merely perpetuates an error that cannot make sense of itself. Kojève rejects the heroes of nonsense, from the underground man, who becomes a durable literary figure in the twentieth century, to the hero of Knut Hamsun's *Hunger*, through Bardamu, to Molloy, to Camus's rather more anemic stranger. These ostensibly modern or postmodern heroes live the absurd, the pointless, not necessarily as something to regret or with a disdain for the ugliness of nihilism. On the contrary, one may forcefully celebrate nihilism as the final advent of freedom, as diverse embodiments of the gesture of negation made by the underground man.[26]

Is this not indeed what is left to freedom, or to the modern free historical individual? Or is the better representative the modern consumer, sensitive to the new trend, the new gadget, the new way to dress? Or is this the post-historical creature for whom all values melt into the delight of acquisition of the latest products? The despairing nihilist becomes the cheerful nihilist of Americanization—the final embodiment of freedom, understood as victory of sheer pointlessness.[27] The highest value is the freedom to recreate oneself in ever more trivial ways, triviality itself being a celebration of the freedom from conflicts, from pain, from the difficult hold of nature.

SELF-OVERCOMING

The bite of Kojève's thought is precisely in its emphasis on the need to overcome the individual, its fervent opposition to the extolling of self-interest that is, by all accounts, the supreme, unchallenged dogma of our time. For Kojève, the individual makes no real sense—the individual is a sign of error, and the kind of error that cannot find satisfaction other than in self-immolation. The individual, then, is a mistake. Kojève is of course not alone in thinking in this way. While, on the surface, he seems vulnerable to ridicule for the extremity of his thought and for the extremity of the hostility it reveals toward the supreme atomic unit of our modern self-understanding, the free historical individual, his thought has close affinities to the venerable tradition of self-sacrifice one finds in both Christianity and Buddhism as well as in some of the most astonishing modern works of art, like those of his Russian predecessors in visual art and the powerful achievements in serial music of composers like Arnold Schoenberg. Indeed, in the fervent atmosphere of the nascent Soviet Union of the 1920s, a whole tendency of radical thought could be found in many realms of cultural production, as well as in the political arena, a clear movement away from the free, historical individual.

Kojève thus stands for the rejection of the modern liberal tradition and its emphasis on what he views as an incoherent individual—incoherent because self-interest cannot be a coherent grounding principle, as I have noted in several contexts. Self-interest is malleable, unreliable, and inherently in conflict with any overriding polity, because self-interest has to place the interest of the one over all others. Even when gestures are made to community, the ultimate principle of community is fear of death, of violent death, as Thomas Hobbes indicated in *Leviathan*. Thus, self-preservation is hallowed, becoming the true alpha and omega of all human relations, and can thus easily be turned to the various myths of "mutual satisfaction" that play a role in the propaganda of "self-interest well understood" or in the essentially contractual models of modern sociality, which assure the stability of social relations or the appropriate apportionment of selfish gain.

From the very beginning of the *Introduction*, Kojève conducts the fiercest possible polemic against this view of the human being, which he seems to have regarded as a kind of bestialization or a refusal of the truly human potential. Nonetheless, one might argue that his countermodel—or, simply, his model—of human development cannot have seemed less convincing to a society steeped in the lore of individualism. His countermodel ends up offering the unattractive model of self-immolation, of self-cancellation, without promise of external award or benefit in heaven. Kojève offers a variant of the Christian sacrifice that could never be fully accepted within Christian society itself—recall Kojève's dramatic comment about the one theological mistake of Christianity: resurrection. Kojève's philosophical propaganda, then, advocates an end to history, an end to man, understood as the self-interested creature of the modern era, without remorse or reward. We are supposed to march forward to our own self-cancellation in a society that resembles a ghastly or ghostly collection of cadavers from which all life has ebbed.

The final question, then, is are we to take Kojève seriously? Why did Kojève present such an extreme model of human activity and destiny? The operative irony of his work, one that I have expressed again and again in this study, is that genuine emancipation is emancipation from the self, the individual, an emancipation that requires, as its very condition of possibility, the most extreme self-abnegation possible. In other words, genuine emancipation requires the taking of measures that the self-interested bourgeois could not possibly accept, because the only real emancipation for the bourgeois is to allow his animal desires free rein, a potentially disgusting spectacle in which the final search for animal immortality cannot possibly achieve the desired result, other than through a transformation of the human being as radical as that contemplated by Kojève.

Although Kojève does not make these objections explicitly, one can easily infer that his response to Nikolai Fedorov, for example, would be mocking, since a community of immortals is hard to imagine. Once released from death, these beings are released from the very animality that pushed them. The end of the pursuit of animal self-interest, in this respect, is animal self-interest itself—I kill myself to become immortal. But the simpler delusion of self-interest is that there is no emancipation involved at all. To free one's animal desires—if these are even desires—is a bestialization, an acquiescence to rule by the body, a rule that makes of reason a tool for the pursuit of selfish interest only, a perversion and destruction of reason.

The rule of self-interest is the rule of animal self-preservation that, with all ironies intact, must head to its own destruction in the creation of an immortal being. The animal dream of freedom ends up in the same sort of immolation of the self as that prescribed by Kojève, the major difference being that the one route is freely chosen while the other is not, being itself a product of delusion. This vexed circumstance itself—that there is no way out of human limitation, of suffering and death, other than by transforming the human into what must be its own constructive death—might explain the emphasis on voluntary self-immolation as the last nobility available to human beings.

It may be that the best coda emerges from the desperate struggle of the underground man, whose drama set the original stage for our subsequent approach to Kojève. The underground man is unable to overcome his self-interest; neither is he capable of completely succumbing to it. He is the impressive description of the muddle, of the one who cannot decide to escape from the muddle. He is the hero of nonsense, the hero of will that is unable, in the end, to impose itself. He prefers infinite negation—and the semblance of freedom it offers—to finality.

The underground man has not the nobility of Alexei Kirillov or Nikolai Stavrogin, both negative or darkly parodic echoes of Christ. He cannot bring himself to take on the greatest burden, to end the muddle, to sacrifice the grotesque spectacle of selfishness, of vanity, and error that must attend a creature unable to give up its desperate desire to live, who rejects its capacity to see the utter senselessness of its existence in favor of the only truly divine act available to it: suicide.

There can be no doubt that the most shocking aspect of Kojève's challenge to the bourgeois is contained in his notion that the purest expression of freedom is the willingness to die, to kill oneself for a purpose that has nothing to do with animal self-preservation. The purpose that has the least to do with animal preservation, of course, is the complete rejection of animal self-preservation itself—the complete rejection of the animal, of nature, of any and all coercive aspects of our bodily or animal existence. Suicide is thus itself the highest, purest, and most powerful expression of the great refusal that is freedom—the divine refusal to be restricted by the creation, the ultimate, terrible liberty of a god.

EPILOGUE

The Grand Inquisitor

Few of Fyodor Dostoevsky's writings could claim to be more famous and enigmatic that Ivan Karamazov's "poetic" fragment "The Grand Inquisitor," which plays a central role in *The Brothers Karamazov.* The fragment has been taken as a parable of twentieth-century totalitarianism, one of the most baleful examples of which is the very Stalinist regime that time and again Kojève claimed to support.[1] Kojève has been accused of facile provocation, and even one of his best students, Raymond Aron, could not be sure of Kojève's political loyalties or, indeed, whether the self-proclaimed Stalinist was truly loyal to the Stalinist regime (a fact that would seem to be belied by his residency in Paris). Whatever be the case, the ghostly specter of the grand inquisitor seems to hang over Kojève's work, offering a rather dire interpretation of that work as promoting an essentially totalitarian political vision.

A central claim, which have I mentioned already, appears in Ivan's poem: "Nothing has ever been more insufferable for man and human society than freedom."[2] We note that it is the grand inquisitor himself who makes this statement; the mysterious stranger says nothing. And why should he? The grand inquisitor seems well pleased with his withering judgment of human beings who are happy to give up their freedom provided that an excuse flattering to their vanity can be provided. In this respect, the grand inquisitor suggests that bread and the power of miracle, mystery, and authority may prove sufficient to provide the appropriate cover for man's own weakness.

We may say that the basic proposition of this famed parable is this: man seeks to rid himself of his freedom; the end of history is to eliminate history. By this, the grand inquisitor seems to mean that man can suffer neither the anguish of uncertainty nor the great responsibility of having to decide without certainty. The certainty of servitude is preferable to the uncertainty of freedom. Man is thus a born slave who cannot tolerate uncertainty. He exercises his freedom so as to extirpate it once and for all, root and branch. One can imagine the punditry to which such a series of claims may lead, especially given the reality of the bureaucratic state in the Soviet Union. Stalinism adopts the attitude of the grand inquisitor by ensuring that all be freed of the pain of freedom.

Kojève may emerge as *the* philosopher of this proposition, the "conscience of Stalin," as he was wont to put it. Kojève's proclamation of the end of history may tempt one to believe that his thinking beckons us toward freedom from freedom, for Kojève's sage is not free. Indeed, if we follow Kojève's argument to its conclusion, the sage is the one for whom freedom is no longer possible—or relevant. The end of history signaled by the advent of the sage is transparently a moment at which freedom will no longer matter. The slave frees himself by overcoming his concern for servitude—but does the slave become less of a slave for doing so?

If we heed the crushing statement of the grand inquisitor—that man will gladly bow down to bread—then the answer must be in the negative. To bow down to bread is to choose animal life over freedom. This choice is the defining choice of the slave, and it directs his life even in his endeavor to overcome nature. The slave seeks to overcome nature by transforming nature through technology. The slave seeks to turn nature from a blind destructive force into an entirely regulated one that can no longer pose any threat to the slave's animal life. In doing so, the slave transforms himself from worker into manager or bureaucrat and occupies himself chiefly with technical problems related to the smooth operation or perfection of the regulatory system he has developed to rule over nature. The slave devotes himself to the furtherance of animal life by ensuring the complete eradication of any possible threat to that animal life. Once all such threats have come under management, the slave becomes free of his fear of death.

This is a crucial moment, as we know. Kojève states that this moment signifies the advent of wisdom, since wisdom is the conscious acceptance of death.[3] Yet the slave does not accept death in any conventional sense. The slave does not muster existential courage, does not resign himself peacefully, does not put his head in the way of the bullet, his neck in the noose. On the contrary, the slave ensures himself that this possibility finally becomes impossible. The slave accepts death only when "death is no more," when death has lost its authority to command and dominate the slave.[4]

With or without terror, the slave ultimately becomes free of his fear of death by abolishing death. The slave thus never frees himself of his fear of death, he merely eliminates that fear by eliminating its object. But, by eliminating his fear of death, the slave has also eliminated any possibility of threat, any possibility of an event occurring that could be harmful to his life. All runs according to plan, and this plan involves no surprises (other than "happy" ones); nothing unpredictable, outside the slave's control, can possibly occur. The slave frees himself of the fear of death by freeing himself of novelty, of chance, of the unexpected. The end of the slave's struggle with the master—the apotheosis of the slave's relation to the master—is the elimination of the *concern* with freedom.

The obvious objection is that freedom from the fear of death is the headiest freedom. We become master over nature. We become a god. But is a god really free? From Kojève's perspective, a god cannot be free because a god has no need to act—a god is fully satisfied. For a god nothing matters, because nothing is at stake. Kojève understands freedom only negatively, in the servile manner, as the negation of something given in favor of something not yet given—freedom from the given. To put this in the crudest terms, the slave negates the given in favor of a given that satisfies. Once this satisfying given has been brought to completion, the slave need no longer negate. If the slave need no longer act, the slave no longer exercises freedom.

Thus, Kojève agrees with the grand inquisitor to the extent that he argues that the slave becomes free only by freeing himself of his freedom. Uncertainty and fear make the slave. To eliminate them is the liberating act. Conversely, the grand inquisitor claims that Christ enslaves by his silence, that Christ's enigmatic quality ensures that those who may follow him cannot be sure that following Christ will vanquish their fear—again the greatest fear of all, the enslaving fear of death.

CHRIST'S CRUELTY

If we put this in other terms, we may say that Christ does not allow for finality whereas the grand inquisitor does. The grand inquisitor maintains that Christ is cruel because he compels human beings to live in suffering. To live without a certain end is a kind of suffering. The grand inquisitor emphasizes the connection of nonfinality with suffering. But he also emphasizes thereby the connection between nonfinality, understood as freedom, with suffering: to be free is to suffer. What is the main point of doing so?

The grand inquisitor frames the question thus: Why prefer the freedom of nonfinality to the freedom of finality? We find ourselves in a rather peculiar situation, with two different, if not opposed, concepts of freedom, one drawing its strength from the lack of an end, the other from the sure prospect of an end. Some have argued that the operative distinction is between "freedom to" or "freedom from," between positive and negative freedom.[5] Positive freedom is beset by the difficulty that it is exercised for an end that, by its very nature, terminates the freedom that allowed the end to be achieved, or the freedom to achieve any end at all. Negative freedom is necessarily enigmatic because it is defined negatively as being freedom from positive action, indeed, from an act that may determine such freedom, thereby diminishing it.

It should be no surprise that we return here to our starting point in Dostoevsky. The man of action is one who constantly limits his freedom, tying himself down to certain ways of exercising his freedom. The man of inaction, the underground man, pursues the negative ideal of freedom as far as he can. He attempts to thwart limitation in whatever form it may take in any given situation. The underground man is thus a hero of negation, as we have noted, and he mocks those who engage in the seemingly contradictory process of limiting their own freedom.

The underground man is in this respect a parody of nonfinality as a kind of liberation, because the underground man is trapped within his own "logic" of negation. He is reactive, as we see in the second part of the novel, and he can be only reactive, because any positive or creative action is necessarily a self-restriction of freedom. To avoid these two problematic alternatives, there is yet a third: to engage in positive action and to undo that action—to "weave and unweave Penelope's web," in the words of Hannah Arendt.[6] Arendt associates this with a liberating notion of thinking. But is it liberating? For one may then simply wind oneself up in a repetitive pattern of building and destroying that is yet another restriction on freedom understood as being absolutely free from any pattern or condition.

Would it be possible to experience such freedom? Likely not, since to experience a sort of "pure" openness would seem to be impossible other than as mystic experience or experience that cannot be addressed by cognition, for cognition has to produce a series of identities that collapse the openness into a specific configuration of things. Mystic experience interrupts or puts aside discussion of any kind in favor of silence; mystic experience is silence (as Kojève indicates). In this respect, the freedom of the mystic moves beyond the parameters of finality and nonfinality because it moves beyond any cognitive or social network—hence, its silence.

To the extent that we can speak of finality or nonfinality, we may do so only in the context of discourse, a context bound to language and determinate norms. This discourse either becomes fully transparent to itself—and when it does, it becomes fully clear to itself such that nothing new or different can ever be encountered—or it does not, in which case the possibility of a new and different configuration cannot simply be dismissed out of hand.

Returning to the grand inquisitor, it may be possible now to view the attraction of finality, of final authority, as eliminating any need for further thought—or as eliminating the potential for endless chatter, in the case where a final account is ruled out from the very beginning. If a final account is in fact ruled out, all accounts may be subject to change at any moment and without warning. We know what we know only "provisionally." Our identity, the world to which we have become accustomed, is only a provisional home. While the provisional character of the account allows for the freedom of conversion, of the discovery of the apparently new, of transformation, it also, though by definition provisional, is of a stronger kind since a final account can never be achieved. This possibility means that no matter what we know, we cannot claim that it is definitive and, more likely, that whatever we know is like a fiction, allowing us some security in the world, some sense of being at home, when in reality there is no chance of finding a home or peace in the world, and never will be any.

To link nonfinality with homelessness brings out the problematic quality of freedom as the result of an inability to find comfort in the world, a sense of homelessness that can be as much delight as burden or terror. To the extent that we see the world withdraw before our eyes, we are stuck with mystery, miracle, and the authority of the unknowable, what is beyond us. What is beyond us remains outside our control; reality retains an aleatory aspect that can be the delight of the new or the terror of the awful and unexpected.

On the other hand, to be at home, to be at an end while still alive, can be nothing but repetition where nothing is at stake, nothing needs resolution. As we noted earlier, repetition in this sense is indistinguishable from ritual. No questions arise, other than of a technical nature, the worthiness of ends having been already assumed. One obeys the ritual, all things have order, space takes precedence over time.

A REVERSAL?

Living is servitude, in either sense, whether to ineffable chance or to repetition. One cannot live and accept death. The only way to accept death is to risk one's life completely. The master is the only one who accepts death, and he remains silent in the crucial sense that his is not a world of change and development but one of stasis. He has said his last word, and there is nothing else for him to say. The slave is the creature of discourse, the one who talks in order to stave off death, like a sort of Scheherazade. And, like Scheherazade, the slave may be silent only at that point when the threat of death is no longer present. If we take the analogy further, the slave only creates while death is still a threat.

Yet, in Ivan's poem, it is the ostensive master who talks and the slave (or prisoner) who is silent. The poem reverses the relation we have just described. And this is an intriguing reversal because it suggests that the one who considers himself master in this case, the grand inquisitor, is nothing of the sort. His need for discourse belies his authority. This point may be merely obvious, but its full significance is more elusive and has to do, it seems to me, with the difference between discourse and action, for the grand inquisitor talks while the mysterious stranger silently acts.

Kojève tells us that philosophy is about action. He roundly mocks those who leave philosophy at the level of theory or who stick to their philosophical cloisters rather than engaging in revolutionary action. These "cloistered minds" are the madmen with which we began in the first chapter of this book. They are the ones who live in discourse, and discourse only.[7]

The grand inquisitor does not belong among the madmen of this kind. The grand inquisitor is indeed a strange figure within the context of Kojève's thinking—the putative sage who talks to the slave as if the slave were master, the sage who talks and cannot stop talking. But this is a deception. The real master is the one who is silent. The one who speaks is still the slave, the one who has not and cannot reach satisfaction.

THE SUICIDE MYTH

As long as there is discourse, there is servitude. Silence is the proper speech of the master. Kojève's call to revolution undercuts itself as long as it remains a call. Kojève's garrulousness is a sign of dissatisfaction—or worse, of impossibility. No matter how he might have tried, Kojève cannot rid his thought of this lingering, damning inconsistency. Like the grand inquisitor, he cannot be silent; he cannot be satisfied by the authority he has attained because it does not and cannot satisfy him. To put this in Kojève's terms, one *cannot accept death while still alive*. The notion that there can be some sort of acceptance of death that accompanies life is a myth, a founding fiction that fails. This founding fiction undergirds the entire edifice of Kojève's thought. If we return to our original terminology, the acceptance of suicide, of utter self-immolation, can only be a decoy of the slavish imagination, as it is for Alexei Kirillov, the model Kojève invokes, ambiguously, in this respect.

In a passage from Kojève's unfinished manuscript *Atheism*, from 1931, two years before he gave the first Hegel lectures, he writes, " 'The human being in the world' is thus given to herself in her consciousness of herself as finite and free, that is, as being able at any moment freely to kill herself. And that is why she lives at every moment only thanks to her free refusal to commit suicide, that is to say that she is free, not only at the moment of suicide, but at any given moment of her existence."[8]

Here Kojève tries to address the problem I have identified: that the acceptance of suicide is merely a fiction, a thought experiment, or, worse, a *Hirngespinst* or pipe-dream that proves nothing at all or is glaringly disproved by the one who continues to live.[9] For if the act of suicide is the only absolutely free act, then the refusal of that act cannot in itself be free—indeed, as I indicate, the refusal of that act must itself undermine any claim to the heady freedom of suicide. Kojève turns this objection around by suggesting that acceptance of death is possible insofar as this acceptance is the precondition of freedom, the reality of which is proved every moment by the decision not to commit suicide.

This argument seems to be little more than a sophisticated ruse. In the simplest terms, it claims that continued life is not prima facie evidence of animal attachment to life. Rather, continued life is the result of a free decision that sustains itself by continued reassertion. This free decision is the decision not to commit suicide. Hence, continued life results from what is supposed to be an *absolutely* free act. The problem here, as above, is precisely that the free act is absolute. The question arises, then, as to how an act can be absolutely free and yet at the same time fit into a continuum of preceding acts. The tension between the act itself and the context of its exercise is difficult, if not impossible, to resolve. If this act is not absolutely free, then it cannot have the significance it is supposed to have as an assertion of a sovereign freedom; to the extent that the act is not absolute or is incomplete, it cannot be free. The freedom of the act can only be assured by its completion. Any negation of that completion, such as the decision not to carry through the act, is equivalent to complete nonperformance. One thus cannot simply say that to decide not to commit suicide is sufficient evidence of the willingness to do so, because it is not. The only sufficient evidence is the completion of the act itself (even taking into account "failed" attempts).

Kojève cannot simply brush aside Dostoevsky's irony with regard to Kirillov. The theoretical suicide is no suicide at all.

FREEDOM FROM FREEDOM

With disarming simplicity, this point calls Kojève's whole elaborate system of thought into question. For the individual suicide that is so important in the context of Kojève's earlier writing becomes the collective suicide of the slave who negates in the desire for wisdom or final freedom (from freedom). One can argue that the slave's overcoming of his own position through work and struggle is cumulative evidence of his freedom because the slave works to eliminate himself as such—the slave's struggle toward wisdom is self-immolation writ large. But this simply cannot be so, because the slave's struggle is a *refusal* of the risk of death. To struggle, to hang on, is indeed proof of a decision not to die, but this proof is not, for all that, a positive proof of the "free refusal to commit suicide." How can it be? One cannot prove a free decision not to commit suicide when that decision is not taken.

The upshot is that the slave, the creature of discourse, will continue to talk as long as possible and will cease to talk only unwittingly. The slave, like the grand inquisitor, cannot shake off his essential origin. The conversion from slave to free creature is not possible other than through the willing and final completion of the act of self-immolation. Christ's death had to be. If he had lived, he would have been an object of ridicule.

The irony is the governing irony of Kojève's work: the freedom from freedom, the final finality, is an impossible goal *as* goal. It is only possible as an impossible goal. The talk continues as long as it continues because we cannot tell ourselves when the goal has been reached. We can only deceive ourselves about the goal having been reached to the degree that we can still talk about it—and how can we deceive ourselves without the capacity for speech? Martin Heidegger may well have the final say, for Heidegger's implacable assertion of finality as an impossible possibility or a possibility whose realization is impossible remains, unrefuted.

"THE BEST PRIZE OF ALL"

Does this vitiating irony disqualify the Kojèvian project? Does it work to marginalize a philosophical project whose own "life" has largely been on the margins, despite its immense influence? I would suggest that this vitiating irony serves to cast the Kojèvian project in a certain light as a sober critique of the modern bourgeois emancipation narrative. As a philosophy in the conventional sense—as a doctrine to live by—Kojève's thinking is quite obviously extravagant. There is further irony in this extravagance, since Kojève's own cultivation of mystery and dramatic presence is flatly opposed by the teaching he labors to unfold. And this goes even for the bureaucrat that Kojève became.

The irony can be taken too far. At his best, Kojève reveals a vital difficulty by emphasizing the problematic nature of both finality and nonfinality—finality reduced to becoming unconscious or animal, nonfinality reduced to wandering aimlessly in discourses that are interminable. One ends up perplexed or, in Kojève's case, making a choice to reject perplexity, which never seems to have succeeded, as the volume of his unpublished work indicates.

In the end, Kojève resembles the tragic figure of *Oedipus at Colonus*. Having glimpsed difficulties that could not admit of reconciliation with each other or with any singular form of life, Kojève became a sort of wanderer, with a proper title and function that disguised his lack of rootedness in any solid conviction other than that uttered by the chorus in *Oedipus at Colonus*:

> The deliverer comes at last,
> When Hades is to have his share,
> Without marriage song, lyre or dance,
> Death at the end.
> Not to be born is the best prize of all.
> But if one is born, the next best thing is
> to return from whence one comes
> As quickly as possible.[10]

The contrast between Kojève's thought and life are captured here. The philosopher who exhorts us to correct the mistake nature made, to return to blessed unconsciousness, stands in marked contrast to the bureaucrat who strove to unify Europe, to create a final state that might well have been the state envisaged by the *Outline of a Phenomenology of Right*. Indeed, the sparkling commentary on Hegel's *Phenomenology of Spirit* stands in marked contrast to the *Outline*. Perhaps Kojève did not have the courage to face what he truly knew, as Nietzsche might have put it.[11]

But such conjectures are idle. What we have before us is a remarkably divided body of work. One may refer to that division as ironical (as Kojève seems to have wished), as inconsistent, or even as farcical. What remains is a testament tied to a "monstrous site," the site of death. Kojève, like the great death-haunted titans of Russian literature, Leo Tolstoy and Dosto-evsky, wanders, afflicted by this site, by the question of why we are the death that lives a human life, the death that hides from itself until it is unable to summon the resources to hide anymore. Like the old prince Bolkonsky in Tolstoy's *War and Peace*, who, before his death, sleeps in a different room every night so as to evade the inevitable, Kojève's inability to decide on a final road, on a way not interrupted or fettered by doubt, is a manner of glimpsing the inevitable without finally succumbing to it. But Kojève did succumb. His supposed antihumanism is a clear vision of our tragic (and darkly comic) position in the world, announced via a commentary on the ostensibly optimistic philosophy of Hegel—a vision Kojève spent the remainder of his life denying, without success.

NOTES

INTRODUCTION

1. An excellent English-language account of Kojève's seminar is given in Ethan Kleinberg, *Generation Existential: Heidegger's Philosophy in France, 1927–1961* (Ithaca, NY: Cornell University Press, 2007), 49–110.

2. Robert Pippin, *Hegel on Self-Consciousness: Death and Desire in the Phenomenology of Spirit* (Princeton, NJ: Princeton University Press, 2010), vii; Michael Forster, *Hegel's Idea of a Phenomenology of Spirit* (Chicago: University of Chicago Press, 1998), 294.

3. Leo Strauss, *On Tyranny*, ed. Victor Gourevitch and Michael Roth (Chicago: University of Chicago Press, 2013), 305.

4. The two main biographies of Kojève are those by Dominique Auffret and Marco Filoni. Neither has been translated into English. See Dominique Auffret, *Alexandre Kojève: la philosophie, l'état, la fin de l'histoire* (Paris: Grasset and Fasquelle, 1990); and Marco Filoni, *Il filosofo della domenica: vita e pensiero di Alexandre Kojève* (Turin: Bollati Boringhieri, 2008).

5. Bene vixit qui bene latuit (He who lived well, hid well) is a Latin motto used by Descartes. It may be taken to reflect either the contemplative nature of philosophical life or—much more likely, in the case of Kojève—the philosopher's overcoming of concern for purely individual, animal life.

6. Kleinberg, *Generation Existential*, 65–68.

7. There is an important irony here, because Dostoevsky himself seems to have been influenced by radical thinkers of the Hegelian left, whose thought seeped into Russia in the 1840s. Thus, Kojève's approach to Hegel offers a distinctively Russian response to Hegelian influence. While Kojève's peculiar Christology shows affinities with Ludwig Feuerbach and Bruno Bauer, it is much more intimately linked to Kojève's Russian philosophical predecessors precisely in terms of its distinctive focus on self-abnegation.

For Dostoevsky's influences, see Nel Grillaert, *What the* God-seekers *Found in Nietzsche: The Reception of Nietzsche's* Übermensch *by the Philosophers of the Russian Religious Renaissance* (Leiden: Brill-Rodopi, 2008), 107–139.

8.   An important specific task outside the general purview of this book is an investigation into Kojève's debts to the tradition of Russian Hegelianism. Both Bernard Hesbois and Philip Grier raise questions about the originality of Kojève's approach by reference, respectively, to the work of Kojève's friend Alexandre Koyré and that of Ivan Il'in, whose capacious work on Hegel may well have influenced Kojève (who, as Grier points out, appears to deny that influence). See Bernard Hesbois, "Le livre et la mort: essai sur Kojève" (PhD diss., Catholic University of Louvain, 1985), 10–11, note 15; and Ivan Il'in, *The Philosophy of Hegel as a Doctrine of the Concreteness of God and Humanity*, ed. and trans. Philip T. Grier, 1:lviii–lix (Evanston, IL: Northwestern University Press, 2010).

9.   And quite consciously so. Kojève is the best reader of Dostoevsky whom no one knows as such, and he profoundly influenced René Girard's later discussions of Dostoevsky as well. His interest in both Dostoevsky and Soloviev are well known in any case, as his biographer Dominique Auffret attests. See Auffret, *Alexandre Kojève*, 180–197; and Filoni, *Il filosofo della domenica*, 34–101. Filoni is particularly good on the Russian context, the thought of the "Silver Age."

10. Kojève conceives of history in a curiously cyclical way, as "happening once" completely and then potentially repeating any number of times. That is, for Kojève, the Hegelian circle can be traversed originally "without blueprint" only *once*, but is repeated thereafter almost "mechanically." See Kojève, *Introduction à la lecture de Hegel*, ed. Raymond Queneau, 2nd ed. (Paris: Gallimard, 1968), 391. Where there is an English translation, I include reference to the pagination of the English edition. Since the English translation omits roughly three hundred pages of the original French text, many references are not followed by an English reference, and I supply translations where appropriate.

11. I say "explicit" here because the book contains what amounts to a running commentary on the relation of Kojève to Heidegger to clarify their opposed positions and, I hope, the implications of those positions. In this latter regard, the comparison with Heidegger is illuminating.

12. Kojève's relation to Heidegger warrants its own book. While it is a commonplace of Kojève scholarship to view his commentary on Hegel as profoundly indebted to both Marx and Heidegger, other writings, such as his unpublished manuscript from 1931, entitled *Atheism*, evince an intense polemic against Heidegger as well. Regarding the commentary, see Dominique Pirotte, "Alexandre Kojève Lecteur de Heidegger," *Les Études Philosophiques* 2 Hegel-Marx (April–June 1993): 205–221.

13. In this respect, I think it is somewhat problematic to claim that Kojève is a positive biopolitical thinker, since elimination of animality as the locus of interest is a rather extreme example of biological "management." While we may argue that Kojève is a transhumanist thinker as well, the concern of transhumanism with complicated variations of our relation to animality far exceeds Kojève's rather modest contribution—in the end Kojève's thought remains profoundly hostile to *all* compromises with

animality, and he rarely presumes to imagine radically new types of being, as transhumanists do. If Kojève seeks to correct the "error" that is humanity, his new "overman" ends up assuming that status in the unheroic form of the static Sage. If anything, Kojève's thought challenges transhumanist fantasies as inherently contradictory, animal fantasies that dream of eliminating the negative features of animality and therewith animality itself. See Giorgio Agamben, *The Open: Man and Animal*, trans. Kevin Attell (Stanford, CA: Stanford University Press, 2004), 12.

14. Of these philosophers, Alain Badiou is no doubt the most outspoken as a defender of the truth against what he refers to as antiphilosophy, perhaps in emulation of Kojève. Badiou's *Manifesto for Philosophy* is a case in point, a polemic that seeks to turn away from the philosophy of errancy without, however, going so far as to declare a final truth. See Badiou, *Manifesto for Philosophy*, trans. Norman Madarasz (Albany: State University of New York Press, 1999).

15. The anti-Hegelianism of French philosophy of the 1960s has much to do with Kojève (as, perhaps, does the reaction to structuralism, which has many affinities with Kojève's thought as well). See J. Derrida, "Différance," in *Margins of Philosophy*, trans. Alan Bass (Chicago: University of Chicago Press, 1984), 1–28; and his brilliant critique of Michel Foucault, J. Derrida, "Cogito and the History of Madness," in *Writing and Difference*, trans. Alan Bass (Chicago: University of Chicago Press, 1978), 31–63. See also Gilles Deleuze and Félix Guattari, *What Is Philosophy?*, trans. Hugh Tomlinson (New York: Columbia University Press, 1996); Michel Foucault, *Discipline and Punish: Birth of the Prison*, trans. Alan Sheridan (New York: Vintage, 1977); and Jim Vernon and Antonio Calcagno, eds., *Badiou and Hegel: Infinity, Dialectics, Subjectivity* (London: Lexington, 2015), 18.

16. Many studies decry Kojève's "nihilism" or "antihumanism," by which they mean his resolute resistance to the free historical individual, understood as the individual self that holds to what Kojève considers the modern myth of self-creation and self-determination. Kojève advocates reification, to use a different vocabulary, but certainly not in the sense of Georg Lukács or Theodor Adorno. For Kojève, the concern with reification betrays a refusal to relinquish self-interest, which Lukács may have sought to correct but Adorno, whose emphasis on suffering as central to morality retains a crucial aspect of self-interest, did not.

17. This view of Hobbes appears vividly in Leo Strauss's early book on Hobbes, which Kojève read. See Leo Strauss, *The Political Philosophy of Hobbes: Its Basis and Genesis* (Chicago: University of Chicago Press, 1952), 15–16; and Alexandre Kojève to Leo Strauss, November 2, 1936, in Strauss, *On Tyranny*, 231–234.

18. Jean-Jacques Rousseau's concerns about the proliferation of desires, in the Second Discourse, are of particular relevance here. The notion of the owner or property holder who declares that a certain property is "his" comes to mind as a basic move in the structure of self-assertion that is at the heart of Rousseau's critique of modern bourgeois society as the society where the "I" triumphs over the "we," where self-interest triumphs over republican virtue. This movement from "I" to "we" is also fundamental to Kojève's interpretation of Hegel, as we shall see.

19. In this sense, Kojève is profoundly opposed to Francis Fukuyama.
20. Fyodor Dostoevsky, *Winter Notes on Summer Impressions*, trans. David Patterson (Evanston, IL: Northwestern University Press, 1997).
21. The translation of Kojève's major manuscript on legal theory, *Outline of a Phenomenology of Right*, by two fine Straussian scholars, constitutes a notable exception.
22. Boris Groys, *Introduction to Antiphilosophy*, trans. David Fernbach (London: Verso, 2012), 145–167; Stefanos Geroulanos, *An Atheism That Is Not Humanist Emerges in French Thought* (Stanford, CA: Stanford University Press, 2010), 130–172.
23. To be fair, Georges Bataille originally made this claim in 1955, in his article "Hegel, la mort et le sacrifice": "The originality and, it must be said, the courage of Alexandre Kojève is to have perceived the impossibility of going any further, *consequently* the necessity of renouncing the production of an original philosophy and thus the interminable recommencement that is the admission of the vanity of thought." Cited in Dominique Pirotte, *Alexandre Kojève: un système anthropologique* (Paris: Presses Universitaires de France, 2005), 159.

1. MADMEN

1. As does the related notion of nonsense, particularly in terms of Kojève's concern in his later works to provide a theory of sense as opposed to silence and nonsense, the latter being described most succinctly as unending or infinite discourse, a discourse than cannot find or limit itself. See Kojève, *Essai d'une histoire raisonnée de la philosophie païenne* (Paris: Gallimard, 1968–1973), 1:23–33, 57–95.
2. Kojève, "Tyranny and Wisdom," in Leo Strauss, *On Tyranny*, ed. Victor Gourevitch and Michael Roth, 135–176 (Chicago: University of Chicago Press, 2013), 153. Hereafter abbreviated as TW. See also J. Derrida, "Cogito and the History of Madness," in *Writing and Difference*, trans. Alan Bass, 31–63 (Chicago: University of Chicago Press, 1978), 36.
3. Kojève's abiding and profound interest in Dostoevsky is well documented. See Dominique Auffret, *Alexandre Kojève: la philosophie, l'état, la fin de l'histoire* (Paris: Grasset and Fasquelle, 1990), 183–197. Auffret reiterates the view that Dostoevsky's role for Kojève was fundamental, at least as important as that of Soloviev and Hegel.
4. This radical change is registered as "the birth of the self-conscious anti-hero in Russian literature." See Robert Louis Jackson, *Dostoevskij's Underground Man in Russian Literature* ('s-Gravenhage: Mouton, 1958), 14. We may consider this figure the hero of nonfinality, giving a different dialectical edge to the underground man as the hero of negation as well.
5. This is perhaps the most distinctively "Russian" aspect of Kojève's approach to Hegel.
6. Plato, *Republic*, trans. Chris Emilyn-Jones and William Preddy, vol. 2 (Cambridge, MA: Harvard University Press, 2013), 112 [516b]. The customary Stephanus numbers are indicated in brackets after all page references to the relevant modern translations.

7. For a more general discussion of madness in Plato and in the philosophical tradition in general, see Ferit Güven, *Madness and Death in Philosophy* (Albany: State University of New York Press, 2005), 13–29.

8. Plato, *Phaedrus*, trans. James H. Nichols Jr. (Ithaca, NY: Cornell University Press, 1998), 49 [245c]; for the Greek text, see Plato, *Phaedrus*, ed. Harvey Yunis (Cambridge: Cambridge University Press, 2011), 51. The translation may be controversial, since it suggests that all soul is essentially one. The Greek could mean also that "every soul is immortal." What is the import of this distinction? In the former case, soul is one—all souls participate in this one soul, are manifestations of it. In the latter case, souls are multiple, while all retaining the same essential being. What is at issue is the relation of the one and the many, an important issue in Plato, since the unity of soul, as an ideal being, suggests that soul as such is unity and is reflected in the empirical world in various embodiments, in flesh and bone. If plurality is merely the result of embodiment, then all soul is one; if not, then there is plurality in the ideal being itself, each individual is ideal.

9. Plato, *Phaedrus*, trans. Nichols, 49–50 [246a].

10. See Plato, *Republic*, 330–337 [414e–415c].

11. Plato, *Phaedrus*, trans. Harold North Fowler (Cambridge, MA: Harvard University Press, 1914), 471–473 [246a–246c].

12. Plato, *Phaedrus*, trans. Fowler, 477–479 [248b–248c].

13. Plato, *Phaedrus*, Fowler edition, 466 [244d] (my translation).

14. The phrase is a slight distortion of James Joyce's celebrated phrase about the exalted role of the artist. See James Joyce, *A Portrait of the Artist as a Young Man* (Harmondsworth: Penguin, 1976), 253.

15. Plato, *Symposium*, trans. Alexander Nehamas and Paul Woodruff (Indianapolis, IN: Hackett, 1989), 58–59 [210c–211d].

16. *Fanā* refers to the state of self-annihilation achieved by the Sufi adept. See Toshihiko Izutsu, *Sufism and Taoism: A Comparative Study of Key Philosophical Concepts* (Berkeley: University of California Press, 1984), 8, 44.

17. Martin Heidegger, "Plato's Doctrine of Truth," in *Pathmarks*, ed. William McNeill (Cambridge: Cambridge University Press, 1998), 155–182. This brief essay was culled from a lecture course Heidegger gave in the winter of 1931–1932. It was, however, not published until after the war, together with the famed "Letter on Humanism." Heidegger's basic claim is that the installation of the Platonic idea as the measure for what constitutes a being is a decisive move in the creation of a hegemonic metaphysics that has prevailed into the twentieth century. Platonism in its various avatars is still the ruling thought of the West. Regarding Kojève's thought, see TW, especially where Kojève locates universalist imperialism in Plato (169–173). Also, as to the connection with deification, pagan and Christian, see John R. Lenz, "The Deification of the Philosopher in Classical Greece," in *Partakers of the Divine Nature: The History and Development of Deification in the Christian Traditions*, ed. Michael J. Christensen and Jeffery A. Wittung (Grand Rapids, MI: Baker Academic, 2007), 47–67. As to Soloviev, see Kojève, "La métaphysique religieuse de V. Soloviev," *Revue d'histoire et de philosophie religieuses*

14 (1934): 534–554; and 15 (1935): 110–152. This text was adapted from Kojève's doctoral dissertation (of more than six hundred pages), which was supervised by Karl Jaspers. See Kojève, *Die religiöse Philosophie Wladimir Solowjews*, manuscript NAF 28320, Fonds Kojève, Bibliothèque nationale de France (box no. 6).

18. See, for example, Jackson, *Dostoevskij's Underground Man*, 49–63. Jackson calls the *Notes* a "pivotal work" in which "Dostoevsky develops the main themes of his great novels."

19. I say "dialectical" not to engage in polemic with the heritage of the Bakhtinian interpretation of Dostoevsky. But a "dull-edged" polemic will emerge, nonetheless, as we bring Kojève's thought more clearly into focus. The crucial Bakhtinian notion of "unfinalizability" must reveal itself as largely incoherent for Kojève, or as a notion that prizes "pseudo sense" over sense, in terms of Kojève's lengthy analysis of discourse in his later works. The argument between Mikhail Bakhtin and formalism has a great deal of similarity to the argument between Bakhtin and Kojève, who is decisively closer to formalist thought than is Bakhtin. For an interesting view of the relation between Kojève and Bakhtin, see Emily Finlay, "The Dialogic Absolute: Bakhtin and Kojève on Dostoevsky's *The Devils*," *The Dostoevsky Journal: An Independent Review* 12–13 (2012–2013), 47–58.

20. F. M. Dostoevsky, *Notes from Underground*, trans. Richard Pevear and Larissa Volokhonsky (New York: Vintage, 1993), 14.

21. Plato, *Phaedo*, trans. R. Hackforth (Cambridge: Cambridge University Press, 1955), 190 [118a]. At the end of his life, Socrates says that he owes a cock to the healing god Asklepios, a gesture that implies gratitude for successful recovery from an illness. In *Twilight of the Idols*, Nietzsche reads this gesture as an admission that equates life with sickness. Hackforth denies the connection, basing his judgment on that of the eminent classicist Ulrich von Wilamowitz-Moellendorff. The denial is not terribly convincing, especially since it comes without argument. Nietzsche is of course not so dismissive. See Friedrich Nietzsche, *Twilight of the Idols* and *The Anti-Christ*, trans. R. J. Hollingdale (New York: Penguin, 1968), 39.

22. The ironic description of the poet from Søren Kierkegaard's *Either/Or* comes immediately to mind: "What is a poet? An unhappy man who hides deep anguish in his heart, but whose lips are so formed that when the sigh and cry pass through them, it sounds like lovely music." See Kierkegaard, *Either/Or: A Fragment of Life*, trans. Alistair Hannay (London: Penguin, 1992), 43.

23. Kojève's comment "Language is born from discontent. Man speaks of Nature that kills him and makes him suffer; he speaks of the State that oppresses him" reflects the sentiments of the underground man, whose moans are his own account of the reasons for those moans. See Kojève, *Introduction à la lecture de Hegel*, ed. Raymond Queneau, 2nd ed. (Paris: Gallimard, 1968), 117. More generally, the claim is that human activity, insofar as it cannot overcome death, is a kind of terror or moaning before the fact of death. Art is similar, a lamentation of our cruel situation that would not exist if that situation were otherwise, if the laws of nature did not oppress us by forcing us into death.

24. See Robert L. Jackson, *Dialogues on Dostoevsky* (Stanford, CA: Stanford University Press, 1996), 29–54.

25. Dostoevsky, *Notes*, 3.

26. Dostoevsky, *Notes*, 17.

27. Dostoevsky, *Notes*, 17.

28. Just as that primary source of comedy, Aristophanes's *Clouds*, shows. The ridiculous followers of Socrates in the *phrontisterion* come to mind—pale, absurd creatures measuring fleas' jumps and gnats' farting. Coarser perhaps is the laughter of the Thracian maid who watches Thales stumble into a pit while he is looking up at the heavens. See Plato, *Theaetetus*, trans. Harold North Fowler (Cambridge, MA: Harvard University Press, 1921), 121 [174a].

29. This point is made with frequency in Heidegger's works, especially where he is eager to distinguish between philosophy and science. See, for example, Martin Heidegger, *What Is Called Thinking?*, trans. J. Glenn Gray (New York: Harper and Row, 1968), 33.

30. Andrey Platonov's poor Voshchev suffers from the disease of reflection and is "removed from production" on that basis. See Platonov, *The Foundation Pit*, trans. Robert Chandler and Olga Meerson (New York: New York Review of Books, 2009), 1.

31. See Joseph Frank, *Dostoevsky: The Stir of Liberation 1860–1865* (Princeton, NJ: Princeton University Press, 1986), 344; Robert Louis Jackson, "Aristotelian Movement and Design in Part Two of *Notes from Underground*," in *Dostoevsky (New Perspectives)*, ed. Robert Louis Jackson (Englewood Cliffs, NJ: Prentice-Hall, 1984), 66–81; and James R, Scanlon, *Dostoevsky the Thinker* (Ithaca, NY: Cornell University Press, 2002), 15, 57–80.

32. In this respect, the affinity with Nietzsche is astonishing. Nietzsche suggests that the highest form of art is the capacity for mockery—indeed, for self-mockery. See Friedrich Nietzsche, *Towards a Genealogy of Morality*, trans. Maudemarie Clark and Alan J. Swenson (Indianapolis, IN: Hackett, 1998), 69.

33. Dostoevsky, *Notes*, 32–34.

34. I refer here to Erasmus's famous work *In Praise of Folly* (1511), the play and evasiveness of which may be read as a distant forerunner to the underground man. This comparison is particularly intriguing if one considers the relation of Erasmus to Sir Thomas More, the author of *Utopia* (published by Erasmus in 1516). There is no folly in utopia.

35. See Martin Heidegger, *What Is a Thing?*, trans. Vera Deutsch (New York: Gateway, 1968). To put this point in its proper context, I may cite the example of Gottfried Leibniz, who sought to expand the hegemony of mathematical operations over the natural world to the world of history, of human behavior. Leibniz developed a fascinating thought experiment. He advocated the construction of a machine that could resolve all disputes or arguments. Leibniz referred to this machine as a "ratiocinator," and his aim was to ensure that the calculus managed by this machine would be so flawless that any dispute would be revealed as having at its basis a mistake that could be proved, or at least revealed, by a simple mathematical operation. As Leibniz put it, we might simply say, "Calculemus" (Let's calculate), and the issue would be resolved. (Leibniz's famous French text uses the French *contons* for *calculemus*.) G. W. Leibniz,

"La vraie méthode," in *Philosophische Schriften* (Berlin: Akademie Verlag, 2006), 4:3–7; and "Synopsis libri cui titulus erit: Initia et Specimina Scientiae novae Generalis pro Instauratione et Augmentis Scientarum ad publicam felicitatem" (Summary of a Book Whose Title Will Be: Beginnings and Proofs of a New General Science for the Establishment and Increase of the Sciences for the Happiness of the Public), in *Philosophische Schriften*, 4:443.

36. Dostoevsky, *Notes*, 28.
37. See Friedrich Nietzsche, *Sämtliche Briefe* (Berlin: Walter de Gruyter, 1986), 8:28.
38. Kojève, "Sofia, filo-sofia i fenomeno-logia," ed. A. M. Rutkevich, in *Istoriko-filosofskii ezhegodnik* (Moscow: Nauka, 2007), 271–324; autograph manuscript in Fonds Kojève, Bibliothèque nationale de France (box no. 20).
39. This is a point Kojève makes in his later *The Concept, Time, and Discourse*. See Kojève, *Le concept, le temps et le discours*, ed. Bernard Hesbois (Paris: Gallimard, 1990), 50.
40. Dostoevsky, *Notes*, 30.
41. As Jorge Luis Borges put the matter: "There is a concept which corrupts and upsets all others. I refer not to Evil, whose limited realm is that of ethics; I refer to the infinite." Borges, "Avatars of the Tortoise," in *Labyrinths: Selected Stories and Other Writings*, ed. Donald A. Yates and James E. Irby (New York: New Directions, 2007), 202.
42. Dostoevsky, *Notes*, 17.

2. THE POSSESSED

1. The best treatment of these "heroes" as being a kind of Left Hegelian *chelovekobog* (man-god) is in Nel Grillaert, *What the* God-seekers *Found in Nietzsche: The Reception of Nietzsche's* Übermensch *by the Philosophers of the Russian Religious Renaissance* (Leiden: Brill-Rodopi, 2008), 107–139.
2. Fyodor Dostoevsky, *Crime and Punishment*, trans. Richard Pevear and Larissa Volokhonsky (New York: Vintage, 1992), 3.
3. The Machiavellian echoes are quite evident: the prince or lawgiver may do what he prohibits others to do. See Niccolò Machiavelli, *The Prince*, trans. Peter Bondanella (Oxford: Oxford University Press, 2008); as to new modes and orders, see also Machiavelli, *The Ten Discourses on Livy*, trans. Harvey C. Mansfield and Nathan Tarcov (Chicago: University of Chicago Press, 1996), 5.
4. "In my opinion, if, as the result of certain combinations, Kepler's or Newton's discoveries could become known to people in no other way than by sacrificing the lives of one, or ten, or a hundred or more people who were hindering the discovery, or standing as an obstacle in its path, then Newton would have the right, and it would even be his duty ... *to remove* those ten or a hundred people." Dostoevsky, *Crime and Punishment*, 259.
5. Dostoevsky, *Crime and Punishment*, 260.
6. Dostoevsky, *Crime and Punishment*, 260–261.

7. See Carl Becker, *The Heavenly City of the Eighteenth-Century Philosophers*, 2nd ed. (New Haven, CT: Yale University Press, 2003).

8. Here I allude to Ippolit Terentiev's marvelous, desperate phrase in part 3 of *The Idiot*: "Can something that has no image come as an image?" Fyodor Dostoevsky, *The Idiot*, trans. Richard Pevear and Larissa Volokhonsky (New York: Vintage, 2002), 409. See also Gary Saul Morson, *Hidden in Plain View: Narrative and Creative Potentials in "War and Peace"* (Stanford, CA: Stanford University Press, 1988), 130.

9. Kojève, "Tyranny and Wisdom," in Leo Strauss, *On Tyranny*, ed. Victor Gourevitch and Michael Roth, 135–176 (Chicago: University of Chicago Press, 2013), 153–154.

10. As noted in chapter 1, Kojève refers to Kirillov at least twice in the Hegel lectures and once in his article "Hegel, Marx and Christianity."

11. See Albert Camus, *The Myth of Sisyphus*, trans. Justin O'Brien (New York: Vintage, 1991).

12. Fyodor Dostoevsky, *Demons*, trans. Richard Pevear and Larissa Volokhonsky (New York: Vintage, 1994), 115–116.

13. Herman Melville, *Moby-Dick*, in *Redburn, White-Jacket, Moby-Dick*, ed. G. Thomas Tanselle (New York: Literary Classics of the United States, 1983), 832.

14. Dostoevsky, *Demons*, 590.

15. Dostoevsky, *Demons*, 622.

16. Dostoevsky, *Demons*, 624.

17. Here I refer to famous comments from Dostoevsky himself: "And thus, all the pathos of the novel is in the prince, he is the hero. Everything else moves around him, like a kaleidoscope" and "Everything is contained in the character of Stavrogin. Stavrogin is everything." See Fyodor M. Dostoevsky, *Polnoe sobranie sochinenii*, 30 vols. (Leningrad: Akademia nauk, 1972–1990), 11:136, 207.

18. Friedrich Nietzsche, *Twilight of the Idols*, in *Twilight of the Idols* and *The Anti-Christ*, trans. R. J. Hollingdale (New York: Penguin, 1968), 34.

19. Dostoevsky, *Demons*, 43.

20. Dostoevsky, *Demons*, 45–46.

21. Samuel Beckett comes to mind, if not Louis-Ferdinand Céline: ugliness, distortion, the grotesque as a careful strategy. Or their predecessor, Nikolai Gogol.

22. See Martin Heidegger, "What Is Metaphysics?," in *Pathmarks*, ed. William McNeill (Cambridge: Cambridge University Press, 1998), 82–96; and J. Derrida, "Cogito and the History of Madness," in *Writing and Difference*, trans. Alan Bass (Chicago: University of Chicago Press, 1978), 33–37.

23. The key treatment of the notion of *bezobrazie*, or formlessness, in Dostoevsky is Robert Louis Jackson, *Dostoevsky's Quest for Form: A Study of His Philosophy of Art* (New Haven, CT: Yale University Press, 1966), 40–70. Jackson shows extraordinarily well the essentially Platonist derivation of Dostoevsky's conception of art. Formlessness, however, remains within the traditional orbit of the form–matter distinction. The more radical notion, that the Platonic forms themselves, in their unmediated purity, can be nothing for us but an empty void, is not explored.

24. One of the novel's key phrases, мне все равно, literally "all is the same to me," is the crucial catchphrase of "deep boredom," as Heidegger describes it in his 120-page account of boredom, presented as part of his 1929–1930 lecture course *The Fundamental Concepts of Metaphysics*. That there is a connection here that may serve as additional proof of Heidegger's intensive engagement with Dostoevsky. See Martin Heidegger, *The Fundamental Concepts of Metaphysics*, trans. William McNeill (Bloomington: Indiana University Press, 2001), 59–174.

25. G. W. Leibniz, *Theodicy*, trans. E. M. Huggard (La Salle, IL: Open Court, 1985), 136.

26. Bakhtin's notion of unfinalizability may be a target of Kojève's critique of nonfinality. As we will see, Kojève maintains that only a finite set of possibilities is available at any given time. There can be no assurance that those possibilities may be inexhaustible or infinite until the impossible moment when that thesis has been proved. For Kojève, then, Bakhtin's claim of the unfinalizable is a fiction, flattering for those who want to believe in the essential openness of human experience.

27. A daring conjecture would align Dostoevsky's notion of a "tear" or "stress point" with Heidegger's notion of the "rift" or *der Riß* (tear), a key constitutive aspect of the work of art. What Dostoevsky initially considers as negative—a twist, laceration, or wound in a person—becomes an important positive aspect of the work of art for Heidegger because it prevents that work from being turned into a simple object or becoming closed off. The analogy is absorbing because Heidegger holds imperfection to be positive and important, against the more prevailing view that Dostoevsky expresses in this passage. See Martin Heidegger, "The Origin of the Work of Art," in *Basic Writings*, trans. David Farrell Krell (New York: Harper Perennial, 2008), 143–203, especially 188–189.

28. Fyodor Dostoevsky, *The Brothers Karamazov*, trans. Richard Pevear and Larissa Volokhonsky (New York: Farrar, Straus and Giroux, 2002), 163–164.

29. See Emmanuel Levinas, *God, Death, and Time*, trans. Bettina Bargo (Stanford, CA: Stanford University Press, 2000).

30. Dostoevsky, *Brothers Karamazov*, 166–167.

31. Dostoevsky, *Brothers Karamazov*, 303.

32. Dostoevsky, *Brothers Karamazov*, 335.

33. Dostoevsky, *Brothers Karamazov*, 56.

34. Dostoevsky, *Brothers Karamazov*, 257.

35. Dostoevsky, *Brothers Karamazov*, 171.

36. As Mephistopheles says in part 1 of *Faust*, "I am part of that force / that always wills evil and does good" (Ich bin Teil von jener Kraft / die stets das Böse will und das Gute schafft).

3. GODMEN

1. Friedrich Nietzsche, *Towards a Genealogy of Morality*, trans. Maudemarie Clark and Alan J. Swenson (Indianapolis, IN: Hackett, 1998), 56–59.

2. V. S. Solovyov, *Lectures on Divine Humanity*, trans. rev. and ed. Boris Jakim (Hudson, NY: Lindisfarne, 1995). References to the Russian text are from V. S. Solovyov,

Sobranie sochinenii, ed. S. M. Soloviev and E. L. Radlov, 2nd ed., 1911–1914 (reprint, Brussels: Izdatel'stvo Zhizn' s bogom, 1966–1970), 3:1–181. Kojève himself refers to these lectures as the "principal source" for understanding the metaphysics of Soloviev, the basis of his thought. See Kojève, "La métaphysique religieuse de Vladimir Soloviev," *Revue d'histoire et de philosophie religieuses* 14 (1934): 537. While Kojève prefers to identify Soloviev with Friedrich Schelling, George L. Kline, for example, characterizes Soloviev as a "neo-Hegelian" and emphasizes Soloviev's debt to Hegel. See George L. Kline, "Hegel and Solovyov," in *George L. Kline on Hegel* (North Syracuse, NY: Gegensatz, 2015).

3. See Kojève, "La métaphysique religieuse de V. Soloviev," *Revue d'histoire et de philosophie religieuses* 14 (1934): 534–554; and 15 (1935): 110–152. This text was adapted from Kojève, *Die religiöse Philosophie Wladimir Solowjews*, manuscript NAF 28320, Fonds Kojève, Bibliothèque nationale de France (box no. 6). Kojève also published *Die Geschichtsphilosophie Wladimir Solowjews* (Bonn: Friedrich Cohen, 1930). Kojève's principal argument against Soloviev is that the latter maintains the subordinate position of divine humanity vis-à-vis the divine, the so-called theory of two absolutes being essentially problematic because they are not equal. See, for example, Kojève, "La métaphysique religieuse" 15 (1935): 124.

4. Paul Valliere, *Modern Russian Theology: Bukharev, Soloviev, Bulgakov* (Edinburgh: T and T Clark, 2000), 114.

5. See V. Solovyov, *The Philosophical Principles of Integral Knowledge*, trans. Valeria Z. Nollan (Grand Rapids, MI.; William B. Eerdmans, 2008), 19. This treatise was written at almost the same time as the lectures and begins with a sharp framing of the issue that presupposes the problem of suffering and evil, of theodicy. Indeed, Soloviev frames his investigation of the good life within the context of human purpose: What is the goal of human existence in general? The determination of purpose in turn determines the contours of what a good life can be—that is, a life that fulfills that purpose. From this perspective alone, it is perhaps somewhat misleading to argue that Soloviev asks about the good life in the Socratic way, since his questioning is infused with the Christian concern for theodicy.

6. Solovyov, *Lectures on Divine Humanity*, 1.

7. The force of action in Soloviev's thought is crucial and seems to have had considerable influence on Kojève. One of the virtues of Oliver Smith's recent study of Soloviev's thought is to focus on the distinctive role action plays in it. See Smith, *Vladimir Soloviev and the Spiritualization of Matter* (Brighton: Academic Studies Press, 2011), 32–36, 95. Smith quotes Judith Kornblatt's important comment, "All Russian religious philosophy insists on the role of action, a task or задача whose accomplishment will mean the reunion of God and creation." See Kornblatt, "Russian Religious Thought and the Jewish Kabbala," in *The Occult in Soviet and Russian Culture*, ed. Beatrice G. Rosenthal (Ithaca, NY: Cornell University Press, 1997), 86. See also Thomas Nemeth, *The Early Solov'ëv and His Quest for Metaphysics* (Cham: Springer, 2014), 115–123; Randall A. Poole, "Vladimir Solov'ëv's Philosophical Anthropology: Autonomy, Dignity, Perfectibility," in *A History of Russian Philosophy 1830–1930*, ed. G. M. Hamburg

and Randall A. Poole (Cambridge: Cambridge University Press, 2010), 131–149; and Valliere, *Modern Russian Theology*, 143–171.

8.   Michael S. Roth puts the issue succinctly: "The significance of Soloviev's dual perspective is clear: by seeing the Absolute as incarnate in Time (Humanity), he places great importance on human history. The structure of history's progress is determined by its End, which is the continual unification of all people in a universal reunification with God." See Roth, *Knowing and History: Appropriations of Hegel in Twentieth-Century France* (Ithaca, NY: Cornell University Press, 1988), 87.

9.   Solovyov, *Lectures on Divine Humanity*, 17.

10. Karl Löwith, *Meaning in History* (Chicago: University of Chicago Press, 1949).

11. Solovyov, *Lectures on Divine Humanity*, 17–18.

12. These narratives are generally narratives of decay—the narrative unfolds as fall or decay from a pristine beginning. One may call this kind of narrative "Edenic" as well.

13. No dialogue deals with the problem of the relation of the realm of ideas with the embodied or material world more powerfully than the *Parmenides*.

14. Solovyov, *Lectures on Divine Humanity*, 30.

15. Solovyov, *Lectures on Divine Humanity*, 38.

16. Solovyov, *Lectures on Divine Humanity*, 40–41.

17. This notion is of course vital to Kojève's philosophical enterprise, though Kojève transforms Soloviev's thinking by turning negation into a positive attribute, as the characteristic of the truly sovereign human who no longer posits a God that is outside or ahead as a "first" absolute. The negative is the character of the truly finite God. As Kojève notes, "The negative being is essentially finite. One can only be human if one dies. But one must die as a human in order to be human. Death must be freely accepted." Kojève, *Introduction à la lecture de Hegel*, ed. Raymond Queneau, 2nd ed. (Paris: Gallimard, 1968), 52.

18. Solovyov, *Lectures on Divine Humanity*, 44. Note the contrast with Kojève indicative of Kojève's atheism.

19. Solovyov, *Lectures on Divine Humanity*, 45.

20. Solovyov, *Lectures on Divine Humanity*, 67–68.

21. Kojève, *Introduction à la lecture de Hegel*, 529; Kojève,"The Idea of Death in the Philosophy of Hegel," trans. Joseph Carpino, *Interpretation* 3, no. 2/3 (Winter 1973): 114.

22. The commitment to absolute intelligibility arises from the "all-or-nothing" tendency of German idealism, best expressed by Schelling, who insists that the isolated or unique particular is contradictory. Kojève affirms this assertion, a point that becomes particularly clear in the postwar writings, as we shall see. One understands the whole only if all the parts are understood, each part in relation to every other part. Without relation, the one to the other, no understanding is possible at all. See F. W. J. Schelling, *Philosophical Investigations into the Essence of Human Freedom* (1809), trans. Jeff Love and Johannes Schmidt (Albany: State University of New York Press, 2006); and Kojève, "Sofia, filo-sofia i fenomeno-logia," ed. A. M. Rutkevich, in *Istoriko-filosofskii*

ezhegodnik (Moscow: Nauka, 2007), 320; autograph manuscript in Fonds Kojève, Bibliothèque nationale de France (box no. 20).

23. See the discussion of *Attempt at a Rational History of Pagan Philosophy* in chapter 8. Kojève calls into question the significance of sense that is only partial insofar as it may change—to say "provisional" in this respect is to say "in error" or "untrue," once the whole picture is available. And if that picture is not available, then no standard of truth or falsehood is available. What sense is left? And how do we distinguish it from non-sense, the dream of the madman, and so on? To absolve ourselves of concern for what is true (or what is "the case") is a peculiar move that may be taken so far as to deny any limitations on our capacity to create realities. Kojève's attitude is direct: one either ends up "mad," acting "as if" the world were what one imagines it to be—surely a dangerous proposition from the practical point of view—or one transforms the world through collective action in conformity with a universally accepted ideal.

24. See Saul Kripke, *Wittgenstein on Rules and Private Language* (Cambridge, MA: Harvard University Press, 1982). Kripke emphasizes the problem of the "internalized" norm or "subjective certainty" in Kojève's terms. In the absence of any external or public standard, how can I know that what I say is what I think I am saying? If I check, I may remember incorrectly or not at all. No adjudicating agency is available, and I am literally lost in myself.

25. Solovyov, *Lectures on Divine Humanity*, 81.

26. There are several important recent texts dealing with this issue. See, for example, Norman Russell, *The Doctrine of Deification in the Greek Patristic Tradition* (Oxford: Oxford University Press, 2004).

27. Solovyov, *Lectures on Divine Humanity*, 95. Augustine's text reads, "dico autem haec tria: esse, nosse, velle. sum enim et scio et volo, sum sciens et volens, et scio esse me et velle, et volo esse et scire" (*Confessiones*, book 13, para. 11).

28. Is Soloviev's approach any more outlandish than, say, Heidegger's reduction of all history to the history of Being?

29. Solovyov, *Lectures on Divine Humanity*, 71.

30. Solovyov, *Lectures on Divine Humanity*, 81.

31. Solovyov, *Lectures on Divine Humanity*, 108, 113, 118.

32. Solovyov, *Lectures on Divine Humanity*, 121. Translation modified.

33. This is Kojève's primary complaint: if there is a God, man cannot become God other than by bringing God down to man, that is, by making a move equivalent to atheism.

34. Immanuel Kant, *Groundwork of the Metaphysic of Morals*, trans. H. J. Paton (New York: Harper and Row, 1964), 88–99, 100.

35. Immanuel Kant, *Religion Within the Limits of Reason Alone*, trans. Theodore M. Greene and Hoyt B. Hudson (New York: Harper and Row, 1960), 23–27. See also Gordon E. Michalson Jr., *Fallen Freedom: Kant on Radical Evil and Moral Regeneration* (Cambridge: Cambridge University Press, 1990), 37–40.

36. See George M. Young, *Russian Cosmism: The Esoteric Futurism of Nikolai Fedorov and His Followers* (Oxford: Oxford University Press, 2012).

37. The Russian texts may be found in volumes 1 and 2 of N. F. Fedorov, *Sobranie sochinenii*, ed. A. G. Gacheva and S. G. Semenova (Moscow: Traditsia, 1995–2000). An abridged translation of *The Philosophy of the Common Task* is N. F. Fedorov, *What Was Man Created For?: The Philosophy of the Common Task*, trans. Elisabeth Kutaissoff and Marilyn Minto (London: Honeyglen, 1990), 33–102. The "Supramoralism" essay may be found in the same volume, at 105–136. For an excellent treatment of Fedorov's thought in English, see Irene Masing-Delic, *Abolishing Death: A Salvation Myth of Russian Twentieth-Century Literature* (Stanford, CA: Stanford University Press, 1992), 76–104. For a comprehensive treatment, see Michael Hagemeister, *Nikolaj Fedorov: Studien zu Leben, Werk und Wirkung* (Munich: Otto Sagner, 1989).

38. The title expresses the typically Fedorovian insistence on completeness. One finds in Fedorov's works a repetitiveness essential to their construction, both as an indication of the simplicity of their underlying point and the obsessive need to make it again and again—to convince completely.

39. Fedorov, *Sobranie sochinenii*, 1:37–308.

40. Kojève, "Tyranny and Wisdom," in Leo Strauss, *On Tyranny*, ed. Victor Gourevitch and Michael Roth, 135–176 (Chicago: University of Chicago Press, 2013), 171–173. See also A. M. Rutkevich, "Alexander Kojève: From Revolution to Empire," *Studies in East European Thought* 69, no. 4 (December 2017): 329–344.

41. Fedorov, *What Was Man Created For?*, 56.

42. As Fedorov notes, "Only when all men come to participate in knowledge will pure science, which perceives nature as a whole in which the sentient is sacrificed to the insensate, cease to be indifferent to this distorted attitude of the conscious being to the unconscious force." And he adds, "Then applied science will be aimed at transforming instruments of destruction into means of regulating the blind death-bearing force." Fedorov, *What Was Man Created For?*, 40; see also 76.

43. Fedorov, *What Was Man Created For?*, 40. This suppression is crucial to Fedorov's project; there has been considerable debate concerning Fedorov's radical theology—is it still a theology or is it the most extreme anthropology possible?

44. Fedorov, *What Was Man Created For?*, 89.

45. This seems a more Confucian than Christian move, unless one takes into account the differing notion of community that applies in the Eastern church.

46. "Singularity" is Ray Kurzweil's term for the moment when human beings will have reached a new kind of being.

47. Fedorov, *What Was Man Created For?*, 77.

48. An interesting study that picks up Solovovien themes from a rather different perspective is Mark Johnston, *Surviving Death* (Princeton, NJ: Princeton University Press, 2010).

49. This seems to be Kojève's view; it is also reflected in a remarkable text from Martin Heidegger from his recently published Black Notebooks: "In this way, the lower forces of the animal first come to prevail, through rationality *animalitas* first comes into play—with the goal to liberate the animality of the not yet finished animal, mankind." See Martin Heidegger, *Anmerkungen I-V (Schwarze Hefte 1942–1948)*, ed. Peter Trawny (Frankfurt: Vittorio Klostermann, 2015), 41.

4. THE LAST REVOLUTION

1. This is characteristic of the reception from the Straussian side as well as from others like Judith Butler, who puts the matter succinctly: "Kojève's lectures on Hegel are both commentaries and original works of philosophy." See Butler, *Subjects of Desire: Hegelian Reflections in Twentieth-Century France* (New York: Columbia University Press, 1987), 63. See also F. Roger Devlin, *Alexandre Kojève and the Outcome of Modern Thought* (Lanham, MD: University Press of America, 2004), xiv–xv; James H. Nichols Jr., *Alexandre Kojève: Wisdom at the End of History* (Lanham, MD: Rowman and Littlefield, 2007), 21–30; and Stanley Rosen, *Hermeneutics as Politics* (Oxford: Oxford University Press, 1987), 103–107. Others are less sanguine, perhaps with good reason. See Philip T. Grier, "The End of History and the Return of History," in *The Hegel Myths and Legends*, ed. Jon Stewart (Evanston, IL: Northwestern University Press, 1996), 183–198; and Joseph Flay, *Hegel's Quest for Certainty* (Albany: State University of New York Press, 1984), 299. Flay bluntly says, "Kojève's influence is unfortunate, for seldom has more violence been done by a commentator to the original." Still others, like Michael Forster, think that Kojève's interpretation is correct or, at the very least, plausible. Barry Cooper offers a balanced approach that accepts Kojève's interpretation as "vulgarized" Hegel but praises its astuteness and power. See Cooper, *The End of History: An Essay on Modern Hegelianism* (Toronto: University of Toronto Press, 1984), 3. George L. Kline affirms the importance of Kojeve's reading as well as its flaws. See Kline, "The Existentialist Rediscovery of Hegel and Marx," in *George L. Kline on Hegel* (North Syracuse, NY: Gegensatz Press, 2015). Perhaps most balanced of all is a more recent reading of Kojève that gives Kojève his due for emphasizing the revolutionary potential in Hegelian thought as a thinking about history. See Eric Michael Dale, *Hegel, the End of History, and the Future* (Cambridge: Cambridge University Press, 2014), 80–109. Still, Dale admits (echoing Flay) that Kojève is better Kojève than Hegel: "Indeed, Kojève's *Introduction à la lecture de Hegel* is not a particularly useful introduction to reading Hegel, if what one wants is Hegel, rather than Kojève. For that matter, Kojève's book is not a particularly good introduction to how to read Hegel via Marx, if what one wants is to understand Marx's appropriation of Hegel, rather than Kojève's. As a guide to Kojève's thought, however, *Introduction à la lecture de Hegel* remains the ideal starting place" (83). This comment repeats similar comments made about Heidegger as well.

2. Kojève seems to admit as much himself. See Kojève, review of G. R. G. Mure's *A Study of Hegel's Logic, Critique* 3, no. 54 (1951): 1003–1007.

3. Martin Heidegger, *Kant and the Problem of Metaphysics*, trans. Richard Taft (Bloomington: Indiana University Press, 1997), xx. Translation modified.

4. See Butler, *Subjects of Desire*, 63, for the defense; and Flay, *Hegel's Quest for Certainty*, 299, for the negative view.

5. Kojève, *Introduction à la lecture de Hegel*, ed. Raymond Queneau, 2nd ed. (Paris: Gallimard, 1968), 529 (hereafter abbreviated as ILH); Kojève, "The Idea of Death in the Philosophy of Hegel," trans. Joseph Carpino, *Interpretation* 3, no. 2/3 (Winter 1973): 114 (hereafter IDH).

6. ILH, 66. All translations of Kojève's text are mine unless otherwise indicated. See also note 10.
7. ILH, 93.
8. ILH, 117.
9. ILH, 135.
10. ILH, 167; Kojève, *Introduction to the Reading of Hegel*, ed. Allan Bloom, trans. James H. Nichols Jr., 2nd ed. (Ithaca, NY: Cornell University Press, 1969), 38 (hereafter abbreviated as IRH). Where I have been able to use it as a base, I have frequently modified Nichols's fine translation for emphasis or clarity with regard to the context in which I quote Kojève. In addition, as I note in this chapter, the English translation omits roughly three hundred pages of the French original; thus, all translations from the French text not translated by Nichols are mine.
11. ILH, 463; IRH, 187.
12. ILH, 550; IDH,134.
13. I note, however, that Kojève attributes a capacity for condensation of the whole into a part to Hegel himself and his "ideogram texts." See ILH, 415.
14. Kojève, "Tyranny and Wisdom," in Leo Strauss, *On Tyranny*, ed. Victor Gourevitch and Michael Roth (Chicago: University of Chicago Press, 2013), 255.
15. ILH, 97. In fairness to Kojève, however, it should be noted that the focus on action in his commentary tends to overshadow concerns with the "passive contemplation" described in the first three chapters of the *Phenomenology*. Indeed, as George L. Kline puts it, "It was Kojève, I think, who first adequately stressed the interrelations among what he called 'contemplation,' 'desire,' and 'action' in Hegel. His point was that (passive) contemplation at the initial stage of consciousness gives way at the stage of self-consciousness to desire, which, in turn, at the stages of self-consciousness and active reason, issues in action. Desire introduces negativity to the dialectical scene, and negativity leads to action." See Kline, "The Dialectic of Action and Passion in Hegel's *Phenomenology of Spirit*," in *George L. Kline on Hegel* (North Syracuse, NY: Gegensatz, 2015). This view runs contrary to that of Robert Pippin, who decries Kojève's interpretation of Hegel precisely on the basis of Kojève's relative neglect of the first three chapters of the *Phenomenology*. See Pippin, *Hegel on Self-Consciousness: Death and Desire in the Phenomenology of Spirit* (Princeton, NJ: Princeton University Press, 2010), 11.
16. Prudence recommends an interpretation of Kojève's approach to Hegel that both stands on its own and points to some of Kojève's supposed deviations from or simplifications of the text. It is evident that Kojève's reputation among Hegel scholars is worth an extended treatment of its own, but that is not the purpose of this study. While Stanley Rosen defends Kojève, claiming that his work is worth many more learned commentaries, the concern among Hegel scholars is surely justified. One may argue that, for scholars such as Terry Pinkard and Robert Pippin, who develop a view of the *Phenomenology* as creating a comprehensive practical philosophy, Kojève's interpretation must seem problematic, if not perverse. Other Hegel scholars seem to view Kojève's interpretation more ambiguously, though one would be hard pressed to find a champion of Kojève in the current Anglo-American discourse on Hegel. For a more positive

view of Kojève's interpretation as justified within its own terms, see, for example, Michael Forster, *Hegel's Idea of a Phenomenology of Spirit* (Chicago: University of Chicago Press, 1998), 248. For a view that follows Kojève in substantial respects, see Catherine Malabou, *The Future of Hegel: Plasticity, Temporality and Dialectic* (New York: Routledge, 2005).

17. Stefanos Geroulanos, *An Atheism That Is Not Humanist Emerges in French Thought* (Stanford, CA: Stanford University Press, 2010), 131. Geroulanos's treatment of Kojève is in general superb and, aside from Groys's, is the most helpful in English. Its most problematic aspect may be that it assumes an underlying understanding of the human as the bourgeois free historical individual, which Kojève is out to eliminate as being more animal than human. Does Kojève's project end up in an "antihumanism" or in a more profound humanism? Geroulanos does not go into this debate. Nonetheless, Kojève's fundamental challenge turns on how one defines the human. Is it more human to respect the servitude to animal desire or to extirpate that desire? Kojève seems to conclude that the latter is more human, and, in so doing, he calls into question the definition of the human upon which Geroulanos relies.

18. We may go even further back to mention Jean-Jacques Rousseau's second discourse, *A Discourse on Inequality*, as another imitation and parody of academic discourse.

19. The article was published as "Autonomie et dépendance de la conscience de soi" (Autonomy and Dependence on Self-Consciousness), *Mesures* (January 14, 1939).

20. This problem is inherent in all interpretation where the original author cannot respond to correct or clarify his text in light of the interpretation. Dialogues with the dead are impossible, other than in the form of a deceptive metaphor.

21. See Jacques Derrida, "Before the Law," in *Acts of Literature*, ed. Derek Attridge (London: Routledge, 1992), 191.

22. It is not clear whether Derrida would refute this account, as if repetition were something to be abhorred. Indeed, Derrida's own concerns with radical novelty are apparent in "Cogito and the History of Madness" as well as in many other arguments he makes against the possibility of unmediated access to what is. The repetition of failure to achieve that access is not negative for Derrida but the source of a certain beneficial humility.

23. The "canonical" text here is of course Leo Strauss, *Persecution and the Art of Writing* (Chicago: University of Chicago Press, 1988).

24. See Eric Michael Dale, *Hegel, the End of History, and the Future*, 80.

25. ILH, 8.

26. ILH, 11; IRH, 3. For the Hegelian text, see G. W. F. Hegel, *Die Phänomenologie des Geistes*, ed. Heinrich Clairmont and Hans-Friedrich Wessels (Hamburg: Felix Meiner, 1988), 127–135; or G. W. F. Hegel, *The Phenomenology of Spirit*, trans. A. V. Miller (Oxford: Oxford University Press, 1977), 111–119. Further references to the *Phenomenology* shall give English pagination and paragraph numbering first, then the pagination of the German text, in brackets.

27. Of course Hegel himself introduces the relation of self-consciousness and desire (*Begierde*) in chapter 4, but Kojève's development of the relation is extraordinary. Moreover,

to begin one's commentary by ignoring the introduction and first three chapters of the *Phenomenology* is itself very provocative; hence accusations that Kojève's interpretation is bad because it ignores crucial aspects of the *Phenomenology*. See, for example, Pippin, *Hegel on Self-Consciousness*, 11. As to desire, see Pippin; and Frederick Neuhouser, "Deducing Desire and Recognition in the *Phenomenology of Spirit*," *Journal of the History of Philosophy* 24, no. 2 (April 1986): 243–262. For another view, see Paul Redding, "Hermeneutic or Metaphysical Hegelianism? Kojève's Dilemma," *The Owl of Minerva* 22, no. 2 (Spring 1991): 175–189.

28. Redding, "Hermeneutic or Metaphysical Hegelianism?"; Ethan Kleinberg, *Generation Existential: Heidegger's Philosophy in France, 1927–1961* (Ithaca, NY: Cornell University Press, 2005), 79.

29. Kleinberg, *Generation Existential*, 69. Kleinberg suggests that Kojève's understanding of Heidegger was "sophisticated, if slightly impressionistic." It may be better to suggest that Kojève's interpretation is tendentious, distorting Heidegger's terminology by interpreting it as an attempt to escape from Hegel or the philosophy of self-consciousness. Kojève's remarkable note on Hegel and Heidegger, an unpublished book review, tends to confirm this thesis. See Kojève, "Note inédite sur Hegel et Heidegger," ed. Bernard Hesbois, *Rue Descartes* 7 (June 1993): 35–46.

30. Gwendoline Jarczyk and Pierre-Jean Labarriere, *De Kojève à Hegel: 150 ans de pensée hégélienne en France* (Paris: Albin Michel, 1996), 64. Kojève's words are striking: "On the one hand, my course was essentially a work of propaganda intended to make a striking impression [*frapper les esprits*]. That's why I consciously emphasized the role of the dialectic of Master and Slave and, in general, treated the content of the *Phenomenology* schematically." Given Kojève's habitual irony, it is hard to say to what extent this passage reflects the truth about the lectures. If, however, one takes Kojève seriously in "Tyranny and Wisdom," it is at the least a fair conjecture to attribute to his arguments a polemical, political intent and not a scholarly one (as that may be traditionally understood).

31. ILH, 11–12; IRH, 4.

32. One should be careful here. The freedom of the beginning is the only point of freedom that seems absolute, and even it cannot be absolute because the beginning is negative, thus conditioned by whatever it negates (even if that negation is a negation of the "absolute" beginning). These conditions come to clarity as the activity of negation continues, and one might argue that the continued process of negation is merely a process of coming to grasp clearly the limitations established by that beginning—indeed, this may be said of Kojève's thinking as a whole insofar as it insists upon self-understanding as explicitation of the implications relevant to or contained in the beginning. While Kojève emphasizes human identity as negative in itself, as empty or *un vide*, the process of negation produces a positive discursive identity and is not, in this sense, merely a "deconstructive identification of *man* with *negation*," as Geroulanos suggests, but rather is that and its opposite, the difference between negation and creation having been effaced when viewed from the final end point, the universal or homogeneous state or the "Book" (which I will discuss in chapter 6). See Geroulanos, *An Atheism*, 151.

33. We must assume that Kojève refers to Hegel's famous equation of self-consciousness and desire in the *Phenomenology* (121, §167 [105]). But as I have noted, Kojève's account seems to "float free" of the Hegelian text, at least for the initial six pages of the French text, which effectively replaces Hegel's own introduction to chapter 4.

34. ILH, 12; IRH, 5.

35. The comparison with Plato is obvious and instructive. In this sense, Kojève engages in a (slightly) veiled commentary on the *Symposium* and the two forms of *erōs*, the lower and the higher.

36. ILH, 66.

37. Nonetheless there does seem to be an element of question begging here, since the story of self-emergence seems to presume the existence of the self that comes to itself in the dialectical process, this being another version of the problem set out previously with regard to the identity of the self to which desire forces a return.

38. Kojève comments on the dialectic in the first appendix to the Hegel lectures. See ILH, 453; IRH, 176.

39. Kojève, following Rousseau, privileges history, defined as the human elimination of nature as such. Indeed, for Kojève, it seems that history has no other sense than as the negation of nature, its antipode. He goes so far as to argue that the retention of a philosophy of nature is Hegel's principal mistake. See ILH, 377–378.

40. The universal and homogeneous state will be discussed further in the following chapters, particularly chapter 8. Still, this is a curious identity because it must be something like an absolute identity, and what can an absolute identity be? Kojève hesitates here, even suggesting at one point that the universal and homogeneous state is a "limit case." See Kojève, *Esquisse d'une phénoménologie du droit* (Paris: Gallimard, 1981), 182 (hereafter abbreviated as EPD); Kojève, *Outline of a Phenomenology of Right*, trans. Bryan-Paul Frost and Robert Howse (Lanham, MD: Rowman and Littlefield, 2008), 165 (hereafter OPR).

41. Here in embryonic form is the tension between finality and negation that will loom large in Kojève. How does one know when negation is complete?

42. ILH, 13; IRH, 6.

43. Friedrich Nietzsche, *Beyond Good and Evil*, trans. Marion Faber (Oxford: Oxford University Press, 1998), 56.

44. Rousseau is arguably the originator of the recognition thesis in his notion of the relation of *amour de soi* and *amour propre*. See Frederick Neuhouser, *Rousseau's Theodicy of Self-Love* (Oxford: Oxford University Press, 2008), 29–53.

45. Robert B. Pippin, *Hegel on Self-Consciousness*, vii. Pippin otherwise distances himself from Kojève's reading of Hegel.

46. ILH, 14; IRH, 7.

47. Of course, the mere possibility of a common object of different desires raises a question as to the origin of the commonality. Different desires would seem to presuppose a difference in the object desired, which also presupposes a common identity transcending the difference. But whence this common identity? If identity is created by negation, by human activity, there cannot be a positive "given" prior to that activity. The

plurality Kojève associates with this activity has to be at odds with any overarching commonality. The common object itself can only be a creation of previous negation, but it is by no means obvious that the prior negation reveals anything like a nature or common underlying identity, a "given," albeit implicit.

48. Again, this identification seems problematic. Is self-preservation not a given for Kojève? And, if so, then how is it given if human (not animal) negation creates the given? As we shall see, self-preservation is not a given for Kojève; it is the result of a specific choice, the decision to surrender in combat rather than to die, and this choice reveals two identities, that of the master, which Kojève associates with the human, and that of the slave, which Kojève associates with the animal. The master rejects any given, whereas the slave hesitates in this respect, and it is not clear why, for Kojeve, the slave chooses to be human—or if this is indeed the case. Kojève's own hesitations about the emancipation of the slave, via either technology or revolutionary terror, illustrate the problem: the slave who conquers death through technology seems more beast than human, while the slave who achieves emancipation through terror looks more human than beast.

49. ILH, 14; IRH, 7.

50. The expression is quite awkward in French as well. I have translated it literally—one might prefer "desire for"—to capture the peculiarity of the genitive.

51. Kojève utilizes the image of a ring, both in the Hegel lectures and in his *Outline of a Phenomenology of Right*, to describe his "dualist ontology": "An image might compel one to admit that the project of a dualist ontology is not absurd. Let us consider a gold ring. There is a hole, and this hole is just as essential to the ring as is the gold: without the gold, the 'hole' (which, moreover, would not exist) would not be a ring; but without the hole the gold (which would nonetheless exist) would not be a ring either." This image recalls the black circle insofar as the center is the "trou" (hole), the emptiness, the absence surrounded by a frame. See ILH, 487; IRH, 214–215.

52. ILH, 14; IRH, 7.

53. ILH, 15; IRH, 8–9.

54. "La seule erreur—théiste—du Christianisme est la résurrection" (The only—theistic—error of Christianity is resurrection). Kojève, "Hegel, Marx and Christianity," trans. Hilail Gildin, *Interpretation* 1, no. 1 (1970): 41.

55. Hegel, *Phenomenology*, 111–119 ($178–196) [127–136].

56. In his famous letter to Tran Duc Thao, Kojeve himself admits that this is an innovation of his own, though Kojève's account is not an implausible one. See Gwendoline Jarczyk and Pierre-Jean Labarriere, eds., *De Kojève à Hegel: 150 ans de pensée hégélienne en France* (Paris: Albin Michel, 1996), 64–65. For differing discussions of desire in Hegel's chapter 4, see, again, Pippin, *Hegel on Self-Consciousness*, 6–53; and Neuhouser, "Deducing Desire," 243–262. For an overview of the issue, see Scott Jenkins, "Hegel's Concept of Desire," *Journal of the History of Philosophy* 47, no. 1 (2009): 103–130.

57. This reading of Kojève shows his affinity with Carl Schmitt, whose insistence that conflict is the foundation of the political (whence emerge, we may surmise, all other modes of human activity) broadens Kojève's exclusive focus on one such relation.

58. Indeed, Kojève goes so far as to translate Hegel's rather neutral "das Sein des Lebens" as *la vie-animale*, a possible if tendentious rendering of the German.

59. ILH, 18; IRH, 11. Commenting on Hegel, *Phenomenology*, 111 (§178) [127–128].

60. Once again, for Kojève there is no nature, no given. Even the relation of master and slave is not a given; rather, it is a productive origin that the philosopher merely describes. Kojève is of course aware that this relation is not obviously decisive to all as a "given" not given necessarily but contingently through human action, and thus requires the "pedagogical" or "propagandistic" activity of the philosopher.

61. ILH, 19; IRH, 13. Commenting on Hegel, *Phenomenology*, 113–114 (§187) [130–131].

62. *Conatus* refers to Spinoza's choice of the Latin verb *conari* (to attempt; to try): "Unaquæque res, quantum in se est, in suo esse perseverare conatur" (Each thing, insofar as it is in itself, endeavors to persist in being). Baruch Spinoza, *Ethics* part 3, prop. 6, in *Spinoza: Complete Works*, trans. Samuel Shirley (Indianapolis, IN: Hackett, 2002), 283.

63. There is nothing new in the thesis that the servant creates culture, that culture is indeed the product of servitude—this much may be gleaned by even a casual reading of Nietzsche's *Towards a Genealogy of Morality*. Here, as elsewhere in Kojève, the *Genealogy* an important point of reference for Kojève's commentary (since the *Genealogy* is in some ways itself a commentary on Hegel).

64. "But one cannot *live* as master." Or better still (from *Outline of a Phenomenology of Right*), "The Master appears in history only in order to disappear. He is only there so that there will be a Slave" (EPD, 242; OPR, 213, translation modified). On "catalyst," see ILH, 175.

65. To be sure, this is a problematic point, because the master, though at an impasse, *needs* the slave to continue his life. Servitude to the slave is the master's eventual undoing, his corruption. Kojève notes that the master "can die as a man, but he can live only as an animal" (ILH, 55).

66. ILH, 28; IRH, 23. Commenting on Hegel, *Phenomenology*, 117 (§194) [134].

67. ILH, 34; IRH, 29–30. Commenting on Hegel, *Phenomenology*, 119 (§196) [136].

5. TIME NO MORE

1. "It is the Slave who will become the historical human, the true human: in the last instance, the Philosopher, Hegel, who will understand the why and the how of definitive satisfaction by means of mutual recognition." Kojève, *Introduction à la lecture de Hegel*, ed. Raymond Queneau, 2nd ed. (Paris: Gallimard, 1968), 54. Hereafter abbreviated as ILH.

2. Kojève writes, "The Sage is the man who is *fully* and *perfectly conscious of himself.*" See ILH, 271; and Kojève, *Introduction to the Reading of Hegel*, trans. James H. Nichols Jr. (Ithaca, NY: Cornell University Press, 1969), 76 (hereafter abbreviated as IRH).

3. Martin Heidegger, *Introduction to Metaphysics*, trans. Gregory Fried and Richard Polt, 2nd ed. (New Haven, CT: Yale University Press, 2014), 163–200.

4. See Mark Johnston, *Surviving Death* (Princeton, NJ: Princeton University Press, 2010), 270–304. As I noted previously, this well-received book examines some of the central issues pertinent to Vladimir Soloviev, Nikolai Fedorov, and Kojève from a perspective that shows strong affinities with both Soloviev and Kojève, though more with Soloviev.

5. Stefanos Geroulanos is particularly helpful in this respect, with his interesting and nuanced reading of Kojève's differing attempts to characterize the end of history (and death of man) narratives. Geroulanos describes three differing approaches, two arising in the Hegel lectures, a third from Kojève's *Notion of Authority*, written in 1942 and unpublished in Kojève's lifetime. In his account, Geroulanos tends to focus on the result as one of enervation (the "last man") or bestialization (a failure to overcome nature), and, in either case, with the death of man as a free historical individual. While Geroulanos's account is no doubt justified within its own terms, I seek to address the problem Geroulanos identifies so effectively in a different manner, as a problem having to do with the dilemma of emancipation, of becoming truly human, the ostensibly free historical individual being, despite these terms—the problem of a slave not yet emancipated but still very much on the way to emancipation. As Kojeve notes, "It is only in negating this existence [man's 'animal existence'] that he [man] is human" (ILH, 53). The problem for Kojeve that I seek to clarify is twofold, since he wavers both on how emancipation may be achieved (through terror, technology, or both) and on what an emancipated state might look like. Do we become like animals, having returned to the freedom from error of nature, the state prior to the combat that creates history, or do we become something wholly different, neither human nor animal? This final irony (which Geroulanos denies) is that the complete negation of nature returns us to a state that is like nature though radically different, since it is created by humanizing *work*.

6. ILH, 144. Commenting on chapter 6, part B.3, in G. W. F. Hegel, *Die Phänomenologie des Geistes*, ed. Heinrich Clairmont and Hans-Friedrich Wessels (Hamburg: Felix Meiner, 1988), 385–394; or G. W. F. Hegel, *The Phenomenology of Spirit*, trans. A. V. Miller (Oxford: Oxford University Press, 1977), 355–363 (§582–597).

7. The images Kojève uses, of "bodies emptied of spirit" or "bees," suggest bestialization. But there is no necessity to come to this conclusion. These images—which we will discuss in chapter 7—seem to form part of Kojève's provocative "propaganda." Considered somewhat more perspicuously, the post-historical state, as Kojève also hints, is more likely impossible to imagine, because the death of man that is the highest expression of the human brings with it the death of the animal as well. As Kojève writes, "A purely human Universe, by contrast, is inconceivable, for without Nature, the Human is nothingness, pure and simple." Kojève, *Esquisse d'une phénoménologie du droit* (Paris: Gallimard, 1981), 244; *Outline of a Phenomenology of Right*, trans. Bryan-Paul Frost and Robert Howse (Lanham, MD: Rowman and Littlefield, 2008), 214, translation modified. This sentence comes right after a discussion of the ring and emphasizes the importance of the relation between the human and nature and, consequently, the unusual aspect of the end of history—that neither can remain at the end.

8. This is one of Kojève's innovative readings of Hegel insofar as Kojève views dialectic not as a method but as the form through which the philosopher—or, better, the

sage—merely describes the "Real," the struggle and work that lead to the final truth of "universal History," at the end of history. See ILH 455, 462, 466; IRH 179, 186, 191.

9.   ILH, 143. Again commenting on Hegel, *Phenomenology*, chapter 6, part B.3.

10.   Tom Rockmore, *Cognition: An Introduction to Hegel's* Phenomenology of Spirit (Berkeley: University of California Press, 1997), 179. The notion that the *Phenomenology* brings philosophy to an end in the attainment of absolute knowledge (or, as Kojève implies, *Sophia*) may seem a commonplace. But the exact result of the *Phenomenology* is a subject of considerable debate; it seems anything but clear. Indeed, it may be fair to say that one's view of the *Phenomenology* (and thus of its impact on philosophy) depends on how one interprets the finality announced in this chapter, and there are many differing interpretations. For various views of the chapter and absolute knowledge, one may consult Michael Forster, *Hegel's Idea of a Phenomenology of Spirit* (Chicago: University of Chicago Press, 1998); Robert Pippin, *Hegel's Idealism* (Cambridge: Cambridge University Press, 1989); Terry Pinkard, *Hegel's Phenomenology: The Sociality of Reason* (Cambridge: Cambridge University Press, 1994); and Catherine Malabou, *The Future of Hegel: Plasticity, Temporality and Dialectic* (New York: Routledge, 2005). But there are many other signal works: Jacques Derrida, *Glas*, trans. John P. Leavey Jr. (Lincoln: Nebraska University Press, 1986); Joseph C. Flay, *Hegel's Quest for Certainty* (Albany: State University of New York Press, 1984); Martin Heidegger, *Hegel's Phenomenology of Spirit*, trans. Parvis Emad and Kenneth Maly (Bloomington: Indiana University Press, 1988); Martin Heidegger, *Hegel*, trans. Joseph Arel and Niels Feuerhahn (Bloomington: Indiana University Press, 2015); Jean Hyppolite, *Genesis and Structure of Hegel's* Phenomenology of Spirit, trans. S. Cherniak and J. Heckman (Evanston, IL: Northwestern University Press, 1974); Charles Taylor, *Hegel* (Cambridge: Cambridge University Press, 1977). Also, as a supplement, see Robert Pippin, "The 'Logic of Experience' as 'Absolute Knowledge' in Hegel's *Phenomenology of Spirit*," in *Hegel's* Phenomenology of Spirit: *A Critical Guide*, ed. Dean Moyar and Michael Quante (Cambridge: Cambridge University Press, 2011), 210–217.

11.   See Allen Speight, *Hegel, Literature, and the Problem of Agency* (Cambridge: Cambridge University Press, 2004), 12. For discussion of the *Phenomenology* as a bildungsroman, see Michael Forster, *Hegel's Idea*, 437; and H. S. Harris, *Hegel's Ladder* (Indianapolis, IN: Hackett Publishing, 1997), 1:10. Whether bildungsroman or biography (of man or God), the subject appears to be spirit itself and not the peculiar Kojèvian Godman, the sage, as the personification or incarnation of spirit.

12.   Kojève is clear that the philosopher or sage merely describes the slave's self-overcoming: "This is to say that the attitude of the philosopher or the "savant" (= Sage) vis-à-vis Being and the Real is that of purely passive *contemplation*, and philosophical or "scientific" activity confines itself to a simple *description* of the Real and Being" (ILH, 449).

13.   Kojève, "Tyranny and Wisdom," in Leo Strauss, *On Tyranny*, ed. Victor Gourevitch and Michael Roth (Chicago: University of Chicago Press, 2013),153.

14.   Kojève, "Tyranny and Wisdom," 153–154.

15.   In this respect, Kojève brings his own status into question. If a philosopher or sage merely describes what is the case, then he does not try to influence or shape it. Yet Kojève's pedagogy is clearly active and seeks to bring about "conversion." That being so, Kojève

takes on an interesting role as the one who proclaims the truth in order to *implement* it; he is the prophet of the new religion. Better: he is prophet of the truth that will replace religion. "Man . . . achieves the absolute Philosophy, which replaces Religion" (ILH, 114).

16.   Kojève, "Hegel, Marx and Christianity," trans. Hilail Gildin, *Interpretation* 1, no. 1 (1970): 42.

17.   ILH, 279; IRH, 85.

18.   The "unthought" or "unsaid" is a cliché of Heidegger's thinking. See, for example, the prefatory comments to Heidegger's celebrated essay "Plato's Doctrine of Truth," in Martin Heidegger, *Pathmarks*, ed. William McNeil (Cambridge: Cambridge University Press, 1998), 155.

19.   ILH, 280; IRH, 86. Kojève identifies the Platonic view with theism and Hegel's with atheism, the Platonic affirming the impossibility of attaining wisdom and, thus, the necessarily *zētētic* nature of the philosophic life, the Hegelian insisting on the attainability of wisdom through human reason alone. Kojève places himself in the Hegelian line, against those, such as Heidegger, to whom he attributes theism in this broad sense. Perhaps his clearest discussion of this difference is in one of the excerpts from the as yet not fully published manuscript *Sofia, filo-sofia i fenomeno-logia* (278–284); autograph manuscript in Fonds Kojève, Bibliothèque nationale de France (box no. 20).

20.   For Kojève, circularity is very important, the criterion that distinguishes Hegel from Plato—or philosophy from theology, in Kojève's terms. As he puts it, "This idea of circularity is, as it were, the only original element brought forth by Hegel" (ILH, 287). He also states, "There is thus for Hegel a double criterion for the realization of wisdom: on the one hand, the universality and homogeneity of the State in which the Sage lives and, on the other, the circularity of his Knowledge"(ILH, 289). As to the state, Kojève notes, "The Sage is only possible in the State that finishes this evolution and where *all* citizens "suppress" themselves . . . where there are no *particular* interests that mutually *exclude* each other" (ILH, 301).

21.   Martin Heidegger, *The Metaphysical Foundations of Logic*, trans. Michael Heim (Bloomington: Indiana University Press, 1984), 45.

22.   Kojève divides chapter 8 into three parts. His divisions do not exist in the original Hegelian text. He divides his own account as follows (English pagination and paragraphing, followed by pagination of the German text): lectures 1 and 2 are introduction; lectures 3 and 4 cover part 1, roughly six pages in the German text (479–485, §788–797 [516–522]); lectures 5, 9, and 10 cover part 2, roughly five pages in the German text (485–490, §798–804 [523–528]); lectures 6 through 8 are an "excursus" on time and the concept, based on two pages of the German text (486–487, §801 [524–525]); and lectures 11 and 12 cover part 3, comprising the final three pages of German text (490–493, §805–808 [528–531]).

23.   ILH, 319. This lecture is omitted from the English translation.

24.   ILH, 300. This lecture is also omitted from the English translation.

25.   See Heidegger, *Introduction to Metaphysics*, 8–9.

26.   Friedrich Nietzsche, *Beyond Good and Evil*, trans. Marion Faber (Oxford: Oxford University Press, 1998), 4.

27.   Michael Roth's fine study brings this point to the fore. Roth, *Knowing and History: Appropriations of Hegel in Twentieth-Century France* (Ithaca, NY: Cornell University Press, 1988), 83. Also see Kojève, ILH, 289: "Hegelian philosophy is a *theo-logy*; only its God is the Sage."

28.   Immanuel Kant, *Groundwork of the Metaphysic of Morals*, trans. H. J. Paton (New York: Harper and Row, 1964), 103–104.

29.   I refer here of course to the celebrated opening of the *Science of Logic*. See G. W. F. Hegel, *The Science of Logic*, trans. George di Giovanni (Cambridge: Cambridge University Press, 2010), 45–82. Also see Kojève's interesting treatment of this beginning in *Le concept, le temps et le discours*, ed. Bernard Hesbois (Paris: Gallimard, 1990), 229–260.

30.   ILH 61, 287; IRH 93.

31.   ILH, 337; IRH, 101. As a helpful guide to basic concerns about the equation of time and concept, see Paul Livingston, *The Logic of Being: Realism, Truth, and Time* (Evanston, IL: Northwestern University Press, 2017), xi–xv, 129–131. Livingston suggests that the "constructivist" equation of time and concept (which seems most germane to Kojève's reading of Hegel) is seriously flawed for reasons of consistency and completeness. The concerns Livingston addresses have considerable bearing on the problems with Kojève's thinking with regard to the completion or end of history. I take up this question throughout, but in greater detail in the discussion of *Attempt at a Rational History of Pagan Philosophy* in chapter 8.

32.   Heidegger, *Metaphysical Foundations*, 42–69.

33.   Kojève was obviously sensitive to this himself. His final major work, *Attempt at a Rational History of Pagan Philosophy*, is an exhaustively detailed examination of the temporalizing of the concept, stretching to more than 1,200 pages. What was a "note" consisting of three lectures in 1938–1939 becomes the major philosophical content of this immense and unfinished work. If nothing else, this late work provides ample evidence that Kojève's "reductions" are not reckless or superficially provocative speculations. His often nonchalant manner leads some to conclude that he is not as careful or serious as he in fact is—he wears his learning lightly and rarely displays the breadth of his knowledge. When one looks at his notebooks for the Hegel lectures, however, an entirely different image emerges. They are astonishingly detailed and careful, constituting more than two thousand pages of minute notes. The texts that we have are in this sense all fragments, the tip of a grand iceberg.

34.   See Heidegger, *Metaphysical Foundations*, 47.

35.   ILH, 364; IRH, 131.

36.   This is a Kojèvian commonplace: mathematics is a form of silence, neither a language nor a discourse. The problem of mathematical analogy for Kojève rests with his insistence on the nontemporal essence of mathematics as opposed to the very temporal existence of the things to which mathematics might apply. Indeed, it would seem that mathematical analogies (which Kojève uses not infrequently) are at best inadequate, at worst impossible. Kojève's attitude toward mathematics in this respect is intriguing, especially given his considerable competence. As I have noted elsewhere, I am not

aware of any reference in Kojève to the great advancements in mathematical logic, the pioneers of which, such as Kurt Gödel, John von Neumann, and Alan Turing, were contemporaries of Kojève. One can only speculate as to the reasons why, since Kojève's avid interest in quantum physics offers a sharp contrast to his apparent disinterest in the mathematical logic that would lead to the computer revolution. My surmise is that Kojève found mathematical logic *as* logic deeply problematic for the same reason he dismisses Spinoza: the mathematization of logic for Kojève would likely amount to the eradication of the temporal dimension of language. Hence, for Kojève, modern mathematical logic is a defensive or reactionary logic that turns away from the revolutionary character of Hegelian logic, the accounting for time. This is of course not the case in quantum physics, and that difference may explain Kojève's interest in quantum physics as well as his neglect of modern mathematical logic. There is likely another reason as well, stated with utmost concision by Hegel himself: "As I have remarked elsewhere, inasmuch as philosophy is to be a science, it cannot borrow its method from a subordinate science, such as mathematics, any more than it can remain satisfied with categorical assurances of inner intuition, or can make use of argumentation based on external reflection." See Hegel, *The Science of Logic*, 9.

37.   ILH, 366; IRH, 133. In a note, Kojève qualifies this judgment somewhat, claiming, "It may be that it is actually impossible to do without Time in Nature; for it is probable that (biological) life, at least, is an *essentially* temporal phenomenon" (ILH 366; IRH 133). This distinction muddies Kojève's association of temporality with human labor. It is at best an equivocation and at worst a contradiction.

38.   ILH, 366; IRH, 133. The Hegelian text reads, "Was die Zeit betrifft, von der man meinen sollte, daß sie, zum Gegenstücke gegen den Raum, den Stoff des andern Teils der reinen Mathematik ausmachen würde, so ist sie der daseiende Begriff selbst." See Hegel, *Phänomenologie*, 34; *Phenomenology*, 27 (§46).

39.   ILH, 366, 368; IRH, 133, 135.

40.   Kojève, *Essai d'une histoire raisonnée de la philosophie païenne* (Paris: Gallimard, 1968), 1:104.

41.   ILH, 368–369; IRH, 136.

42.   ILH, 371; IRH, 139.

43.   ILH, 540. As Kojève puts it elsewhere, "It is by resigning himself to death, by revealing it through his discourse, that Man arrives finally at absolute Knowledge or at Wisdom, in thus completing History." Kojève, "The Idea of Death in the Philosophy of Hegel," trans. Joseph Carpino, *Interpretation* 3, no. 2/3 (Winter 1973): 124.

44.   ILH, 287. For Kojève, returning to the beginning, reading the Book is the silence of repetition, since the "new word" is impossible.

45.   ILH, 293.

46.   Kojève associates this with the theological attitude or with a theistic attitude in philosophy.

47.   As Kojève's friend Leo Strauss argues, there is no possibility of an argument between faith and philosophy since the central assumption of faith is to believe "in spite of."

48. Indeed, here we see clearly the "corruptness" of the underground man, who is not content purely to act but feels compelled to justify his rejection of rationality. He thus invites contradiction, for he tries (or feigns) to give a rational account of why one cannot give a rational account based on the intrinsic impossibility of the latter. The underground man, as such, is the master of endless talk, and his refusal to end is a direct challenge to any notion of completion. The linguistic equivalent of his declaration that 2 x 2 = 5 is a bending of grammar that ends up in nonsense, as I discussed in chapter 1 and will discuss again in chapter 8.

49. Stanley Rosen is perhaps the harshest, declaring that Kojève's "system was unworthy of his intelligence and even of his illuminating commentaries on the *Phenomenology*." See Rosen, "Kojève's Paris: A Memoir," in *Metaphysics in Ordinary Language* (New Haven, CT: Yale University Press, 1999), 277. Rosen's honesty is refreshing, however, and his view is not to be dismissed, given that Rosen knew Kojève fairly well. Rosen suspects that Kojève's end of history is somewhat like a regulative ideal or the play of a farceur. If there is clear evidence for the claim that it is a regulative ideal, it is (naturally enough) harder to justify the characterization as a joke or farce, especially given the seriousness of Kojève's later attempts to defend his views.

6. THE BOOK OF THE DEAD

1. "Briefly: the perfect State and, consequently, all of History, are there only so that the Philosopher can achieve Wisdom by writing a *Book* ("Bible") containing *absolute* knowledge." Kojève, *Introduction à la lecture de Hegel*, ed. Raymond Queneau, 2nd ed. (Paris: Gallimard, 1968), 302; see also 326. Hereafter abbreviated as ILH.

2. ILH, 289.

3. ILH, 410–411. Translation mine; this lecture is not included in the English translation.

4. "Man denies survival: the *Wahrheit* [truth] of man disappears with the disappearance of his animal existence. But it is only in negating this existence that he is human" (ILH, 53).

5. Kojève himself seems to anticipate concerns in a long, perhaps parodic note to the eleventh lecture, part of which I reproduce here (retaining Kojève's unusual hyphenated constructions):

> The role that I attribute to the "Book" can appear exaggerated if one only takes chapter 8 into account. To justify my interpretation, I would thus like to cite a passage that is located at the end of the Preface (*Vorrede*) of the PhG where Hegel says this (page 58, 1:7–15): "We must be convinced that the truth has as its destiny to make-itself-a-path when its time has come, and that it appears only if its time has come; and that, accordingly, the truth never appears too soon and that it never finds a public that-is-not-ripe [for it]. And [we must] also [be convinced] that the individual needs this effect [produced on the public] so that what is still only its solitary cause produces-its-proofs-and-declares-itself-true

(*bewähren*) for it [-self] by means of this effect and [so that] it can produce-experience of the fact that the conviction, which at first belongs only to particularity, is something universal."

This is quite clear. In order to declare itself true, philosophy must be universally recognized, that is recognized in the final account by the universal and homogeneous *State*. The empirical-existence (Dasein) of Knowledge—this is not the private *thinking* of the Sage but his *word* (*parole*), universally *recognized*. And it is evident that this "recognition" can only be obtained by publication of a book. Now, by existing in the form of a book, Knowledge effectively detaches itself from its author, that is, from the Sage or from the Man. (ILH, 414)

6.   Kojève speaks of the Book as containing the "System der Wissenschaft," having two parts: the phenomenology and the logic, with the former being an "introduction" and the latter the "science itself" (ILH, 483–484). So it may well be better to speak of the Book as having two mutually implicating parts. It is even more difficult to get around the problem of Kojève's commentary itself (and his subsequent work), for the reasons mentioned at the end of chapter 5. To add, explain, and elaborate is to indicate the degree to which the end not only is not obviously apparent but also is not yet achieved, since every addition, explanation, and elaboration becomes effectively a new text in the Book (which then threatens to become interminable). Indeed, if a commentary goes no further even than to make explicit what already lies in the narrative of history, it adds to the Book, since something was missing to invite the additional explanation or explicitation in the first place. On the curious identity of the Book, see Dominique Pirotte, *Alexandre Kojève: un système anthropologique* (Paris: Presses Universitaires de France, 2005), 26.

7.   Philip T. Grier, "The End of History and the Return of History," in *The Hegel Myths and Legends*, ed. Jon Stewart (Evanston, IL: Northwestern University Press, 1996), 186–191; Joseph Flay, *Hegel's Quest for Certainty* (Albany: State University of New York Press, 1984), 299.

8.   Stefanos Geroulanos, *An Atheism that Is Not Humanist Emerges in French Thought* (Stanford, CA: Stanford University Press, 2010), 130–132; Boris Groys, *Introduction to Antiphilosophy*, trans. David Fernbach (London: Verso, 2012), 145–167; James H. Nichols, *Alexandre Kojève: Wisdom at the End of History* (Lanham, MD: Rowman and Littlefield, 2007), 11–13. One could argue that Kojève's major difference with Soloviev is in his collapsing of the "two absolutes" of Soloviev into one "finite" absolute—the citizen of the universal and homogeneous state, the sage. Against Soloviev, Kojève's interpretation of Christianity holds that it evolves naturally into atheism through the assumption of divine identity as the final emancipation of the slave. Christianity leads to the divinization of the slave that is in turn the creation of a finite deity. Hence, Kojève agrees that becoming God, or deification, is the proper end of Christian thinking, but only as a finite God and in a different sense than might be understood more generally in the Russian tradition. This tradition is capably surveyed by Nel Grillaert, who also

points to the presence of Left Hegelian influence in Dostoevsky's heroes, especially Kirillov. Grillaert, *What the* God-seekers *Found in Nietzsche: The Reception of Nietzsche's* Übermensch *by the Philosophers of the Russian Religious Renaissance* (Leiden: Brill-Rodopi, 2008), 107–139.

9. For an overview, see Marshall Poe, " 'Moscow the Third Rome': The Origins and Transformations of a Pivotal Moment," in *Jahrbücher für Geschichte Osteuropas* Neue Folge 49, no. 3 (2001): 412–429.

10. This is a rather fanciful reading of both the Third Rome idea and Kojève. But there is an affinity between the assertion of a distinctly Russian identity in the realm of Christendom and Kojève's appropriation of Hegel to the Russian deification narrative (which he also inverts insofar as it is God that becomes man, the infinite thus surrendering to the finite).

11. See Geroulanos, *An Atheism*, 136–141; Groys, *Introduction to Antiphilosophy*, 166–167; Shadia Drury, *Alexandre Kojève: The Roots of Postmodern Politics* (New York: St. Martin's, 1994), 12–15.

12. See Dominique Auffret, *Alexandre Kojève: la philosophie, l'état, la fin de l'histoire* (Paris: Grasset and Fasquelle, 1990), 243–244.

13. Kojève, "Hegel, Marx and Christianity," trans. Hilail Gildin, *Interpretation* 1, no. 1 (1970): 41. Kojève develops this point more generally in the lectures from 1936–1937:

> Man will want to make the world in which he lives agree with the ideal expressed in his discourse. The Christian World is the world of Intellectuals and Ideologues. What is an ideology? It is not a *Wahrheit* (an objective truth), nor is it an error, but something that can *become* true by Struggle and the Work that will make the World conform to the ideal. The test of Struggle and Work renders an ideology true or false. It will be worth noting that at the end of the revolutionary process what is realized is not the ideology pure and simple from which one began but something that differs from it and is the truth (the "revealed *reality*") of this ideology. ILH, 117.

14. "Hegel can refer to the *fact* that he is himself a Sage. But can he truly *explain* it? I doubt it. And I thus doubt that he is the Sage completing History, for it is precisely the capacity to *explain* oneself that characterizes Wisdom." ILH, 400.

15. This aspect of Kojève's text offers evidence of its modernity as a text that directly mirrors its content.

16. Aristotle, *Metaphysics*, trans. Hugh Tredennick (Cambridge, MA: Harvard University Press, 1933), 1:2.

17. "Religion is therefore a epiphenomenon of human Work. It is essentially a historical phenomenon. Accordingly, even in its theo-logical form, Spirit is essentially *becoming*. There is thus no God revealed outside of History." ILH, 390.

18. ILH, 540. See also "The Idea of Death in the Philosophy of Hegel," trans. Joseph Carpino, *Interpretation* 3, no. 2/3 (Winter 1973): 124. Hereafter abbreviated as IDH.

19. Sigmund Freud, *Civilization and Its Discontents*, trans. David McLintock (London: Penguin, 2002), 3.

20. See Leo Strauss, "Notes on Lucretius," in *Liberalism Ancient and Modern* (Chicago: University of Chicago Press, 1995), 85.

21. Plato, *Republic*, trans. Chris Emilyn-Jones and William Preddy (Cambridge, MA: Harvard University Press, 2013), 2:14–19.

22. Friedrich Hölderlin, *Hyperion*, in Hyperion *and Selected Poems*, ed. Eric L. Santner (New York: Continuum, 1990), 23.

23. ILH, 436; Kojève, *Introduction to the Reading of Hegel*, trans. James H. Nichols Jr. (Ithaca, NY: Cornell University Press, 1969), 159 (hereafter abbreviated as IRH).

24. ILH, 388.

25. See Geroulanos, *An Atheism*, 169–172. Geroulanos's approach is very refreshing because he takes Kojève's avowed Marxism as a red herring. To my mind, one might take Kojève's Marxism in the same way as his Hegelianism: it is both homage and correction. Kojève's final state, the ostensive realization of work, is a challenge to a crude notion of liberation that one may associate with Marx, according to which material satisfaction suffices to create "happiness." Nonetheless, it would be going too far to suggest that Kojève was not Marxist or not attracted to the Marxist final state. Proof for this is provided by the second excerpt from Kojève's still largely unpublished manuscript from 1940–1941, *Sofia, filo-sofia i fenomeno-logia*, which explicitly makes the connection between omniscience (and hence, the final state) and "Marxist-Leninist-Stalinist philosophy." See Kojève, *Sofia, filo-sofia i fenomeno-logia*, ed. A. M. Rutkevich, *Voprosy filosofii* 12 (2014): 79; autograph manuscript in Fonds Kojève, Bibliothèque nationale de France (box no. 20).

26. ILH, 443; IRH, 167–168.

27. F. M. Dostoevsky, *The Brothers Karamazov*, trans. Richard Pevear and Larissa Volokhonsky (New York: Farrar, Straus and Giroux, 2002), 1.

28. Theodor Adorno, *Metaphysics: Concepts and Problems*, trans. Edmund Jephcott (Stanford, CA: Stanford University Press, 2002), 33–35.

29. Hannah Arendt, *The Life of the Mind* (San Diego, CA: Harcourt, Brace, 1977), 2:6–7.

30. This is where Geroulanos's antihumanism thesis may run into difficulties, because it simply assumes a point of view—that of individual freedom attached to humanism (or bourgeois humanism, whatever that might be)—which Kojève seeks to refute and which, at the very least, Kojève shows to be problematic, if not incoherent. For the ostensibly free historical individual is in reality a servant to the body, to the overwhelming fear of death. In fairness, however, it must be said that Geroulanos's charge of antihumanism hits deeper if one regards Kojève's "humanism" as an extreme form of pessimism concerning the human—and it is hard not to do so.

31. Martin Heidegger, *Introduction to Metaphysics*, trans. Gregory Fried and Richard Polt, 2nd ed. (New Haven, CT: Yale University Press, 2014), 50.

32. ILH, 384–385.

33. ILH, 391.

34. Piet Tommissen, ed., *Schmittiana*, vol. 6 (Berlin: Duncker and Humblot, 1998), 34.

35. ILH, 554; IDH, 139.

36. ILH, 418–419.

37. F. M. Dostoevsky, *Notes from Underground*, trans. Richard Pevear and Larissa Volok-honsky (New York: Vintage, 1993), 7.

38. See Groys, *Introduction to Antiphilosophy*, 166–167. Groys might be read to suggest that the Kojevian cycle repeats a series of ends of history. It seems to me that this interpretation risks turning Kojève's thinking into a thinking of cycles divorced from each cycle, as it would have to be to provide a general thinking of cycles—the repetition, that is, of an abstract paradigm. The evidence that Kojève seeks a general thinking of this type is at best equivocal; indeed, Kojève avows that his thinking is an explicitation of a given history—just as Hegel's is—and thus is immanent to the conceptual history it describes and of which it is a part. Kojève's discussion of dialectic, not as a method but as description—given in the famed essay "The Dialectic of the Real and the Phenomenological Method in Hegel," which is included in the appendix to the lectures—seems to confirm this line of thinking. As a result, the only kind of repetition that Kojève's thinking allows is the exact repetition of one history, complete and final in and of itself. By this, I do not mean a repetition that shows a similarity in difference but rather a final, complete history that repeats itself in every detail, rather like Friedrich Nietzsche's eternal return of the same. Still, as in Nietzsche's eternal recurrence, the first narrative is the crucial one. The Book it writes is read thereafter verbatim, again and again. Kojève is clear: "But while not being cyclical, time is necessarily *circular*; in the *end* one attains the identity of the *beginning*. . . . Just like Time, History, and Man, Knowledge [La Science] is thus *circular*. But if the historical Circle is gone through but one time, the Circle of Knowledge is a *cycle* that repeats eternally. There is a *possibility* of repetition of Knowledge, and this repetition is even *necessary*. Indeed, the content of knowledge relates only to itself: the Book *is* its own content." ILH, 393.

39. ILH, 385. What the human achieves, the programmed human (animal) repeats (or that which remains beyond both in the post-historical—post-Book—"period"): "The time where the Man-reader-of-the-Book remains is thus the cyclical (or biological) Time of Aristotle, but not linear, historical, Hegelian Time." Kojève is ambiguous: Is the post-historical being man, animal, or "something" else, like "bodies emptied of spirit"?

40. Of course, Kojève notes that thinking can never be "mine." In his lectures on Pierre Bayle, from 1936–1937, Kojève writes, "Man is only man to the extent he *thinks*; his thinking is only *thinking* to the extent that it does not depend on the fact that it is *he* who thinks." See Kojève, *Identité et réalité dans le "Dictionnaire" de Pierre Bayle*, ed. Marco Filoni (Paris: Gallimard, 2010), 15–16. This trope becomes a central point in Jacques Derrida, *Monolingualism of the Other; or, the Prosthesis of Origin*, trans. Patrick Mensah (Stanford, CA: Stanford University Press, 1998). With regard to language, Derrida makes a claim similar to Kojève's, stating, "I have only one language; it is not mine" (1).

41. Jacques Derrida, "Cogito and the History of Madness," in *Writing and Difference*, trans. Alan Bass (Chicago: University of Chicago Press, 1978), 36. One wonders to what extent Derrida's Hegel is that of Kojève. Derrida himself is equivocal. See Jacques Derrida, *Specters of Marx: The State of the Debt, the Work of Mourning and the New International*, trans. Peggy Kamuf (New York: Routledge, 1994), 70–75.

42. ILH, 529; IDH, 114.

43. Within Kojève's own terms, his claim for the importance of the relation is fair because Kojève lines up with "substance" terms like "nature," "master," "eternity," and "space," as opposed to the operative vocabulary for the subjective, such as "man," "slave," "time," and "negation."

44. ILH, 535–536; IDH, 119–121.

45. ILH, 540, 548, 550, 554; IDH, 124, 132, 134, 137.

46. See Kojève, "Hegel, Marx and Christianity," 28.

7. NOBODIES

1. See Bernard Hesbois, "Le livre et la mort: essai sur Kojève" (PhD diss., Catholic University of Louvain, 1985), 30, note 12. Hesbois's unpublished dissertation is the best single work on Kojève's later thought.

2. Kojève, *Introduction à la lecture de Hegel*, ed. Raymond Queneau, 2nd ed. (Paris: Gallimard, 1968), 38 (hereafter abbreviated as ILH). This very Hegelian conception of narrative has emerged recently in Roberto Mangabeira Unger and Lee Smolin, *The Singular Universe and the Reality of Time* (Cambridge: Cambridge University Press, 2014), 13–15.

3. Kojève, "Note inédite sur Hegel et Heidegger," ed. Bernard Hesbois, *Rue Descartes* 7 (June 1993): 35.

4. It is important to keep in mind the ambivalent status of this overcoming, which I have discussed in the preceding chapters.

5. ILH, 550; Kojève, "The Idea of Death in the Philosophy of Hegel," trans. Joseph Carpino, *Interpretation* 3, no. 2/3 (Winter 1973): 134 (hereafter abbreviated as IDH).

6. Again, Martin Heidegger is the significant opponent, whose Bremen lectures from 1949 attack this very notion of identity as, at base, differentiating among things only insofar as they take up different positions in a mathematized landscape. See, especially, Heidegger, "Positionality," in *Bremen and Freiburg Lectures*, trans. Andrew J. Mitchell (Bloomington: Indiana University Press, 2012), 23–43.

7. This is of course a key Heideggerian point. See also Jacques Derrida, *Aporias*, trans. Thomas Dutoit (Stanford, CA: Stanford University Press, 1993), 55–81.

8. It is indeed hard to avoid the Nietzschean echo here. Like Kojève's Hegel, the eternal return is the repetition of only one narrative arc. But if Friedrich Nietzsche's eternal return is aimed at individual lives, Kojève's account is aimed at the life of a collective: " 'Alles *endliche* ist dies, sich selbst aufzuheben' [Everything *finite* is an overcoming/sublating of itself], says Hegel in the *Encyclopedia*. It is only *finite* Being that suppresses itself dialectically. If, then, the Concept is Time, that is, if conceptual-understanding is *dialectical*, the existence of the Concept—and consequently of Being revealed by the Concept—is essentially *finite*. Therefore History itself must be essentially finite; collective Man (humanity) must die just as the human individual dies;

universal History must have a definitive *end*." ILH, 380; Kojève, *Introduction to the Reading of Hegel*, trans. James H. Nichols Jr. (Ithaca, NY: Cornell University Press, 1969), 148 (hereafter abbreviated as IRH).

9. Kojève, *Le concept, le temps et le discours*, ed. Bernard Hesbois (Paris: Gallimard, 1990), 54.

10. Kojève employs the French *supprimer* to translate *Aufhebung*. I translate that term here as "overcoming," but *supprimer* typically means "eliminate," "eradicate," or "remove." Kojève uses the term to indicate that what is partial in a view is overcome or eliminated in a new, more holistic view, and so on, until all partiality is ultimately eliminated. Conversely, Kojève insists that what is thereby preserved is the universality in any given view. See ILH, 457; IRH, 180.

11. A point made in Boris Groys, *Introduction to Antiphilosophy*, trans. David Fernbach (London: Verso, 2012), 147.

12. Kojève, *Kant* (Paris: Gallimard, 1973), 47. Kojève translates *wu-wei* as "faire le non-faire" (to act not acting, or to do not doing). He interprets this notion in an unusual way, as a retreat from action, whereas a more conventional interpretation might apply the concept to action that is not planned but is "immediate" and "natural." See Edward Slingerland, *Effortless Action: Wu-Wei as Conceptual Metaphor and Spiritual Ideal in Early China* (Oxford: Oxford University Press, 2007).

13. Boris Groys, *The Communist Postscript*, trans. Thomas Ford (London: Verso, 2010).

14. ILH, 554; IRH, 137.

15. ILH, 275; IRH, 80.

16. ILH, 32; IRH, 28.

17. F. M. Dostoevsky, *Notes from Underground*, trans. Richard Pevear and Larissa Volokhonsky (New York: Vintage, 1993), 25, 35.

18. This is a major point in *Attempt at a Rational History of Pagan Philosophy*: history either never starts, or it starts and never stops, or it starts and stops (history as a completed "circle"). For Kojève, only the third variant has any coherence, the first being silence and the second endless chatter, since, without a final picture of the whole, one never knows whether what one knows is what one claims to know—the exact predicament of the underground man subject to infinity.

19. This note has been the object of considerable discussion. For three examples, see Jacques Derrida, *Specters of Marx*, trans. Peggy Kamuf (New York: Routledge, 1994), 70–75; James H. Nichols, *Alexandre Kojève: Wisdom at the End of History* (Lanham, MD: Rowman and Littlefield, 2007), 83–89; and Stanley Rosen, *Hermeneutics as Politics* (Oxford: Oxford University Press, 1987), 93.

20. ILH, 28, 34; IRH, 23, 27.

21. Robert Brandom, *Making It Explicit: Reasoning, Representing and Discursive Commitment* (Cambridge, MA: Harvard University Press, 1998), 5.

22. ILH, 436–437; IRH, 161–162.

23. ILH, 385. Kojève refers to the time experienced by the readers of the Book as being equivalent to Aristotelian "biological" (and cyclical) time as opposed to the Hegelian

linear time. The basic distinction seems to be between the initial course of history and subsequent repetition, the initial course being a linear "first run" and the repetition cyclical "copies." Giorgio Agamben perceives this distinction somewhat ambiguously based on the manifest tensions in Kojève's work. Agamben views Kojève as creating an "anthropophorous" notion of animality whereby the animal "carries" the human as the human comes to eliminate or "transcend" it. Thus, Agamben sees also no biopolitical concern in Kojève (other than to reject the premises of biopolitics as an attitude toward nature and the body that pursues cultivation of both for certain purposes), and he questions what becomes of animality in the post-historical state. He writes suggestively in this respect: "Perhaps the body of the anthropophorous animal (the body of the slave) is the unresolved remnant that idealism leaves as an inheritance to thought." See Agamben, *The Open: Man and Animal*, trans. Kevin Attell (Stanford, CA: Stanford University Press, 2003), 12.

24. See Frederic Jameson, *Postmodernism* (Durham, NC: Duke University Press, 1992), 97–130.

25. Jean-Jacques Rousseau, *Discourse on the Origin, and the Foundations of Inequality Among Men*, in *The Major Political Writings of Jean-Jacques Rousseau*, trans. John T. Scott (Chicago: University of Chicago Press, 2012), 65–90.

26. See, for example, Stefanos Geroulanos, *An Atheism That Is Not Humanist Emerges in French Thought* (Stanford, CA: Stanford University Press, 2010), 157–188.

8. ROADS OR RUINS?

1. As we know, Kojève freely admits this. See Kojève, "Hegel, Marx and Christianity," trans. Hilail Gildin, *Interpretation* 1, no. 1 (1970): 41. His argument is essentially that history must come to an end if it is to make sense, if it is to evince rationality by serving as the victory of rationality. Otherwise, history can be nothing more than a tale of endless conflict with no overarching course or shape. What he is less open about is that the consequence of the victory of rationality is either the extreme limitation of the vestiges of slave being—by curtailing the prevalence of self-interest or self-preservation in what we would call a totalitarian state—or their elimination. We might say that the limitation is the province of law and the elimination is the province of philosophy.

2. Kojève, *Essai d'une histoire raisonnée de la philosophie païenne* (Paris: Gallimard, 1968), 1:16. Hereafter abbreviated as EHPP.

3. In a 1961 letter to Leo Strauss, Kojève writes, "In the meantime I have completed my *Ancient Philosophy*. Over 1,000 pages. Taubes has had them photocopied. In my view it is by no means 'ready for publication.' But if Queneau insists, I will not refuse. (To refuse would, in this case, also amount to taking oneself seriously!)" See Strauss, *On Tyranny*, ed. Victor Gourevitch and Michael Roth (Chicago: University of Chicago Press, 2013), 304. Hereafter abbreviated as OT.

4. Martin Heidegger, *Nietzsche* (Pfullingen: Günther Neske, 1961), 1:17.

5. Kojève, "The Emperor Julian and His Art of Writing," trans. James H. Nichols Jr., in *Ancients and Moderns: Essays on the Tradition of Political Philosophy in Honor of Leo Strauss*, ed. Joseph Cropsey (New York: Basic Books, 1964), 95–113.

6. Kojève, "Tyranny and Wisdom," in OT, 153.

7. Stanley Rosen remarks, "I have come to the conclusion that my initial intuition, formed during the year of my study and weekly contact with him, was correct: Kojève's system was unworthy of his intelligence and even of his illuminating commentaries on the *Phenomenology*. Not only this, but I believe that he knew its unworthiness, or at least suspected it, or knew it once but had allowed himself to forget it in the pleasures of his own success. See Rosen, "Kojève's Paris," in *Metaphysics in Ordinary Language* (New Haven, CT: Yale University Press, 1999), 277. Kojève, for his part, seems to have taken to Rosen, as evidenced by his comments to Leo Strauss. See OT, 305.

8. Certainly, in the limit case of a perfectly homogeneous society, in which all conflict among its members is excluded by definition, one would be able to do without Right. See Kojève, *Esquisse d'une phénoménologie du droit* (Paris: Gallimard, 1981), 182 (hereafter abbreviated as EPD); and Kojève, *Outline of a Phenomenology of Right*, trans. Bryan-Paul Frost and Robert Howse (Lanham, MD: Rowman and Littlefield, 2008), 165 (hereafter OPR).

9. Kojève to Leo Strauss, September 19, 1950, in OT, 256. Kojève makes this same point elsewhere. See Kojève, review of G. R. G. Mure's *A Study of Hegel's Logic, Critique* 54 (1951): 1003.

10. Perry Anderson, "The Ends of History," in *A Zone of Engagement* (London: Verso, 1992), 279–375.

11. EPD, 237–266; OPR, 205–231.

12. In addition to this, Robert Howse suggests that certain treatments of Kojève's work suffer because they ignore this work. I have to agree with this assessment, since the vision of the final state provided in the *Outline* shows the extent to which the treatment of that state in the Hegel lectures is not itself conclusive.

13. EPD, 586; OPR, 479.

14. Carl Schmitt, *The Leviathan in the State Theory of Thomas Hobbes*, trans. George Schwab and Erna Hilfstein (Chicago: University of Chicago Press, 2008). This remarkable text, first published in 1938, provides an interpretation of the state projected by Hobbes that bears an astonishing resemblance to the universal superstate Kojève projects and which is anathema to Schmitt.

15. EPD, 22–25; OPR, 37–40.

16. In this case, the reliance on Schmitt is explicitly avowed by Kojève. See EPD, 144; OPR, 134.

17. EPD, 154; OPR, 143.

18. EPD, 258–266; 267–324; OPR, 225–231; 233–262.

19. EPD, 255; OPR, 222–224.

20. EPD, 253; OPR, 221.

21. EPD, 311; OPR, 265–266.

22. Kojève, *Introduction à la lecture de Hegel*, ed. Raymond Queneau, 2nd ed. (Paris: Gallimard, 1968), 143–144. Hereafter abbreviated as ILH.

23. Karl Marx, *Capital*, trans. Ben Fowkes (London: Penguin, 1990), 1:165.

24. Georg Lukács, *History and Class Consciousness*, trans. Rodney Livingstone (Cambridge, MA: MIT Press, 1971), 83–222; and Martin Heidegger, *Mindfulness*, trans. Parvis Emad and Thomas Kalary (London: Continuum, 2006), 12.

25. The Kojève archive at the Bibliothèque nationale de France shows the extent to which Kojève continued to write after the war.

26. The second excerpt covers the part of the introduction that follows the text published in 2007. See "Philosophy as the Striving for Complete Consciousness; That Is, Philosophy as the Way to Total Knowledge" (Философия как стремление к завершенной сознательности, т.е. философия как путь к совершенному знанию), *Voprosy filosofii* 12 (2014): 78–91.

27. Kojève, "Sofia, filo-sofia i fenomeno-logia," ed. A. M. Rutkevich, in *Istoriko-filosofskii ezhegodnik* (Moscow: Nauka, 2007), 307; autograph manuscript in Fonds Kojève, Bibliothèque nationale de France (box no. 20).

28. Jorge Luis Borges, *Labyrinths: Selected Stories and Other Writings*, ed. Donald A. Yates and James E. Irby (New York: New Directions, 2007), 152, 154.

29. Kojève adduces an excellent example:

> This extraordinary *wealth*, not to say extravagance, of the "contents" of Notions referred to as "general" is at first unsettling. But it is not unique. One finds oneself in the presence of an analogous situation when one deals with the mathematical algorithms called "Tensors."
>
> When one wishes to apply an Algorithm to whatever is in a geometric Space (or Space-time), one must introduce an appropriate "subject" with a "point of view"; and one does so in the middle of a System of coordinates. Just as in the World in which we live Things change aspect depending on the subject to which they reveal themselves (via perception) and depending on the point of view at which the former is placed, entities located in geometric Space (or, more generally, in nonphysical Space-time) change their "aspects" too as a function of changes in the Systems of coordinates. But just as Things in our world remain what they are in themselves despite changes in aspect, entities in geometric Space also have "invariant" constitutive elements. These are the elements that a Tensor expresses (= symbolizes). Now, the Tensor expresses not by "abstracting" from Systems of coordinates, that is, from geometrically possible "subjects" and "points of view" and, thus, from different "aspects" of the entity in question, but by *implicating all* at once. (Kojève, *Le concept, le temps et le discours*, ed. Bernard Hesbois [Paris: Gallimard, 1990], 113. Hereafter abbreviated as CTD.)

30. Martin Heidegger, *Contributions to Philosophy (of the Event)*, trans. Richard Rojcewicz and Daniela Vallega-Neu (Bloomington: Indiana University Press, 2012), 1.

31. This omission is unfortunately unavoidable within the confines of my study and of this final section, where I concentrate on Kojève's elaboration of the temporalizing of the

concept, first introduced in the final Hegel lectures from 1938–1939. This chapter as a whole pursues the continuation of the two basic narratives addressed in the Hegel lectures—the master and slave and the ascent to wisdom—the former finding completion in the *Outline*, the latter in the discussion of the crucial "subnarrative" (temporalizing of the concept) that is the backbone of *Attempt at a Rational History of Pagan Philosophy*. This is a shame, because *The Concept, Time, and Discourse* is an important and distinctive work in its own right (and one that is slated to appear in English translation in January 2018).

32. See Bernard Hesbois's introduction to CTD, 9. It should be noted that Kojève thought of Immanuel Kant as presenting an emblematically Christian philosophy, an attempt to reconcile reason and will that gave birth to the reconciliation offered by Hegel. See Kojève, *Kant* (Paris: Gallimard, 1973), 54.

33. Dominique Pirotte provides a fine account of the *Attempt* in his excellent study of Kojève's thought. Pirotte, *Alexandre Kojève: un système anthropologique* (Paris: Presses Universitaires de France, 2005), 111–161.

34. This admission of the possible impossibility of the project is very curious. It supports one of Stanley Rosen's more withering comments, suggesting that Kojève was himself "at bottom a skeptic in the modern sense of the term, and very close to nihilism" (Rosen, "Kojève's Paris," 276). Rosen suggests that Kojève's "System" is, if anything, insincere, the product of a skeptic (though, to be sure, a most unusual skeptic). This comment fits in the same genre of comments as those made by Leo Tolstoy about Fyodor Dostoevsky, that Dostoevsky's novels were so strained because they are works of one who wanted to believe but could not. Yet I think it would be more accurate to view Kojève's skepticism or nihilism, if these are properly attributable to him, as being of a totally different kind—that the end of his thinking is to free the world of the mistake that is the human being. In this respect, Kojève resembles Jonathan Swift, not Dostoevsky, and his "nihilism" is his conviction that the aim of human existence is self-extermination as a boon to nature, which, in the human being, has created a devastating viral mistake.

35. EHPP, 1:11.

36. EHPP, 1:11–12.

37. EHPP, 1:33–34.

38. Again Kojève asserts his basic dogma that a true account must be a final one. He thereby avoids the skeptical arguments of David Hume. But is this emphasis on the absolute not problematic? Why can we not claim that current knowledge is good until proven otherwise? This rather more pragmatic approach seems to permit the justification of an opinion at a given time, even if that opinion later turns out to be false. Kojève finds this vexing because it means that the same statement is at T^1 true and at T^2 false. Kojève develops the notion of a "parathesis" to deal with this problem, and he notes that a parathesis is a sort of "pseudo sense" during the time when it is held to be true.

39. EHPP, 1:33.

40. Kojève makes this point forcefully in his discussion of Kant as a theistic philosopher. In an extremely interesting discussion of *Critique of Judgment*, Kojève concludes, "And

Kant has only camouflaged (yet very "cunningly") this skeptical character of his Philosophy of the theoretically "infinite task" and of "moral" or "practical" "infinite progress" See Kojève, *Kant*, 92.

41. Kojève creates a rather complicated set of typographic differences to distinguish among the "notion" of the concept, its sense, and its morpheme. The Hegelian system of knowledge begins with a notion of the concept, a claim that the concept *is*, and then proceeds to fill out its sense—the history of its definition. The morpheme simply refers to the given word used in different languages, such as *Begriff* or понятие. See EHPP, 1:14.

42. See EHPP, 1:14–33; and CTD, 43–48. Kojève does not take an explicit position about the term "sense" in the context of the extensive literature on the subject in analytic philosophy. It is not clear that he was aware of Gottlob Frege's distinction between "sense" and "reference." This is hardly surprising, since Kojève's approach is dialectical, not analytic, and as such forms part of the tradition of thought that the earliest analytic philosophers struggled against. Indeed, one of the intriguing lacunae in Kojève's work is his lack of engagement with modern mathematical logic, a somewhat surprising lacuna, given Kojève's extensive interest in mathematics, yet one likely justified, as I noted earlier, by Kojève's rejection of nondialectical logic, or the kind of "logic" Kojève identifies in Spinoza as "acosmic."

43. See CTD, 43–48.

44. EHPP, 1:28–31.

45. EHPP, 1:34–57. The term "antiphilosophy," which would become so celebrated with Alain Badiou, seems to originate in Kojève's treatise.

46. EHPP, 1:35.

47. The political analogy is almost irresistible here, given that the concern with a final discourse is almost exactly parallel to the kind of adjudicative system Kojève creates in the *Outline*.

48. EHPP, 1:44.

49. Friedrich Nietzsche, *The Gay Science*, trans. Walter Kaufmann (New York: Vintage, 1974), 38.

50. EHPP, 1:63.

51. See J. G. Fichte, *Introductions to the* Wissenschaftslehre *and Other Writings, 1797–1800*, trans. Daniel Breazeale (Indianapolis, IN: Hackett, 1994), 111–113.

52. Regarding the problem of limits, see Graham Priest, *Beyond the Limits of Thought*, 2nd ed. (Oxford: Oxford University Press, 2003), particularly chapters 7 and 8.

53. This is a very important—and somewhat surprising—move, given Kojève's use of mathematical analogies throughout the *Attempt*. The basic point is clear: mathematics is not discourse. It is not discourse because it is abstract and partial; it avoids the dialectical interaction that is fundamental to discourse and the unfolding of experience precisely as the complete articulation of interaction in the concept. Still, Kojève's resistance to mathematics is curious, given the important developments in mathematical logic bearing on the problems of the whole, which Kojève attempts to address. Paul Livingston puts the issue well with regard to Badiou's mathematical discourse on totality in *Being and Event*, when he differentiates between Badiou's solution to the

paradoxes of the whole in favor of logical consistency and multiplicity (thus the absence of a final whole) and another approach that favors the whole over logical consistency. Kojève, surely against his own intention, and especially the notion of dialectical parathesis he invents, appears to end up in the latter group. Indeed, his entire approach to the completing history turns on the problem of completion understood as a problem of seamless or complete self-inclusion—the absolute. The paradoxes associated with self-inclusion make it impossible to preserve both completion and consistency at the same time, but only the one or the other, ostensibly cheating dialectical fusion or absolution. See Livingston, *The Politics of Logic: Badiou, Wittgenstein, and the Consequences of Formalism* (New York: Routledge, 2012), 56–58, 60. Also see, more generally, Graham Priest, *Beyond the Limits of Thought*, 2nd ed. (Oxford: Oxford University Press, 2003), 102–140.

54. Allen Wood quips, with regard to the thesis–antithesis–synthesis terminology: "To use this jargon in expounding Hegel is almost always an unwitting confession that the expositor has little or no first-hand knowledge of Hegel." See Wood, ed., introduction to G. W. F. Hegel, *Elements of the Philosophy of Right*, trans. H. B. Nisbet (Cambridge: Cambridge University Press, 1991), xxxii. Terry Pinkard makes a similar comment at the beginning of his comprehensive biography of Hegel. See Pinkard, *Hegel: A Biography* (Cambridge: Cambridge University Press, 2000), xi. There can be little doubt that Kojève's use of this "arid formula" that "misrepresents the structure of his [Hegel's] thought," as Pinkard puts it, is controversial and cannot but lead to accusations of excessive simplification.

55. EHPP, 1:59.

56. EHPP, 1:65.

57. EHPP, 1:55.

58. Pirotte, *Alexandre Kojève*, 112.

59. We recall here that Kojève identifies space with nature and the absence of time. Man is a "hole" in space but in effect first opens space through time, an interaction that is another way of describing the relation of the temporal to the eternal. See ILH, 364–380.

60. EHPP, 1:309–312.

61. EHPP, 1:308.

62. "Scientific experience is thus merely a pseudo-experience. And it can't be otherwise, since vulgar science is in fact concerned not with the concretely real but an *abstraction*." See ILH, 453–455.

63. ILH, 485.

64. This rejection is a prime example of Kojève's divergence from Hegel, or of the Marxist current in Kojève's interpretation of Hegel. It is important to note that Kojève takes a stance on a venerable question in Marxism by emphasizing the power of subjective agency to complete a project of self-fulfillment. Kojève thereby challenges any deterministic network, the Marxian history of History. But this should already be evident in Kojève's insistence on there being different roads to the same goal.

65. See G. W. F. Hegel, *The Phenomenology of Spirit*, trans. A. V. Miller (Oxford: Oxford University Press, 1977), 50, §78 [English text]; G. W. F. Hegel, *Die Phänomenologie des*

Geistes, ed. Heinrich Clairmont and Hans-Friedrich Wessels (Hamburg: Felix Meiner, 1988), 61 [German text].

66.   It is no coincidence that this question bears more than a passing relation to an ancient metaphysical question—What is the relation of the one to the many?—a question that has occasioned an enormous and still unfinished literature, that is indeed a philosophical literature unto itself, stretching from Plato's *Parmenides* to Alain Badiou's *Being and Event*. Of course, mediation is central to Hegel's account of experience in *The Phenomenology of Spirit*, for the experience of consciousness is largely one of progressive differential unification that proceeds to a higher level with self-consciousness and, finally, the ascent to absolute knowledge.

67.   EHPP 1:304.

68.   See EHPP 2:64–110.

69.   EHPP 1:303.

70.   EHPP 3:425.

71.   Kojève, *Kant*, 9. This short book is an absorbing work in its own right. I cannot even begin to do justice to it here.

72.   ILH, 40.

73.   I will discuss this issue at greater length in chapter 9. For the moment, I suggest that his proposition is perhaps questionable. Both Albrecht Dihle and Hannah Arendt attribute the discovery of the modern notion of will to Augustine in his *de libero arbitrio*. For Augustine will—*voluntas*—describes the capacity to disobey God. Is this capacity to disobey, however, the same as the will Kojève associates with Kant? In both cases, will is *negation*, in the one instance, of God's will or of God himself. In the case of Kant, it is the assumption of a Godlike position in relation to the world, achieved by negating limitation (a move which itself suggests the difference between the human and the divine). Still, the similarities outweigh the differences and suggest that Augustine and Kant are closer than Kojève admits. In the absence of Kojève's history of Christian philosophy, however, the question is moot. See Albrecht Dihle, *The Theory of the Will in Classical Antiquity* (Berkeley: University of California Press, 1982), 123; and Hannah Arendt, *The Life of the Mind* (San Diego, CA: Harcourt, Brace 1977), 2:87.

74.   Kojève, *Kant*, 95–99.

75.   EPD, 182; OPR, 165.

76.   The comparison may seem fanciful, though it must be admitted that Samuel Beckett, too, was preoccupied with the more-or-less purgatorial state to which Kojève seems to fall prey. The fact that both were in Paris and may have passed within similar circles has given rise to speculation, especially since Kojève's influence in the immediate postwar period was so pervasive. See Richard Halpern, *Eclipse of Action: Tragedy and Political Economy* (Chicago: University of Chicago Press, 2017), 227–230.

77.   The contrast with Georg Lukács is instructive. And one may sympathize with Stefanos Geroulanos's suspicions about Kojève's Marxism. While the issue is far too complicated to address adequately here, I think it may suffice to assert that Kojève's reading of Hegel is very much in accord with Karl Marx's view, as expressed in the 1844 manuscripts, though with an end result that, if not equivocal about the end state, is then

potentially corrosive to the Marxist objective. But to suggest that Kojève is a reaction-ary or a "Marxist of the right" is quite problematic, given the underlying radicality of Kojève's position, which does nothing to flatter self-interest, nationalism, or systemic inequality, as the right is wont to do. Moreover, the 1940–1941 manuscript in Russian openly praises the Marxist end state with no hint of irony or retraction from the goal of realization of such a state under Stalin's leadership. See Kojève, *Sofia, filo-sofia i fenomeno-logia*, ed. A. M. Rutkevich, *Voprosy filosofii* 12 (2014): 79; autograph manu-script in Fonds Kojève, Bibliothèque nationale de France (box no. 20).

78. "The suppression of Man (that is, of Time, that is, of Action) in favor of static-Being (that is, Space, that is, Nature) is thus the suppression of Error in favor of Truth. And if History is certainly the history of human errors, Man himself is perhaps only an error of Nature that 'by chance' (freedom?) was not immediately eliminated." ILH, 432; Kojève, *Introduction to the Reading of Hegel*, ed. Allan Bloom, trans. James H. Nich-ols Jr., 2nd ed. (Ithaca, NY: Cornell University Press, 1969), 156.

9. WHY FINALITY?

1. The creation of a revolutionary collective subject is a crucial aspect of Alain Badiou's thought. See, for example, Badiou, *Being and Event*, trans. Oliver Feltham (London: Continuum, 2006), 391–409. I borrow the term "aleatory rationalism" from the editors' postface to a collection of essays by Badiou. See Badiou, *Theoretical Writings*, ed. and trans. Ray Brassier and Alberto Toscano (London: Continuum, 2004), 253. See also Ed Pluth, "Alain Badiou, Kojève, and the Return of the Human Exception," *Filozofski Vest-nik* 30, no. 2 (2009): 197–205.

2. One has only to consider the dire predictions regarding the progress of artificial intel-ligence and the possibility of so-called superintelligence dwarfing human capabilities. See James Barrat, *Our Final Invention: Artificial Intelligence and the End of the Human Era* (New York: St. Martin's Griffin, 2015).

3. This is a view popular among critics of Straussian inclination.

4. The most important philosophical exploration of this issue is F. W. J. Schelling's 1809 *Philosophical Investigations into the Essence of Human Freedom*.

5. Kojève, *Introduction à la lecture de Hegel*, ed. Raymond Queneau, 2nd ed. (Paris: Gal-limard, 1968), 40. Hereafter abbreviated as ILH.

6. Augustine, *On Free Choice of the Will*, trans. Thomas Williams (Indianapolis, IN: Hackett, 1993).

7. Lactantius, *De ira dei*, in *Patrologia latina, cursus completus*, ed. J. P. Migne (Paris: 1844), 7:121. My translation.

8. Augustine, *City of God Against the Pagans*, trans. R. W. Dyson (Cambridge: Cambridge University Press, 1998), 484 (book 11, chap. 26).

9. ILH, 419.

10. There is a considerable debate on this issue. While both Albrecht Dihle and Hannah Arendt—to name but two important figures—argue that Augustine's notion of will,

and the notion of freedom that flows from it, are innovations, Michael Frede takes a different view, suggesting that a notion of will was evident already in Stoic texts. I follow Dihle and Arendt, since it seems to me that the notion of will emergent in Augustine has a great deal to do with excusing the Christian God from responsibility for evil, a context that is absent in Pagan antiquity. See Albrecht Dihle, *The Theory of the Will in Classical Antiquity* (Berkeley: University of California Press, 1982), 123–144; Hannah Arendt, *The Life of the Mind* (San Diego, CA: Harcourt, Brace, 1977), 2:84–110; and Michael Frede, *A Free Will: Origins of the Notion in Ancient Thought*, ed. A. A. Long (Berkeley: University of California Press, 2012), 1–18.

11. Friedrich Nietzsche, *The Will to Power*, trans. Walter Kaufmann and R. J. Hollingdale (New York: Vintage, 1973), 401–402; Hans Blumenberg, *The Legitimacy of the Modern Age*, trans. Robert M. Wallace (Cambridge, MA: MIT Press, 1985), 133. Blumenberg states, "The problem of the justification of God has become overwhelming, and that justification is accomplished at the expense of man, to whom a new concept of freedom is ascribed expressly in order to let the whole of an enormous responsibility and guilt be imputed to it."

12. ILH, 327.

13. Martin Heidegger, "On the Essence of Truth," in *Pathmarks*, ed. William McNeill (Cambridge: Cambridge University Press, 1998), 150.

14. Friedrich Nietzsche, *Beyond Good and Evil*, trans. Walter Kaufmann (New York: Vintage, 1989), 11–12. I have substantially modified the translation.

15. F. M. Dostoevsky, *The Brothers Karamazov*, trans. Richard Pevear and Larissa Volokhonsky (New York: Farrar, Straus and Giroux, 2002), 252.

16. See J. Derrida, *Aporias*, trans. Thomas Dutoit (Stanford, CA: Stanford University Press, 1993), 72–81.

17. Heidegger, "Essence of Truth," 145.

18. Arendt, *Life of the Mind*, 1:88.

19. Friedrich Nietzsche, *Towards a Genealogy of Morality*, trans. Maudemarie Clark and Alan J. Swenson (Indianapolis, IN: Hackett, 1998), 14–18.

20. Alexandre Kojève, *The Notion of Authority*, trans. Hager Weslati (London: Verso, 2014), 2.

21. Georg Lukács is the pioneer here, his concept of reification exercising enormous influence (perhaps even on Heidegger, as Lucien Goldmann suggests). See Lukács, *History and Class Consciousness*, trans. Rodney Livingstone (Cambridge, MA: MIT Press, 1971), 83–222; Theodor Adorno, *Negative Dialectics*, trans. E. B. Ashton (New York: Continuum, 1973), 40; and Frederic Jameson's comments on this section of Adorno's text, in Jameson, *Late Marxism: Adorno or the Persistence of Dialectic* (London: Verso, 1990), 21–22.

22. The 1844 manuscripts suggest that the Marxist utopia may require the overcoming of material need as a condition of possibility. In this respect, Kojève's reading of Marx, slight as it is, may be plausible. See Karl Marx and Friedrich Engels, "Economic and Philosophic Manuscripts of 1844," in *The Marx-Engels Reader*, ed. Robert C. Tucker,

2nd ed. (New York: W. W. Norton, 1978), 81–93. Also see Karl Marx, *Ökonomisch-philosophische Manuskripte* (Frankfurt: Suhrkamp, 2009), 112–130.

23. Martin Heidegger, "Letter on 'Humanism,'" in *Pathmarks*, 239; Lukács, *History and Class Consciousness*, 188–189.

24. F. M. Dostoevsky, *Notes from Underground*, trans. Richard Pevear and Larissa Volok-honsky (New York: Vintage, 1993), 28–29.

25. Martin Heidegger, *Contributions to Philosophy (of the Event)*, trans. Richard Rojcewicz and Daniela Vallega-Neu (Bloomington: Indiana University Press, 2012), 5, 356–358; Heidegger, "What Is Metaphysics?," in *Pathmarks*, 93.

26. See, for example, Gianni Vattimo, *Nihilism and Emancipation*, ed. Santiago Zabala (New York: Columbia University Press, 2004).

27. Heidegger's comments, found in the latest of the so-called Black Notebooks, are extreme and include Russia as part of the coming "greater Fascism" (*der Großfaschismus*). See Heidegger, *Anmerkungen I–V (Schwarze Hefte 1942–1948)*, ed. Peter Trawny (Frankfurt: Vittorio Klostermann, 2015), 249.

EPILOGUE

1. F. M. Dostoevsky, *The Brothers Karamazov*, trans. Richard Pevear and Larissa Volok-honsky (New York: Farrar, Straus and Giroux, 2002), 246–264. See Dominique Auf-fret, *Alexandre Kojève: la philosophie, l'état, la fin de l'histoire* (Paris: Grasset and Fasquelle, 1990), 183, 255. Auffret, of course, appreciates the immense influence of Dos-toevsky on Kojève and that Kojève himself mentioned this famous episode in Dosto-evsky's fiction as "a classic to become acquainted with."

2. Dostoevsky, *Brothers Karamazov*, 252.

3. "Accordingly, Hegelian absolute Knowledge or Wisdom and the conscious acceptance of death, understood as complete and definitive annihilation, are but one and the same thing." Kojève, *Introduction à la lecture de Hegel*, ed. Raymond Queneau, 2nd ed. (Paris: Gallimard, 1968), 540.

4. The phrase "time is no more" may be interpreted as referring to the elimination of death. Kojève's equation of the concept with time suggests that the end of the one sig-nals the end of the other—or that the fusion of concept and time is the end of con-sciousness, the end of time, and thus the end of death.

5. See Martin Heidegger, *Schelling's Treatise on the Essence of Human Freedom*, trans. Joan Stambaugh (Akron: Ohio University Press, 1985), 83–84.

6. Hannah Arendt, *The Life of the Mind* (San Diego, CA: Harcourt, Brace, 1977), 1:88. Kojève addresses the comic nature of this insistence on making and unmaking by plac-ing it close to contradiction, as when someone asks a waiter to "bring and not bring me a beer." But contradiction depends on simultaneity, whereas Arendt's comment allows for the activity by giving a discrete temporal sequence to the two opposed actions. Still, it is not hard to argue that the making and unmaking of a thing, as a

serial occurrence, achieves the same blockage of an action as does contradiction because it repeats a process of position and negation of that action as a whole.

7. Kojève, "Tyranny and Wisdom," in Leo Strauss, *On Tyranny*, ed. Victor Gourevitch and Michael Roth (Chicago: University of Chicago Press, 2013), 154–155. See also Kojève, "The Emperor Julian and His Art of Writing," trans. James H. Nichols Jr., in *Ancients and Moderns: Essays on the Tradition of Political Philosophy in Honor of Leo Strauss*, ed. Joseph Cropsey (New York: Basic Books, 1964), 100–101.

8. Kojève, *L'athéisme*, trans. Nina Ivanoff (Paris: Gallimard, 1998), 162. This remarkable unfinished work rehearses many of the themes of the Hegel lectures. For an account that does justice to the work, see Dominique Pirotte, *Alexandre Kojève: un système anthropologique* (Paris: Presses Universitaires de France, 2005), 31–53.

9. Perhaps there is a parodic echo of Friedrich Nietzsche's aphorism (no. 157) from *Beyond Good and Evil*: "The thought of suicide is a powerful solace: it helps us through many a bad night." See Nietzsche, *Beyond Good and Evil*, trans. Marion Faber (Oxford: Oxford University Press, 1998), 70.

10. Sophocles, *Oedipus at Colonus*, in *The Plays and Fragments*, ed. Sir Richard C. Jebb (reprint, Amsterdam: Servio, 1963), 192–194. This is my rather free translation of lines 1220–1225 in the Greek.

11. See Friedrich Nietzsche, *Twilight of the Idols* and *The Anti-Christ*, trans. R. J. Hollingdale (New York: Penguin, 1968), 33.

BIBLIOGRAPHY

WORKS BY KOJÈVE

Ateizm. Edited by A. M. Rutkevich. Moscow: Praxis, 2007.

Esquisse d'une phénoménologie du droit. Paris: Gallimard, 1981.

Essaie d'une histoire raisonnée de la philosophie païenne. 3 vols. Paris: Gallimard, 1968–1973.

"Filosofia kak stremlenie k zavershennoi soznatel'nosti, t.e. filosofia kak put' k sovershennomu znaniu." *Voprosy filosofii* 12 (2014): 78–91.

"Hegel, Marx and Christianity." Translated by Hilail Gildin. *Interpretation* 1, no. 1 (1970): 21–42.

"Hegel, Marx et le Christianisme." *Critique* 2 (1946): 339–366.

"The Idea of Death in the Philosophy of Hegel." Translated by Joseph Carpino. *Interpretation* 3, no. 2/3 (Winter 1973): 114–156.

Identité et realité dans le "Dictonnaire" de Pierre Bayle. Edited by Marco Filoni. Paris: Gallimard, 2010.

Introduction à la lecture de Hegel. Edited by Raymond Queneau. 2nd ed. Paris: Gallimard, 1968.

Introduction to the Reading of Hegel. Edited by Allan Bloom. Translated by James H. Nichols Jr. 2nd ed. Ithaca, NY: Cornell University Press, 1969.

Kant. Paris: Gallimard, 1973.

Kolonialismus in europäischer Sicht. Schmittiana, vol. 6, 125–140.

L'athéisme. Translated by Nina Ivanoff. Paris: Gallimard, 1998.

L'empereur Julien et son art d'écrire. Paris: Fourbis, 1990.

"L'empire latin: Esquisse d'une doctrine de la politique française." *La Règle du Jeu* (1990).

L'idée du déterminisme dans la physique classique et dans la physique moderne. Edited by Dominique Auffret. Paris: Librairie générale francaise, 1990.

"L'origine chrétienne da la science moderne." In *Mélanges Alexandre Koyré*, vol. 2, 295–306. Paris: Hermann, 1964.

"La métaphysique religieuse de Vladimir Soloviev." *Revue d'histoire et de philosophie religieuses* 14 (1934): 534–554.

"La métaphysique religieuse de Vladimir Soloviev." *Revue d'histoire et de philosophie religieuses* 15 (1935): 110–152.

La notion de l'autorité. Edited by François Terré. Paris: Gallimard, 2004.

Le concept, le temps et le discours. Edited by Bernard Hesbois. Paris: Gallimard, 1990.

"Le dernier monde nouveau." *Critique* 111/112 (1956): 702–708.

"Les peintures concrètes de Kandinsky." *Revue de Métaphysique et de Morale* (1985): 149–171.

"Les romans de la sagesse." *Critique* 60 (1952): 387–397.

"Note inédite sur Hegel et Heidegger." Edited by Bernard Hesbois. *Rue Descartes* 7 (June 1993): 35–46.

Outline of a Phenomenology of Right. Translated by Bryan-Paul Frost and Robert Howse. Lanham, MD: Rowman and Littlefield, 2008.

Review of G. R. G. Mure's *A Study of Hegel's Logic. Critique* 54 (1951): 1003–1007.

"Sofia, filo-sofia i fenomeno-logia." [Excerpt 1.] Edited by A. M. Rutkevich. In *Istoriko-filosofskii ezhegodnik*, 271–324. Moscow: Nauka, 2007. Autograph manuscript in Fonds Kojève, Bibliothèque nationale de France (box no. 20).

"Sofia, filo-sofia i fenomeno-logia." [Excerpt 2.] Edited by A. M. Rutkevich. In *Voprosy filosofii* 12 (2014): 78–91. Autograph manuscript in Fonds Kojève, Bibliothèque nationale de France (box no. 20).

"Tyranny and Wisdom." In Leo Strauss, *On Tyranny*, edited by Victor Gourevitch and Michael Roth, 135–176. Chicago: University of Chicago Press, 2013.

WORKS ON KOJÈVE

Agamben, Giorgio. *The Open: Man and Animal.* Translated by Kevin Attell. Stanford, CA: Stanford University Press, 2003.

Anderson, Perry. "The Ends of History." In *A Zone of Engagement*, 279–375. London: Verso, 1992.

Auffret, Dominique. *Alexandre Kojève: la philosophie, l'état, la fin de l'histoire.* Paris: Grasset and Fasquelle, 1990.

Burns, Timothy W., and Bryan-Paul Frost. *Philosophy, History and Tyranny: Reexamining the Debate Between Leo Strauss and Alexandre Kojève.* Albany: State University of New York Press, 2016.

Butler, Judith. *Subjects of Desire: Hegelian Reflections in Twentieth-Century France.* New York: Columbia University Press, 1987.

Cooper, Barry. *The End of History: An Essay on Modern Hegelianism.* Toronto: University of Toronto Press, 1984.

Dale, Eric Michael. *Hegel, the End of History, and the Future.* Cambridge: Cambridge University Press, 2014.

Derrida, Jacques. *Specters of Marx: The State of the Debt, the Work of Mourning and the New International*. Translated by Peggy Kamuf. New York: Routledge, 1994.

Devlin, F. Roger. *Alexandre Kojève and the Outcome of Modern Thought*. Lanham, MD: University Press of America, 2004.

Drury, Shadia. *Alexandre Kojève: The Roots of Postmodern Politics*. New York: St. Martin's, 1994.

Filoni, Marco. *Il filosofo della domenica: vita e pensiero di Alexandre Kojève*. Turin: Bollati Boringhieri, 2008.

Fukuyama, Francis. *The End of History and the Last Man*. New York: Free Press, 1993.

Geroulanos, Stefanos. *An Atheism That Is Not Humanist Emerges in French Thought*. Stanford, CA: Stanford University Press, 2010.

Groys, Boris. *Introduction to Antiphilosophy*. Translated by David Fernbach. London: Verso, 2012.

Hesbois, Bernard. "Le livre et la mort: essai sur Kojève." PhD diss., Catholic University of Louvain, 1985.

Jarczyk, Gwendoline, and Pierre-Jean Labarriere, eds. *De Kojève à Hegel: 150 ans de pensée hégélienne en France*. Paris: Albin Michel, 1996.

Kleinberg, Ethan. *Generation Existential: Heidegger's Philosophy in France, 1927–1961*. Ithaca, NY: Cornell University Press, 2005.

Nichols, James H. *Alexandre Kojève: Wisdom at the End of History*. Lanham, MD: Rowman and Littlefield, 2007.

Niethammer, Lutz. *Posthistoire: Has History Come to an End?* Translated by Patrick Camiller. London: Verso, 1994.

Nowak, Piotr. *Ontologia sukcesu. Esej przy filozofii Alexandre'a Kojève'a*. Gdansk: Słowo/Obraz Terytoria, 2006.

Pirotte, Dominique. *Alexandre Kojève: un système anthropologique*. Paris: Presses Universitaires de France, 2005.

Redding, Paul. "Hermeneutic or Metaphysical Hegelianism? Kojève's Dilemma." *The Owl of Minerva* 22, no. 2 (Spring 1991): 175–189

Rosen, Stanley. *Hermeneutics as Politics*. Oxford: Oxford University Press, 1987.

——. *Metaphysics in Ordinary Language*. New Haven, CT: Yale University Press, 1999.

Roth, Michael. *Knowing and History: Appropriations of Hegel in Twentieth-Century France*. Ithaca, NY: Cornell University Press, 1988.

Rutkevich, A. M. "Alexander Kojève: From Revolution to Empire." *Studies in East European Thought* 69, no. 4 (December 2017): 329–344.

——. "Vvedenie v chtenie A. Kozheva." In *"Phenomenologia dukha" Gegel'a v kontekste sovremennogo gegelvedenia*. Moscow: Kanon, 2010.

Tommissen, Piet, ed. *Schmittiana*. Vol. 6. Berlin: Duncker and Humblot, 1998.

OTHER RELEVANT WORKS

Adorno, Theodor W. *Hegel, Three Studies*. Translated by S. W. Nicholson. Cambridge, MA: MIT Press, 1993.

——. *History and Freedom*. Translated by Rodney Livingstone. Cambridge: Polity Press, 2006.

——. *Metaphysics: Concepts and Problems*. Translated by Edmund Jephcott. Stanford, CA: Stanford University Press, 2002.

——. *Negative Dialectics*. Translated by E. B. Ashton. New York: Continuum, 1973.

Altizer, Thomas, J. J. *The Apocalyptic Trinity*. New York: Palgrave Macmillan, 2012.

Arendt, Hannah. *The Life of the Mind*. 2 vols. San Diego, CA: Harcourt, Brace, 1977.

Aristotle. *Metaphysics*. Translated by Hugh Tredennick. 2 vols. Cambridge, MA: Harvard University Press, 1933.

Augustine. *City of God Against the Pagans*. Translated by R. W. Dyson. Cambridge: Cambridge University Press, 1998.

——. *On Free Choice of the Will*. Translated by Thomas Williams. Indianapolis: Hackett, 1993.

Badiou, Alain. *Being and Event*. Translated by Oliver Feltham. London: Continuum, 2006.

——. *Manifesto for Philosophy*. Translated by Norman Madarasz. Albany: State University of New York Press, 1999.

——. *Theoretical Writings*. Edited and translated by Ray Brassier and Alberto Toscano. London: Continuum, 2004.

Barrat, James. *Our Final Invention: Artificial Intelligence and the End of the Human Era*. New York: St. Martin's Griffin, 2015.

Becker, Carl. *The Heavenly City of the Eighteenth-Century Philosophers*. 2nd ed. New Haven, CT: Yale University Press, 2003.

Bloch, Ernst. *Subjekt-Objekt*. Frankfurt: Suhrkamp Verlag, 1962.

Blumenberg, Hans. *The Legitimacy of the Modern Age*. Translated by Robert M. Wallace. Cambridge, MA: MIT Press, 1985.

Borges, Jorge Luis. *Labyrinths: Selected Stories and Other Writings*. Edited by Donald A. Yates and James E. Irby. New York: New Directions, 2007.

Bradshaw, David. *Aristotle East and West: Metaphysics and the Division of Christendom*. Cambridge: Cambridge University Press, 2004.

Brandom, Robert. *Making It Explicit: Reasoning, Representing, and Discursive Commitment*. Cambridge, MA: Harvard University Press, 1998.

Butler, Judith. *Subjects of Desire: Hegelian Reflections in Twentieth-Century France*. New York: Columbia University Press, 1987.

Camus, Albert. *The Myth of Sisyphus*. Translated by Justin O'Brien. New York: Vintage, 1991.

Christensen, Michael J., and Jeffery A. Wittung, eds. *Partakers of the Divine Nature: The History and Development of Deification in the Christian Traditions*. Grand Rapids, MI: Baker Academic, 2007.

Deleuze, Gilles, and Félix Guattari. *What Is Philosophy?* Translated by Hugh Tomlinson. New York: Columbia University Press, 1996.

Derrida, J. *Acts of Literature*. Edited by Derek Attridge. London: Routledge, 1992.

——. *Aporias*. Translated by Thomas Dutoit. Stanford, CA: Stanford University Press, 1993.

——. "Cogito and the History of Madness." In *Writing and Difference*, translated by Alan Bass, 31–63. Chicago: University of Chicago Press, 1978.

——. *Glas*. Translated by John P. Leavey Jr. Lincoln: University of Nebraska Press, 1986.

——. *Margins of Philosophy*. Translated by Alan Bass. Chicago: University of Chicago Press, 1984.

——. *Monolingualism of the Other; or, the Prosthesis of Origin.* Translated by Patrick Mensah. Stanford, CA: Stanford University Press, 1998.

Dihle, Albrecht. *The Theory of the Will in Classical Antiquity.* Berkeley: University of California Press, 1982.

Dostoevsky, F. M. *The Brothers Karamazov.* Translated by Richard Pevear and Larissa Volokhonsky. New York: Farrar, Straus and Giroux, 2002.

——. *Crime and Punishment.* Translated by Richard Pevear and Larissa Volokhonsky. New York: Vintage, 1992.

——. *Demons.* Translated by Richard Pevear and Larissa Volokhonsky. New York: Vintage, 1994.

——. *The Idiot.* Translated by Richard Pevear and Larissa Volokhonsky. New York: Vintage, 2002.

——. *Notes from Underground.* Translated by Richard Pevear and Larissa Volokhonsky. New York: Vintage, 1993.

——. *Polnoe sobranie sochinenii.* 30 vols. Leningrad: Akademia nauk, 1972–1990.

——. *Winter Notes on Summer Impressions.* Translated by David Patterson. Evanston, IL: Northwestern University Press, 1997.

Fedorov, N. F. *Filosofia obshchego dela.* Edited by V. A. Kozhevnikov and N. P. Peterson. 2 vols. 1906, 1913. Reprint, Lausanne: L'Age d'homme, 1985.

——. *Sobranie sochinenii.* Edited by A. G. Gacheva and S. G. Semenova. 4 vols. plus supplement. Moscow: Progress/Traditsia, 1995–2000.

——. *What Was Man Created For?: The Philosophy of the Common Task.* Translated by Elisabeth Kutaissoff and Marilyn Minto. London: Honeyglen, 1990.

Fichte, J. G. *Introductions to the* Wissenschaftslehre *and Other Writings, 1797–1800.* Translated by Daniel Breazeale. Indianapolis, IN: Hackett, 1994.

Flaubert, Gustave. *Correspondance.* Edited by Jean Bruneau. Paris: Gallimard, 1991.

Flay, Joseph. *Hegel's Quest for Certainty.* Albany: State University of New York Press, 1984.

Forster, Michael. *Hegel's Idea of a Phenomenology of Spirit.* Chicago: University of Chicago Press, 1998.

Foucault, Michel. *Discipline and Punish: Birth of the Prison.* Translated by Alan Sheridan. New York: Vintage, 1977.

Frank, Joseph. *Dostoevsky: The Stir of Liberation 1860–1865.* Princeton, NJ: Princeton University Press, 1986.

Frede, Michael. *A Free Will: Origins of the Notion in Ancient Thought.* Edited by A. A. Long. Berkeley: University of California Press, 2012.

Freud, Sigmund. *Civilization and Its Discontents.* Translated by David McLintock. London: Penguin, 2002.

Gacheva, A. G., and S. G. Semenova, eds. *N. F. Fedorov: Pro et contra.* 2 vols. Saint Petersburg: RKGI, 2004–2008.

Gadamer, Hans-Georg. *Hegel's Dialectic: Five Hermeneutical Studies.* Translated by P. Christopher Smith. New Haven, CT: Yale University Press, 1982.

Gillespie, Michael Allen. *Hegel, Heidegger, and the Ground of History.* Chicago: University of Chicago Press, 1984.

Grillaert, Nel. *What the* God-seekers *Found in Nietzsche: The Reception of Nietzsche's Übermensch by the Philosophers of the Russian Religious Renaissance.* Leiden: Brill-Rodopi, 2008.

Groys, Boris. *The Communist Postscript.* Translated by Thomas Ford. London: Verso, 2010.

Gustafson, Richard F., and Judith Deutsch Kornblatt. *Russian Religious Thought.* Madison: University of Wisconsin Press, 1996.

Güven, Ferit. *Madness and Death in Philosophy.* Albany: State University of New York Press, 2005.

Hagemeister, Michael. *Nikolaj Fedorov: Studien zu Leben, Werk und Wirkung.* Munich: Otto Sagner, 1989.

Halpern, Richard. *Eclipse of Action: Tragedy and Political Economy.* Chicago: University of Chicago Press, 2017.

Hamburg, G. M., and Randall A. Poole, eds. *A History of Russian Philosophy 1830–1930.* Cambridge: Cambridge University Press, 2010.

Harris, H. S. *Hegel's Ladder.* 2 vols. Indianapolis, IN: Hackett, 1997.

Hegel, G. W. F. *Die Phänomenologie des Geistes.* Edited by Heinrich Clairmont and Hans-Friedrich Wessels. Hamburg: Felix Meiner Verlag, 1988.

——. *Die Phänomenologie des Geistes.* Edited by Johannes Hoffmeister. Leipzig: Felix Meiner Verlag, 1927.

——. *Die Wissenschaft der Logik.* Edited by Hans-Jürgen Gawoll. 2nd ed. 3 vols. Hamburg: Felix Meiner Verlag, 1999.

——. *Die Wissenschaft der Logik.* Edited by Georg Lasson. 2nd ed. 2 vols. Leipzig: Felix Meiner Verlag, 1934.

——. *Elements of the Philosophy of Right.* Edited by Allen W. Wood. Translated by N. B. Nisbet. Cambridge: Cambridge University Press, 1991.

——. *Enzyklopädie der philosophischen Wissenschaften (1830).* Edited by Friedhelm Nicolin and Otto Pöggeler. Hamburg: Felix Meiner Verlag, 1991.

——. *Grundlinien der Philosophie des Rechts.* Edited by Horst D. Brandt. Hamburg: Felix Meiner Verlag, 2013.

——. *The Phenomenology of Spirit.* Translated by A. V. Miller. Oxford: Oxford University Press, 1977.

——. *The Science of Logic.* Translated by George di Giovanni. Cambridge: Cambridge University Press, 2010.

——. *Werke.* Edited by E. Moldenhauer and K. Michel. 20 vols. Frankfurt: Suhrkamp Verlag, 1970–1971.

Heidegger, Martin. *Anmerkungen I-V (Schwarze Hefte 1942-1948).* Edited by Peter Trawny. Frankfurt: Vittorio Klostermann, 2015.

——. *Basic Writings.* Translated by David Farrell Krell. New York: Harper Perennial, 2008.

——. *Being and Time.* Translated by John Macquarrie and Edward S. Robinson. New York: Harper, 1962.

——. *Bremen and Freiburg Lectures.* Translated by Andrew J. Mitchell. Bloomington: Indiana University Press, 2012.

——. *Contributions to Philosophy (of the Event).* Translated by Richard Rojcewicz and Daniela Vallega-Neu. Bloomington: Indiana University Press, 2012.

——. *The Fundamental Concepts of Metaphysics.* Translated by William McNeill. Bloomington: Indiana University Press, 2001.

——. *Hegel.* Translated by Joseph Arel and Niels Feuerhahn. Bloomington: Indiana University Press, 2015.

——. *Hegel's Phenomenology of Spirit.* Translated by Parvis Emad and Kenneth Maly. Bloomington: Indiana University Press, 1988.

——. *Introduction to Metaphysics.* Translated by Gregory Fried and Richard Polt. 2nd ed. New Haven, CT: Yale University Press, 2014.

——. *Kant and the Problem of Metaphysics.* Translated by Richard Taft. Bloomington: Indiana University Press, 1997.

——. *The Metaphysical Foundations of Logic.* Translated by Michael Heim. Bloomington: Indiana University press, 1984.

——. *Mindfulness.* Translated by Parvis Emad and Thomas Kalary. London: Continuum, 2006.

——. *Nietzsche.* 2 vols. Pfullingen: Günther Neske, 1961.

——. *Pathmarks.* Edited by William McNeill. Cambridge: Cambridge University Press, 1998.

——. *Schelling's Treatise on the Essence of Human Freedom.* Translated by Joan Stambaugh. Akron: Ohio University Press, 1985.

——. *What Is a Thing?* Translated by Vera Deutsch. New York: Gateway, 1968.

——. *What Is Called Thinking?* Translated by J. Glenn Gray. New York: Harper and Row, 1968.

Hölderlin, Friedrich. *Hyperion and Selected Poems.* Edited by Eric L. Santner. New York: Continuum, 1990.

Hook, Sidney. *From Hegel to Marx.* New York: Columbia University Press, 1994.

Hyppolyte, Jean. *Genesis and Structure of Hegel's* Phenomenology of Spirit. Translated by S. Cherniak and J. Heckman. Evanston, IL: Northwestern University Press, 1974.

Il'in, Ivan. *The Philosophy of Hegel as a Doctrine of the Concreteness of God and Humanity.* Edited and translated by Philip T. Grier. 2 vols. Evanston, IL: Northwestern University Press, 2010.

Izutsu, Toshihiko. *Sufism and Taoism: A Comparative Study of Key Philosophical Concepts.* Berkeley: University of California Press, 1984.

Jackson, Robert Louis. *Dialogues on Dostoevsky.* Stanford, CA: Stanford University Press, 1996.

——. *Dostoevskij's Underground Man in Russian Literature.* 's-Gravenhage: Mouton, 1958.

——. *Dostoevsky (New Perspectives).* Englewood Cliffs, NJ: Prentice-Hall, 1984.

——. *Dostoevsky's Quest for Form: A Study of His Philosophy of Art.* New Haven, CT: Yale University Press, 1966.

Jameson, Fredric. *The Hegel Variations: On the Phenomenology of Spirit.* London: Verso, 2010.

——. *Late Marxism: Adorno or the Persistence of Dialectic.* London: Verso, 1990.

——. *Postmodernism.* Durham, NC: Duke University Press, 1992.

Jenkins, Scott. "Hegel's Concept of Desire." *Journal of the History of Philosophy* 47, no. 1 (2009): 103–130.

Johnston, Mark. *Surviving Death.* Princeton, NJ: Princeton University Press, 2010.

Joyce, James. *A Portrait of the Artist as a Young Man.* Harmondsworth: Penguin, 1976.

Kant, Immanuel. *Groundwork of the Metaphysic of Morals.* Translated by H. J. Paton. New York: Harper and Row, 1964.

——. *Religion Within the Limits of Reason Alone*. Translated by Theodore M. Greene and Hoyt B. Hudson. New York: Harper and Row, 1960.

Kierkegaard, Søren. *Either/Or: A Fragment of Life*. Translated by Alistair Hannay. London: Penguin, 1992.

Kline, George L. *George L. Kline on Hegel*. North Syracuse, NY: Gegensatz, 2015.

Kornblatt, Judith Deutsch. *Divine Sophia: The Wisdom Writings of Vladimir Solovyov*. Ithaca, NY: Cornell University Press, 2009.

Kripke, Saul. *Wittgenstein on Rules and Private Language*. Cambridge, MA: Harvard University Press, 1982.

Lactantius. *De ira dei*. In *Patrologia latina, cursus completus*. Edited by J. P. Migne. 217 vols. Paris: 1844.

Lauer, Quentin, SJ. *A Reading of Hegel's Phenomenology of Spirit*. New York: Fordham University Press, 1976.

Leibniz, G. W. *Philosophische Schriften*. 6 vols. Berlin: Akademie Verlag, 2006.

——. *Theodicy*. Translated by E. M. Huggard. La Salle, IL: Open Court, 1985.

Levinas, Emmanuel. *God, Death, and Time*. Translated by Bettina Bargo. Stanford, CA: Stanford University Press, 2000.

Livingston, Paul. *The Logic of Being: Realism, Truth, and Time*. Evanston, IL: Northwestern University Press, 2017.

——. *The Politics of Logic: Badiou, Wittgenstein, and the Consequences of Formalism*. New York: Routledge, 2012.

Louth, Andrew. *Modern Orthodox Thinkers: From the Philokalia to the Present*. Downers Grove, IL: InterVarsity Press, 2015.

Löwith, Karl. *Meaning in History*. Chicago: University of Chicago Press, 1949.

Lukács, Georg. *The Destruction of Reason*. Translated by Peter Palmer. Atlantic Highlands, NJ: Humanities Press, 1981.

——. *History and Class Consciousness*. Translated by Rodney Livingstone. Cambridge, MA: MIT Press, 1972.

——. *The Young Hegel*. Translated by Rodney Livingstone. Cambridge, MA: MIT Press, 1976.

Macherey, Pierre. *Hegel or Spinoza*. Translated by Susan M. Ruddick. Minneapolis: University of Minnesota Press, 2011.

Machiavelli, Niccolò. *The Prince*. Translated by Peter Bondanella. Oxford: Oxford University Press, 2008.

——. *The Ten Discourses on Livy*. Translated by Harvey C. Mansfield and Nathan Tarcov. Chicago: University of Chicago Press, 1996.

Maker, William. *Philosophy Without Foundations*. Albany: State University of New York Press, 1994.

Malabou, Catherine. *The Future of Hegel: Plasticity, Temporality and Dialectic*. New York: Routledge, 2005.

Marcuse, Herbert. *Hegel's Ontology and the Theory of Historicity*. Translated by S. Benhabib. Cambridge, MA: MIT Press, 1987.

——. *Reason and Revolution*. Oxford: Oxford University Press, 1942.

Marx, Karl. *Capital*. Translated by Ben Fowkes. 3 vols. London: Penguin, 1990.

———. *Ökonomisch-philosophische Manuskripte*. Frankfurt: Suhrkamp, 2009.

———. *Werke*. Edited by Benedikt Kautsky and Hans-Joachim Lieber. 7 vols. Stuttgart: Cotta-Verlag, 1962.

Marx, Karl, and Friedrich Engels. *The Marx-Engels Reader*. Edited by Robert C. Tucker. 2nd ed. New York: W. W. Norton, 1978.

Masing-Delic, Irene. *Abolishing Death: A Salvation Myth of Russian Twentieth-Century Literature*. Stanford, CA: Stanford University Press, 1992.

McDowell, John. *Mind and World*. Cambridge, MA: Harvard University Press, 1994.

Melville, Herman. *Redburn, White-Jacket, Moby-Dick*. Edited by G. Thomas Tanselle. New York: Literary Classics of the United States, 1983.

Michalson, Gordon E, Jr. *Fallen Freedom: Kant on Radical Evil and Moral Regeneration*. Cambridge: Cambridge University Press, 1990.

Morson, Gary Saul. *Hidden in Plain View: Narrative and Creative Potentials in "War and Peace."* Stanford, CA: Stanford University Press, 1988.

Moyar, Dean, and Michael Quante, eds. *Hegel's Phenomenology of Spirit: A Critical Guide*. Cambridge: Cambridge University Press, 2011.

Mure, G. R. G. *A Study of Hegel's Logic*. Oxford: Oxford University Press, 1959.

Nemeth, Thomas. *The early Solov'ëv and His Quest for Metaphysics*. Cham: Springer, 2014.

Neuhouser, Frederick. "Deducing Desire and Recognition in the *Phenomenology of Spirit*." *Journal of the History of Philosophy* 24, no. 2 (April 1986): 243–262.

———. *Rousseau's Theodicy of Self-Love*. Oxford: Oxford University Press, 2008.

Nietzsche, Friedrich. *Beyond Good and Evil*. Translated by Marion Faber. Oxford: Oxford University Press, 1998.

———. *Beyond Good and Evil*. Translated by Walter Kaufmann. New York: Vintage, 1989.

———. *The Gay Science*. Translated by Walter Kaufmann. New York: Vintage, 1974.

———. *Sämtliche Briefe*. 8 vols. Berlin: Walter de Gruyter, 1986.

———. *Towards a Genealogy of Morality*. Translated by Maudemarie Clark and Alan J. Swenson. Indianapolis, IN: Hackett, 1998.

———. *Twilight of the Idols* and *The Anti-Christ*. Translated by R. J. Hollingdale. New York: Penguin, 1968.

———. *The Will to Power*. Translated by Walter Kaufmann and R. J. Hollingdale. New York: Vintage, 1973.

O'Regan, Cyril. *The Heterodox Hegel*. Albany: State University of New York Press, 1994.

Pinkard, Terry. *Hegel: A Biography*. Cambridge: Cambridge University Press, 2000.

———. *Hegel's Phenomenology: The Sociality of Reason*. Cambridge: Cambridge University Press, 1994.

Pippin, Robert. *Hegel on Self-Consciousness: Death and Desire in the Phenomenology of Spirit*. Princeton, NJ: Princeton University Press, 2010.

———. *Hegel's Idealism*. Cambridge: Cambridge University Press, 1989.

Plato. *Phaedo*. Translated by R. Hackforth. Cambridge: Cambridge University Press, 1955.

———. *Phaedrus*. Translated by Harold North Fowler. Cambridge, MA: Harvard University Press, 1914.

———. *Phaedrus*. Translated by James H. Nichols Jr. Ithaca, NY: Cornell University Press, 1998.

——. *Phaedrus*. Edited by Harvey Yunis. Cambridge: Cambridge University Press, 2011.

——. *Republic*. Translated by Chris Emilyn-Jones and William Preddy. Vol. 2. Cambridge, MA: Harvard University Press, 2013.

——. *Symposium*. Translated by Alexander Nehamas and Paul Woodruff. Indianapolis, IN: Hackett, 1989.

——. *Theaetetus*. Translated by Harold North Fowler. Cambridge, MA: Harvard University Press, 1921.

Platonov, Andrey. *The Foundation Pit*. Translated by Robert Chandler and Olga Meerson. New York: New York Review of Books, 2009.

Pluth, Ed. "Alain Badiou, Kojève, and the Return of the Human Exception." *Filozofski Vestnik* 30, no. 2 (2009): 197–205.

Poe, Marshall. " 'Moscow the Third Rome': The Origins and Transformations of a Pivotal Moment." *Jahrbücher für Geschichte Osteuropas* Neue Folge 49, no. 3 (2001): 412–429.

Priest, Graham. *Beyond the Limits of Thought*. 2nd ed. Oxford: Oxford University Press, 2003.

Rockmore, Tom. *Cognition: An Introduction to Hegel's* Phenomenology of Spirit. Berkeley: University of California Press, 1997.

Rosenthal, Beatrice G., ed. *The Occult in Soviet and Russian Culture*. Ithaca, NY: Cornell University Press, 1997.

Rousseau, Jean-Jacques. *The Major Political Writings of Jean-Jacques Rousseau*. Translated by John T. Scott. Chicago: University of Chicago Press, 2012.

Russell, Norman. *The Doctrine of Deification in the Greek Patristic Tradition*. Oxford: Oxford University Press, 2004.

Scanlon, James R. *Dostoevsky the Thinker*. Ithaca, NY: Cornell University Press, 2002.

Schelling, F. W. J. *Philosophical Investigations into the Essence of Human Freedom*. 1809. Translated by Jeff Love and Johannes Schmidt. Albany: State University of New York Press, 2006.

Schmidt, Alfred. *The Concept of Nature in Marx*. Translated by Ben Fowkes. London: Verso, 2014.

Schmitt, Carl. *The Concept of the Political*. Translated by George Schwab. Chicago: University of Chicago Press, 2007.

——. *The Leviathan in the State Theory of Thomas Hobbes*. Translated by George Schwab and Erna Hilfstein. Chicago: University of Chicago Press, 2008.

Slingerland, Edward. *Effortless Action: Wu-Wei as Conceptual Metaphor and Spiritual Ideal in Early China*. Oxford: Oxford University Press, 2007.

Smith, Oliver. *Vladimir Soloviev and the Spiritualization of Matter*. Brighton: Academic Studies Press, 2011.

Solovyov, V. S. *The Burning Bush: Writings on Jews and Judaism*. Edited and translated by Gregory Yuri Glazov. Notre Dame, IN: University of Notre Dame Press, 2016.

——. *The Crisis of Western Philosophy*. Translated by Boris Jakim. Hudson, NY: Lindisfarne, 1996.

——. *Freedom, Faith, and Dogma: Essays by V. S. Soloviev on Christianity and Judaism*. Translated by Vladimir Wozniuk. Albany: State University of New York Press, 2009.

——. *The Heart of Reality: Essays on Beauty, Love, and Ethics by V. S. Soloviev.* Translated by Vladimir Wozniuk. Notre Dame, IN: University of Notre Dame Press, 2003.

——. *Lectures on Divine Humanity.* Translation revised and edited by Boris Jakim. Hudson, NY: Lindisfarne, 1995.

——. *The Philosophical Principles of Integral Knowledge.* Translated by Valeria Z. Nollan. Grand Rapids, MI: William B. Eerdmans, 2008.

——. *Politics, Law, and Morality: Essays by V. S. Soloviev.* Translated by Vladimir Wozniuk. New Haven, CT: Yale University Press, 2014.

——. *Sobranie sochinenii.* Edited by S. M. Soloviev and E. L. Radlov. 2nd ed. 12 vols. 1911–1914. Reprint, Brussels: Izdatel'stvo Zhizn' s bogom, 1966–1970.

——. *War, Progress, and the End of History.* Translated by Alexander Bakshy. Revised by Thomas. R. Beyer Jr. Hudson, NY: Lindisfarne, 1990.

Sophocles, *The Plays and Fragments.* Edited by Sir Richard C. Jebb. Reprint, Amsterdam: Servio, 1963.

Speight, Allen. *Hegel, Literature, and the Problem of Agency.* Cambridge: Cambridge University Press, 2004.

Spinoza, Baruch. *Spinoza: Complete Works.* Translated by Samuel Shirley. Indianapolis, IN: Hackett, 2002.

Stekeler, Pirmin. *Hegels Phänomenologie des Geistes: Ein dialogischer Kommentar.* 2 vols. Hamburg: Felix Meiner Verlag, 2014.

Stern, Robert. *Hegel's Phenomenology of Spirit.* London: Routledge, 2001.

Stewart, Jon, ed. *The Hegel Myths and Legends.* Evanston, IL: Northwestern University Press, 1996.

Strauss, Leo. *Liberalism Ancient and Modern.* Chicago: University of Chicago Press, 1995.

——. *Persecution and the Art of Writing.* Chicago: University of Chicago Press, 1988.

——. *The Political Philosophy of Hobbes: Its Basis and Genesis.* Chicago: University of Chicago Press, 1952.

Taylor, Charles. *Hegel.* Cambridge: Cambridge University Press, 1977.

Toews, John E. *Hegelianism: The Path Toward Dialectical Humanism 1805–1841.* Cambridge: Cambridge University Press, 1981.

Unger, Roberto Mangabeira, and Lee Smolin. *The Singular Universe and the Reality of Time.* Cambridge: Cambridge University Press, 2014.

Valliere, Paul. *Modern Russian Theology: Bukharev, Soloviev, Bulgakov.* Edinburgh: T and T Clark, 2000.

Vattimo, Gianni. *Nihilism and Emancipation.* Edited by Santiago Zabala. New York: Columbia University Press, 2004.

Vernon, Jim, and Antonio Calcagno, eds. *Badiou and Hegel: Infinity, Dialectics, Subjectivity.* London: Lexington, 2015.

Williams, Robert R. *Hegel's Ethics of Recognition.* Berkeley: University of California Press, 2012.

Young, George M. *Russian Cosmism: The Esoteric Futurism of Nikolai Fedorov and his Followers.* Oxford: Oxford University Press, 2012.

INDEX